How Would You Decide?

10 Famous Trials That Changed History

by
J. Craig Williams

Foreword
By
Erwin Chemerinsky

How Would You Decide? 10 Famous Trials That Changed History© 2024

by J. Craig Williams, Esq. All rights reserved.

No part of this publication may be reproduced, distributed, or transmitted in any form or by any means, including without limitation either copying, recording, or other electronic or mechanical methods, all without the prior, written permission of the publisher, Crimson Cloak Publishing, except in the case of brief quotations embodied in book and podcast reviews as well as certain other non-commercial uses permitted by United States copyright law. Neither this book nor the podcast is in the public domain.

ISBN: 978-1-68160-780-1 (Paperback)

ISBN: 978-1-68160-779-5 (Hardcover)

Library of Congress Control Number: 2024911839

Book design by Carly McCracken. 'Cover art inspired by In Dispute Podcast show art, designed and produced by Legal Talk Network.'

First print edition 2024.

For permission requests, write to the publisher, addressed: "Attention: Permissions Coordinator" at the address below.

Crimson Cloak Publishing

P.O. Box 36

Pilot Knob, MO 63663

United States of America

www.crimsoncloakpublishing.com

What's Your Verdict?

visit www.10FamousTrials.com to register your vote how you would decide each trial and decide the Trial of the Century.

- and also -

Enjoy listening to In Dispute – 10 Famous Trials That Changed History, the podcast audio drama miniseries of each trial on the Legal Talk Network, adapted by Nathan Todhunter, narrated by J. Craig Williams, and joined by approximately 100 voice actors playing the parts of the judges, lawyers, and witnesses using actual trial testimony. www.LegalTalkNetwork.com

DISCLAIMER

This nonfiction book contains descriptions of war, murder, violence, child abuse, sex, cheating, cursing, crime, religion, crucifixion, torture, gun fights, knife fights, stabbings, hangings, stonings, jailing, massacres, hate speech, drugs, gossip, insults, disgusting behavior, betrayals, blood, guts, and just about every other human (and some non-human) vice you can imagine.

Many of the words in this book are highly offensive, but those words are the same historical words that were spoken as they were accurately transcribed originally and then adapted into the quotes cited here. Those quoted words are not sensitized to today's standards and remain offensive. To stay consistent with the way those words were used in the context of the quotes and to avoid confusion, the author in some instances used in his writing the same offensive word from these quotes.

What was said back then does not have the same sensitivities as we do today and will be offensive to some readers. If you can understand, accept, and forgive the offensiveness that this book necessarily quotes from these historical trial transcripts and analyzes, then read on. If on the other hand, you are triggered by any of these things, then stop reading now.

This book contains transcripts, court documents, and other references as cited from their source and accurate to the original; they may contain unintentional errors in spelling, grammar punctuation and/or have omissions and/or misquotes. The author encourages readers to verify independently any suspect information and contact him if you find a mistake so he can correct it for the next edition.

The author is a lawyer. Nothing in this book or its related podcast series constitutes legal advice and does not constitute an attorney-client relationship with him or his law firm.

CONTENTS

DISCLAIMER 3
CONTENTS 4
Expanded Table of Contents 5
Dedication 12
Acknowledgements 13
Foreword 14
Introduction 17
CHAPTER 1 The Trial of Jesus 21
CHAPTER 2 Salem Witch Trials 37
CHAPTER 3 Rex v. Preston and Rex v. Wemms, et al., the two Boston Massacre Trials of Captain Thomas Preston and eight other British Redcoats 64
CHAPTER 4 The Tipping Points of the Civil War and its Aftermath: the Dred Scott Decision, the Trial of John Brown and Plessy v. Ferguson 92
CHAPTER 5 The O.K. Corral Shootout Trial of Wyatt Earp and Doc Holliday 121
CHAPTER 6 The Chicago Black Sox Trial 171
CHAPTER 7 State v. Scopes ("The Monkey Trial") 224
CHAPTER 8 The Lindy Chamberlain Trial 282
CHAPTER 9 The McMartin Preschool Trial 336
CHAPTER 10 The O.J. Simpson Trial for the Murder of Nicole Brown Simpson and Ronald Goldman 385
CONCLUSION 461
About the Author 464
Appendix A 465
Appendix B 468
Electronic Version, Book websites and Bonus Materials 473
Endnotes 475

Expanded Table of Contents

Chapter 1

<u>The Trial of Jesus</u>—Piecing together the most influential trial in history from five differing accounts, written with obvious biblical perspectives well after the 30 C.E. trial happened, we walk back in time to hear the trial testimony. Apart from the mystical, religious significance of the event, here's how a modern-day trial lawyer applies an unvarnished view of the legal procedures employed by High Priest Joseph Caiaphas and Roman Governor Pontius Pilate in their conviction of Jesus for blasphemy. Would his trial turn out differently today based on modern legal precedent and criminal procedure?

Chapter 2

<u>The Salem Witch Trials</u>—You can't really call them trials with this kind of procedure, but has criminal law advanced much further? Consider that the <u>Miranda</u> warning case has been overruled by the courts in just about every aspect except by name. See how the evidence admitted in 1692 varies from today's criminal proceedings, notably excepting the name of the charge: witchcraft. Here's how the process (used) to work:

1. The individual "afflicted" by witchcraft made a complaint to the Magistrate about a suspected witch. That complaint would sometimes be made through a third person.

2. The Magistrate issued a warrant for the arrest of the accused witch.

3. The accused witch was taken into custody and examined by two or more Magistrates. If after listening to testimony the Magistrate believed the accused witch is probably guilty, then the accused was sent to jail for possible reexamination and to await trial.

4. The case was next presented to the Grand Jury, and the jurors examined the witch. The examinations were automatically entered into evidence.

5. If the accused witch was indicted by the Grand Jury (which was virtually guaranteed), then the Court of Oyer and Terminer tried the accused witch. A jury, instructed by the "Judges," decided the accused witch's guilt (again, virtually guaranteed).

6. The Court sentenced the convicted witch or wizard. In each case in Salem, the sentence was hanging, set on a particular date.

7. The Sheriff and his deputies carried out the hanging.

Go back in time with me and listen to the judges question the witches. Did they admit the right kind of evidence needed to convict the witches? Did you know a minister was hung as a wizard?

Chapter 3

Rex v. Wemms, *et al.*, the Boston Massacre Trial of Captain Thomas Preston and seven other British redcoats—For the paltry sum of eighteen guineas, about twenty dollars now, future-president-to-be John Adams, then a 34-year-old lawyer in Boston, took on the unpopular defense of these almost surely-to-be-hung soldiers. In 1770, while the United States was seeking its freedom from England, this case marked our first trial on an international stage. Founded on his precise questioning of some forty witnesses and with his eloquent argument mixing law, logic and politics, Adams argued the soldiers were not guilty based on self-defense.

Lawyer Adams obtained an acquittal of six of the eight soldiers arguing: "A judgment of death against those soldiers would have been as foul a stain upon this country as the executions of the Quakers or witches . . . As the evidence was, the verdict of the jury was exactly right." Only the two soldiers who fired into the crowd were found guilty. Would our country have gained the respect of the Europe of colonial times had Adams not convinced the jury to disregard their passions and decide based on the facts? Did this unpopular defense ruin Adams' law practice as many predicted? How would the American Civil Liberties Union have handled this case?

Chapter 4

The Tipping Point for the Civil War and its Aftermath—**The Dred Scott Decision**—In 1856, a slave sued to gain his freedom, but in what has been called one of the worst historical decisions of the United States Supreme Court, the Court itself ruled Scott was not a citizen, and denied him access to the court system. John Brown's actions came on the heels of this decision, taking matters into his own hands.

The Trial of John Brown—The 1859 trial of abolitionist John Brown in Virginia should have been no more than a blip in the history books, but Brown turned out to be larger than life. Partly due to his own flawed zealousness and the efforts of several luminaries around him, including Ralph Waldo Emerson and Henry David Thoreau, John Brown's sentence of death for treason, inciting rebellion, and murder became a lightning rod that galvanized the North into action against the South and started us on the march toward the war between brothers. The courtroom trial started out as a comical farce attended by 600 curious and boisterous court-watchers, but ended with sullen observers wondering if they were doing the right thing.

Slavery ended in large part to events started by Brown's actions, but his death also fostered some unintended consequences. Watching the execution was a young Virginia Military Institute cadet, John Wilkes Booth, who later became infamous in his own right. You may have studied Lincoln's Gettysburg Address in school, but have you heard Brown's oratorical response to the court's verdict of death against him? Brown's closing remarks have been called "one of the most memorable courtroom speeches" and "one of the two greatest American speeches." After Brown spoke in the pre-Civil War courtroom in Virginia, only one spectator clapped when the judge sentenced Brown to death, and that citizen was quickly silenced.

Plessy v. Ferguson—Not until 1896 did our Supreme Court right the injustice done to Dred Scott, which the Court overturned in this famous case.

How do Supreme Court decisions shape historical events? In Civil War times, the high court corrected a horrendous, racially motivated decision. Are there lessons to draw from these cases today?

Chapter 5

The O.K. Corral Shootout Trial of Wyatt Earp and Doc Holliday—Lawmen tamed the Old West with bravery and guns, but did you know Wyatt Earp, his brothers, and Doc Holliday were later tried in court for killing the Clanton gang? You may have seen the movies, but you haven't seen the true trial of these larger-than-life men facing the gallows after the shootout. Their lawyers had a few tricks up their sleeve that saved Wyatt from cross-examination and positioned their case with a favorable court for a decision, saving them from the hangman's noose.

You'll get the chance to decide whether the lawmen were saved by their lawyers or really the town's business-minded judge. What other forces were in play? Did a young female witness sway the judge's mind?

Chapter 6

The Black Sox Trial—Nine players of the Chicago White Sox threw the 1919 World Series and caused a cheating scandal that forever changed the game of baseball, but why? Even though these Boys of Summer didn't take the stand in their defense, they were found not guilty by a jury. Not to be dissuaded, however, the Commissioner of baseball got his revenge and struck the names of the "Eight Men Out" from baseball's roster of players forever.

You may think you know the facts and the outcome, but what about the courtroom intrigue of these famous players? How did the prosecution's objections defeat the ballplayer's attempts to introduce evidence? Were their confessions extracted fairly? Was Shoeless Joe Jackson in on the fix? How did Club manager Charles "The Old Roman" Comiskey's greed factor into mix?

Say it ain't so.

Chapter 7

<u>**State v. Scopes**</u> **("The Monkey Trial")**—You couldn't ask for a better test case or lineup of players. On the side of science, we have the legendary, 70-year-old trial lawyer Clarence Darrow for the defense seeking to uphold the theory of evolution. On the side of religion, there's the famous orator, Congressman William Jennings Bryan who prosecuted biology teacher John Scopes' violation of the anti-evolution

statute in Tennessee. Evolutionary theorist Charles Darwin was absent from the proceedings, but his writings were squarely in the middle.

Did we descend from apes? Could we teach our children Darwin's theory of evolution, or were public schools required to teach the Adam and Eve version of events? After an almost comical trial where he put Bryan on the stand outside the courthouse in 1925, Darrow asked the jury for a surprising verdict of guilty of his own client so Scopes could appeal the loss to the Tennessee Supreme Court. Bryan may have technically won the case, but in reality, he lost when the Tennessee Supreme Court reversed the verdict, dismissed the case, and virtually all states refused to enact similar laws that prevented teaching Darwin's theory of evolution. Here's what can go wrong when you try to set up test cases in court.

Did Darrow lose the battle to win the war? Did Bryan not see the forest for the trees? Can you now spot a test case that lawyers engineer for a particular result and do lawyers still use these tactics?

Chapter 8

The Lindy Chamberlain Trial—Late in August 1980, a mother's cry rose from a quiet, inky-black, dark night at a campsite near Australia's famous Uluru/Ayer's Rock virtually in the middle of the continent: "My God, my God, the dingo's got my baby!" Mother Lindy Chamberlain was tried in court while the nation found itself arguing in the newspapers over her role in her ten-week-old baby Azaria's death. Convicted to almost universal applause across the continent, Lindy was sentenced to life in prison. Her co-defendant husband Michael Chamberlain's sentence was suspended.

Some six years later during search around the base of Uluru/Ayer's Rock during an unrelated investigation of a hiker's death, the police found baby Azaria's matinee jacket, stained with her blood, and mixed with dingo saliva. With that evidence, Lindy was released from jail and awarded $1.3 million Australian dollars for wrongful imprisonment. Was that enough money? How could the investigation and the science go so wrong? Should public opinion affect the outcome of a trial?

Chapter 9

The McMartin Preschool Trial—The pendulum of child abuse concern had swung far to one side and in 1987, four teachers from the

McMartin preschool faculty found themselves in the sights of Parent Judy Johnson. She was a woman later recognized as a paranoid schizophrenic, but who initially appeared as a concerned mother claiming child abuse of her two-and-a-half-year-old son at the preschool, later asserting highly inflamed allegations that the teachers performed satanic rituals with the kids.

Despite no medical signs of abuse and her son's inability to identify the alleged abuser, Manhattan Beach, California police fueled the fire with an apparently unfounded letter sent to other parents, which started a "snowball of suspicion rolling." Seven years and more than fifteen million dollars later, the State of California prosecutors still had no convictions. They had succeeded, however, in emotionally damaging hundreds of children and ruining the reputations of four preschool teachers in the process and demolishing the school looking for tunnels.

How did the so-called expert psychologists and doctors present questionable findings based on unsubstantiated interviews? Did the media fan the fire with headlines without questioning the prosecutors? Did anyone win?

Chapter 10

The O.J. Murder Trial—America's fascination with a fallen football-star-turned-sometime-sports-TV-celebrity transformed into a riveting international obsession that highlighted the cracks and ugly underbelly of our judicial system. We'll look at the:

1. chase;
2. trial and the dream team;
3. children;
4. civil case; and,
5. the acquittal—can we trust the system?

Apart from the farce of the 1995 trial (was it really that long ago?), the TV rating system itself readjusted after 133 days of televised courtroom testimony. That event turned viewers into Simpson trial fanatics and was dubbed the "Super Bowl of murder trials." Some 95 million viewers tuned in to watch a painfully slow police chase of O.J.'s white Ford Bronco crawl across county lines in California. More than 91% of those watching television were watching the Simpson trial the day the jury returned its verdict. Called "a great trash novel come to life," the televised trial held sway over those who would never even pick up a gossip rag like the *National Enquirer*.

It was a daily topic of discussion in the bars, around the watercooler when offices were full, and a *de rigueur* topic to discuss at almost all social events. Did O.J. really kill Nicole and Ron? Did the bloody glove fit? Were O.J.'s highly-paid "dream team" of lawyers the real reason he was acquitted? Does justice depend on money?

Dedication

To Christine Bartley Williams, my wife, life partner and fellow wayfarer along life's path. Her contributions to this book, its podcast miniseries, and my life are immeasurable and for which I am forever grateful.

And also, to my extended family, my father, the Reverend Doctor James Robert Williams, my mother, Marilyn, my grandparents Jim, Leola, Lemuel, and Hilda, as well as my children Julie and Amanda, my grandchildren, Naomi Jo, Tiago, Kingston, and Stallard, and our two dogs, Laguna and Viggo. Family is life.

Acknowledgements

After the success of my first two books, *How to Get Sued: An Instructional Guide*, and *The Sled*, the concept of this book first came into being as the brainchild of HTGS' peerless editor, Susan Barry. She conceived the idea and pitched it with such enthusiasm that I couldn't resist researching and writing it. It started as her baby, and with the guidance of her fellow and equally peerless editor, Kelli Christansen, it was born.

Then Carly McCracken of Crimson Cloak Publishing ran with that edited draft, and with the sharp editorial eye of Kate McCracken, it came into focus. Carly designed the book cover art and together we created the book now in your hands.

A team effort made this book possible. Noted legal scholar and The University of California, Berkeley, School of Law (Boalt Hall) Dean Erwin Chemerinsky wrote the following Foreword and gave thoughtful suggestions to research and polish the text.

My wife, Christine, contributed most of all. She supported me wholeheartedly throughout and without her, neither I, this book, nor the podcast would exist. Click.

Most of all, dear reader, my thanks go to you for your support by buying my books. Stay tuned for the sequels!

Foreword

Long before there was television and streaming video, people went to courthouses to watch trials for entertainment. As long as there has been television, there have been shows featuring lawyers and courtrooms, programs like Perry Mason, Matlock, L.A. Law, and Law & Order. This is not surprising, because trials are inherently dramatic and sometimes riveting. They are a contest with a winner and a loser. There is suspense as to who the jury will find victorious. The lawyers and participants are often compelling, even mesmerizing figures. Sometimes, the major issues of the day are fought over in the context of a trial in a remote courtroom in places like Harpers Ferry, West Virginia, or Dayton, Tennessee.

J. Craig Williams has written of ten of the most interesting and most important trials in world history. He has done a magnificent job of bringing to life the character and the drama of the courtrooms. Some will be familiar to many readers. The last chapter, on the O.J. Simpson case, brings back vivid memories of an amazing cast of characters and how a nation was captivated like never before by a criminal case. By contrast, the early chapters on the trial of Jesus and the Salem witch trials piece together historical materials to allow the reader a sense of what really happened hundreds of years ago.

Craig could not have done a better job of selecting his material. Although it is possible to quibble with any top ten list, no one could deny that these trials were memorable and are worthy of study. Some of the trials described in this book truly changed world and national history. The trial of Jesus which led to his crucifixion was the foundation for a religion as important, and perhaps more important, than any in world history. The events in Boston in 1770, known as the Boston Massacre (described in Chapter 3), helped precipitate the Revolutionary War. The trial of the abolitionist John Brown in 1859 (described in Chapter 4) likewise played a role in precipitating the Civil War, or at least reflected inevitable immanency.

Not surprisingly, trials often touch on the deeper social issues of the times and are a place where those matters are fought over. The O.J. Simpson trial was as much about celebrity, gender violence, and race in late twentieth century America as it was about a double murder. The Scopes Trial over evolution (described in Chapter 7) was about the tension between science and religion at a time of great scientific progress and developments. The Boston Massacre Trial was really about the tensions between a colonial power and a colony seeking its independence. The John Brown trial was about the abhorrence of slavery, a deep flaw in the foundation of this nation from its outset. The O.K. Corral Shootout Trial of Wyatt Earp and Doc Holliday ultimately were about bringing justice to new parts of the country that had often operated outside the bounds of the law.

Some of the chapters are a reminder that our criminal justice system is designed and operated by humans, so it is inevitable that mistakes will be made. The story of the Salem witch trials (in Chapter 2) is a powerful reminder of how essential it is to have fair and just procedures; the author rightly draws parallels to the McMartin Preschool Case (Chapter 9). In both, prosecutors who were sure of their conclusions created procedures to try to validate the results they wanted to achieve. The reality is that in any human system there will be mistakes and we must have a criminal justice system designed to prevent and remedy them.

Some of the cases described in this book captured the public's attention because of the celebrities involved. The story of the Black Sox Scandal (Chapter 6) came at a time when the nation was increasingly interested in professional sports and involved prosecution of some of the greatest stars of Major League Baseball back then. The Lindy Chamberlain trial (Chapter 8), like the O.J. trial decades later, dominated headlines like never before. The O.J. trial became the obsession of a nation, even though it was really just a trial for a double murder in a country where such trials literally occur every day. But no screenwriter could have invented the story of O.J. Simpson or a cast of characters like Judge Lance Ito, Marcia Clark, Chris Darden, Johnnie Cochran, Alan Dershowitz, Barry Scheck, Mark Fuhrman, and Kato Kaelin.

J. Craig Williams' book is masterful in that it is simultaneously tremendously informative and enormously enjoyable. I learned a great deal from these pages and was entertained throughout. I hope that you enjoy it as much as I did.

Erwin Chemerinsky
*Founding Dean and Distinguished Professor of Law,
University of California, Irvine,
School of Law, and now Dean of the University of
California, Berkeley, School of Law (Boalt Hall)*

Introduction

During my first-year criminal law class at the University of Iowa College of Law, Professor Jon Carlson ended one of our hour-long classes by asking the twenty-five law students in the classroom whether we remembered someone interrupting his lecture shortly after it got started. If we did remember the event, then he asked us to identify the person.

There's an old adage that if you ask five lawyers for their opinion, you'll get five different opinions. It applies to our observational powers, as well—and perhaps not just those of lawyers or law students in a classroom.

As you would expect, a good many of us did not remember anyone interrupting the lecture (there was, in fact, an interruption). Of those who did remember, few could agree whether the person was a man or a woman, tall or short, fat, or thin, or even the length and color of the person's hair or the clothes the person wore. We were equally conflicted about whether the person brought something in and gave it to Professor Carlson, took something away, or simply had him sign something on a clipboard.

In short, because we weren't paying attention ... well, we weren't paying attention. We had no particular reason to remember this class interloper because we were there for something else and didn't expect anything other than a law school lecture to occur with a professor in the front and us students taking notes.

I daresay we all have similar observational skills.

Indeed, Professor Carlson's test describes exactly how life happens. We're here for one thing, yet something else occurs that we don't expect. Occasionally that "something else" is a crime or other injurious act that ends up in court, and when we're asked to testify about it, our "observational skills" come into play. How good are yours? Just ask Joe Pesci in *My Cousin Vinny*.

Give our apparent "lack of observation" some thought. In fact, let's run our own little test. Pause for a moment here and think of the last person you saw who's now out of your sight. Pick someone you're likely to see again later today or tonight. Then write down the particulars of the questions we just covered above, and as many other relevant observational details that you can remember. Describe as much as you can. And see if you can remember what that person said last. Write it down and then check back to see if you're right.

Throughout this book, we'll see conflicting testimony, like Professor Carlson's end-of-class test. People rarely remember the same event in the same way. Add to this lack of observational skills a possible desire to influence the outcome of a trial (either through political beliefs, for money, or due to your own prejudices and ideologies), swirl in the effect of heavy media coverage and you'll wonder how we ever manage to reach the truth when famous cases come to court. Some would say we rarely get the verdict right, but with modern-day protections, you might be surprised.

Sure, there are some well-known cases discussed here that have left us all scratching our collective heads. I didn't say our justice system is perfect. It's not. In many instances, it's far from perfect. But it is one of the best systems developed for reaching the truth, even though it occasionally fails. In fact, you'll see that we've come a long way from inquisitions and hanging witches and wizards to get at the truth, which typically resulted in anything but the truth. In the chapter on Lindy Chamberlin, you'll see another country's legal system. Is it that much different from ours?

Read on, and you'll see masterful lawyers reaching the truth as their clients saw it, not necessarily the pure truth of the event. As just one example, if you write the number six on a piece of paper in front of you, it looks like the number nine to the person across the table. Both are right, yet both are wrong. How would you decide?

But that's a whole other book—you'll have to stay tuned for the sequels about more famous cases. There seems to be no end.

CHAPTER 1
The Trial of Jesus

No one knows exactly what happened in the trial of Jesus—or for that matter, whether one or two trials occurred, one religious and one secular. Beyond the many disagreements, books, articles, and beliefs, it appears most scholars and religions agree that Jesus existed, went through one if not two trials, and was crucified. Beyond those several common points, our collective secular beliefs and sacred faiths are wildly divergent.

Unfortunately, there are no contemporaneously written texts to consult; only brief religious and historical accounts written at least a lifetime or more after Jesus' death. Even if we had access to a trial transcript, Jewish or Roman court reporters of the time surely would have had different purposes: alternatively, to alienate Jews or Romans or, conversely, to please Jews or Romans. As you will see in the later Boston Massacre chapter, the accused (a soldier) will tell two different stories, one to their superiors and one to their accusers. Even other possibilities in telling the story of Jesus' death are easy to imagine: to convert others to Christianity, dissuade them from conversion, or enhance any number of other religions or belief sets.

Surely my attempt to analyze this trial will alienate some readers because they will assume I am picking a side, leaving out facts, including only selected facts or simply getting it wrong. Admittedly, I am the son of a Congregational minister, so presumably I have at least that bias, but due to his guidance, I grew up exposed to many different religions and even different divisions within Christianity. In addition to regularly attending my father's church and my mother's Sunday school classes as a child and young man whether I liked it or not, I have attended innumerable masses, worshiped in temples, churches, observed prayers in mosques, talked around campfires, studied Buddhism and Taoism, listened to agnostics, and read the Quran, the Book of Mormon, and studied the Bible at length, even the traitorous Christian book, *The Harlot by the Side of the Road*, a favorite source for my father's sermons.

With all that widely varied dogma rattling in my head, I now find my religion in the outside world and particularly in the First Amendment to the U.S. Constitution—we each have the freedom to practice our own religion as we see fit, all 4,500 plus of them. I believe we each have the correct belief system and that I am in no position to judge one over the other, especially whether the Church of the Flying Spaghetti Monster has it right. The mysteries and genuineness of our individual religions I leave in your capable hands.

So, with those disclaimers, and especially the one at the front of this book, let me define the purpose of this chapter a bit further. I seek not to place blame, but rather only to ask questions that will make you think and perhaps cause you to conduct some theological and scholarly research on your own. As much as I am able, I intend to be fair, open-minded, and impartial in presenting these various religious and historical accounts, and expect you, the reader, to cast a critical eye on the sources I quote for the information provided. You must necessarily apply your own belief system (or lack of one) to what you read—and even what you don't read—but my attempt is to take a lawyer's view of the trials, colored with my own training and experience as a twenty-first century U.S. trial lawyer. In lawyer's jargon, the religious aspect of the trial of Jesus has little, if any, relevance to my analysis.

The trial of Jesus appears both in Jewish and Roman histories. Josephus Flavius, a Jewish historian, wrote:

> At this time there appeared Jesus, a wise man, if indeed one should call him a man. For he was a doer of startling deeds, a teacher of the people who receive the truth with pleasure. And he gained a following both among many Jews and among many of Greek origin. He was the Messiah. And when Pilate, because of an accusation made by the leading men among us, condemned him to the cross, those who had loved him previously did not cease to do so. For he appeared to them on the third day, living again, just as the divine prophets had spoken of these and countless other wondrous things about him. And up until this very day the tribe of Christians, named after him, has not died out.[1]

Roman historian Tacitus records the prosecution of some fifty cases of treason during Emperor Tiberius' reign. Tacitus wrote:

Christus, from whom the name had its origin, suffered the extreme penalty during the reign of Tiberius at the hands of one of our procurators, Pontius Pilate, and a most mischievous superstition, thus checked for the moment, again broke out not only in Judaea, and the first source of the evil, but even in Rome, where all things hideous and shameful from every part of the world find their centre and become popular.[2]

The Judges

Scholars agree that at the time of Jesus' trial, Jerusalem was under Roman rule, although Rome tolerated, to a degree, the practice of Judaism. At the time of his trial, Jesus was 33 years old. The main players in the trial of Jesus included High Priest Joseph Caiaphas and Pontius Pilate. Caiaphas was about eight years older than Pilate, who was 43. Pilate was the sixth Roman prefecture (we would know him as a Governor) of Judea, at the time a subdivision of Syria. In addition to his military duties, Pilate oversaw both civil and criminal trials. Caiaphas likewise owed split allegiances. Rome appointed him to act as liaison between the Roman authorities and the Jewish population, but on the other hand, he was the chief religious authority for Jews. As the son of Annas, an earlier high priest of the Jewish Sanhedrin governing body, Caiaphas came from the Sadducean aristocracy and served as the head of the Great Sanhedrin, a group of seventy-one high priests and lay elders. Researchers believe, however, that about only forty high priests and lay elders heard evidence as part of the trial of Jesus.[3] The Great Sanhedrin was the equivalent of our combined Supreme Court, Executive Branch, and Congress wrapped into one. There were no "checks and balances."

Trial Procedure

After his late-evening arrest by a crowd the chief priests sent to the Garden of Gethsemane, the crowd brought Jesus before the Sanhedrin for a hearing. No one seems to agree on the reasons for his arrest, which may stem from his visit to the Jerusalem Temple during the Passover festival. Cynical speculation leads to the conclusion that his arrest may have resulted from fears over his rising popularity among locals.

On one hand, scholars believe that Jesus may have participated in an armed rebellion, symbolically protested commercialism, predicted the end of the Temple, taught revolutionary ideas, uttered the name of God (YHWH), or even proclaimed himself to be the Messiah. On the other hand, the four gospel accounts (the Bible's New Testament Books of Matthew, Mark, Luke, John, and to some degree Acts [Peter's version]) describe Jesus attacking moneychangers and pigeon-sellers on the Temple grounds, also protesting the commercialism of Temple worship.

Many Christian texts point to the Mishnah Tractate, which is a set of Jewish rabbinical oral traditions (laws) written about 200 years after Jesus' death, as the definitive set of procedures that the Sanhedrin would have followed in conducting Jesus' trial. Perhaps, though, not all those procedures existed two centuries earlier. Christians point to many deviations from those procedures as violations of Jesus' rights. As two examples, trial under Jewish law in the Mishnah Tractate prohibited nighttime proceedings and required at least two separate hearings. Jesus had one trial at night, violating both procedures.

Scholars point out that Mishnah procedures require stoning as the prescribed form of death, not crucifixion, and note that the 200-year gap casts doubt that these procedures were in place at the time of Jesus' first trial or hearing. In any event, these two Jewish laws formed the basis for our current constitutional protections that now require a public trial, rules of evidence, and constitutional criminal procedures. During the arraignment, the judge reads the charges and describes to the accused his or her constitutional rights. The preliminary hearing occurs next, where the judge makes an initial determination of probable cause the crime was committed before proceeding to trial. Then at trial, constitutional protections continue to exist in at least the right to a jury trial, and rules of evidence apply.

Whether Jewish law from the Mishnah Tractate and the older Code of Moses applied to Jesus' trial is a matter of some debate. There are several interesting Jewish laws that, if applied, may have caused a different outcome. Like English law, Jewish law would typically not admit into evidence an accused's forced confession, believing it unreliable. In the chapter about the Boston Massacre, we will hear again about the application of the English version of this law.

Suffice it to say here that using an accused's pretrial deposition in trial is an exception to the supposed prohibition against using a forced confession. Our Fifth Amendment in the Bill of Rights grants the accused the right not to testify in a criminal trial, but as a practical matter, juries question the exercise of that right. Indeed, under California evidentiary law a criminal jury cannot even know the accused asserted the Fifth Amendment, although because we watch TV and stream video, most jurors know that's exactly why a defendant doesn't have to testify. "I plead the Fifth Amendment" is a popular refrain on so many television shows that it is frequently just recited, "I plead the Fifth." An individual also can assert that right in a civil trial, but, if used, the judge can instruct that civil jury to infer that the individual is guilty.

Rabbinical law also allowed an accused to employ counsel. In none of the scholarly or biblical texts do we read about either Jesus' request for an attorney or whether was one appointed for him, a right that did not exist then. Whether an attorney would have made a difference before the Sanhedrin or Pontius Pilate raises a question never answered, but worth considering. Imagine asserting an objection to either the Council or the Roman prefect; They would just have ignored it. This Jewish law forms the basis for one of the modern-day *Miranda* warnings that a criminal accused of a crime is entitled to be represented by a lawyer.

As a lawyer, I can't imagine having Jesus as a client. Let alone the burden of the judgment of the ages, I'm not sure I'd want to run the risk that losing the case would have resulted in his crucifixion and ultimately his death. Even among criminal lawyers, there are those who will not defend anyone who faces the death sentence—and I'd have to say I'm one of those. But I'm getting away from the trial itself, so we'll discuss that later. Before we get to the testimony, though, let's cover a bit of the procedural background.

Sanhedrin Testimony

Neither hearsay nor circumstantial evidence was admissible under the terms of the Mishnah Tractate. The Gospels note that members of the rowdy crowd and, perhaps, direct witnesses testified about Jesus' statements in the Temple to the effect of "I will destroy the Temple."[4] Under current evidence rules, those statements constitute hearsay (an out-of-court statement offered to prove the truth of the matter asserted), but become admissible at least under the excited utterance exception, if not others.

Obviously, current evidentiary rules do not apply in Jesus' trial, but the policy behind the hearsay exceptions is nothing new either. Modern trials are replete with circumstantial evidence. As we will see again in the chapter about the trial of Australian Lindy "the-dingo-ate-my-baby" Chamberlain, the prosecution built its entire case from circumstantial evidence.

Let's take the concept of a lawyer representing Jesus to its logical conclusion: do you assert the hearsay objection and keep that testimony against him out of the trial?

In response to Sanhedrin questions about whether he was the son of God, Jesus responded, "You are right in saying I am."[5] If the Mosaic Code applied to this trial, then Jesus had the right to refuse to respond to this question. In that situation, and given Jesus' Temple education as a youth who studied Jewish laws, it seems logical to assume he knew he had the right to refuse to testify. By choosing to respond to the question though, we can assume Jesus voluntarily waived that right and chose to testify against himself, knowing the consequences. Modern trials are full of examples where criminal defendants elect to testify, so this waiver is certainly not unusual. A question not addressed by any account, however, springs from an alternative not present: What would have happened if Jesus would have asserted his right not to testify?

What would have happened if Jesus had the benefit of an attorney and followed that attorney's advice not to testify? What would have happened if the lawyer obtained a "not guilty" verdict?

According to various versions of the four gospels, based on Jesus' statements to the Sanhedrin that were alleged to constitute blasphemy, the Sanhedrin found him guilty and eligible for death by stoning. Only Roman law had the power to pronounce and carry out death sentences, however. The question becomes, then, whether it made any difference to die underneath the press of stone or die on the cross? We will see the torture again by the "press of stone" in the Salem Witch Trials chapter. With the benefit of hindsight, we know the effect of Jesus' death on the cross, but perhaps the authorities were trying to send a different message than we have now. Perhaps Jesus himself sought the death penalty by painful crucifixion. The cross is a more powerful symbol of sacrifice than a pallet of stones. We have seen many instances since where criminal defendants sentenced to death welcome the verdict and sentence, seemingly willing to suffer the penalty.

To obtain a death sentence for Jesus, the Sanhedrin had to bring its accusation before the Roman prefect, who then had a duty to review the entire "lower court" proceeding as a separate trial court. The final power to determine Jesus' innocence or guilt rested in the Roman Governor's hands. Scholars disagree with the accounts that elevate the proceedings before the Sanhedrin to the level of a trial and argue instead that they only took preliminary evidence, similar to our modern-day preliminary hearing.

Modern-day Judaism treats Jesus as largely irrelevant to its religion when compared to Christianity. Most scholars identify Christianity's split from Judaism to the former's belief in a dual or triumvirate deity, while the latter encourages only monotheistic beliefs. Consequently, Jewish scholars and texts do not provide much information about either Jesus or his trial. What information does exist comes mainly from Christian texts written during the formative years after its separation from Judaism. Those writings arose amid establishing its independence from Judaism, many years if not decades after Jesus' crucifixion occurred. One of Christendom's foremost scholars, Rudolf Bultmann, argued the synoptic gospels' theology of Jesus' life offered it more as stories and myths, urging believers to split history from faith.[6] This argument is soundly discredited by fundamentalist and evangelical Christian beliefs. Islam, on the other hand, treats Jesus as a human prophet, not divine, but offers little about his trial.

You will have to judge for yourself whether Professor Carlson's "observation" example cited in the Introduction has any validity and applicability to the trial of Jesus. What crimes did the crowd see him commit? With that, let's get to the trial transcript, such that it is.

The Dominant Gospels' Version of the Trial Before Pontius Pilate

Without much evidence from Judaic texts, little other than the three synoptic gospels, Matthew, Mark and Luke, exists to draw a consistent set of circumstances of Jesus' trial.[7] The so-called maverick gospel, John, which differs from the three others in many respects, also alters the timeline of events and places Jesus' action of clearing the Temple of moneychangers at the start of his ministry[8] compared to the other three.[9] The synoptic gospels, generally favored by more liberal Christians, agree that this event almost immediately preceded Jesus' arrest and presumably formed the basis for his arrest. John's version of Jesus' trial likewise differs significantly from the other three gospels.[10] Other gospels, such as ones from Thomas and Mary, exist, but those are more historical in nature. With these caveats, we turn to Mark—mostly accepted as the oldest of the four dominant gospels—to examine the trial of Jesus before Pontius Pilate.

It's hard to pick which one of these versions to follow, but since we need at least one transcript to review, here is Mark's version of Jesus' trial before Pilate:

> 1. And as soon as it was morning the chief priests, with the elders and scribes, and the whole council held a consultation; and they bound Jesus and led him away and delivered him to Pilate.
>
> 2. And Pilate asked him, "Are you the King of the Jews?" And he answered him, "You have said so."[11]

Here, any judge worth his or her salt—to coin a phrase—would have stricken that answer as non-responsive and ordered the witness to answer yes or no to the question asked. None of the Gospels indicate any challenge to Jesus' answer, even from Pilate as his judge.

> 3. And the chief priests accused him of many things.
>
> 4. And Pilate again asked him, "Have you no answer to make? See how many charges they bring against you."
>
> 5. But Jesus made no further answer, so that Pilate wondered.
>
> 6. Now at the feast he used to release for them one prisoner for whom they asked.
>
> 7. And among the rebels in prison, who had committed murder in the insurrection, there was a man called Barabbas.
>
> 8. And the crowd came up and began to ask Pilate to do as he was wont to do for them.
>
> 9. And he answered them, "Do you want me to release for you the King of the Jews?"
>
> 10. For he perceived that it was out of envy that the chief priests had delivered him up.

> 11. But the chief priests stirred up the crowd to have him release for them Barabbas instead.
>
> 12. And Pilate again said to them, "Then what shall I do with the man whom you call the King of the Jews?"
>
> 13. And they cried out again, "Crucify him."
>
> 14. And Pilate said to them, "Why, what evil has he done?" But they shouted all the more, "Crucify him."
>
> 15. So Pilate, wishing to satisfy the crowd, released for them Barabbas; and having scourged Jesus, he delivered him to be crucified.[12]

As an aside, it's interesting that we lawyers, judges and court reporters still use numbered pages and lines to cite trial transcripts some 2,000 years later.

Jesus' Sanhedrin trial was apparently not without other witnesses, who the synoptic Gospels call out as false witnesses. Nevertheless, we have this allegedly blasphemous statement uttered against Jesus by unnamed witnesses: "At the last came two false witnesses and said, 'This fellow [Jesus] said, I am able to destroy the temple of God, and to build it in three days.'"[13] While you might think to assert a hearsay objection here, you would be both right and wrong. The statement meets the test for hearsay, that is an out-of-court statement offered for the truth of the matter it asserts. It is competent evidence though, because it meets one of the many exceptions to the hearsay rule—it is admission by the opposing party (Jesus) against his interest.

Maybe it's a good thing lawyers weren't there.

Although many have examined these passages for their religious significance and delivered innumerable sermons about them, there are several legal issues present that literature has given short shrift. Regardless of religious significance, truth or mythological nature of the matters stated, the legal issues (in modern parlance) in these sixteen verses include jurisdiction, an arraignment, a preliminary hearing, a speedy trial, the privilege against self-incrimination, the right to face accusers, hearsay evidence, the burden of proof, direct and circumstantial evidence, a jury trial, double jeopardy, parole, cruel and unusual punishment, sentencing, and, finally, the right to appeal.

This book's legal analysis steers clear of Roman criminal law because Mark does little, if anything, to demonstrate his knowledge of it. Instead, he attempts to place blame elsewhere, and that analysis is likewise beyond the scope of this chapter. Indeed, Pilate had the option of applying Roman law or religious law.[14] The Roman law against treason that would have applied to Jesus was known as the *Lex Julia Majestatis*, passed in 48 B.C.E.

There are two Latin criminal terms that bear some examination: *actus reus* and *mens rea*. Combined, they form the two essential elements of a crime. *Actus reus* means "guilty act" and *mens rea* means "guilty mind." Under modern law, both elements must exist for guilt to be pronounced. While you would think these elements come from Roman law since we're using Latin to explain them, they derive from the much later English law of the sixteenth century. English jurist Edward Coke first wrote the legal maxim, "*non facit reum nisi mens sit rea*, which means, "the act is not culpable unless the mind is guilty."

Perhaps that's why Rome fell.

To be convicted of a crime under English law after the sixteenth century, the accused must both commit the act and intend the consequences, elements still required today. At the time of Jesus' trial, the law was not so distinct and refined. Even so, evidence of both elements of Jesus' criminal act and his intent is not readily apparent, although earlier passages in the various gospels point to several of his alleged crimes against Roman, Mosaic, and Judaic laws.

The "many accusations" against Jesus included his act of chasing the moneylenders out of the Temple, which at the time was an act of desecration, despite the opposite social policy today. His claim to be the son of God constituted blasphemy. His refusal to recognize Caesar or pay taxes to Rome flaunted Roman law and rule. Certainly, under laws of the time, these acts constituted the *actus reus* element. These crimes were all capital offenses at the time and presumably required some showing of intent to commit them, but Jesus' knowledge of those laws would have established his *mens rea* necessary to fulfill the second element. Jewish children of the time were taught in the Temple, learned to read, analyze, and study the Talmudic scriptures and Jewish law. At 12 years old, the Gospel of Luke noted that Jesus was growing in understanding from his visits to the Temple "both listening and asking questions."[15] Whether we agree now that the acts Jesus undertook constitute crimes or whether the punishment fits the crimes are considerations that were not present at the time of his trial.

To turn to the other legal issues at hand, it appears Jesus was arraigned before both the Sanhedrin and Pilate, although in a cursory manner at best. It appears the two bodies were not overly concerned with jurisdiction over Jesus, since both heard the charges against him. It is equally unclear what charges Jesus faced, although there appear to have been many possibilities. In the Sanhedrin proceedings, Jesus was accused of blasphemy. Yet, in Mark's transcript of the Roman trial, Pilate focuses instead on treason. Which crime Jesus committed, or both, is at best unclear, but blasphemy was not a Roman crime.[16] Today, the accused must be informed of the charges.

In another of the synoptic gospels, Jesus faced the charge of treason for failure to pay tribute (taxes) to Rome, which created a conundrum. If he refused to pay tribute, then he admitted treason. If he paid tribute, then he betrayed his own teachings. Jesus instead avoided both pitfalls and responded, "Render therefore unto Caesar the things which are Caesar's; and unto God the things that are God's."[17] The division in this statement finds its way into our own Constitution as the forerunner of the separation of church and state and freedom of religion in the First Amendment of the Bill of Rights.

Jesus certainly received a speedy trial, given that he was arrested and tried within a day. He was technically denied the opportunity not to testify against himself, however. I say "technically" because his answers to both the Sanhedrin and Pilate may not have constituted admissible testimony. He said, "You have said so," which foisted the charge back to the accusers and was not necessarily an admission of guilt. In legal parlance, Jesus did not answer the question asked.

Noticeably absent from Mark's version of the trial before Pilate is any witnesses against Jesus other than the Sanhedrin priests. Although Jesus faced his accusers, these men were not percipient witnesses but rather could introduce only inadmissible hearsay evidence. Presumably, they did not personally witness Jesus' alleged crimes, which allegations Pilate apparently disregarded in any event. Likewise, Jesus did not cross-examine his accusers, a right he would have had under Roman law, according to Paul's account of his own final trial in Acts. Paul quotes Porcius Festus, the procurator (governor) of Judea after Pilate, where Festus responded to a question from King Agrippa about the evidence against Paul:

> To [Paul] I answered, it is not the manner of the
> Romans to deliver any man to die, before that he

> which is accused have the accusers face to face, and have license to answer for himself concerning the crime laid against him.[18]

Maybe Festus was a lawyer.

In Mark's account of the trial of Jesus, there appears to be no direct or circumstantial evidence introduced and the only evidence, if it even rises to that level, are the statements of the priests about Jesus' actions. Basing a death sentence on hearsay demonstrates the value of the rule we follow now.

Direct evidence can be testimony from a witness of the event or a physical item of evidence. Circumstantial evidence has been defined in modern law as:

> . . . direct evidence of a fact from which a person may reasonably infer the existence or nonexistence of another fact. A person's guilt of a charged crime may be proven by circumstantial evidence, if that evidence, while not directly establishing guilt, gives rise to an inference of guilt beyond a reasonable doubt.[19]

Under modern law, Jesus could be convicted of these crimes only upon proof beyond a reasonable doubt. Given Mark's short transcript of the trial, sufficient evidence to reach that level of proof appears to be sorely lacking:

> In ancient Roman law, the principle of burden of proof expressed itself through different maxims, such as *ei qui affirmat non ei qui negat incumbit probatio* (onus of proof is on him who affirms, and not on him who denies) and *actori incumbit probatio* (the claimant carries the burden of proof).[20]

More Latin. You'd think this book was a class. In California we have remarkably similar "Maxims of Jurisprudence."[21] As a close example of the latter, the statute reads, "He who takes the benefit must bear the burden."[22]

It also appears from Mark's version that Pilate offered Jesus a sort of jury trial, given his questions to the crowd seeking to determine Jesus' guilt. Pilate retained the final power to decide Jesus' fate, and he elected to sentence Jesus to death, although he equivocated and consented to cries for death from the crowd as prompted by the Sanhedrin priests. In addition to the obligation to enforce Roman law, the emperor charged Pilate with maintaining the peace in this province, so it is not surprising that Pilate consented to the wishes of the crowd to release Barabbas and crucify Jesus.

Can we consider that crowd the modern-day equivalent of a jury? Did the Sanhedrin priests exercise the equivalent of our peremptory challenges so the crowd "outvoted" those who wanted to save Jesus? Did they pay members of the crowd to ask for Barabbas' release? What if Jesus' followers had understood how to stack the jury/crowd in favor of Jesus and the apostles had been so trained by jury consultants?

In addition to the issue of whether Jesus was granted a jury trial, questions arise whether he was placed in double jeopardy for being tried by both the Sanhedrin and the Roman government. Was the Sanhedrin's "consultation" a conviction, or in the manner of a preliminary hearing did the Sanhedrin bind him over for trial? Pilate's questions of Jesus constituted what we now consider a trial. Under the laws of at least the European Union, the United States and India, an individual cannot be punished twice for the same crime, however.[23] Some commentators point out that Pilate first scourged (whipped) Jesus and then sent him to be crucified. According to other texts, whipping was part of crucifixion, designed to hasten death.[24] If so, then double jeopardy would not attach to the conviction because it was part of the punishment for the crime. On the other hand, either whipping or his crucifixion alone would now be viewed as cruel and unusual punishment. Taking a further step back, the Sanhedrin did not punish Jesus; Only Roman authority sentenced Jesus.

As part of his trial, Pilate offered the crowd the opportunity to "parole" one of two criminals: either Barabbas or Jesus. Pilate incorrectly assumed the crowd would pick Jesus since Barabbas had been convicted of murder, a more serious crime than Jesus had committed. The crowd, perhaps stirred by planted rabble-rousers, chose Barabbas. In his Gospel account, Mark offers the parole of one criminal as a means of avoiding punishment for another. The concept appears in few places in the history of jurisprudence and is relevant here, in a Roman custom during Passover of freeing a prisoner.

In any event, Mark's transcript, confirmed by the other gospels, shows that Pilate was willing to acquit Jesus and release him. Even today's governors in the 50 states have the power of parole and pardon, and in the U.S. the President too has the power to pardon a criminal. Do you think Jesus could have received a pardon if he would have sought one?

Jesus' trial also raises interesting questions about the concept of cruel and unusual punishment. The idea of cruel and unusual punishment is unique to modern law; it was not at all present in Roman times—whipping and crucifixion were accepted forms of punishment. Today, many would argue that stoning, scourging and crucifixion each alone constitute both cruel and unusual punishment. We are left to wonder how the Romans would have viewed death by other earlier methods, such as the rack, stoning, burning, beheading, and hanging (as we will see in the chapter about the Salem witch trials of the 1600s) or any other number of methods of execution carried out over the years.

We believe we have come a long way over the last 2,000 years. In the next 2,000 years, though, how will our descendants view hanging (3), electrocution (155), a firing squad (2), the gas chamber (11) and lethal injection (965)? The numbers in parentheses are the number of death sentences carried out in the United States via those respective methods between just 1976 and 2008, according to the Death Penalty Institute. The Old Testament and several other religious texts offer a differing perspective: an eye for an eye and a tooth for a tooth.[25] Some countries continue to practice retribution, one of the four goals of criminal law. The others are rehabilitation (therapy), deterrence (cost), and incapacitation (jail).

Finally, we look at the issue of appeals. Although an appellate system was in place during the time of Jesus' trial, he was not a Roman citizen, unlike Paul, who was. Jesus could not appeal to Rome for a review of Pilate's decision, which was final. As a Jew, Jesus was not entitled to invoke the protections or standard procedures of Roman law. As the Bible relates, his appeal was limited to a higher power. Yet through Roman law, Jesus faced at least an arraignment, was read an indictment, examined by a prosecutor, offered a defense, was given a verdict, and an opportunity for parole—all standard criminal procedures of the time and to some degree now although our evidentiary standards are much different and distinct.

Today, criminal appeals can take years, even decades in the case of death sentences. In the United States, one prisoner was on death row for twenty years pending his appeals, some even longer. How would the Gospels have treated a long incarceration for Jesus?

Chapter Conclusion

The two trials went wrong in many ways if you apply modern standards. Jesus was not afforded a true, open-to-the-public arraignment so he and others could hear the charges against him. He was forced to testify against himself, even though his answers were cryptic. The Gospels allege the testimony against him was false, but under today's standards that decision lies in the hands of the fact finder, here Pontius Pilate. Neither the Sanhedrin nor the Roman Governor truly offered him the opportunity to consult with counsel and he did not receive a trial by a jury of his peers as we understand those rights today. His punishments were cruel, if not unusual by the way we look at things today, even though generally accepted at the time. The two punishments fall within our definition of double jeopardy. He had no right of appeal—or at least none was offered or otherwise apparently available, according to the Gospels. Had the right of appeal existed, there were many (modern) grounds to overturn the decision while Jesus waited on death row in jail.

Although the offer of a pardon was not offered directly to Jesus, it was offered to the crowd of onlookers and soundly rejected by them. While the crowd constituted a jury in the loosest sense of the concept, the Gospels suggest the outcome was rigged against Jesus and not the true vote of those who would sit in judgment of him. Realizing now Jesus' significance to the Christian faith, such a decision would intimidate anyone sitting in judgment, which may be something to keep in mind the next time you're on a jury.

In one trial, I remember a juror's excuse for not wanting to sit on a jury; she told the judge she didn't think she could sit in judgment of anyone—that task was solely God's province. She was promptly excused from the jury pool. But for justice and the rule of law to work, we must sit in judgment of one another when called to do so. At other times, perhaps best illustrated by gossip in a social context, it may not be appropriate to sit in judgment of others.

Contributing to these omissions was both Jesus himself, on one hand, and the priests and the Governor on the other. Reading between the lines of Mark's recitation of the story of Jesus' trial, you can argue that Jesus chose the route of a martyr and did not sufficiently challenge the outcome of the trial, as if it was preordained—a concept not lost on the Christian faith. Mark's story overtly attempts to cast the Sanhedrin priests in the capacity of those who simply wanted Jesus out of the way to eliminate a challenge to their authority, and the Roman Governor likewise seems concerned about the same result, questioning Jesus' role as King of the Jews.

Even assuming Jesus had been provided and exercised all the rights afforded to him under modern law, would the outcome have been any different? Would Jesus have been crucified or simply gone on to live a life on death row not remembered today? If he had not died, would his teachings have continued? What else would he have taught? Who would have been listening to him when he reached 80 years old? Would he still have disciples who recorded his every word? Some of those questions are dangerous to ask the Christian faithful, but on the other hand largely irrelevant to the world's other religions. They're questions I won't answer for you but commend instead to your good judgment and consideration. They are certainly interesting questions to consider and expand on, and equally interesting to follow to their logical conclusion: how would the world's other religions be different today? Would Jesus' message still have the reach it presently has? If not, would another prophet, messiah, or towering religious figure have filled the gap? Would we even have a New Testament?

It is unfair to judge the trial of Jesus by our modern standards, but nonetheless instructive. In this analysis, we can become more aware of how we apply current concepts of justice to ancient stories and belief systems, allowing us to deepen our faith and take away a more informed ideal of applying the basic justice of "right and wrong" in our dealings with each other. That ideal, after all, is the core message of this trial, and it is one I have asked every jury in each of my trials.

Yes, the judge will read a set of jury instructions that outline the law as it applies to each case, but my question to the jury is simpler: "What is right and what is wrong?" At some point in time in each juror's life they learned right and wrong from their families, their peers, and their faith. Right and wrong is an inherent belief system. Even the Marvel Universe thinks so; without it there would be no struggle between the forces of good and evil.

Remember to enter your vote on the outcome of this trial on www.10FamousTrials.com and see how other readers voted.

CHAPTER 2
Salem Witch Trials

Step into the Shoes of a Witch

You are a fine, upstanding member of the community and well-respected by all, having lived for years in Salem, part of the Massachusetts colony in the year 1692. Unfortunately, you've just been accused of a supernatural crime that will almost certainly end with your death by hanging as a result of grand jury proceedings you knew nothing about. But don't worry, things will be worse before they get better, if you can even look at it that way.

After your indictment and arrest, you'll be thrown in jail in the middle of a brutally cold New England winter where the temperatures are below freezing. Because you are a woman with virtually no money and little standing in society, you won't be able to pay your jail fees, so you'll get only the food your family brings to you—on occasion. You will be bitter cold because you can't afford the firewood and to top it off, the jail leaks, allowing the wind and snow to enter your cell. Plus, you may languish in jail for four or five months before you go to trial. Perhaps by then it will warm up if you're still alive.

Oh, you want to know about your constitutional rights? Well, remember, it's 1692. We don't have a constitution yet in the Massachusetts Colony. In other words, you do *not* have the right to remain silent, and everything you say can and will be used against you. You do *not* have the right to have an attorney present during questioning. The court will *not* appoint an attorney for you, even if you can't afford one. In fact, there's not an attorney available for about 3,000 miles across an ocean. The authorities don't care if you don't understand your rights, or for that matter, whether you have any rights. They just want to convict you.

In fact, the judge of the court is instead a town merchant with no legal training, who was appointed to the position by an uneducated treasure hunter (also known as the Governor of the Colony—maybe not much different from some other more recent U.S. governors). When the judge has questions about the evidence, he turns to ministers for advice, not judges, or lawyers. That's religious ministers in case you were wondering, not government ministers. In fact, the judges seem more concerned with finishing the trials than they are about taking evidence, since you are already presumed guilty.

When you finally get to attend your trial, you won't be allowed to cross-examine the witnesses who testify against you. In fact, your husband and your daughter may testify against you. The members of the community who now scorn you will ask questions of you and the other witnesses during your trial. They will also offer comments to impugn your character, interpreting your previous kind acts as the reason they lost cattle or why their other family members got sick and died, both common occurrences for the times.

The main witnesses who testify against you will likely be teenage, angst-ridden children, who will entertain the onlookers with their staged convulsive fits. Those fits will miraculously stop when you touch them and provide the judges with conclusive evidence to prove you are guilty. Additionally, the children will testify that your ghost came to them in the night and asked them to sign their names in the devil's book, further convincing the judges that you are guilty. The judges won't believe your denials of guilt and assertions of innocence, and no one will testify on your behalf. Just to make sure you are guilty, other women will strip you in the "privacy" of your jail cell and find a mole on your body as the final piece of evidence to seal your guilt.

Once convicted, you will have no right of appeal. If you are educated enough to know how to write and somehow manage to get your petition to the Governor (yes, the same uneducated one as above) asking for a pardon, he will ignore it. Your church will then excommunicate you, and your minister, together with leaders of your now former church, will come to your cell to give you the news just before your hanging.

On Gallows Hill, the crowd will mock you. Once dead, your body will be thrown into an open pit. You would be lucky if someone tosses a few shovelfuls of dirt over your body. Your family may come at night to retrieve your body and bury it in a shallow but certainly unmarked grave. If you owned property, it will be sold, and the sheriff may take more than his share for conducting the sale. Your family may receive a pittance as payment for your death years later after everyone realizes you really were innocent, but even then, it will take your descendants nearly 300 years to clear your name of guilt.

Welcome to the late 17th century in New England. Skip forward for a moment, if you like, to the McMartin preschool trial chapter and see if we've come much further.

Historical Background

In 1692, seventy-two years after the Pilgrims landed in Plymouth, Massachusetts, in their quest to escape religious persecution, another type of trial arose. All hell broke loose in the Massachusetts Colony, and in the seaport of Salem and the more inland and agricultural Salem Village (now known as Danvers, Massachusetts). Townspeople turned against one other and accusations of witchcraft flew around the Colony, resulting in nineteen deaths by hanging; one death from pressing under rocks and five who died because they stayed too long in prison, all due to the hysteria. In the process, legal proceedings were largely ignored.

Broomsticks, satanic rituals, and seemingly "afflicted" children stirred puritanical imaginations, deepened by petty rifts between powerful families and rival congregations. To inquire into the torrent of citizen complaints about the number of prisoners in jail, Massachusetts Bay Colony Governor William Phips appointed a man with no legal training to preside over the trials. This man, William Stoughton, was both a town merchant and Lieutenant Governor of the Colony. Judge Stoughton would allow evidence of specters—ghosts—into the proceedings. Instead of acting as judges, he and several others appointed themselves prosecutors and questioned defendants, allowed public onlookers to interrupt the trials with evidence and questions, refused to allow attorneys to represent the defendants, and forced the accused to testify against themselves.

Much can be said about the historical backdrop of the time, but a few things bear mention first. There were many outside forces at play. The Massachusetts Bay Colony Charter at first allowed self-rule and made land grants to the colonists. The Crown restored its own Charter in 1692 when it appointed Sir William Phips Governor of the Colony, but the colonists were unsure whether the prior land grants would be respected. For himself, Phips started life as a poor shepherd, but upon his discovery of sunken treasure off the Bahamas as a ship's captain, he won a knighthood from King James II and his appointment as Governor from William and Mary. Perhaps not surprising, ten percent of Phips' discovery went to the Crown. Having started as a shepherd and without formal education, Phips was ill-equipped to deal with the requirements of his government and had little support from England, where he was eventually called back to trial to answer for his failures.

The English crown was in flux, as well as the colonies. King James II had been deposed some three years earlier in 1689, and William III of the House of Hanover and Mary II ascended to the throne, signaling a switch from Catholicism to Protestantism. Settlers in New England had suffered through the bloody King Phillip's War. "King Phillip" was the English name for Metacom, the leader of the native American Wampanoag tribe from the Nantucket and Cape Cod area of Massachusetts (and one of my ancestors, some 14-15 generations ago) in 1675 and 1676, only to fight again in the French and Indian Wars, which raged in the colonies from 1689 to 1697. The wars ravaged the colonists' lives, money, and temperament, in part driving the fears that led to the witch trials.

In early January 1692, just before the first allegations of witchcraft arose in Salem, nearby colonists suffered a vicious attack that became known as the Candlemas Massacre. About 150 Abenaki Indians, commanded by officers of New France, attacked the York Garrison in Maine, killed about 100 of the English settlers, and burned much of the town. The remaining villagers were taken hostage, about 80 in all, and forced to walk some 200 miles to French Canada, where they were ransomed by Captain John Alden of Boston. Alden was the son of John Alden and Priscilla Mullins of the Plymouth Colony and a Mayflower descendent, the two idolized in Thanksgiving history dinners. Alden himself would be accused of witchcraft, but escaped from jail and later won a pardon after the hysteria died down. While the colonists may have fought English wars, they did not adopt much of its law and what they did adopt was seriously misinterpreted in the witch trials.

English common law, written in two mid-century sets of treatises by Sir Edward Coke, chief justice of Common Pleas and King's Bench, had difficulty making its way across the Atlantic. In fact, early colonists viewed lawyers as unnecessary and more trouble than they were worth. One notable law, however, would be imported: the 1641 English law that made witchcraft a crime punishable by death.

On the other side of the Atlantic in the Massachusetts, two father-and-son ministers, Reverends Increase Mather and Cotton Mather, played a significant role in the witch trials. Both consistently preached about the influences of sin on the colonists and their backsliding ways. In a refrain heard over the years and ever since, the younger generation was simply going to the devil, according to the two ministers.

Just prior to the outbreak of the witch trials in Salem, Reverend Cotton Mather, the minister in Boston's North Church, helped fan the flames of witchcraft with his book, *Memorable Providences, Relating to Witchcrafts and Possessions.* In that publication, Mather detailed his investigation of Goodwife Ann Glover, a widowed Irish washer woman and her witchcraft. Reverend Mather's introduction noted:

> A Faithful Account of many Wonderful and Surprising Things, that have befallen several Bewitched and Possessed Persons in New-England. Particularly, A Narrative of the marvellous Trouble and Releef Experienced by a pious Family in Boston, very lately and sadly molested with Evil Spirits.[1]

Along with most New England homes, Mather's bestselling book was on Reverend Samuel Parris' bookshelf in Salem Village. Parris, perhaps unwittingly, stirred tensions in the inland, agricultural Salem Village where the townspeople had for years sought to form their own congregation. They wanted to separate from Salem Town, which was the nearby, more populous and prosperous seafaring town. Once the inland congregation won that right, they called Parris as their minister in 1689, but became divided over the decision to deed the parsonage and its two acres to Parris. The powerful Putnam family favored the deed, with the Nurse family against. The Hatfields and McCoys are another variant of this time-worn tale of fights between families. Both Salem Village families had themselves engaged in their own disputes over land grants. To make matters worse, Parris had little experience as a minister, having spent a good number of years as a lackluster merchant in Barbados.

Midwinter in late January and early February of 1692, the roots of the witchcraft trials first gained their chokehold in the Parris parsonage. Reverend Parris' nearly teenage daughter, Elizabeth, experienced apparently unexplained convulsive fits and was believed to have a fever. One modern-day researcher marshaled circumstantial evidence pointing to convulsive ergotism, "a disorder resulting from the ingestion of grain contaminated with ergot, may have initiated the witchcraft delusion."[2] Ergot is a mold known to contaminate rye and the mold can be derived into LSD and other hallucinogens. Whether the moldy rye triggered the fits is a matter of great debate, and something you shouldn't try at home.

The Witch Hunt

Nevertheless, the non-scientific puritans blamed Elizabeth's fits on witchcraft, and they pointed first to the Parris' family slave, Tituba, an Indian from Barbados, who Reverend Parris brought with him to Salem when he accepted in 1688 an invitation to preach at the Salem Village church. Tituba originally came "from an Arawak village in South America where she was captured as a child, taken to Barbados as a captive and sold into slavery."[3] Parris bought her in Barbados along with her husband, Indian John, who would later be accused of witchcraft as well. Prior to any allegations, Tituba had enthralled Betty and her cousin, Abigail Williams, with palmistry, fortune-telling, tales of voodoo, and other dark magic, largely known to her because of her exposure to several Caribbean cultures.

More children began to exhibit the same bizarre behavior as Elizabeth, including her friend twelve-year-old Ann Putnam, Jr., the daughter of Sergeant Thomas Putnam and his wife, Ann Putnam. Thomas Putnam also served as clerk of the newly established parish and was one of the leaders of the faction who brought Parris to Salem, having earlier led efforts to oust the prior minister, Reverend George Burroughs. Other children involved include seventeen-year-old Mercy Lewis, who had previously been in the family of the Reverend Burroughs while he was in the Village. At the time the trials started, Mercy Lewis was a servant in Sergeant Putnam's family. Other afflicted children included Mary Walcott, the daughter of Captain Jonathan Wolcott, deacon of the parish. Reverend Burroughs had been removed from the parish due to his unconventional religious beliefs (the Reverends Mather thought he was a Baptist) and he had failed to repay money lent to him by Thomas Putnam. Burroughs had moved to Maine, but was later arrested and brought back to Salem for trial as a wizard, supposedly the "ringleader" of the accused witches, having been so accused by Ann Putnam, Jr. As a man and head of his household, Thomas Putnam relayed his daughter's accusations to the Magistrate.

To determine the basis for Elizabeth's affliction, Parris' neighbor, Mary Sibly, advised Tituba and her husband Indian John to take the child's urine, mix it with a cake with rye and feed it to a dog, which was believed to identify the witch causing Elizabeth's affliction. Mrs. Sibly's advice was founded on an old English tradition known then as "white magic." On February 25, 1692, Tituba baked the cake. When Reverend Parris discovered the attempt, he beat Tituba.

In response to the affliction of their daughter Ann, On February 29, 1692, the Putnams brought charges of witchcraft against Tituba, Sarah Good, and Sarah Osborne, as well as other women in the Village. Good was homeless and a beggar, about 70 years old and the wife of William Good, a laborer. She mumbled words under her breath and scolded the townspeople if they failed to give her alms, who in turn believed her mumbled words to be curses directed at them.

To avoid further beatings, Tituba confessed that the "devil urged her to sign a book . . . and also work mischief with the children,"[4] all admissions tantamount to being a witch, a suspicion already widely held. Tituba's testimony also mentioned flying broomsticks. By her confession, Tituba was jailed but avoided death because the Puritans believed she would be judged by God, and their mortal judgment was therefore unnecessary. Tituba remained in jail for some thirteen months because Parris refused to pay her jail fees. Parris then took matters before his congregation.

The Fears of Religion

In the words of Reverend Parris, the Puritans feared "Satan and his wiles and devices." Witchcraft was the common enemy, but that fear failed to bring the community together; it instead divided the townspeople. The Salem Village Church Record contains an entry about Mary Sibly, written by Clerk Thomas Putnam, chronicling her confession to the congregation as read by Reverend Parris. In the entry, Putnam related how the good reverend took to task Sister Sibly for her behavior. She repented and the congregation tacitly voted to forgive her.

But notice how Reverend Parris shifted the blame for the witchcraft outbreak from his household:

27. March. Sab. 1692. Sacrament day.

After the common Auditory was dismissed, & before the Church's communion at the Lords Table, the following testimony against the Error of our sister Mary Sibly, who had given direction to my Indian man in an unwarrantable way to find out Witches, was read by the Pastor.

It is altogether undenyable that our Great & Blessed God, for wise & holy ends hath suffered many persons, in several families, of this little Village, to be grievously vexed, & tortured in body, & to be deeply tempted, to the endangering of the destruction of their souls; & all these amazing feats (well known to many of us) to be done by Witchcraft, & Diabolical operations. It is also well known that when these calamities first began, which was in my own family, the affliction was several weeks before such Hellish operations, as Witchcraft was suspected. Nay it never broke forth to any considerable light, untill Diabolical means was used by the making of a Cake by my Indian man, who had his direction from this our sister Mary Sibly: Since wch Apparitions have been plenty, & exceeding much mischief hath followed. But by this means (it seems) the Devil hath been raised amongst us, & his Rage is vehement & terrible, & when he shall be silenc'd the Lord only knows. But now that this our sister should be instrumental to such distress, is a great grief to myself, and our godly Honoured & Reverend neighbours, who have had the knowledge of it. Nevertheless, I do truly hope, & believe, that this our sister doth truly fear the Lord, & am well satisfied from her, that what she did, she did it ignorantly, from what she had heard of this nature from other ignorant, or worse persons. Yet we are in duty bound, to protest against such actions, as being indeed a going to the Devil, for help against Devil, we having no such directions from Nature, or Gods word, it must therefore be, & is, accounted by godly Protestants, who write or speak of such matters as Diabolical, & therefore calls this our sister to deep humiliation for what she has done, & all of us to be watchful against Satans wiles & Devices.

> Therefore, as we in duty, as a Church of Christ are deeply bound, to protest against it, as most directly contrary to the Gosple, yet in as much as this our sister did it in ignorance as she professeth, & we believe, we can continue her in our holy Fellowship, upon her serious promise of future better advisedness and caution, & acknowledging that she is indeed sorrowfull for her rashness herein.
>
> Brethren, If this be your mind that this iniquity should be thus born witness against, manifest it by your usual signe of lifting up your hands.
>
> The Brethren voted generally, or universally: None made any exceptions.
>
> Sister Sibly, If you are convinced that you herein did sinfully, & are sorry for it: Let us hear it from your own mouth.
>
> She did manifest to satisfaction her error & grief for it.
>
> Brethren. If herein you have received satisfaction, testify it by lifting up of your hands.
>
> A general vote passed: no exception made.
>
> **Note.** 25. March 1692 I discoursed said sister in my study about her grand error abovesaid, & also then read to her what I had written as above to read to the Church, & said sister Sibly assented to the same wth tears & sorrowful confessions.[5]

Despite Sister Sibly's confession and apparent remorse, witchcraft fever was about to strike Salem Village in earnest. With his daughter still "afflicted," Parris called in the Village doctor, William Griggs, who diagnosed Elizabeth as "bewitched," an easy diagnosis since he didn't know what was wrong. Soon thereafter, two other girls in the town became similarly afflicted, complaining also of "pinching" and "biting," while exhibiting convulsive fits. But it was not just religion that spurred the witch hunt. In the words of the Salem Witch Museum, "factions among Salem Village fanatics and rivalry with nearby Salem Town, a recent smallpox epidemic and the threat of attack by warring tribes created a fertile ground for fear and suspicion."[6]

That claim might be an understatement.

The First Set of Witch Trials

The Putnams' charges resulted in a warrant issued by Magistrates John Hathorne and Jonathan Corwin for the arrest of Sarah Good, which charged her "with suspicion of witchcraft done to Elizabeth Parris, Abigail Williams, Ann Putnam and Elizabeth Hubbard, at sundry times within this two months."[7]

Good was the first alleged witch examined during the witch trials. Hathorne and Corwin originally set her examination at the tavern of Lieutenant Nathaniel Ingersoll in Salem Village. When a hundred or so onlookers showed up, they adjourned to the larger meetinghouse, where they examined Tituba, Sarah Osborne, and Sarah Good on March 1 and 5, 1692. As reported by Ezekiel Cheever, here is the examination of Sarah Good, as conducted by John Hathorne, who speaks first:

> Q: Sarah Good, what evil spirit have you familiarity with?
>
> A: None.
>
> Q: Have you made no contracts with the devil?—
>
> A: No.
>
> Q: Why do you hurt these children?
>
> A: I do not hurt them. I scorn it.
>
> . . .
>
> Q: Why did you go away muttering from Mr. Parris' house?
>
> A: I did not mutter, but thanked him for what he gave my child.
>
> Q: Have you no contract with the devil?
>
> A: No.

[Reporter Stephen Sewell's note] Hathorne desired the children to look upon her and see if this were the person that hurt them, and so they all did look upon her and said that this was one of the persons that did torment them. Presently they were all tormented.

> Q: Sarah Good, do you not see now what you have done? Why do you not tell us the

truth? Why do you thus torment these poor children?

A: I do not torment them.

...

Q: How came they thus tormented?

A: What do I know? You bring others here and now you charge me with it.

Q: Who was it?

A: I do not know but it was some you brought into the meeting house with you.

Q: We brought you into the meetinghouse.

A: But you brought in two more.

Q: Who is it then that tormented the children?

A: It was Osborne.

Q: What is it you say when you go muttering away from person's houses?

A: If I most tell I will tell.

Q: Do tell as, then.

A: If I must tell, I will tell. It is the commandments: I may say my commandments, I hope.

Q: What commandment is it?

A: If I most tell you, I will tell; it is a psalm.

Q: What psalm?

[Reporter's note] After a long time she muttered over some part of a psalm.

Q: Who do you serve?

A: I serve God.

Q: What God do you serve?

A: The God that made heaven and earth (though she was not willing to mention the word "God").

[Reporter's note] Her answers were in a very wicked, spiteful manner, reflecting and retorting against the authority with base and abusive words; and many lies she was taken in. It was here said that her husband [William Good] had said that she was either a witch or would be one very quickly. The worshipful Mr. Hathorne asked him his reason why he said so of her, whether he had ever seen anything by her. He answered: "No, not in this nature, but it was her bad carriage to him; and indeed," said he, "I may say with tears, that she is an enemy to all good."[8]

Not only did her husband testify against her, but the Magistrates also examined her daughter, Dorcas Good (a dispute exists among various texts, which alternatively lists her name as Dorothy Good, and disputes exist whether she was four or five years old). It is hard to imagine a nearly 70-year-old woman had a daughter, unless the little girl was "taken in" by the Good family. In any event, recorded testimony from Dorcas quotes her testimony against her mother, Sarah Good, as follows:

> She [Sarah Good] "had three birds, one black, one yellow, and these birds hurt the children and afflicted persons."[9]

The vocabulary in her testimony is obviously not that of a little girl, but rather that of a somewhat inaccurate adult court reporter. Earlier, Tituba's testimony had included tales of a little yellow bird with the devil that had scratched her. Dorcas herself would also be accused of witchcraft by Mercy Lewis, Mary Wolcott and Ann Putnam, Jr., all virtually in the same words:

> The deposition of Mercy Lewis, aged about nineteen years, who testefieth and saith that on the 2d of April, 1692, the apperishtion of Dorrithy Good, Sarah Good's daughter, came to me and did afflict me, urging me to write in her book and several times since Dorothy Good hath afflicted me, biting, pinching and choaking me, urging me to write in her book.[10]

On March 7, Sarah Osborne, Sarah Good, Dorcas, and Tituba were sent to a Boston prison. By allowing the testimony about an "apparition," Hathorne and Corwin had admitted what was then called spectral evidence, which was highly controversial at the time and completely inadmissible now. The current test of admissibility is largely based on the perceived trustworthiness of the testimony. The village people believed that a witch gave the devil permission to use her "shape" to afflict another. The objection to this evidence rested on the obvious untrustworthiness of the testimony, since an accuser could simply claim the alleged witch's apparition appeared to the accuser. In line with local beliefs, however, the Magistrates (and later the court appointed by the Governor) concluded the devil could not use a "shape" without the witches' permission, which was sufficient to convict a person of witchcraft.

That's what lawyers call circular, or syllogistic, reasoning. The supposed rule proves itself.

Supported by this "evidence," Hathorne and Corwin continued their investigation of the others accused of witchcraft. Hathorne's questions approached an inquisitional style and showed little respect for either the accused or belief that they had any presumption of innocence, contrary to our Constitution. The theory that we have somehow progressed from those archaic beliefs may be founded on paper, but not in reality. Most present-day criminal defense attorneys report that only lip service is paid to the presumption of innocence. Instead, the accused must actively prove his or her innocence, especially when a jury considers that the police arrested the person for the crime, the prosecutor elected to try the case, and the judge has found probable cause that the defendant must stand trial. At the start of a criminal trial, even now, there is truly little presumption of innocence left.

After all, if you didn't do anything wrong, why would you be in the defendant's chair?

Still, court proceedings have come a long way in three hundred years, thankfully. Both Hathorne and Corwin were magistrates or what we know as justices of the peace, but neither were trained in the law. While they may have been successful Salem Village merchants, they won appointments to their positions in part due to their political connections. Trained lawyers and judges were virtually nonexistent in the colonies. Indeed, the first law school in the colonies would not be established until 1779 at the College of William and Mary in Virginia, named after the former English rulers. On the other hand, Queens' College of Cambridge, England, where English law was first taught, was formed some 560 years ago, but successful solicitors, barristers and, judges in England had little reason to relocate to the colonies in the 1600s and the early 1700s.

While reality today may not presume innocence, there are at least attorneys and judges trained in the law to ensure defendants receive fair trials, which stands in stark contrast to the proceedings in the Salem Village witch trials. As with most aspects of the law, there are exceptions. Today and mostly in rural and sparsely populated areas with no lawyers, we still have justices of the peace who are not trained in the law, and, like Hathorne and Corwin, won their appointments through political connections or elections. Unlike the Salem Village witch trials, most proceedings today are conducted with constitutional procedural protections.

Most of the time, anyway.

In May of 1692, the Magistrates Hathorne and Corwin signed arrest warrants for a number of people who were ultimately caught and brought before them—but at least two, George Jacobs Jr. and Daniel Andrews, could not be caught. Like today, allegations against those who are suspected of crimes tend to reach the ears of the accused sooner than most others. Jacobs and Andrews were more than lucky to have learned of the warrants early and left town to avoid the hangman's noose. On the other hand, having left Salem Village for small-town Wells, Maine after a dispute arose over his beliefs and a debt, Reverend George Burroughs was arrested in early May, hauled back to Salem, and tossed in jail after allegations against him by Ann Putnam, Jr., relayed to the Magistrate by her father, Thomas Putnam, to whom Borroughs owed a debt. At some point, although it is not clear when, John Alden and Phillip English, who have both been examined by Hathorne and Corwin's court, escaped from jail and did not return to Salem Village.

The Court of Oyer and Terminer

As the witch hunt fever began in and around Salem in 1692, the magistrate-style trials caused some 62 accused witches to clog the jails. In response to the imprisonment of so many, on May 27, 1692, Massachusetts Bay Colony Governor William Phips convened a Court of Oyer (to hear) and Terminer (to decide) to inquire into the matter. That court convened in Salem Village, and the judges included Lieutenant Governor William Stoughton, Nathaniel Saltonstall, Bartholomew Gedney, Peter Sergeant, Samuel Sewall, Wait Still Winthrop, John Richards, John Hathorne and Jonathan Corwin (who substituted in for another judge who resigned in disgust after the first trial). Stoughton acted as the chief judge.

In the trials, Stoughton went beyond the norms of an English courtroom. He admitted spectral evidence (evidence of ghosts), allowed private conversations between accusers and judges, permitted spectators to interrupt the procedures with personal remarks, forbade defense counsel for the accused, and placed judges in the role of prosecutors and interrogators of witnesses. His admission of evidence regarding specters may appear to lack common sense to us now, but perhaps his lack of legal training and the overly puritanical religious environment coupled with the colonists' multiple fears contributed to this mistake. It is likewise unclear why Stoughton suffered little political damage from his role in the trials. In 1694, Stoughton became acting governor when Phips returned to London to defend his administration against claims of corruption. Defying rational thought, Stoughton nevertheless ran the courtroom in a way that contributed to the injustices suffered.

On June 2, 1692, the first of the witches tried by the newly established Court of Oyer and Terminer was Bridgett Bishop. As part of her trial, the court appointed a "jury of matrons" to examine her body. The matrons found an excrescence of flesh—something growing out of another without use or contrary to the order of production.[11] What we commonly understand as a mole, Puritans of the time thought was where the devil suckled for nourishment, then called a "witches teat."

Additional testimony against Bishop included allegations of what was, at the time, considered "black magic:"

> Two witnesses testified that on taking down the cellar wall in the old Bishop house where Bridget lived in 1685, they found in holes in the wall several poppits [a type of rag doll] made up of rags and hog's brussels with headless pins in them with the points out. Poppits were believed to represent the person whom the witch desired to afflict, and by sticking pins into those images the mischief was supposed to be mysteriously and safely accomplished.[12]

Stoughton also failed to control the other judges who participated in the trials. In fact, Hathorne's questioning grew even more prejudicial.

> Hathorne: How do you know that you are not a witch?
>
> Bishop: I do not know what you say. . .I know nothing of it.

> Hathorne: Why look you, you are taken now in a flat lye.

Hathorne's initial query quoted above is known as a "negative pregnant" question, which implies its affirmative opposite and is virtually impossible to disprove. This style of questioning is frequently lampooned by lawyers, who sarcastically respond, "When did you stop beating your wife?" to which there is no satisfactory answer and proves its foolishness. Hathorne's conclusion that Bishop has lied simply proves the bias of the results-oriented court. She was tried and convicted the same day, and Chief Judge William Stoughton signed her death warrant. A photograph of his personal seal on her death warrant is included below.[13] Just eight days later, on June 10, 1692, Bridget Bishop was hung on Gallows Hill. Less than a week later, on June 16, Roger Toothaker, jailed earlier, died in prison.

Shortly thereafter, Reverend William Milbourne, a Baptist minister in Boston, publicly petitioned the General Assembly in June 1692, challenging the use of spectral evidence by the court. Milbourne had to post £200 bond or be arrested for "contriving, writing and publishing the said scandalous Papers."[14] In response, twelve ministers of the colony advised the court not to rely on spectral evidence for convicting suspected witches.[15]

Ministers acting as judges. What will they think of next? Inquisitions? At this point, "The further trials were put off to the adjournment, the 30th of June. The governor and council thought proper, in the meantime, to take the opinion of several of the principal ministers upon the state of things as they then stood. This was an old charter practice."[16] On June 15, 1692, the ministers wrote back, as penned by Cotton Mather:

> The Return of Several Ministers Consulted by his Excellency, and the Honorable Council, upon the present Witchcrafts in Salem Village.
>
> I. The afflicted state of our poor neighbors that are now suffering by molestations from the invisible world, we apprehend so deplorable that we think their condition calls for the utmost help of all persons in their several capacities.
>
> . . .
>
> III. We judge that in the prosecution of these, and all such witchcrafts, there is need of a very critical

and exquisite caution, lest by too much credulity for things received only upon the Devil's authority there be a door opened for a long train of miserable consequences, and Satan get an advantage over us, for we should not be ignorant of his devices.

IV. As in complaints upon witchcrafts there may be Matters of Inquiry which do not amount unto Matters of Presumption, and there may be Matters of Presumption which yet may not be reckoned Matters of Conviction, so 'tis necessary that all proceedings thereabout be managed with an exceeding tenderness towards those that may be complained of, especially if they have been persons formerly of an unblemished reputation.

V. When the first inquiry is made into the circumstances of such as may lie under any just suspicion of witchcrafts, we could wish that there may be admitted as little as is possible of such noise, company, and openness as may too hastily expose them that are examined, and that there may be nothing used as a test for the trial of the suspected the lawfulness whereof may be doubted among the People of God, but that the directions given by such judicious writers as Perkins and Bernard be consulted in such a case.

VI. Presumptions whereupon persons may be committed, and, much more, convictions whereupon persons may be condemned as guilty of witchcrafts, ought certainly to be more considerable than barely the accused person being represented by a specter unto the afflicted, inasmuch as 'tis an undoubted and a notorious thing that a Demon may, by God's permission, appear even to ill purposes in the shape of an innocent, yea, and a virtuous man. Nor can we esteem alterations made in the sufferers by a look or touch of the accused to be an infallible evidence of guilt, but frequently liable to be abused by the Devil's legerdemains.

...

VIII. Nevertheless, we cannot but humbly recommend unto the government the speedy and vigorous prosecution of such as have rendered

> themselves obnoxious, according to the direction given in the Laws of God and the wholesome statutes of the English nation for the detection of witchcraft.[17]

Despite the ministers' objections, the court resumed its proceedings and continued to admit spectral evidence and required the accused witches to touch the accusers. Stoughton felt confident spectral evidence should be admitted, and cited several authorities in defense of his position, including the Bible. While the Bible may seem an odd legal citation, like all good writers, the court recognized its audience. In New England, the following "authorities" were used in support of Witchcraft:

> Keeble, Common Law, Chapter on Conjuration, pp. 217- 220.
>
> Sir Matthew Hale's Tryals of Witches, 1682.
>
> Glanville's Collection of Sundry Trials of Witches in England and Ireland in the years 1658-61-64-81.
>
> Bernard's Guide to Jurymen.
>
> Baxter and Burton, Histories about Witches.
>
> Cotton Mather, Memorable Providences relating to Witchcraft.

Of course, these authorities in turn rested upon "Holy Writ" (the Bible) itself.[18]

Notably, Sir Matthew Hale, K.T., was an English jurist who just ten years earlier had published an account where he admitted spectral evidence to convict and hang some thirteen women accused of witchcraft in a 1664 trial. At the end of June and beginning of July, the grand jury issued indictments against Sarah Good, Elizabeth Howe, Susannah Martin, Elizabeth Procter, John Procter, Martha Carrier, Sarah Wilds, and Dorcas Hoar. Of those, Sarah Good, Elizabeth Howe, Susannah Martin, and Sarah Wildes, along with Rebecca Nurse, went to trial and they were found guilty and executed on July 19, 1692.

At Sarah Good's hanging, Reverend Nicholas Noyes sought her confession as a witch, saying, "You are a witch, and you know you are a witch." She responded, "You are a liar. I am no more a witch than you are a wizard, and if you take away my life, God will give you blood to drink."[19] Twenty-five years later, Noyes died of a hemorrhage and choked on his own blood.

After their trial, Sarah Good, Elizabeth Howe, Sarah Wildes, Susannah Martin, and Rebecca Nurse were hanged on Gallows Hill on June 29.

The trials were far from over. On July 2, 1692, Ann Pudeator was examined at Beadle's Tavern in Salem Village before the Magistrates, but despite their demands, she refused to confess to the charges of witchcraft. Accuser Sarah Churchill testified that Ann Pudeator took her to the devil's book to sign when Sarah was at the home of George Jacobs, Sr., and the Magistrates admitted more spectral evidence. Mrs. Pudeator could neither counter this evidence, nor withstand charges of causing diseases. In his testimony against Mrs. Pudeator, Lieutenant Jeremiah Neal alleged:

> She [Ann Pudeator] has been an ill-carriage woman, and since my wife has been sick of the small pox, this woman has come to my house pretending kindness. She asked whether she might use our mortar. My wife and I consented to it, but I afterwards repented of it, for my wife was the worse. My wife grew worse until she died.[20]

Testimony against Ann Pudeator is likewise noteworthy because of the unique "touch test" used by the Magistrates to determine whether the afflictions the children suffered could be transferred back to the alleged witch. Ann Pudeator was required to touch accusers Ann Putnam, Jr., and Mary Warren, whereupon the children stopped writhing, as if the afflictions were miraculously returned to the supposed witch's body.

> Ann Putnam fell into a fit, and said Pudeator was commanded to take her by the wrist, and did; and said Putnam was well presently. Mary Warren fell into two fits quickly, after one another; and both times was helped by said Pudeator taking her by the wrist."[21]

There are no reports in the records of the witch trials whether any type of scientific control was used for this "test," such as blindfolding the children or having different people touch the child. This form of evidence is called demonstrative evidence, which will see most famously used in the trial of O.J. Simpson regarding the notorious bloody glove, as discussed in chapter 10. Judges today are understandably worried about the use of demonstrative evidence as an alternative to testimonial evidence. Questions are frequently raised whether the conditions of the in-court demonstration are sufficiently the same as the actual event. When coupled with its dramatic effect on a jury, demonstrative evidence can create an unconscious bias. Demonstrative evidence such as used in the Salem witch trials would not be admitted today because of the lack of scientific credibility.

Other evidence was also admitted against the accused, remarkably including bite marks, perhaps the first of its kind in America. Bite marks are still considered valid evidence in modern criminal cases due to their uniqueness, which criminalists claim is similar to fingerprints. It is hard to imagine that this evidence admitted in the witch trials was applied in the same scientific and precise fashion as it is today:

> The Testimonies of the other Sufferers concurred with these [other accusers]; and it was Remarkable, that whereas Biting was one of the ways which the Witches used for the vexing of the Sufferers, when they cry'd out of G. B. [Reverend George Burroughs] biting them, the print of the Teeth would be seen on the Flesh of the Complainers, and just such a sett of Teeth as G. B's would then appear upon them, which could be distinguished from those of some other mens.[22]

The Prisoner's Attempts to Avoid Death

On July 23, John Proctor and others in prison write to Reverends Increase Mather, James Allen, Joshua Moody, Samuel Willard, and John Bayley, seeking their support for a request for a change of venue for the trials. Motions to change venue are commonly used today in high-profile cases to transfer the matter to a different jurisdiction where predispositions and prejudices are not fully formed. Such was John Proctor's attempt.

But Proctor's request was unsuccessful, and on August 19, Reverend George Burroughs, John Proctor, George Jacobs Sr., John Willard, and Martha Carrier were also hung on Gallows Hill. Before his execution, Reverend Burroughs recited the Lord's Prayer perfectly, a task supposedly impossible for either a witch or a wizard, but Reverend Cotton Mather reminded those watching that Burroughs' conviction still stood.

> His [Reverend George Burroughs'] prayer (which he concluded by repeating the Lord's Prayer) was so well worded, and uttered with such composedness and such (at least seeming) fervency of spirit, as was very affecting, and drew tears from many, so that it seemed to some that the spectators would hinder the execution. The accusers said the black man stood and dictated to him. As soon as he was turned off, Mr. Cotton Mather, being mounted upon a horse, addressed himself to the people, partly to declare that he [Mr. Burroughs] was no ordained minister, and partly to possess the people of his guilt, saying that the Devil often had been transformed into an angel of light; and this somewhat appeased the people, and the executions went on.[23]

Not all who were condemned to die were willing to go quietly. Mary Eastick penned a handwritten petition to Governor Phips asking for a pardon, but the Governor refused to spare her. Here is her attempt at a pardon, edited into more modern English for readability, but retaining as much of the original text as reasonable:

> The humble petition of Mary Eastick unto his Excellencies Sir William Phipps and to the honored Judge and Bench now sitting in Judicature in Salem and the Reverend ministers humbly showeth: That whereas your poor and humble Petitioner, being condemned to die do humbly beg of you to take it into your judicious and pious considerations that your poor and humble petitioner knows my own innocence. Blessed be the Lord for it, and see plainly the wiles and subtlety of my accusers. I cannot but judge charitably of others that are going the same way myself if the Lord steps not mightily in. I was confined a whole month upon the same account that I am condemned now for, and then cleared by the afflicted persons as some of your honors know and in two days times I was cried out upon by them and have been confined and now am condemned to die. The Lord above knows my innocence then and likewise does now as at the great day will be known to men and Angels. I petition your honors, not for my own life for I know I must die and my appointed time is set but the Lord, he knows it is that if be

possible no more innocent blood may be shed, which undoubtedly cannot be avoided. In the way and course you go in I question not but your honors do to the utmost of your powers in the discovery and detecting of witchcraft and witches and would not be guilty of innocent blood for the world by my own innocence. I know you are in the wrong way. The Lord in his infinite mercy direct you in this great work if it be his blessed will that no more innocent blood be shed. I would humbly beg of you that your honors would be pleased to examine these afflicted persons strictly and keep them apart some time and likewise to try some of these confessing witches, I am confident there are several of them has belied themselves and others as will appear if not in this world, I am sure in the world to come whither I am now going and I question not but you will see an alteration of these things they say myself and others having made a league with the devil, we cannot confess I know and the Lord knows as will thoroughly appear they belie me and so I question not but they do others. The Lord above who is the searcher of all hearts knows that as I shall answer it at the tribunal Seat that I know not the least thing of witchcraft, therefore I cannot I dare not belie my own soul. I beg your honors not to deny this my humble petition from a poor dying innocent person and I question not but the Lord will give a blessing to your endeavors.[24]

The concept of pardon from government authorities has not changed much over the years—the condemned continue to claim their innocence, and thanks to advanced technology like DNA testing, sentences have been commuted and the innocent freed. In 1692, however, it took much more than a single plea to prevent the continued convictions and hanging of supposed witches. But hanging was not the only form of punishment meted out.

The punishment of hanging was insufficient for many in the local church. Reverend Parris' church records reflect the members' unwillingness to allow a witch in their congregation.

> 11. September. Lords day
>
> Sister Martha Kory taken into the Church. 27. April. 1690 was after Examination upon suspicion of

> Witchcraft. 21. March. 1691-2 committed to Prison for that Fact, & was condemned to the Gallows for the same yesterday: And was this day in Publick by a general consent voted to be excommunicated out of the Church; & Lft. Nathanael Putnam, & the 2 Deacons chosen to signify to her, with the Pastor the mind of the Church herein. Accordingly this 14. Septr. 1692. The 3. aforcsd Brethren went with the Pastor to her in Salem Prison, whom we found very obdurate justifying her self, & condemning all that had done any thing to her just discovery, or condemnation. Whereupon after a little discourse (for her imperiousness would not suffer much) & after Prayer, (which she was willing to decline) the dreadful sentence of Excommunication was pronounced against her.[25]

Martha Kory went to the gallows on September 22, 1692, along with seven others: Mary Eastey, Martha Corey, Ann Pudeator, Samuel Wardwell, Mary Parker, Alice Parker, Wilmot Redd, and Margaret Scott. The church also excommunicated members Giles Corey and Rebecca Nurse. Reportedly none of the deaths of the people executed as witches were concurrently recorded in Salem's record books.

A few days earlier, on September 19, 1692, 80-year-old Giles Corey, a Salem Village farmer, refused to enter a plea at his arraignment, which had the effect of refusing to consent to the court's jurisdiction. In essence, the court could not take jurisdiction over an individual unless that individual consented to jurisdiction by entering a plea. Courts have always been notoriously queasy about jurisdiction. Presently, federal courts can only take jurisdiction if that power is granted by statute or if the issue in the case involves a question about the interpretation of federal law, parties from different states, along with several other restrictive methods. Modern state courts, on the other hand, can take jurisdiction a bit more freely, but usually only over citizens after proper service of a summons, warrant or other judicial process. Entering a plea is no longer necessary to establish jurisdiction, but appearing in court is a sure way to do it, harkening back to the procedure used in the witch trials.

Relying on English law, the Court of Oyer and Terminer incorrectly believed it was permissible to use *peine forte et dure*, which is pressing the accused beneath an increasingly heavy load of stones. They employed that law and tactic to justify their attempt to make Giles Corey enter a plea. The English statute relates back to the primitive alternative of trial by ordeal instead of trial by jury. Parliament first enacted the law in 1215 but repealed it in 1772, but then decided that a refusal to enter a plea equated to a plea of guilty. The law in England 50 years later reversed that decision, which is the current state of the law both in England and in the United States. Despite the pressing, Mr. Corey refused to enter a plea to ensure his heirs would inherit his property. Had he been found guilty, his property would have escheated to the state. Corey is reportedly the only citizen in the United States to have ever suffered the punishment of *peine forte et dure* at the hands of a court.

The court convicted several others of witchcraft, including Elizabeth (Bassett) Proctor and Abigail Faulkner, but they received temporary reprieves due to their pregnancies and were scheduled to be spared from the gallows until they had given birth. Five other women were convicted in 1692, but their sentences were never carried out: Ann Foster (who later died in prison), her daughter Mary Lacy Sr., Abigail Hobbs, Dorcas Hoar, and Mary Bradbury.

The Beginning of the End

As accusations of witchcraft spiraled out of control to wider and wider circles, even Governor Phips' wife, Lady Mary Phips, was accused as a witch. Soon after, in early October 1692, Phips ordered spectral evidence and testimony excluded from future trials. Three weeks later on October 29, 1692, Phips prohibited further arrests of witches, released most of the accused witches still in prison and dismissed the Court of Oyer and Terminer.

About a month later, Phips created the Superior Court of Judicature, Court of Assize and General Gaol [jail] Delivery and convened the court in Salem Village to try those remaining in jail who were accused of witchcraft. Stoughton was once again on the court, but no spectral evidence was allowed. No one else was hanged, although Stoughton's court found several guilty and he again wrote warrants for their execution. In May 1693, in response to the death warrants, Phips pardoned them. One accused woman, Lydia Dustin, died in jail, unable to pay her jail fees despite her pardon. Ironically, as one of its last trials, the court heard charges against Mary Watkins for falsely accusing her mistress, Mrs. Swift, of witchcraft. Swift admitted the charges under examination and was apparently sold into slavery to satisfy her jail fees.[26]

And Lady Mary Phips was safe.

With this ignominious end, the initial chapter was closed on the Salem witch trials, and Reverend Increase Mather felt compelled to write a defense of the judges and trials, but condemned their use of spectral evidence. In his book commonly known as "America's first tract on evidence,"[27] *Cases of Conscience Concerning Evil Spirits,* Reverend Mather said, "It were better that Ten Suspected Witches should escape, than that one Innocent Person should be Condemned."[28]

Sir William Blackstone wrote much earlier, "It is better that ten guilty persons escape than that one innocent suffer."

The Requests for Compensation and Apologies

After the trials were over, many relatives of those hung, jailed, or accused petitioned the State of Massachusetts for compensation for lost loved ones and damage to their reputations. In response, the state agreed to pay approximately £600 to various relatives, and in 1697 acknowledged a day of atonement for its actions.

In 1706, Ann Putnam, Jr. sought membership in the Salem Village Church, but she first apologized for her role in the trials. Instead of accepting responsibility, she ironically blamed Satan when she stood before her church. Reverend Parris' successor, Reverend John Greene read her apology to the church members. Edited for readability:

> I desire to be humbled before God for that sad and humbling providence that befell my father's family in the year about ninety-two; that I, then being in my childhood, should, by such a providence of God, be made an instrument for the accusing of several persons of a grievous crime, whereby their lives were taken away from them, whom, now I have just grounds and good reason to believe they were innocent persons; and that it was a great delusion of Satan that deceived me in that sad time, whereby I justly fear I have been instrumental, with others, though ignorantly and unwittingly, to bring upon myself and this land the guilt of innocent blood;

> though, what was said or done by me against any person, I can truly and uprightly say, before God and man, I did it not out of any anger, malice, or ill will to any person, for I had no such thing against one of them; but what I did was ignorantly, being deluded by Satan.
>
> And particularly, as I was a chief instrument of accusing Goodwife Nurse and her two sisters, I desire to lie in the dust, and to be humble for it, in that I was a cause, with others, of so sad a calamity to them and their families; for which cause I desire to lie in the dust, and earnestly beg forgiveness of God, and from all those unto whom I have given just cause of sorrow and offense, whose relations were taken away or accused.[29]

The church admitted Miss Putnam, whose parents had both died earlier and left her to raise her siblings. Miss Putnam remained a spinster throughout her life. After two months of debate, the church also voted to posthumously revoke its earlier excommunication of Martha Kory, but the church records indicate several members' feelings were still strong: "There was a major part [who] voted [in favor, but] 6 or 7 dissented."[30] In 1712, the church reversed the excommunication of its now deceased members, Rebecca Nurse and Giles Corey.

In the ensuing years after the trials, many attempted to make amends for their behavior. On January 14, 1697, a fasting day proclaimed by the Massachusetts court, Reverend Samuel Willard read Salem witch trial Judge Samuel Sewell's apology to the congregation of Boston's South Church "to take the Blame & Shame" of the "late Commission of Oyer & Terminer at Salem."[31] Thomas Fiske and eleven other trial jurors also asked forgiveness.[32] Finally, in October 2001, the Massachusetts Legislature passed Chapter 122 of the Acts of 2001 for the Commonwealth of Massachusetts, which included the names of all who were wrongfully convicted of witchcraft in the State's finding of innocence.

Some three hundred years later, many will again wonder whether we have learned our lesson about the validity of testimony from children and satanic worship when the McMartin preschool trials begin, as discussed below in Chapter 9. After spending some seven years and more than $15 million in attorney fees in that case, we may still not have the answer to those questions, despite the history lesson of the Salem witch trials.

The witch hunts are far from over. Just look around to see if you can find allegations of one or two.

Chapter Conclusion

It's a bit frightening to go back in time and realize how the lack of modern-day constitutional protections can so easily lead to your death. These collective verdicts that led to sentences of hanging went horribly wrong due to a cascading series of terrible decisions: fears and unfounded beliefs, the appointment of ill-trained judges, their willingness to allow untested and illogical evidence into the trial, the lack of an attorney to defend the accused, no jury, and no right to appeal. Some would argue that the pendulum of protections has today swung too far in the opposite direction, but few disagree the Salem witch trials were nothing less than a farce.

The tough economic times, strict religious sects, dangerous wars, corrupt officials, in-fighting among various community factions, fear of the unknown, and malevolent children all contributed to the witch hunts.

And you thought I was talking about 1692!

The one take-away from this chapter centers on how easy it would have been to avoid these mistakes if lawyers and the rule of law had a place in the trial. William Shakespeare's famous line, "The first thing we do, let's kill all the lawyers" points out how topsy-turvy the world would be without lawyers. Had rules of evidence, the right to a defense lawyer, and trained judges been in place, the Salem witch trials would have ended quite differently—the so-called witches likely would have been acquitted. By the way, the premise to Shakespeare's "let's kill all the lawyers" is "if you want anarchy…"

Remember to enter your vote on the outcome of this trial on www.10FamousTrials.com and see how other readers voted.

CHAPTER 3
Rex v. Preston and Rex v. Wemms, et al., the two Boston Massacre Trials of Captain Thomas Preston and eight other British Redcoats

On a cold, moonlit night near an icy Boston harbor in 1770, wearing the redcoats that earned them their nickname, a small platoon of English soldiers stood in a rag-tag semi-circle. They came to protect a lone sentry who had retreated to Boston's Old State House from a gathering crowd of colonists infuriated with everything English. Coming to his aid, the soldiers stood shoulder-to-shoulder, with bayonets mounted aiming their loaded muskets at the colonists, breathing staccato clouds of formless mist that evaporated into the inky night as an even larger, riotous crowd of patriots gathered in front of them.

British Officer of the Day Captain Thomas Preston, sword drawn, positioned himself in front of his soldiers, hoping to diffuse a dangerous situation and calm the angry colonists. On the receiving end of those pointed bayonets gathered a surly crowd of some 200 rough New England dockworkers and young miscreants, rebelling at higher taxes, lost jobs, and foreign rule. They first took out their frustrations on the sentry, but now faced the barrels and bayonets of newly arrived King's soldiers protecting the sentry.

Apparently staged by radical patriots seeking to oust the English government, ringleaders such as Samuel Adams roused the crowd into action. The Patriots sought to create a catalyst to foment a revolution, and they found it that fateful night. Adams could not have anticipated the events he and others instigated, especially their effect on his second cousin, John Adams.

The crowd hurled snowballs, chunks of ice, and oyster shells at the soldiers. As their numbers grew, the rabble taunted the red "lobster backs" to fire their muskets. The colonists thought themselves protected by British law that forbade the soldiers from attacking without orders from a local civilian magistrate, who was not present that evening. Falsely emboldened, the colonists yelled "Fire!" and insulted the soldiers' heritage and lack of bravery. Swelled by an unchecked gang mentality, the crowd inched closer to the formed-up platoon.

In his closing argument during the soldiers' trial, defense lawyer John Adams described the crowd as "a motley rabble of saucy boys, negroes and mullatoes, Irish teagues and outlandish jack tars."[1] On that fateful evening, it was a sailor and ship's mate who first urged the charge, taunting and then clubbing an English solider.

The sailor, Crispus Attucks, grabbed a bat used by dockworkers to beat their ropes into twisted strands, and stood at the edge of the crowd immediately next to the redcoats. Attucks swung his bat and knocked that soldier, Private Hugh Montgomery, to the ground. As he rose, the Private yelled to his brothers-in-arms, "Fire, damn you, fire," and soldiers' musket shots rang out.

When the smoke cleared from the soldiers' now-empty musket barrels, five Bostonians lay on the cold, hard ground with their red blood freezing in the white snow. Three were dead, including Attucks, and two more mortally injured who would die within the fortnight. Six more were also injured but would later recover from their wounds. These shots, deaths and injuries became known as the Boston Massacre and galvanized a young nation to fight a more powerful and distant adversary, eventually winning this country's independence.

Conventional thinking of the time predicted these English soldiers would hang from the shortest yardarm of a ship moored in Boston harbor. Instead, John Adams, then a 34-year-old Boston lawyer and cousin of instigator Samuel Adams, saw trouble brewing and took on a most unpopular defense of the soldiers, later losing half his law practice because his clients protested his choice.

That's dedication to justice and history itself.

Historians disagree about the events I've related and am about to relate, but as a trial lawyer, I see things differently than these groups. As time marched on, details of the event morphed into the stuff of legends. Countless books and movies have portrayed the events of the Boston Massacre and ensuing trials. But not all the books and movies agree on the events themselves. For example, the HBO special *John Adams* took liberties with the actual events. The miniseries had one trial, when there were, in fact, two trials. Even more contrary to the television version, the second trial ended with two of the eight soldiers convicted of manslaughter. The miniseries found the soldiers "not guilty." Adams' supposed perfect TV record was pure Hollywood.

Revisionist history is nothing new to either TV or politics. Thankfully, a transcript of the soldiers' trial exists in the Library of Congress, and other publications there contain snippets of history allowing a modern-day, legal look at the trials. To put the trial in context, let's first examine the background of the trials.

Because the patriots hated the English, most visibly represented by the redcoats who shot five of the patriots' fellow countrymen late on the evening of March 5, 1770, the jury's decision was all but certain. Boston was still in the grip of an icy-cold winter and mobs of angry, pre-Revolutionary War patriots and civilians roamed the streets of Boston, freely taunting the soldiers because English proclamations supposedly prevented retaliation. A week before the Boston Massacre occurred, however, one colonist was shot by British soldiers in a similar tussle.

The outcome of the Boston Massacre trials of the soldiers and their captain seemed a sure thing well before Hollywood rewrote the script. Colonists predicted that the accused British soldiers would all hang for the murder of the five unarmed patriots, especially when judged by a Boston jury. John Adams took a different view and orchestrated their trials in a way that defied conventional thinking.

The Mood Before the Massacre

To understand the Boston Massacre, several other historic events in the prior three years must first come into focus. Initially, the British Parliament passed the Townshend Tax Acts on June 29, 1767. These Acts imposed more taxes on products imported into the Colonies, such as lead, glass, paper, spirits, rum, wine, molasses, sugar, and, as most of us remember, tea. Parliament also imposed duties on court documents, certificates, licenses, deeds, playing cards, pamphlets, books, calendars, newspapers, and even dice. The colonists were firmly under the thumb of British rule, but Bostonians rebelled and refused to pay the taxes. In response, England sent a heavy presence of British troops to Boston following the Stamp Act Riots.

As we know from the musical Hamilton, "Cuz when push comes to shove, I will kill your friends and family to remind you of my love."[2]

Most notably, John Hancock refused to pay taxes on May 9, 1768, some two years before the Boston Massacre, when he brought his aptly named sloop, *Liberty*, into port carrying a shipment of Portuguese Madeira wine. British law required Hancock to pay customs duty on his shipment, but as part of a locally organized boycott by Boston merchants, he instead unloaded and transported the wine to his warehouse without paying the duty. British customs officials then branded Hancock a smuggler and seized *Liberty*, which lead to a public outcry fueled mostly by Hancock's frustration. His and other patriots' defiance of customs officers in turn led to even more British troops stationed in Boston in September and October of 1768, to the increased disgust of the colonists.

Maybe that's where we got our dislike of taxes. I knew we imported one thing too many from England.

Realize for a moment the motivation of the British customs officials. Called the "Commissioners of Customs," they were appointed in Britain but lived in the colonies and drew their pay from the customs they collected in America. Ostracized by their colonist neighbors, most commissioners viewed their jobs solely to make money before returning to England as richer men. They cared nothing for politics and colonist sympathies unless it put revenue into their pockets. Faced with a sure loss of this revenue from colonists who "just needed to learn a lesson," the Commissioners called in the troops.

General Thomas Gage, then the Commander-in-Chief of the British forces stationed in the colonies, responded to demands from the Commissioners of Customs for more troops to ensure the collection of taxes for the King George III. Gage ordered regiments under the command of British Lieutenant Colonel William Dalrymple to Boston from Halifax, England, slated to arrive in September of 1768. These two regiments were known as the 14th West Yorkshire Fusiliers and the 29th Worcestershire Regiment of Foot. Soldiers from this latter regiment were the ones involved in the Boston Massacre.

Not satisfied with just two regiments, Gage also ordered the presence of the 64th and 65th Regiments, with an addition of a detachment from the 59th Regiment and a train of artillery with two cannons. These troops were scheduled to arrive in Boston some six weeks later from Ireland. In all, some 700 troops were sent to deal with the 15,000 recalcitrant, nontax-paying Boston citizens, who had been fighting for the exact opposite.

As we know from Patrick Henry's famous speech in 1765, some five years before the Boston Massacre, there should be "no taxation without representation." Bostonians also wanted fewer redcoats in the city, not more.

Instead, they lost on both counts, and on October 1, 1768, two years before the Massacre, the British troops arrived in Boston to restore order and collect taxes for the Commissioners of Customs and ultimately King George III. Describing their arrival, famous Patriot Paul Revere wrote that the British troops "formed and marched with insolent parade, drums beating, fifes playing, and colours flying, up King Street. Each soldier having received 16 rounds of powder and ball."[3] Revere, as we shall see, was the master of patriot propaganda, if not also his own.

When British Colonel Dalrymple requested to assign his redcoats to the homes of Boston citizens as they had been in New York under the Quartering Act, the Boston city council demurred. It declared its citizens were not required to furnish quarters until all available barracks space was filled. Because Castle William, named for William III of Orange, a former King of England (now simply "Castle Island"), had plenty of empty berths, the council members reasoned, so the soldiers could quarter there. For the town council, Castle William had the added advantage that it was outside the city. The townspeople had not forgotten how the British redcoats behaved during the French and Indian War when those troops were housed with the citizens. The colonists thought the career soldiers as mercenary, surly, and mean; certainly not fit company for their wives and daughters.

Massachusetts Governor Bernard, appointed by and loyal to the Crown (called a "Loyalist"), wanted the troops quartered in the colonists' homes as more pressure to pay the King's taxes. He countered that housing soldiers at Castle William thwarted decisions made in London, but the Boston selectmen held firm and refused to consent. Without housing readily available, the Governor instead offered General Gage empty factory buildings throughout the city. Troops of the 29th, unable to berth even in town, instead pitched tents on Boston Common. The stench from their latrines wafted through Boston, further frustrating the colonists.

There's little doubt why we now have the Third Amendment to the Constitution, which reads, "No soldier shall, in time of peace be quartered in any house, without the consent of the owner, nor in time of war, but in a manner to be prescribed by law." Like the remainder of the Bill of Rights, this simple statement carries more background than the thirty-two words of this amendment otherwise reveals.

Bostonians disliked the British soldiers for other reasons. They took jobs away from the colonists by working part-time in off-duty hours and accepting lower wages than local workers. Boston's dockworkers feared the soldiers as well. The redcoats enforced English press gang laws, which authorized British ship captains to seize just about anyone and force them into service aboard British Navy ships.

Once settled, the British troops then regularly patrolled the streets of Boston, rudely treating the colonists and outrightly disrespecting the lower-class dockworkers. Secure now with troops behind them, the Commissioners of Customs more easily collected taxes with higher success, demoralizing shop owners and manufacturers who passed on the higher taxes to the colonists, ultimately frustrating the wider Boston population.

These various affronts to the populace accumulated with more frequency and severity, culminating with the Boston Massacre. That evening's events, however, were sparked by a comparatively simple interaction between two people, but one directly symbolic of the looming problems between the two countries. The Boston Massacre started with an otherwise nondescript confrontation—the complaints of a local Boston wigmaker's apprentice to a British Lieutenant Captain demanding payment for his master's work on the wig.

The Boston Massacre

On March 5, 1770, an icy cold, dark, and dreary Boston night, Private Hugh White stood a lonely sentry's watch on Boston's King Street, just outside the Customs House, where the Commissioners collected their taxes and stored their levies, awaiting transport to England. Both the soldier and the Customs House stood as a barely tolerated reminder of King George III and Parliament's oppressive taxes against the colonists.

As was common at the time, an off-duty Lieutenant Captain walked about in uniform. Nearby a local wigmaker's apprentice,

Edward Garrick, spotted the British officer, Lieutenant Captain John Goldfinch, and called out, saying, "There goes the fellow who hath not paid my master for dressing his hair."[4]

Goldfinch walked on without acknowledgment. Historical accounts note that Goldfinch had paid the bill. Emboldened by Goldfinch's failure to respond, Garrick continued his insults and complained to three other passing colonists that this English officer had not paid his bill.

Perhaps feeling a need to defend his superior, nearby British Sentry Private Hugh White responded to Garrick's criticisms in Goldfinch's place, "He is a gentleman, and if he owes you anything he will pay for it."[5]

Garrick countered with, "There are no gentlemen left in the regiment."[6]

In response, the Sentry left his post and confronted Garrick, engaging in a heated exchange of words. With the butt end of his musket, the redcoat ensured the delivery of his message, struck Garrick, and knocked him down. As Garrick lay in the snow and cried in pain, one of the passers-by, Bartholomew Broaders, took up the argument with the Sentry.

"Bloody lobster back! Lousy rascal! Lobster son of a bitch!" Broaders yelled at White, who was quickly joined by others.[7]

Attracted by the melee, a crowd of about 50 colonists gathered from nearby bars and houses. Pouring in the street, they threw chunks of ice and other missiles at Private White, who retreated for his safety to his sentry box, loaded his musket and waved it to keep the now angry colonists away. The crowd continued to grow, and, in fear for his life, White retreated to the Customs House on King Street where the nearby British Main Guard slept.

Pause here for a moment and look around Boston. Apart from this altercation, two other initially unrelated disturbances almost simultaneously erupted a few blocks away from King Street, with sentries and small platoons also retreating to the Main Guard for protection. One crowd sprouted into a confrontation a few blocks north. In Dock Square, another club-carrying crowd of some 200 men likewise headed to the Customs House. Samuel Adams had been hard at work that night.

Then someone rang the fire bell at the Old Brick Meeting House, which drew curious onlookers expecting to see flames. Other bells in nearby church steeples rang, drawing a crowd of between 300 to 400 colonists. As Officer of the Day, British Captain Thomas Preston would later state in his deposition on March 13, 1770, "About 9 of the guard came to and informed me the town inhabitants were assembling to attack the troops, and that the bells were ringing as the signal for that purpose and not for fire, and the beacon intended to be fired to bring in the distant people of the country."[8] All streamed toward King Street, the Customs House, and the Main Guard.

At the Main Guardhouse, Captain Thomas Preston watched the powder-keg situation. As he testified in his deposition:

> . . . I saw the people in great commotion, and heard them use the most cruel and horrid threats against the troops. In a few minutes after I reached the guard, about 100 people passed it and went towards the Custom House where the king's money is lodged. They immediately surrounded the sentry posted there, and with clubs and other weapons threatened to execute their vengeance on him. I was soon informed by a townsman their intention was to carry off the soldier from his post and probably murder him. . . . This I feared might be a prelude to their plundering the king's chest.[9]

Preston continued:

> I immediately sent a non-commissioned officer and 12 men to protect both the sentry and the king's money, and very soon followed myself to prevent, if possible, all disorder, fearing lest the officer and soldiers, by the insults and provocations of the rioters, should be thrown off their guard and commit some rash act.[10]

Something got lost in the translation, though. In fact, it was Preston, Lieutenant James Basset, Corporal William Wemms and Privates Hugh Montgomery, John Carroll, James Hartigan, William McCauley, William Warren, and Matthew Kilroy who moved from the Main Guardhouse to the Customs House in a column of twos, then with bayonets drawn. This relief column moved forward to a lone sentry from the now-empty sentry box. The crowd of colonists pressed around the soldiers as they formed a semi-circle and joined up with Private White, all with their backs to the locked doors of the Customs House and the King's ransom.

The rabble had separated briefly to let the bayoneted guns and men through to reach the Sentry, but hurled insults at them. Preston continued to describe the scene in his deposition just a week after the event:

> The mob still increased and were more outrageous, striking their clubs or bludgeons one against another, and calling out, come on you rascals, you bloody backs, you lobster scoundrels, fire if you dare, G-d damn you, fire and be damned, we know you dare not, and much more such language was used. At this time I was between the soldiers and the mob, parleying with, and endeavouring all in my power to persuade them to retire peaceably, but to no purpose. They advanced to the points of the bayonets, struck some of them and even the muzzles of the pieces, and seemed to be endeavouring to close with the soldiers. On which some well behaved persons asked me if the guns were charged. I replied yes. They then asked me if I intended to order the men to fire. I answered no, by no means, observing to them that I was advanced before the muzzles of the men's pieces, and must fall a sacrifice if they fired . . .[11]

Not everyone sees things the same way. According to an "Anonymous Account of the Boston Massacre, A Short Narrative of the Horrid Massacre in Boston, Printed by Order of the Town of Boston," in March 1770, the event was quite different. Some believe Samuel Adams helped write this document, given his instigation of the events leading up to the event:

> The officer on guard was Capt. Preston, who with seven or eight soldiers, with fire-arms and charged bayonets, issued from the guardhouse, and in great haste posted himself and his soldiers in front of the Custom House [. . .]. In passing to this station the soldiers pushed several persons with their bayonets, driving through the people in so rough a manner that it appeared they intended to create a disturbance. This occasioned some snowballs to be thrown at them which seems to have been the only provocation that was given. Mr. Knox (between

whom and Capt. Preston there was some conversation on the spot) declares, that while he was talking with Capt. Preston, the soldiers of his detachment had attacked the people with their bayonets and that there was not the least provocation given to Capt. Preston of his party; the backs of the people being toward them when the people were attacked. He also declares, that Capt. Preston seemed to be in great haste and much agitated, and that, according to his opinion, there were not then present in King street above seventy or eighty persons at the extent.[12]

The Anonymous Account continues:

The said party was formed into a half circle; and within a short time after they had been posted at the Custom House, began to fire upon the people. . . . Captain Preston is said to have ordered them to fire, and to have repeated that order. One gun was fired first; then others in succession and with deliberation, till ten or a dozen guns were fired; or till that number of discharges were made from the guns that were fired. By which means eleven persons were killed and wounded, as above represented.[13]

The *Boston Gazette and Country Journal* reported its slightly different version of the facts five days later on Monday, March 12, 1770, faithfully reproduced in Appendix A.

Despite what the differing accounts say, all agree on one thing. The British soldiers fired at the Boston colonists and five were killed. The dead included Crispus Attucks, a sailor of African American and Native American descent; Samuel Gray, a rope-maker; and James Caldwell, a mate on a ship. All three died immediately. A ricocheting musket ball struck seventeen-year-old Samuel Maverick at the back of the crowd and he died a few hours later in the early morning of March 6, 1770. The shots also wounded thirty-year old Patrick Carr, a leather worker and Irish immigrant who died two weeks later. All the victims are buried at Granary Burying Ground where there is a memorial honoring them in Boston Commons.

The Boston Gazette and Country Journal published their obituaries a week after their deaths.

After the Massacre, justice at first moved swiftly—and then slowly. Preston and his men were arrested the same evening the shots were fired. All were charged with murder. Tensions were high, and a committee of citizens, led by Samuel Adams, formed to seek removal of the troops from Boston. Realizing the danger of the situation, Governor Bernard relented and regarrisoned the British troops at Castle William in the harbor outside the city. He also postponed the trials by some eight months, and the soldiers remained in jail pending their trial.

Under British law, none of the defendants would be allowed to speak as witnesses on their own behalf at the trial because they had an interest in the case. Nevertheless, the prosecutor and defending attorneys took their depositions.

Why take their depositions if they weren't allowed to testify? Two reasons: propaganda and evidence rules. Much the same way that many trials today are first tried in popular media, local bars, over the water cooler, and social media, John Adams realized the benefit of getting his clients' stories out. Second, at that stage of the development of the law, statements given by an accused had to be made under oath to be admissible.

A week after his arrest, Captain Preston gave this account of the beginnings of the event in his deposition:

> On my asking the soldiers why they fired without orders, they said they heard the word fire and supposed it came from me. This might be the case as many of the mob called out fire, fire, but I assured the men that I gave no such order; that my words were, don't fire, stop your firing. In short, it was scarcely possible for the soldiers to know who said fire, or don't fire, or stop your firing. On the people's assembling again to take away the dead bodies, the soldiers supposing them coming to attack them, were making ready to fire again, which I prevented by striking up their firelocks with my hand.[14]

As with the Third Amendment, the guarantees of the Fifth Amendment sprung from this and other criminal trials of the time and throughout history. Under the Fifth Amendment, a jury cannot take an adverse inference from a criminal defendant's refusal to testify, and the defendant cannot be made to testify. Each defendant has the right to elect whether to testify, a right not granted by English law of the time.

While in jail for eight months waiting for the trial to start, Captain Preston wrote to the *Boston Gazette and Country Journal*. In an early letter to the paper, Preston extended his "thanks . . . to the inhabitants of this town—who throwing aside all party and prejudice, have with the utmost humanity and freedom stept forth advocates for truth, in defense of my injured innocence." His letters initially built up goodwill with Bostonians, and we are left to wonder whether John Adams had a hand in this propaganda, too. Today, rich criminal defendants hire public relations firms.

Trying cases in the media is nothing new. But Captain Preston spoke differently to two masters. To his English superiors, he wrote:

> It is a matter of too great notoriety to need any proofs that the arrival of his Majesty's troops in Boston was extremely obnoxious to its inhabitants. They have ever used all means in their power to weaken the regiments, and to bring them into contempt by promoting and aiding desertions, and with impunity, even where there has been the clearest evidence of the fact, and by grossly and falsely propagating untruths . . .

On June 25, 1770, the *Boston Gazette* published his letter to his superior, which virtually erased the favorable sentiments Preston had developed in his earlier letter to the colonists.

Subterfuge and intrigue are nothing new to the human condition, either. As John Adams tried to build his case, revolutionaries such as Samuel Adams and Paul Revere tried equally to discredit the soldiers' cases.

The sway of the media has long affected criminal trials—just wait until we get to the O.J. chapter if you've forgotten.

Separate Trials

For reasons unknown, Captain Preston was tried separately from the soldiers. On October 21, the soldiers objected in a letter to the court: "We poor distressed prisoners beg that ye would be so good as to let us have our trial at the same time with our Captain, for we did our Captain's orders, and if we do not obey his command should have been confined and shot for not doing it." Although this request was denied, today there exists no written explanation for it.

Modern ethical rules require an attorney for each separate defendant, so by present-day standards, John Adams should not have represented all nine criminal defendants. Indeed, the very fact that the line soldiers complained about the separate trials should have raised the question of an ethical conflict of interest in Adams' mind, but historical records do not disclose his reasoning on this point.

As it turned out, the soldiers were right to fear separate trials. Captain Preston's best defense lay in his denial that he gave any orders to fire. Preston, in fact, claimed exactly that in his deposition, arguing that he would have never issued that order while he stood between his men and the colonists. John Adams advanced that theory in Preston's trial.

John Adams' conflict of interest in representing both the captain and the soldiers in separate trials arose from the soldiers' need to blame Captain Preston and Captain Preston's need to blame them. Directly contrary to their captain's best argument, the soldiers' best defense arose from their claim that they had simply followed their captain's orders, a defense commonly asserted in military situations over the years. Obviously, legal ethical standards in the 1770s were much different than our present-day rules.

Or perhaps not.

Preston's separate trial started eight months after the Boston Massacre and lasted for one week, from October 24, 1770, to October 30, 1770. The second trial of the soldiers started about a month after Preston's acquittal, on November 27, 1770, and ended two weeks later on December 14, 1770. All would be tried according to English law because the colonies still were under British rule and the U.S. Constitution was years from adoption.

The Lawyers

Robert Treat Paine and Samuel Quincy prosecuted for the Crown. John Adams defended both Preston and the soldiers in their separate trials. Joining him as defense counsel for Preston was Robert Auchmuty, Jr., a judge of the Vice-Admiralty Court and Loyalist to the Crown. Auchmuty would later die in exile in London. Samuel Quincy left Massachusetts with the British in 1776 and also later died in exile in England.

As lawyers for the defense of the soldiers with Adams was a much younger Josiah Quincy, Jr. (prosecutor Samuel's younger brother) and Sampson Salter Blowers, another Loyalist.

After the revolution, Blowers moved to Nova Scotia in exile and became the chief justice of that court.

Even the young Quincy's loyalties were questioned by his father:

> My dear Son, I am under great affliction, at hearing the bitterest reproaches uttered against you, for having become an advocate for those criminals who are charged with the murder of their fellow-citizens. Good God! Is it possible? I will not believe it . . . Your anxious and distressed parent, Josiah Quincy.[15]

In response and citing a litany of famous patriots his father would surely know:

> Honored Sir, . . . I refused all engagement, until advised and urged to undertake it, by an Adams, a Hancock, a Molineux, a Cushing, a Henshaw, a Pemberton, a Warren, a Cooper, and a Phillips . . . I dare affirm, that you, and this whole people will one day REJOICE, that I became an advocate for the aforesaid "criminals," charged with the murder of our fellow citizens. I am, truly and affectionately, your son, Josiah Quincy Jun.[16]

Although Thomas Paine represented King George III, he was later elected to the Continental Congress and signed the Declaration of Independence. John Adams also signed the Declaration of Independence, served as an ambassador to France and as George Washington's vice president, and became the second President of the United States. Before the revolutionary war, Josiah Quincy went to England to advocate the colonists' position but died on the return voyage prior to the Revolutionary War.

Rex v. Preston Trial Testimony

As in the following trial of the soldiers, the judges impaneled a jury of all men to try Captain Preston.

In this first trial, the jurors had to determine whether Preston gave the order to fire on the civilians. Although no transcript of this six-day trial is known to exist, historians have pieced together snippets of the testimony from other sources.[17] Court reporter John Hodgson originally transcribed the trial in shorthand, but as John Adams observed, "The British government have never permitted it to see the light, and probably never will." Preston's trial is believed to be the first in the colonies to have lasted longer than one day.

The Crown's Case

As with all criminal trials, the prosecution started first. Samuel Quincy opened and first called Edward Garrick, the apprentice wigmaker. After describing his altercation with the Sentry, Private Hugh White, Garrick admitted his taunts. He ultimately described the blow struck by the end of White's musket and testified that he saw soldiers in the streets carrying swords before Preston marched his men to the Customs House. The Crown then called its next witness, Thomas Marshall, who supported Garrick's statement and added that although Preston most certainly did have time to order his men to cease fire between the first and subsequent shots, he did not.

Samuel Quincy started as all good trial lawyers do: with a bang. He called his lead witness and sought to establish that the deaths were a result of a dispute over payment for a wig. That statement would lend support for his closing argument. Then, knowing what was coming based on Preston's deposition, Quincy sought to take the wind out of the sails of the defense's case. Trial lawyers steal thunder either by admitting the circumstances claimed by the defense, or directly refuting it. Quincy went for the jugular.

Although Preston did not testify at trial, Preston steadfastly denied in his deposition that he ordered his men to fire. Indeed, three defense witnesses would bolster his claim, though four witnesses for the prosecution swore Preston gave the fatal order.

Deadly Testimony

Prosecution eyewitness Daniel Calef testified:

> I was present at the firing. I heard one of the Guns rattle. I turned about and looked and heard the officer who stood on the right in a line with the Soldiers give the word fire twice. I looked the Officer in the face when he gave the word and saw his mouth. He had on a red Coat, yellow Jacket and Silver laced hat, no trimming on his Coat. I saw his face plain, the moon shone on it.[18]

Calef's testimony had squarely identified Preston, "The Prisoner is the Officer I mean."[19]

Daniel Calef unequivocally claimed that he had "looked the officer in the face when he gave the word" to fire. The next witness, Robert Goddard, also claimed firmly that Preston, standing behind his men, had given the order to fire. Prosecution witnesses who followed also gave damning testimony. Peter Cunningham said Captain Preston ordered his men to prime and load their muskets:

> Captain came and ordered the Men to prime and load. He came before 'em about four or five minutes after and put up their Guns with his Arm. They then fired and were priming and loading again. I am pretty positive the Capt. Bid 'em Prime and load. I stood about four feet off him.[20]

Cunningham later confirmed his statement by saying that the man who had ordered the troops to fire was definitely an officer by reason of the way he was dressed.

William Wyatt and John Cox, also witnesses for the Crown, both insisted Captain Preston gave the order to fire. William Wyatt said, "I saw about one hundred people in the street huzzaing, crying fire, damn you fire...The officer then stamped and said, 'Damn your bloods fire be the consequence what it will.' Immediately the first gun was fired."[21]

There you have it. A plethora of witnesses all pointing the finger at Preston. A strong finish to the first day. The following day's testimony adduced in the Crown's case was not as powerful. Witness Theodore Bliss said Preston had been standing in front of the guns. Bliss heard someone shouting "Fire" but did not think it was the Captain. Henry Knox testified that the crowd was shouting, "Fire, damn your blood, fire." And Benjamin Burdick said he heard the word "Fire" come from behind the men, all pointing to someone other than the Captain.[22]

Not the best way to end your case. Trial lawyers prefer to start and end with strong testimony to leave a lasting impression on the jury. Ending with weak testimony shows that your case is, well, weak.

A good trial lawyer on the other side of the case will seize on that weakness, as John Adams did.

Captain Preston's Defense

Adams and Josiah Quincy put on their case the following day. They presented witnesses who described the angry crown that rampaged the streets the night of March 5, 1770. The first witness for the defense, John Edwards, stated firmly that it was British Corporal William Wemms who had given the men the order to prime and load their muskets.

Another, Joseph Hilyer, said, "The soldiers seemed to act from pure nature, . . . I mean they acted and fired by themselves."[23]

Adams did what every criminal defense lawyer worth his salt would do: offer the SODDI defense—"Some Other Dude Did It," in more modern parlance. Point the finger elsewhere. It wasn't my client's order to fire, Adams claimed in closing.

It was Richard Palmes who gave the Loyalist jurors what they wanted to hear:

> . . .I saw Capt. Preston at the head of 7 or 8 Soldiers at the Custom house drawn up, their guns breast high and bayonets fixed . . . I saw something resembling snow or ice strike the grenadier on the captain's right . . . He [the grenadier] instantly stept one foot back and fired the first gun . . . After the gun went off I heard the word fire . . . I don't know who gave the word fire.[24]

Andrew, servant to Oliver Wendell, confirmed Palmes' testimony:

I jump'd back and heard a voice cry fire and immediately the first gun fired. It seemed to come from the left wing from the second or third man on the left. The officer was standing before me with his face towards the people. I am certain the voice came from beyond him.[25]

With these statements, Adams clinched the testimony necessary to establish his main argument: someone other than Captain Preston gave the order. Still, Adams faced conflicting testimony. Prosecution witnesses fingered Preston. Defense witnesses blamed someone else. When you're faced with conflicting testimony, another part of the story requires you to paint your witness as a fine, upstanding citizen.

Defense witness Benjamin Lee said:

> I saw Capt. Preston as soon as the Soldiers were ranged. A man went up and asked him if he was going to fire. [Preston said, "]No Sir upon my honor if I can any way avoid it.["] I knew the Captain by sight and name . . . He had his Regimentals, a hat on, his breast plate and Sash round his body and Sword in his hand.[26]

We call it wrapping your client in the flag. The trouble here, though, is that the English flag was presumably not highly favored with local Bostonians. Character evidence is a tricky thing, especially in murder trials. Even so, Adams brought a friend to the stand, Thomas Handaside Peck, who said of Preston:

> I was at home when the guns were fired. I heard 'em distinct. I went up to the main guard and addressed myself to the captain and said to him "What have you done?" He said, "Sir, it was none of my doings, the Soldiers fired of their own accord. I was in the Street and might have been shot." His character is good as a gentleman and soldier. I think it exceeds any of the corps.[27]

Finally, Adams sought to paint Preston in a sympathetic light. According to Edward Hill, after the firing, he saw Preston push up a musket and say, "Fire no more. You have done mischief enough." Adams would also call upon prosecution witness Theodore Bliss' testimony about Captain Preston's position in the melee. Preston himself claimed he stood between his men and the crowd and that he would have caused his own injury had he given the order to fire while standing in front of his men.

Bliss confirmed Preston's deposition testimony:

> I am sure the captain stood before the men when the first gun was fired. I had no apprehension the captain did give order to fire when the first gun was fired. I thought, after the first gun, the captain did order the men to fire but do not certainly know. I heard the word fire several times but know not whether it came from the captain, the soldiers or people. Two of the people struck at the soldiers after the first gun. I don't know if they hit 'em. There were about 100 people in the street. The muzzles of the

guns were behind him. After the first gun, the captain went quite to the left and I to the right.[28]

Adams had done what all good lawyers do in trials: introduce testimony that bolsters your side of the case and makes sense. He also made sense of favorable testimony offered by the other side. By placing Captain Preston directly in the line of fire, Adams could convincingly argue the good captain would never had ordered his soldiers to fire because he would have been among the first shot and killed. Adams also brought out testimony from common Bostonians, offering more a believable scenario than the testimony offered by the prosecution that the angry crowd had their backs turned to the redcoats.

That, quite simply, is the best a trial lawyer can do: weave a logical story from the testimony of the witnesses that takes common sense and mixes it with the facts as we would believe them to have occurred based on how people really behave. It's the same way we argue cases now.

Closing Arguments

Typical of the times, Samuel Quincy did not close the Crown's case with a summation of the evidence. Instead, he quoted from legal treatises:

> Not such killing only as proceeds from premeditated hatred or revenge against the person killed, but also in many other cases, such as is accompanied with those circumstances that shew the heart to be perversely wicked, is adjudged to be of malice prepense, and consequently murder.[29]

Snooze away here because that's likely what the jurors did. Pompous legal phrases without explanation are as boring now as they were then, and they typically succeed only in putting a jury to sleep. Even with the stilted language of the times, Samuel Quincy's argument didn't persuade anyone.

Unlike modern trials where only one lawyer can stand up for each side, both John Adams and Josiah Quincy presented closing arguments. Quincy poked at the jurors:

> "You lobster," "You Bloody back," "You coward" and "You dastard," are but some of the expressions proved. What words more galling? What more cutting and provoking to a soldier? To be reminded of the colour of his garb, by which he was

> distinguished from the rest of his fellow citizens; to be compared to the most despicable animal that crawls upon the earth, was touching indeed a tender point. . . . A soldier and a coward! . . . Gentlemen of the jury, for heaven's sake, let us put ourselves in the same situation! Would you not spurn at that spiritless institution of society, which tells you to be a subject at the expense of your manhood?[30]

As mentioned, no remaining record appears to exist of John Adams' closing argument in this trial, although in the following trial of the soldiers, his closing argument there gives an indication of what he would have said in Preston's case:

> Facts are stubborn things; and whatever may be our wishes, our inclinations, or the dictates of our passions, they cannot alter the state of facts and evidence: nor is the law less stable than the fact; if an assault was made to endanger their lives, the law is clear, they had a right to kill in their own defence; if it was not so severe as to endanger their lives, yet if they were assaulted at all, struck and abused by blows of any sort, by snow-balls, oyster-shells, cinders, clubs, or sticks of any kind; this was a provocation, for which the law reduces the offence of killing, down to manslaughter, in consideration of those passions in our nature, which cannot be eradicated. To your candour and justice I submit the prisoners and their cause.[31]

The jury returned a verdict of not guilty against Captain Preston. Our small country took a giant leap onto the world stage. We became a people governed by reason, not by unchecked passion.

Rex v. Wemms, *et al.* Trial Testimony: The Soldiers' Jury

The jury again was all men. The court exhausted the *venire* (jury pool) before sitting a complete jury. In all, the lawyers exercised ten peremptory challenges against various jurors whom the court sought to impanel. There are two ways for lawyers to remove a potential juror before the trial starts. Peremptory challenges do not require the lawyer striking the individual juror to explain why the lawyer exercised the challenge, unless the challenge appears to be based on ilegal practices. A "for cause" challenge requires the lawyer to convince the judge that the challenged juror is too biased to render a fair verdict.

Without any more jurors to draw from out of the pool, the court selected five talesmen (onlookers) from among the court spectators. The talesmen were both merchants and strong Loyalists, not about to convict the King's men. The jurors lived in nearby towns such as Roxbury, Dedham, and Hingham, and only two of the twelve jurors were from Boston proper. The court packed the jury in Captain Preston's favor and itself struck three of the sworn jurors.

Recognize here how this obvious prejudice occurred. The Crown appointed the judges, but unlike the merchants, they were loyal to the Crown. The surest way to avoid a conviction is to ensure those who will make the decision—the jurors—have their minds predisposed to the appropriate conclusion. Lawyers today attempt to do the same thing through peremptory challenges, although it is much more difficult.

Now we just use jury consultants. We think we've come a long way.

As in colonial times, some judges today likewise exercise much of the decision-making power over who sits on a jury. To be sure, lawyers still have several peremptory challenges we can use to knock out a potential juror before the jury is chosen, but in criminal matters, those challenges must be used carefully. You cannot challenge a juror based on race, for example. Even so, lawyers in high-profile cases use jury consultants to seat ideal jurors, predicting the outcome from a crystal ball of factors tied to various prejudices a juror may hold.

Colonial juries typically did not present a problem for the Crown. Indeed, in many cases, England simply removed accused criminals to be tried in England instead of allowing the case to proceed in the colonies. It was this practice of divesting Americans of jury trials that led the framers of the Constitution to include the right to a jury trial. That right first appears in Article III, Section 2, for trial by jury in criminal cases. Then in the Fifth Amendment, which provides for grand juries in criminal cases, and in the Sixth Amendment, which guarantees the right to trial by jury in felony federal criminal cases. Finally, the right to a trial appears in the Seventh Amendment, which provided for a jury trial in civil cases where the amount in controversy exceeded $20 (now changed to $75,000).

We imported much of our country's laws from England, but we corrected a respectable number of them, too. Some of them, anyway. We still have that military jail down in Cuba…

Loyalists realized the powder-keg situation existed because of the Boston Massacre. Colonists would not tolerate the Crown's removal of the soldiers to England for trial. Given our current political discussions, we may have forgotten this lesson of how the colonists dealt with wartime atrocities that occurred on foreign soil, always a tricky situation for a still-young country, its soldiers, and their families. Nevertheless, with the trial of the soldiers in the Boston Massacre case, we sought to show the world we were worthy of the larger citizenship.

The Crown's Case Against its own Soldiers

The Crown opened with a concise introduction and proceeded to call a lengthy list of witnesses. The second witness, Ebenezer Bridgham, was questioned by Samuel Quincy and testified:

Q: Did you apprehend the soldiers in danger, from anything you saw?

A: I did not, indeed.

. . .

Q: You said, you saw several blows struck upon the guns, I should like you would make it more plain.

A: I saw the people near me on the left, strike the soldiers' guns, daring them to fire and called them cowardly rascals for bringing arms against naked men; bid them lay aside their guns [. . .].

Q: Did you see any person fall?

A: Yes, I saw [Samuel] Gray fall.[32]

Witness after witness testified for the prosecution, many of whom testified without import because the lawyers simply were questioning witnesses without ever having talked to them prior to the trial. Many testified as patriots, following the lead of those who wanted the soldiers found guilty. Many others testified with their observations of the events, like Bridgham. The transcript of the trial available in the Library of Congress runs for some 146 pages in all.

Here's another invitation to flip ahead to the end of the O.J. chapter and read through the statistics compiled in that case. See if you think trials are more efficient now.

Evidence for the Defense

Key evidence introduced for the defense at the trial was the dying statement of Patrick Carr, one of the victims in the massacre. Whether Carr's testimony would be admitted into evidence depended on the hearsay rule, because Carr was not present in the courtroom for obvious reasons. Legal historians believe this testimony is the first recorded use of the "dying declaration" exception to the hearsay exclusionary rule. Carr's attending physician, Doctor John Jeffries testified for the defense:

Q: Was you Patrick Carr's surgeon?

A: I was . . .

Q: Was he [Carr] apprehensive of his danger?

A: He told me . . . he was a native of Ireland, that he had frequently seen mobs, and soldiers called upon to quell them . . . he had seen soldiers often fire on the people in Ireland, but had never seen them bear half so much before they fired in his life....

Q: When had you the last conversation with him?

A: About four o'clock in the afternoon, preceding the night on which he died, and he then particularly said, he forgave the man whoever he was that shot him, he was satisfied he had no malice, but fired to defend himself.[33]

As it is today, it was then: a finding of murder requires a finding of intent—here described as malice—before a man can be convicted of murder resulting in a sentence of death. In addition, Carr's dying declaration gave Adams the ability to argue for a lesser-included charge of manslaughter, claiming the soldiers felt threatened by the mob.

At the conclusion of the trial, two judges instructed the jury of twelve men, and in particular Justice Oliver commented on this testimony, "This Carr was not upon oath, it is true, but you will determine whether a man just stepping into eternity is not to be believed, especially in favor of a set of men by whom he had lost his life."[34] The basis for the dying declaration exception to the hearsay rule lies in the belief that a dying person has no reason to lie. Carr's belief that there was no malice in the man who shot him would have allowed the jury to find the soldiers not guilty, and if threatened, then convicted of the lesser charge of manslaughter.

Adams' Closing Argument

Adams argued from the soldier's perspective. If the mob endangered the soldiers, he reasoned, then they had the legal right to fight back and consequently were innocent. If they were provoked but not endangered, then they were, at most, guilty of manslaughter. Without a finding of malice, the jurors could not convict the soldiers of murder.

He argued the defense's evidence and pointed out to the jurors the conflicting testimony presented by the Crown:

> . . . .however, it is apparent, that witnesses are liable to make mistakes, by a single example before you. Mr. *Bass,* who is a very honest man, and of good character, swears positively that the tall man, *Warren,* stood on the right that night, and was the first that fired; and I am sure you are satisfied by this time, by many circumstances, that he is totally mistaken in this matter; this you will consider at your leisure. The witnesses in general did not know the faces of these persons before; very few of them knew the names of them before, they only took notice of their faces that night. How much certainty there is in this evidence, I leave you to determine.[35]

Here is an ultimate lesson in tact, one lost on many trial lawyers today; John Adams called Mr. Bass a liar, but did so in a most kind way, using flattery: "[he] is a very honest man, and of good character, swears positively. . ." With that kind of lead in, the jurors knew Adams was not attacking the man. Adams sliced his attack solely at Mr. Bass' testimony, not at Mr. Bass.

Adams argued for twelve hours over two days. Marcia Clark, Christopher Darden, Johnnie Cochran, and the O.J. dream team combined argued about the same amount of time. Worn out by the long speech, Court Reporter John Hogsdon noted with bare kindness:

> Mr. Adams proceeded to a minute consideration of every witness produced on the crown side; and endeavoured to shew, from the evidence on that side, which could not be contested by the council for the crown . . . But it would swell this publication too much, to insert his observations at large, and there is the less necessity for it, as they will probably occur to every man who reads the evidence with attention.[36]

Hogsdon, at least, was convinced—which is quite an admission because this man had documented innumerable trials and would have been the most qualified juror in the room, if he had been in the position of so serving. As a trial lawyer, you know you've won when the court staff is on your side.

In all, six of the eight soldiers were acquitted. The only two soldiers proven to have fired, Privates Hugh Montgomery and Matthew Killroy, were found guilty of manslaughter, a charge lesser than murder due to the jury's belief that they did not act with the required "malice," just as Adams had argued.

Upon their conviction and staring down death sentences, the soldiers claimed the "benefit of the clergy" defense. After proving they were literate enough to read from the Bible, the two soldiers reduced their convictions from murder to manslaughter. These two privates were punished by branding "M" on their thumbs to prevent them from using the same defense again and were discharged from the British Army, a comparatively minor punishment.

Had Carr's dying declaration testimony not been allowed, this "benefit of the clergy" might likely have been refused. For his part, John Adams called his defense of British soldiers in 1770 "one of the most gallant, generous, manly, and disinterested actions of my whole life, and one of the best pieces of service I ever rendered my country."

The Boston Massacre from the Patriot's View

Even today, not everyone sees the two trials as I laid them out here. Many correctly note that Britain's stranglehold on the colonies was sucking the colonies' economy dry. Parliament and the King ignored the many entreaties of the colonists to lessen the punishing taxes. English law failed to address the more enlightened thinkers of New England, who were equally without a voice in British government. On top of the brutal taxes and laws ignorant of their effect on the colonies, England piled on more insults and installed an occupying army in the colonies. Leaders and free thinkers had enough and sought to put an end to British rule.

Before the "Boston Massacre" name became common, the incident also was called "the Bloody Massacre in King Street," taken from the title of the famous Paul Revere gravure, a masterful piece of anti-British propaganda. As a prime example of Revere's bias, his engraving placed Captain Preston behind the line of soldiers, contrary to testimony both from civilians and Preston. The Massacre occurred on what is now the intersection of Devonshire and State streets in downtown Boston, where a circle of cobblestones is laid outside the Old State House.

On the fourth anniversary of the Boston Massacre on March 5, 1774, patriot John Hancock spoke these words, largely considered the most powerful of his career:

> . . . it was easy to foresee the consequences which so naturally followed upon sending troops into America to enforce obedience to acts of the British Parliament, which neither God nor man ever empowered them to make. It was reasonable to expect that troops, who knew the errand they were sent upon, would treat the people whom they were to subjugate, with a cruelty and haughtiness which too often buries the honorable character of a soldier in the disgraceful name of an unfeeling ruffian. The troops, upon their first arrival, took possession of our Senate House, and pointed their cannon against the judgment hall, and even continued them there whilst the supreme court of judicature for this province was actually sitting to decide upon the lives and fortunes of the King's subjects. Our streets nightly resounded with the noise of riot…[37]

Hancock's speech squarely presented his argument for the basis of the Amendment prohibiting the quartering of soldiers. Later that year in September, the First Continental Congress met in Philadelphia. The following year in 1775, the "shot heard 'round the world" was fired at Concord, Massachusetts at the beginning of the Revolutionary War. That event led ultimately to the Declaration of Independence on July 4, 1776, just to put everything in context.

Still pained by the Massacre, Bostonians continue to hold memorial services on its anniversary. Every year on its March 5 anniversary, the Bostonian Society reenacts the Boston Massacre. The reenactment takes place on the actual site of the massacre, directly in front of the Old State House.

Chapter Conclusion

Colonists bent on war with England saw these acquittals as unfavorable decisions since the result robbed them of a rallying cry to further foment revolution, denying them useful propaganda. The English, on the other hand, saw the jury's verdicts as vindication of their actions and perhaps as one of America's first, tentative steps on to the world stage. Some trials, like this one, transcend those directly involved.

Still, many, if not all the decisions reached in courtrooms are like this one; good for one side and bad for another. Judges have lamented that each of their decisions makes a friend for only a brief period, but an enemy for life. Whether a verdict is a wrong decision typically depends on what side you're on.

In this case, the outcome was largely dependent on one man: John Adams. Had he not taken on this unpopular case, the soldiers would likely have been convicted and probably hung. The victims of the massacre would have been hailed as heroes instead of rabble-rousers. Even today, we attempt to cast this case as the "Boston Massacre," an obvious attempt to disregard the actual outcome of the trial. Don't get me wrong here. I was born in Worcester, Massachusetts, a somewhat distant Boston suburb and consequently proud of our role in the American Revolution, but it's hard to correlate the acquittals as an intentional massacre.

On the other hand, had all the soldiers been convicted, the American Revolution may have occurred just that much sooner. Convictions may have had other consequences, as well. As the losing lawyer, John Adams most likely would have been forgotten by history. The Boston Massacre trials were one of the tipping points of his career, vaulting him first to Vice President under George Washington and then as America's second President. That history-changing course was not one of the foremost things on his mind when his law practice suffered as a consequence of his role in the cases and he tried to make ends meet for his family.

Remember to enter your vote on the outcome of this trial on www.10FamousTrials.com and see how other readers voted.

CHAPTER 4
The Tipping Points of the Civil War and its Aftermath: the Dred Scott Decision, the Trial of John Brown and Plessy v. Ferguson

Dred Scott v. Sandford

As a prelude to the following section on the trial of John Brown, this summary offers the context to John Brown's actions and covers the events that led up to Brown's attack on Harper's Ferry. The United States Supreme Court's decision in Dred Scott v. Sandford, reported at 60 U.S. 393 (1856),[1] issued when Brown was 56, was just three years before his seizure of Harper's Ferry. Dred Scott's desire to end his bounds of slavery led him to sue for his freedom, and his lawsuit wound its way up to the Supreme Court. In the court's words:

> A free negro of the African race, whose ancestors were brought to this country and sold as slaves, is not a "citizen" within the meaning of the Constitution of the United States. When the Constitution was adopted, they were not regarded in any of the States as members of the community which constituted the State, and were not numbered among its "people or citizens." Consequently, the special rights and immunities guaranteed to citizens do not apply to them. And not being "citizens" within the meaning of the Constitution, they are not entitled to sue in that character in a court of the United States, and the Circuit Court has not jurisdiction in such a suit.

In other words, because Scott's status as an African American was deemed to fall outside the definition of a "citizen," he could not invoke the federal "diversity of citizenship" rules to trigger federal court jurisdiction to sue for his freedom. Based on this technicality, the court ruled 7-2 against him. The court didn't stop there, also ruling on several other issues.

Despite being effectively repealed, the court nullified the Missouri Compromise and ruled it exceeded the powers of Congress due to its attempt to prohibit slavery and involuntary servitude and grant both freedom and citizenship to African Americans. The court also ruled that African Americans were "property." According to the opinion, "the Constitution of the United States recognizes slaves as property, and pledges the Federal Government to protect it." Chief Justice Taney, who delivered the opinion of the Supreme Court, argued that prohibitions on slavery violated the Fifth Amendment by depriving slave owners of their property without due process of law.

The case arose because Dred Scott had moved from Virginia, a slave state at the time, to the northern territories, where slavery was outlawed, giving him the right to make a claim for freedom, but which Scott apparently never made. Congress had not recognized the free status of a slave who had moved from the south to the north. The Northwest Ordinance and the Missouri Compromise, in effect at the time, simply established boundary lines where slavery was prohibited and permitted. Ultimately Scott made an offer to buy his freedom from his master's widow, Irene Sandford Emerson, but she refused the offer. Scott then took his bid for freedom to the courts.

Scott won his case at the trial level but was overruled on both subsequent appeals. The year following the court's decision, Abraham Lincoln, then a candidate for Congress, and incumbent Stephen A. Douglas, traded barbs in the famous Lincoln-Douglas debates about the ruling and issues of slavery. In his June 26, 1857 speech at Springfield, Illinois, Lincoln exposed his beliefs on ". . . that part of the Declaration of Independence which declares that 'all men are created equal.'"

Now, let us hear Douglas' view of the same subject, as found in the printed report of his late speech:

> "No man can vindicate the character, motives and conduct of the signers of the Declaration of Independence except upon the hypothesis that they referred to the white race alone, and not to the African, when they declared all men to have been

> created equal; that they were speaking of British subjects on this continent being equal to British subjects born and residing in Great Britain; that they were entitled to the same inalienable rights, and among them were enumerated life, liberty and the pursuit of happiness. The Declaration was adopted for the purpose of justifying the colonists in the eyes of the civilized world in withdrawing their allegiance from the British crown, and dissolving their connection with the mother country."

My good friends, read that quote carefully over a leisure hour, and ponder well upon it to see what a train wreck and mangled ruin it makes of our once glorious Declaration.

Lincoln lost the election but succeeded in establishing a national name for himself. Early on, well before his presidency, Lincoln signaled his beliefs about slavery.

Abolitionist John Brown carefully watched these events before his capture of Harper's Ferry in 1859. Brown's actions preceded the Civil War by just two years, when Abraham Lincoln became president in 1861. During the war between brothers, some 620,000 lives would be lost—more than all lives lost in all the wars fought by the United States combined. After the Civil War, the United States enacted two amendments to its Constitution to remedy the <u>Dred Scott</u> ruling.

Passed by Congress and ratified by the states in 1865 and 1868, the Thirteenth and Fourteenth Amendments to the Constitution overruled the <u>Dred Scott</u> decision some twelve years later. Section 1 of the Thirteenth Amendment reads:

> Neither slavery nor involuntary servitude, except as a punishment for crime where of the party shall have been duly convicted, shall exist within the United States, or any place subject to their jurisdiction.

Section 1 of the Fourteenth Amendment reads:

> All persons born or naturalized in the United States, and subject to the jurisdiction thereof, are citizens of the United States and of the State wherein they reside. No State shall make or enforce any law which shall abridge the privileges or immunities of citizens of the United States; nor shall any State

deprive any person of life, liberty, or property, without due process of law; nor deny to any person within its jurisdiction the equal protection of the laws.

In 1872, ultimately the Supreme Court itself acknowledged in the Slaughterhouse Cases[2] that the Dred Scott decision had been overruled by Section 1 of the Fourteenth Amendment:

The first observation we have to make on this clause is, that it puts at rest both the questions which we stated to have been the subject of differences of opinion. It declares that persons may be citizens of the United States without regard to their citizenship of a particular State, and it overturns the Dred Scott decision by making all persons born within the United States and subject to its jurisdiction citizens of the United States. That its main purpose was to establish the citizenship of the negro can admit of no doubt.

With this background, let's turn to the trial of John Brown in 1859, which happened just three years after the Dred Scott decision and well before the court overruled that decision.

The Trial of John Brown in Charlestown, Virginia

The 1859 trial of abolitionist John Brown in Virginia might not have been much more than a blip in the history books if Brown had not turned out to be larger than life. Partly due to his own flawed zealousness and several luminaries around him (including Ralph Waldo Emerson and Henry David Thoreau) John Brown's death sentence for treason, inciting rebellion, and murder became a lightning rod that galvanized the North into action against the South. Together with the Dred Scott decision, John Brown started the country on the march toward civil war. Brown's courtroom trial may have started out as a comical farce attended by six hundred curious and boisterous court-watchers, but it ended with sullen observers wondering if they were doing the right thing.

Although slavery came to an end in large part due to events started by Brown's actions, his martyrdom also created a significant, unintended consequence. Watching the execution was a young Virginia Military Institute cadet who borrowed a uniform to gain entrance: John Wilkes Booth, who later became infamous in his own right.

History has many unusual intersections.

You may have read Lincoln's Gettysburg Address, but have you heard Brown's response to his guilty verdict? You can below, near the end of this chapter. Brown's closing remarks have been called "one of the most memorable courtroom speeches" and "one of the two greatest American speeches." After Brown spoke in the pre-Civil War courtroom in Virginia, only one spectator clapped when the judge sentenced Brown to death, but was roundly silenced.

Innumerable historians, articles, scholars, two movies, a play, an album, a TV miniseries, African Americans, whites, and the Congress cannot agree whether Brown was, in the words of President Lincoln, a "misguided fanatic,"[3] or as Malcolm X said, the only white man possibly deserving to join his Organization for Afro-American Unity. It is not the place of this chapter to categorize John Brown or his place in history, but instead to examine the trial from a lawyer's perspective so you can judge for yourself how he became such a controversial figure.

Events Leading to the Attacks at Harper's Ferry

Let's turn first to an abbreviated history of the time to set the stage for Brown's raid on Harper's Ferry. Five years before the raid in 1854, Congress approved the Kansas-Nebraska Act, which repealed the Missouri Compromise. The Supreme Court later acknowledged the unconstitutionality of the Missouri Compromise in the Dred Scott decision. The Kansas-Nebraska Act delegated to the citizens of those two states the right to determine whether they would allow slavery. The Missouri Compromise prohibited slavery in the Western Territories, but as a compromise, it exempted Missouri from the prohibition.

Some two years after this Congressional act, on May 22, 1856, a posse of about seven hundred fifty Southerners mounted an attack in Kansas that became known as the "Sack of Lawrence," in part as a show of force to those who had banned slavery and in response to shots fired at a local sheriff by anti-slavery settlers in Lawrence. On the very same day in distant

Washington, D.C. tempers boiled over too, arising from Massachusetts Senator Charles Sumner's fire-and-brimstone anti-slavery speech and vilification of a relative. In response, South Carolina Congressman Preston Brooks beat Sumner with his cane in the United States Capitol building.

Days later, on May 24 and 25, 1856, John Brown was involved with the Pottawatomie Massacre in Kansas, where five pro-slavery settlers were killed. Together, the Sack of Lawrence and this massacre became known as "Bleeding Kansas." The following year, in 1857, the United States Supreme Court decided Dred Scott v. Sandford.

These events, together with strong anti-slavery sentiments in the North and West and equally strong pro-slavery sentiments in the South, formed the backdrop for John Brown's second attack and his now-famous trial. Brown's second attack at the federal armory in Harper's Ferry, West Virginia sought to free slaves by force if necessary. The site is just forty-five miles northwest of Washington, D.C., at the confluence of the Potomac and Shenandoah rivers in the states of West Virginia, Virginia, and Maryland near the Blue Ridge Mountains.

Harper's Ferry

On October 16, 1859, Brown and a group of eighteen armed men, including free slaves, made their way to Harper's Ferry, where they cut telegraph wires and easily captured two bridges, the federal armory, and arsenal, as well as the U. S. Rifle Works on Hall's Island, which was being guarded by one man. Nearly 100,000 rifles and muskets were stored there. Brown had planned to capture the armory and rifle works, seize the guns to arm his men and slaves, and continue through the South, freeing slaves as he went and destroying the South's economy given its dependence on slave labor.

Brown's first symbolic act was to capture Colonel Lewis Washington, the great grandnephew of President George Washington, and John Allstadt, whom he took as hostages and then freed their slaves. "I wanted you particularly for the moral effect it would give our cause having one of your name, as a prisoner," Brown said to Washington.[4]

In the attack, Brown's group happened to kill train conductor and free African American, Heyward Shepard, who was investigating why his train was not allowed to cross a bridge. Hearing shots after midnight, Doctor John Starry walked from his nearby home to the armory, only to be captured while trying to treat Shepard. Starry, unable to treat Shepard due to his severe wounds, was released and went to notify the townspeople, who gathered their guns and pinned down Brown at the armory. Local citizens and Brown's men engaged in various skirmishes the following day.

Townsfolk quickly dispatched word of the attack to Washington, D.C., where the officer of the day, Lieutenant Israel Green gathered his marines and headed by train to Virginia to meet with nearby officers and proceed to regain the fort at Harper's Ferry. Nearby militias from Virginia arrived in force. With the armory buildings surrounded by ninety marines and two howitzers, Brevet Colonel Robert E. Lee, then charged by President James Buchanan to secure the armory and rifle works, handwrote his surrender demand to Brown on a single sheet of plain white, blue-lined paper.

> H^{d}qrs. Harper's Ferry
>
> 18 Oct 1859
>
> Colonel Lee U.S.A., comm' the troops sent by the President of the United States to suppress the insurrection at this place, demands the surrender of the persons in the Armory buildings.
>
> If they will peaceably surrender themselves, restore the pillaged property; they shall be kept in safety to await the orders of the President.
>
> Col. Lee represents to them in all frankness that it is impossible for them to escape; that the armory is surrounded on all sides by troops; and that if he is compelled to take them by force he cannot answer for their safety.
>
> (signed) R.E. Lee
>
> Col. Comm' U. S. Troops[5]

To capture Brown and his men, Lee and Lieutenant J.E.B. Stuart ordered twelve marines to storm the nearby engine house where Brown had retreated. Although both sides suffered casualties, including two of Brown's sons, Lee won and captured Brown. Lee then took Brown to the Charlestown, Virginia jail.

Charlestown later was annexed into West Virginia, but should not be confused with its capital. This Charlestown is in the eastern panhandle of present-day West Virginia. For their part in his capture, Doctor Starry and Lieutenant Israel Green would testify against Brown in his trial.

In all, seventeen people were killed in the raid: two slaves, three townsmen, a slaveholder, one marine, and ten of Brown's men, including two of his sons. One of his sons escaped.

After Brown's capture, Charlestown was in an uproar, fueled by the mistaken belief that Brown's raid was the forerunner of a Northern invasion of the South. According to the court clerk's report, "The reason given for hurrying the trial, is, that the people of the whole country are kept in a state of excitement, and a large armed force is required to prevent attempts at rescue."[6]

In a process like the Boston Massacre trials, several individuals spoke to Brown while he was in jail on October 18, 1859, a week before the trial started. These conversations were not necessarily part of a deposition, but a three-hour interview, as reported by the *New York Herald*, which included Virginia Governor Henry Wise, Senator James Murray Mason, Congressman Clement Laird Vallandigham of Ohio and Congressman Charles James Faulkner of Virginia, along with Officers Brevet Colonel Robert E. Lee, Lieutenant J. E. B. Stuart, Colonel Lewis Washington, Harper's Ferry District Attorney Andrew Hunter (who would prosecute Brown's trial), and a Doctor Biggs, as well as newspaper reporters.[7] Although it appears Brown was willing to speak, no member of Brown's defense team was present during this interview.

Remember here, <u>Miranda v. Arizona</u> (the *Miranda* rights case) wasn't decided until 1966.

The Trial

Before the trial started, Brown was arraigned on three state charges: treason against Virginia, inciting slaves to rebellion, and murder. In response to the charges, Brown said, "If you want my blood, you can have it any moment, without this mockery of a trial. I have had no lawyer. I have been unable to take advice of any one."[8] Brown plead not guilty to the three charges and

Presiding Judge Richard Parker set the trial to start on Wednesday, October 26, 1859.

As the trial started, some six hundred onlookers swamped the courtroom, many of whom were newspaper reporters who eagerly recited every tidbit to a country on the edge of war. As tensions grew from the inflamed headlines, the court put an end to the reporting. Brown's case may have been one of the first where an American court issued a gag order, although they had been used throughout history and regularly issued in monarchies and dictatorships. Interestingly, Congress debated the issue, whether such gag orders would even apply in Congress:

> ...with the growth of antislavery feeling after the founding of the American Anti-Slavery Society in 1833, the House [of Representatives] was deluged with thousands of antislavery petitions, most of which requested the abolition of slavery in the District of Columbia. Southerners, with the aid of Northern Democrats, secured passage of the gag rules, which prevented the discussion of antislavery proposals in the House. The fight to secure the right of petition, waged virtually singlehandedly, and brilliantly, by John Quincy Adams, aroused the North, and the gag rules were repealed.[9]

That repeal had no sway with southern courts. According to the transcript of Brown's trial, "It is rumored that Brown is desirous of making a full statement of his motives and intentions, through the press, but the court has refused all further access to him by reporters, fearing that be may put forth something calculated to influence the public mind, and to have a bad effect upon slaves."[10] As the court reporter readily reported, the situation was a powder-keg waiting to explode. The court rushed headlong into the trial, intent on bringing it to a rapid end.

Brown and his compatriots, however, were in no shape to stand trial:

> The prisoners, as brought into the court, presented a pitiable sight—Brown and Stephens being unable to stand without assistance. Brown has three sword-stabs in his body, and one saber-cut over the heart. Stephens has three balls in his head, and had two in his breast and one in his arm. He was also

cut on the forehead with a rifle bullet, which glanced off leaving a bad wound.[11]

Nonetheless, Doctor Biggs certified Brown fit to stand trial. Brown attended the start of the trial lying on a cot in the courtroom. His attempts to delay his fate had not worked.

The trial started out as a farce, according to reports by Northern journalists. Brown's first prosecutor, Charles Harding, with his feet propped up on the table, frequently fell asleep and once jolted awake calling out for tobacco. When he showed up at trial drunk and with a bruised face from a barroom brawl the night before, Judge Parker replaced him with the more capable and dignified Andrew Harper. Still, onlookers in the courtroom ate peanuts and chestnuts and threw the shells on the floor, spat tobacco juice while the bailiff shouted for order, and frequently interrupted the proceedings. It almost sounds like the Salem Witch Trials.

The Jury

For the benefit of Northern observers, the court reporter took pains to note the composition of John Brown's jury: "They were all from distant parts of the country, mostly farmers—some of them owning a few slaves, and others none."[12]

The Objections

Brown's counsel, Virginian Lawson Botts, raised an objection about the State of Virginia's jurisdictional authority to try Brown due to his capture on federal—not state—property. The court brushed aside counsel's objections, noting that Virginia citizens had died on the streets of Virginia, not on federal property. The defense likewise objected to the charge of treason against Virginia because Brown was not a resident of the state. Judge Parker likewise swept that objection aside by noting Brown had established residence by renting the Kennedy farm (even though it was in a different state on nearby Maryland soil), that Brown had "did not come divested of his responsibilities"[13] as a citizen of the United States, and that he had fired upon Virginia troops.

No predispositions there.

Finally, although Judge Parker appointed counsel for Brown, Brown rejected those lawyers, and in return, Judge Parker ordered the trial to proceed without a defense lawyer. Judge Parker's choice to start the trial without counsel for Brown was contrary to the law at the time, but Brown's refusal of counsel from Southern lawyers, whose advice he did not trust, is quite like the circumstances of criminal court proceedings today. In fact, an accused criminal defendant can reject counsel and elect to proceed *in pro per* (Latin: for oneself). Given the state of complicated trial procedure, evidence rules, and appellate law, trial judges today must advise the defendant against self-representation and dissuade the attempt; though if the defendant insists, the trial will proceed without defense counsel.

Much is made in the trial transcript about Brown's request for a Northern lawyer and his several requests for a delay of the trial to wait for counsel to arrive and recover from his wounds. Judge Parker, who did not believe counsel was on the way, instead started the trial, and appointed Attorney Botts, a prominent local Southern lawyer from Charlestown to represent Brown. Prior to the trial, Botts had enrolled in Virginia Military Institute, but withdrew and instead studied law and established a practice in Charlestown. Botts would later serve as a Confederate officer with the 2nd Virginia Infantry Regiment during the Civil War. During the trial, Judge Parker also had appointed as Brown's defense counsel Virginians Charles J. Faulkner and Charlestown Mayor Thomas C. Green. They all stepped down from Brown's defense when in open court Brown expressed no confidence in them.

Just at the beginning of the trial, a young, inexperienced lawyer from Boston arrived in Charlestown, but he had not brought his credentials as an attorney. Twenty-one-year-old lawyer, George Hoyt, who was sent to scout out escape possibilities rather than defend Brown, first spoke up in the afternoon of the third day of the trial. John W. Le Barnes, one of the so-called "Secret Six" abolitionists, had hired and sent young Hoyt to Virginia. As Brown sought to discharge his Southern lawyers, Hoyt stepped in and argued that it would be "ridiculous" for him to carry on the defense of Brown because he had not read the indictment, discussed defense strategy with his client or his client's other lawyers, and had "no knowledge of the criminal code of Virginia."[14] Hoyt sought a continuance to allow more experienced Northern counsel time to arrive In response to Hoyt's plea, Judge Parker granted a one-day continuance, which instead allowed two other defense attorneys, Virginian Samuel Chilton and Ohioan Hiram Griswold, time to arrive at the trial and appear on Brown's behalf.

With citation to hastily researched authorities including Archibald's Criminal Pleading, Chilton brought a motion attempting to force the prosecution to elect just one of the three charges against Brown as its theory of the case, arguing that he couldn't defend three different charges in one case. Judge Parker refused the motion, and noted, "The very fact that the offence can be charged in different counts, varying the language and circumstances, is based upon the idea that distinct offences may be charged in the same indictment."[15] As was generally accepted then, Judge Parker's position continues to be the law today. According to the transcript, Chilton told Judge Parker that he would not have stepped in to defend Brown if he had known prior counsel had resigned. He thought he would appear to assist in Brown's defense, not lead it. Judge Parker rejected his protest and ordered the trial to continue and the lawyer to remain in his seat as counsel for Brown.

Forced representation by an attorney still happens today. I've been handcuffed to a chair during a proceeding to prevent me from walking out.

Virginia attorney Chilton then sought to offer insanity as a defense for Brown, citing unsupported declarations from Ohio family members of insanity in Brown's family, but Brown fired Chilton as well, wanting no claim of insanity as his defense. Brown railed at his supposed defense lawyers and said:

> I will add, if the court will allow me, that I look upon it as a miserable artifice and pretext of those who ought to take different course in regard to me, if they took any at all, and I view it with contempt more than otherwise. As I remarked to Mr. Green, insane persons, so far as my experience goes, have but little ability to judge of their own sanity. If I am insane, of course, I should I know more than all the rest of the world. But I do not think so . . . [and I reject] any attempt to interfere in my behalf on that score.[16]

In other words, if you know enough to ask the question…

The Prosecution's Case

A good prosecutor anticipates the defenses likely to be brought up and tries to defeat those defenses in the prosecution's case in chief. It's called stealing the other side's thunder as we've seen in the Boston Massacre trials. Here, Brown's stated reason for capturing Harper's Ferry was to free the slaves and start a revolt against plantation owners. Because the armory and rifle works had so many arms, Brown needed people to use those arms. Brown didn't bring an army with him but planned instead to arm the slaves as part of his revolt—a severe crime in and of itself in the South. District Attorney Andrew Hunter knew he had to show Brown as a loner and madman, and that not even the slaves would join his revolt. Hunter knew his fellow citizens and could count on their testimony.

Hunter called John Allstadt, one of the first two plantation owners seized by Brown. As part of his testimony, Mr. Allstadt said:

> ... the negroes were placed in the watch-house with spears in their hands; the slaves showed no disposition to use them. [I] was afterward transferred to the engine-house; several negroes were there [and] saw [one] making port-holes by Brown's order; the other negroes were doing nothing, and had dropped their spears ...[17]

Similar testimony was solicited during the prosecution's case from other witnesses to show that the slaves wanted no part of Brown's raid and remained loyal to their owners.

Brown started to examine witnesses himself while he lay on his cot. Although unusual, no one objected to Brown's queries, and he was allowed to proceed. In today's criminal and civil proceedings, parties who are represented by counsel are not allowed to participate in questioning witnesses. Not only did Brown question the next witness—John P. Dangerfield, a member of the opposing army and one of Brown's prisoners—but Brown also offered the court his own explanation for his actions. He asked whether the witnesses observed him firing in anything other than a defensive mode. Dangerfield testified that he saw Brown's two sons die, but that Brown also shot members of the surrounding army who approached the engine house with a flag of truce. One of Brown's sons also had been shot while under a flag of truce.

The trial transcript notes:

> A general colloquy ensued between the prisoner, lying on his cot, and the [next] witness [Mayor Mills], as to the part taken by the prisoner [Brown] in not unnecessarily exposing his hostages to danger. No objection was made to Brown's asking these questions in his own way, and interposing verbal explanations relative to his conduct. The [trial] witness [Mayor Mills] generally corroborated [Brown's] own version of the circumstances attending the attack on the engine-house, but could not testify to all the incidents that [Brown] enumerated. [Mayor Mills] did not hear [Brown] say that he surrendered. [The trial] witnes'' wife and daughter were permitted to visit him unmolested, and free verbal communication was allowed with those outside. We were treated kindly, but were compelled to stay where we didn't want to be. Brown appeared anxious to effect a compromise.[18]

Admittedly, Brown's direct involvement in the trial is highly irregular and the record has no evidence that Brown was ever advised of his Fifth Amendment right against self-incrimination. Indeed, it appears by all counts the court simply forgot this right. Brown was interviewed prior to the start of trial, and statements from his interview were admitted into evidence. In all fairness to the trial court, however, it likewise appears Brown freely would have waived that right. He wanted a soapbox. As far as Brown was concerned, this trial was his opportunity to be heard and the U.S. Constitution be damned.

Conversely, no equivalent individual right appears in Brown's own Provisional Constitution, which was admitted into evidence though Brevet Colonel Robert E. Lee's affidavit that detailed Brown's papers and tracts recovered from the Kennedy Farm in Maryland. Using the alias "Isaac Smith," Brown had rented the Farm on July 3, 1859, prior to his invasion of Harper's Ferry and used it as a staging point. After capturing Brown and his men, Colonel Lee also recovered some two hundred Sharp's rifles, revolvers, and pikes (spears) Brown had stored on the Farm, and likewise introduced that evidence in the trial.

Brown's former hostage, Colonel Lewis Washington, who testified on the second day of the trial, likewise confirmed the existence of Brown's desire to enact a new, Provisional Constitution from his pre-trial interview with Brown. Washington also confirmed the prosecutor's recitation of the facts. The transcript simply reads, "He detailed the circumstances as previously stated."[19] Wealthy Virginians feared the North's attempts to interfere with slavery and equally feared an attack on their homes and way of life. The prosecutor played to this fear and solicited Colonel Washington to implicate Brown's attempt to free the slaves, treasonous in the South. Washington testified, "Brown said he had enough to arm about 1,500 men; the Governor asked if he expected that number; he said no doubt that number, and five thousand if he wanted them . . ."[20] Not only did District Attorney Hunter establish Brown's treason, but he struck a chord on the already taut strings that barely held the South together, fearing the loss of slavery and their way of life. With this single line of testimony, Colonel Washington sealed Brown's fate.

Hunter then went on to prove Brown's involvement with his Provisional Constitution, a treasonous document contrary to the United States Constitution. Brown sought to establish a separate government through his Provisional Constitution. Hunter read portions of that document into evidence and called Sherriff Campbell to verify Brown's handwriting. Campbell confirmed he could verify Brown's signature because he had copied letters for Brown in jail. Brown interrupted the proceedings again, and "said he would himself identify any of his handwriting, and save all that trouble."[21] He was ready to face the music.

Not one to be upstaged, Hunter declined the offer and put on his proof through Sherriff Campbell but Brown interrupted again, "Either way, as you please."[22] Hunter must have sensed Brown's attempt at martyrdom, and Brown knew well the predetermined outcome and consequently was unwilling to respect the court's protocols. Hunter likewise understood his audience: he played as much to the Northern journalists as he did to the jury. By offering the Provisional Constitution as evidence, Hunter could prove Brown was equally a challenge to the North as he was to the South. Moreover, because Brown was on trial for murder and treason, his conviction could be seen wholly separate from the reasons he threatened the South.

To his plan, Hunter sought evidence from Virginia citizens about the individuals killed and offered Alexander Kelly, who, according to the court reporter, "described the manner of Thomas Boerley's being killed on Monday. Brown's party fired at witness, and witness returned the fire. Boerley was with witness, and was armed with a gun. Saw him soon after he was shot. The shot came from the direction of Shenandoah street."[23]

A good trial attorney will not cross-examine a witness if nothing can be gained, as it was with Mr. Kelly. Likewise, there little benefit to allow a witness to repeat testimony elicited on direct examination unless the trial attorney can show by some reason that it shouldn't be believed. This unwritten rule exists in part because in this case District Attorney Andrew Hunter would have the chance to "redirect" (rehabilitate) Mr. Kelly's testimony and allow him to repeat it again. Damaging testimony is best left alone unless there is an unimpeachable rebuttal.

In 1859 as is the case today, criminal trials proceed in a manner quite different than civil trials; there are no depositions taken. The lawyers learn the facts of the case through investigation or at trial. With that prelude, it is easier to understand what happened next, and why.

District Attorney Hunter called Albert Grist, a prisoner taken by Brown. Grist testified favorably toward Brown, and said:

> Brown said his object was to free the slaves; told him there were not many there; he replied, "The good book says we are all free and equal," and if we were peaceable we should not be hurt; there was some firing about that time; afterward, about three o'clock, witness was sent to tell the conductor that the train might pass unmolested; saw Mr. Beckham, and delivered the message; Brown then dismissed me; did not go home, being afraid some of Brown's men, not knowing this, might shoot me; saw Hayward brought in, wounded.[24]

Not to be outdone with favorable testimony, Hunter still had a hidden card up his sleeve. He recalled Mr. Kelly, who promptly put another nail in Brown's coffin, saying, "Saw Geo. W. Turner killed on High street; he was shot while in the act of leveling his gun; the shots came from the corner of Shenandoah and High streets; the men who fired had rifles; one had a shawl on [identifying Brown]."[25]

Ending with strong testimony, the prosecution rested. The defense took up the mantle three days into the trial, just after the start of the afternoon session at 3 p.m. on Friday, October 28, 1859.

The best cases are ones where you can get your point across quickly. Think about that adage when we get to the seven-year long McMartin Preschool trial.

Brown's Defense

Brown's defense counsel, Charlestown Mayor Thomas Green, tried to introduce witnesses to soften Brown's involvement and elicited testimony about the death of one of Brown's men, Dauphin Thompson, the brother of Brown's eldest daughter's husband. In response to the testimony the court reporter noted, "[Brown here cried over the circumstances connected with the death of Thompson.]" (Brackets in original, by the court reporter).

A jury can be sympathetic to true tears, as were John Brown's for his loss of his sons. But don't try to fool jurors. They can see right through crocodile tears.

The defense tried to show the actions of the citizens as a counterpoint to Brown's actions. Another man named Hunter (a witness, not the prosecutor) testified about the citizens' treatment of one of Brown's men who had escaped the armory, only to be caught by local militia and held for trial.

> After Mr. [Fountain] Beckham, who was my grand-uncle, was shot, I was much exasperated, and started with Mr. Chambers to the room where the second Thompson [William] was confined, with the purpose of shooting him. We found several persons in the room, and had leveled our guns at him, when Mrs. Foulke's sister threw herself before him, and begged us to leave him to the laws. We then caught hold of him, and dragged him out by the throat, he saying: "Though you may take my life, 80,000,000,000 will rise up to avenge me, and carry out my purpose of giving liberty to the slaves." We carried him out to the bridge, and two of us, leveling

> our guns in this moment of wild exasperation, fired, and before he fell, a dozen or more balls were buried in him; we then threw his body off the trestle work, and returned to the bridge to bring out the prisoner, Stephens, and serve him in the same way; we found him suffering from his wounds, and probably dying; we concluded to spare him, and start after others, and shoot all we could find; I had just seen my loved uncle and best friend I ever had, shot down by those villainous Abolitionists, and felt justified in shooting any that I could find; I felt it my duty, and I have no regrets.[26]

It is not likely this testimony had the desired effect, because many townspeople (and members of the jury) felt the same way. They rightly saw Brown as both an outsider and rabble-rouser threatening to destroy their way of life and passions were high. It is difficult to second-guess the defense's tactics because Brown admitted most of the actions charged against him. In this situation, as is the case still today, when a defendant admits the crime the job of the defense is simply to lessen the punishment. In today's capital murder cases, for example, defense counsel consider life imprisonment a victory when compared to a death sentence. In Brown's case, the defense counsel used the same tactics. They had tried to change venue, delay the trial to let time pass and passions cool, and argue insanity as a defense, all to no avail.

A wrinkle in the case next arose because no further witnesses were available to the defense. The court reporter noted:

> Several witnesses for the prisoner were here called, and did not answer the subpoenas. They had not been returned.
>
> Brown arose from his mattress, evidently excited, and standing on his feet, addressed the court, as follows:
>
> "May it please the court: I discover that, notwithstanding all the assurances I have received of a fair trial, nothing like a fair trial is to be given me, as it would seem. I gave the names as soon as I could get at them, of the persons I wished to have called as witnesses, and was assured that they would be

subpoenaed. I wrote down a memorandum to that effect, saying where those parties were; but it appears that they have not been subpoenaed as far as I can learn; and now I ask if I am to have anything at all deserving the name and shadow of a fair trial, that this proceeding be deferred until to-morrow morning; for I have no counsel, as I before stated, in whom I feel that I can rely, but I am in hopes counsel may arrive who will attend to seeing that I get the witnesses who are necessary for my defense. I am myself unable to attend to it. I have given all the attention I possibly could to it, but am unable to see or know about them, and can't even find out their names; and I have nobody to do any errand, for my money was all taken when I was sacked and stabbed, and I have not a dime. I had two hundred and fifty or sixty dollars in gold and silver taken from my pocket, and now I have no possible means of getting anybody to go my errands for me, and I have not had all the witnesses subpoenaed. They are not within reach, and are not here. I ask at least until to-morrow morning to have something done, if anything is designed if I am ready for anything that may come up."

Brown then lay down again, drew has blanket over him, and closed his eyes and appeared to sink in tranquil slumber.[27]

Mr. Hoyt, the young attorney from Boston, then rose to make the request for a delay because no defense witnesses were available, a point joined in by Attorney Botts, then still counsel of record for Brown. The prosecutor knew exactly how to respond, using a tactic still in use today: agree to whatever the defense wanted to prove because it would have no effect. To steal these witnesses' thunder, District Attorney Hunter responded that he would agree the witnesses would testify Brown had acted leniently.

I beg leave to say, in reference to this application, that I suppose the court, even under these circumstances, will have to be satisfied in some way, through counsel or otherwise, that this testimony is material testimony. So far as any witness has been examined, the evidence relates to

> the conduct of Captain Brown in the treating his prisoners with leniency, respect and courtesy, and this additional matter, that his flags of truce—if you choose to regard them so—were not respected by the citizens, and that some of his men were shot. If the defense choose to take that course, we are perfectly willing to admit these facts in any form they desire. Unless the court shall be satisfied that this testimony (which, I have no doubt, is every particle of it here), which could be got, is really material to the defense, I submit that the application for delay on that score should not be granted. Some of these witnesses have been here, and might have been asked to remain. A host of witnesses have been here, and have gone away without being called on to testify.[28]

In other words, even if the Commonwealth of Virginia admitted the facts these witnesses were expected to testify about, then it mattered not—they were irrelevant to the charges. Given that it was late in the day when this row arose, the court adjourned for the evening, but did not grant the requested continuance of several days and rather suspended the proceedings only for the evening.

That's the mark of an attorney who knows exactly who's on the jury and how they'll likely vote.

The court reconvened at ten a.m. Saturday, October 29, 1859, for the fourth day of trial. As noted above, Samuel Chilton of Washington City (now known as Washington, D.C.) and Henry Griswold of Cleveland, Ohio made their appearances for Brown and qualified to practice before the court.

The defense counsel, including Mr. Hoyt, made objections to the introduction of certain letters from Captain John Brown that already had been introduced by witnesses for the prosecution. District Attorney Hunter promptly withdrew several of the exhibits. Trial procedure remains the same; evidence is commonly introduced by witnesses and "marked for identification" until the end of the trial when the attorneys present argument to admit or exclude the exhibits into evidence, the "formal" process the court uses to receive evidence and allow the jury to review it as they deliberate. Sometimes evidence is "published" to the jury during the trial, and it is handed around the jury box. Some judges admit evidence as each individual exhibit is introduced, but it is evident from the manner

Hunter used to withdraw the exhibit that this Virginia Court employed the former process of waiting until the end of trial before the jurors retire to deliberate.

The new defense team next called several witnesses seeking, in essence, to prove what District Attorney Hunter already had offered as a stipulation: Captain Brown treated his prisoners with leniency, respect, and courtesy, his flags of truce were not respected by the citizens, and some of his men were shot.

Mayor Mills, the master armorer of the seized armory, testified for the defense about the Virginia citizens' treatment of the men Brown had sent out to negotiate a truce:

> ...a paper was drawn up, embracing certain terms, and borne by Mr. Brua to the citizens outside; the terms were not agreed to; the last time Mr. Brua was out, there was severe firing, which, I suppose, prevented his return; Brown's son went out with a flag of truce, and was shot; he came back wounded; [Brown] attended him, and gave him water; [I] heard Brown frequently complain that the citizens had acted in a barbarous manner; he did not appear to have any malicious feeling; he undoubtedly seemed to expect reinforcements; said it would soon be night, and he would have more assistance; his intentions were to shoot nobody unless they were carrying or using arms; if they do, let them have it; this was while the firing was going on.[29]

Brown then woke up enough to participate:

> Capt. Brown here asked the witness whether he saw any firing on his part which was not purely defensive.
>
> Witness: It might be considered in that light, perhaps; the balls came into the engine-house pretty thick.
>
> Question by Counsel: Did you not frequently go to the door of the engine-house?
>
> No, indeed. (Laughter.)
>
> A general colloquy ensued between the prisoner, lying on his cot, and the witness, as to the

> part taken by the prisoner in not unnecessarily exposing his hostages to danger. No objection was made to Brown's asking these questions in his own way, and interposing verbal explanations relative to his conduct. The witness generally corroborated his own version of the circumstances attending the attack on the engine-house, but could not testify to all the incidents that he enumerated. He did not hear him say that he surrendered. Witnes'' wife and daughter were permitted to visit him unmolested, and free verbal communication was allowed with those outside. We were treated kindly, but were compelled to stay where we didn't want to be. Brown appeared anxious to effect a compromise.[30]

The prosecution did not cross-examine a single defense witness. Hunter's tactic was palpable: he had proven the Commonwealth's case, and he wanted the jury to know it. There was no need to disprove any of the testimony offered for the defendant.

The prosecution's belief became evident when the defense rested later in the afternoon and the attorneys and the court discussed whether to start closing arguments or put them over until Monday. No proceedings would go forward on Sunday, of course. In fact, the court consulted the jurors, who were very anxious to get home. Mr. Harding, the other prosecutor for the Commonwealth, observed that, "He was willing, however, to submit the case to the Jury without a single word, believing they would do the prisoner justice."[31]

Nevertheless, Mr. Harding gave a forty-five-minute closing argument before the court adjourned until Monday morning, when the defense counsel would argue Brown's closing argument in the case. Harding's choice is trial lawyering at its best. Whenever counsel for either side has the opportunity, it is always best to leave the jury with your side of the case during any extended break. There is always much jockeying between counsel about who gets in the last word.

The following Monday, Mr. Chilton argued Brown's case for four and one-half hours. While he argued all the points raised during the testimony and the various motions presented to the court, Mr. Chilton almost, if not quite, apologized for his role in the case:

> Still [Mr. Chilton] would say that he had no sympathy with the prisoner. His birth and residence, until within a few years, had been in Virginia, in connection with the institution of slavery. Although now a resident of the District of Columbia, he had returned to his native State to spend the remainder of his days, and mingle his dust with her soil. No other motive operated on him than a disinterested one to do his duty faithfully.[32]

The court reporter next noted that Mr. Hunter offered a rebuttal, but it must not have been significant because the reporter did not record Mr. Hunter's words. Even the court reporter was not without his own eloquence at the conclusion of the trial:

> When Mr. Hunter closed his peroration to the Jury, without further remark, at an intimation from the judge, they immediately withdrew to consider their verdict. After an absence of three-quarters of an hour (during which the court took a recess) they returned into court with a verdict. At this moment the crowd filled all the space from the couch inside the bar, around the prisoner, beyond the railing in the body of the court, out through the wide hall and beyond the doors. There stood the anxious but perfectly silent and attentive populace, stretching head and neck to witness the closing scene of Old Brown's trial. It was terrible to look upon such a crowd of human faces, moved and agitated with but one dreadful expectancy--to let the eyes rest for a moment upon the only calm and unruffled countenance there, and to think that he alone of all present was the doomed one, above whose head hung the sword of fate. But there he stood, a man of indomitable will and iron nerve, all collected and unmoved, even while the verdict that consigned him to an ignominious doom was pronounced upon him.[33]

The jury returned just forty-five minutes after Judge Parker sent them out to deliberate. Much is made today of short and long deliberations, with the feeling, generally that a short deliberation means a verdict of guilty and a long deliberation means not guilty based on the likelihood of a dispute among the jurors. In my experience, the only thing a short deliberation offers is the certainty of the verdict—it is not overly coextensive with guilt or innocence. The jury found Brown guilty. The reporter again noted the mood of the citizens:

> Not the slightest sound was heard in the vast crowd as this verdict was thus returned and read. Not the slightest expression of elation or triumph was uttered from the hundreds present, who, a moment before, outside the court, joined in heaping threats and imprecations on his head; nor was this strange silence interrupted during the whole of the time occupied by the forms of the court. Old Brown himself said not even a word, but, as on any previous day, turned to adjust his pallet, and then composedly stretched himself upon it.[34]

Counsel noted their exhaustion and the court put the matter over to the following day, Wednesday, November 2, 1859, the sixth day of trial. When the trial resumed the clerk then asked Mr. Brown whether he had anything to say why sentence should not be pronounced upon him. Mr. Brown immediately rose, and in a clear, distinct voice, said:

> I have, may it please the court, a few words to say. In the first place, I deny everything but what I have all along admitted, of a design on my part to free slaves. I intended certainly to have made a clean thing of that matter, as I did last winter when I went into Missouri, and there took slaves without the snapping of a gun on either side, moving them through the country, and finally leaving them in Canada.
>
> I designed to have done the same thing again on a larger scale. That was all I intended to do. I never did intend murder or treason, or the destruction of property, or to excite or incite the slaves to rebellion, or to make insurrection. I have another objection, and that is that it is unjust that I should suffer such a penalty.
>
> Had I interfered in the manner which I admit, and which I admit has been fairly proved—for I admire the truthfulness and candor of the greater portion of the witnesses who have testified in this

case—had I so interfered in behalf of the rich, the powerful, the intelligent, the so-called great, or in behalf of any of their friends, either father, mother, brother, sister, wife, or children, or any of that class, and suffered and sacrificed what I have in this interference, it would have been all right, and every man in this court would have deemed it an act worthy of reward rather than punishment.

This court acknowledges, too, as I suppose, the validity of the law of God. I see a book kissed, which I suppose to be the Bible, or at least the New Testament, which teaches me that all things whatsoever I would that men should do to me, I should do even so to them. It teaches me further to remember them that are in bonds as bound with them. I endeavored to act up to that instruction.

I am yet too young to understand that God is any respecter of persons. I believe that to have interfered as I have done, as I have always freely admitted I have done in behalf of His despised poor, is no wrong, but right.

Now, if it is deemed necessary that I should forfeit my life for the furtherance of the ends of justice, and mingle my blood farther with the blood of my children and with the blood of millions in this slave country whose rights are disregarded by wicked, cruel, and unjust enactments, I say let it be done.

Let me say one word further. I feel entirely satisfied with the treatment I have received on my trial. Considering all the circumstances, it has been more generous than I expected.

But I feel no consciousness of guilt. I have stated from the first what was my intention, and what was not. I never had any design against the liberty of any person, nor any disposition to commit treason or excite slaves to rebel or make any general insurrection. I never encouraged any man to do so, but always discouraged any idea of that kind.

Let me say also in regard to the statements made by some of those who were connected with me,

> I fear it has been stated by some of them that I have induced them to join me, but the contrary is true. I do not say this to injure them, but as regretting their weakness. Not one but joined me of his own accord, and the greater part at their own expense. A number of them I never saw, and never had a word of conversation with till the day they came to me, and that was for the purpose I have stated.
>
> Now, I am done.[35]

From the clerk's transcript:

> While Mr. Brown was speaking, perfect quiet prevailed, and when he had finished the Judge proceeded to pronounce sentence upon him. After a few primary remarks, he said, that no reasonable doubt could exist of the guilt of the prisoner, and sentenced him to be hung in public, on Friday, the 2d of December next.
>
> Mr. Brown received his sentence with composure.
>
> The only demonstration made was by the clapping of the hands of one man in the crowd, who is not a resident of Jefferson County. This was promptly suppressed, and much regret is expressed by the citizens at its occurrence.[36]

Henry David Thoreau, in speaking about Brown's then impending death observed the dangers our country faced then and perhaps now:

> Our foes are in our midst and all about us. There is hardly a house but is divided against itself, for our foe is the all but universal woodenness of both head and heart, the want of vitality in man, which is the effect of our vice; and hence are begotten fear, superstition, bigotry, persecution, and slavery of all kinds.[37]

Brown's wife joined him for his last meal on December 1, 1859, but was denied permission to stay the night. Just before his execution by hanging, Brown penned his final words in a note left with his jailer:

Charlestown, Va. 2nd December, 1859. I, John Brown, am now quite certain that the crimes of this guilty land will never be purged away but with blood. I had, as I now think vainly, flattered myself that without very much bloodshed it might be done. Truly it could be said and sung.[38]

Numerous papers thereafter reported, and as Brown supporter Henry David Thoreau also wished after Brown's death, "All is quiet at Harper's Ferry." Just a year and a half later, the Civil War erupted on April 12, 1861, when Confederate forces attacked Fort Sumter. As John Brown predicted, the evils of slavery would last much longer after the Civil War, as we will see in the next case.

Plessy v. Ferguson and its Predecessors and Successor

Some argue John Brown's actions at Harper's Ferry started a chain reaction that led to the Civil War and the civil rights movement. While certainly the case in chronological sequence, there were many setbacks along the way and some false hopes. In 1879, the Supreme Court handed down a pair of decisions in Strauder v. West Virginia[39] and *Ex Parte* Virginia,[40] both holding that states violated the Fourteenth Amendment when they excluded persons from serving on juries on account of their race.

In direct contrast to these decisions favoring the Constitution, the Civil Rights Cases[41] struck down provisions of the Civil Rights Act of 1875, which entitled all persons to full and equal enjoyment of public accommodations. The court ruled Congress exceeded its authority to enact this law, explaining the 14th Amendment was limited to wrongful acts by states, not private individuals. Only one justice dissented from this ruling.

Things went from bad to worse thirteen years later. In Plessy v. Ferguson,[42] the court held a Louisiana statute, a so-called Jim Crow law, that required separate intrastate passenger railcars for the white and colored races neither abridged the privileges or immunities nor deprived African Americans of the equal protection of the laws under the 14th Amendment. This decision brought the phrase "Separate but Equal" into the lexicon of the judicial system and American society. For nearly six decades until the Supreme Court's 1954 desegregation decision in Brown v. Board of Education,[43] "Separate but Equal" remained the law of the land, but a chapter many sought to end.

The Citizen's Committee to Test the Separate Car Act solicited Homer Adolph Plessy to act as a plaintiff in a test case by because he was only one-eighth black through his great-grandmother and otherwise passed for white. On June 7, 1892, he bought a train ticket to travel from New Orleans to Covington, Louisiana and stepped aboard a passenger railcar belonging to the East Louisiana Railroad. Under Louisiana's 1890 Act 111, only white patrons could use the car. Mr. Plessy was arrested, jailed, and tried. He lost at both the trial court before Judge John Howard Ferguson and again at the Louisiana Supreme Court. He appealed to the United States Supreme Court and lost there as well.

As in the civil rights cases, Kentuckian Justice Marshall Harlan, a former slave owner, was again the lone dissenter in the Plessy case. His words ring clear:

> . . . in view of the constitution, in the eye of the law, there is in this country no superior, dominant, ruling class of citizens. There is no caste here. Our constitution is color-blind, and neither knows nor tolerates classes among citizens. In respect of civil rights, all citizens are equal before the law. The humblest is the peer of the most powerful. The law regards man as man, and takes no account of his surroundings or of his color when his civil rights as guarantied by the supreme law of the land are involved. It is therefore to be regretted that this high tribunal, the final expositor of the fundamental law of the land, has reached the conclusion that it is competent for a state to regulate the enjoyment by citizens of their civil rights solely upon the basis of race.

He also predicted, "In my opinion, the judgment this day rendered will, in time, prove to be quite as pernicious as the decision made by this tribunal in the Dred Scott Case." After the court's ruling, Mr. Plessy pled guilty to the charge and paid the $25.00 fine some four years after the case first started. Even after the 1954 Supreme Court decision, it would take many more years for society to dismantle this case.

Chapter Conclusion

John Brown's intentions were good, but the means he used to reach them were misguided at best. As my father frequently said, good intentions pave the road to Hell. Likewise, however, Judge Parker gave short shrift to Brown's request for independent defense counsel and rushed the case to its foregone conclusion. Whether Brown would have been convicted in any event is certain, especially given his own admissions in the trial. Emerson and Thoreau vaulted Brown into his role in history because of his choices and apparent intent to become a martyr for his cause.

While the outcome may not have been different, the court ignored or at least bypassed many procedural protections we take for granted now. Brown did not appeal his death sentence, a required automatic appeal now. Had he appealed, the verdict would likely have been overturned given the procedural anomalies in the trial. Even then, on retrial, Brown's prior admissions would have assured his conviction, and may have been treated by a court of appeal as reason enough to disregard the procedural irregularities.

The law, especially appellate law, has many predispositions at the ready to justify the outcome. After a semester of reading property law cases, I didn't need to read any further when the opinion started with, "Plaintiff is a widow ..." The window always won.

Slavery was an issue in the forefront of the times, and Brown's death certainly brought the issue into sharper relief for Northerners, galvanizing them into action against the South in the Civil War. The Dred Scott decision precipitated Brown's actions and stoked the embers that led to the war to end slavery, but as Plessy v. Ferguson demonstrated, prejudices run long and deep. Not even Brown v. Board of Education resolved the long-simmering racial divide, a fight we still struggle with today.

Dred Scott, Homer Plessy, John Brown, Oliver Brown, Rosa Parks, Dorothy Cotton, Jo Ann Robinson, Martin Luther and Coretta Scott King, Malcolm X, John Lewis, Cesar Chavez, and many others have fought this battle. How far have we come?

Remember to enter your vote on the outcome of these trials on www.10FamousTrials.com and see how other readers voted.

CHAPTER 5
The O.K. Corral Shootout Trial of Wyatt Earp and Doc Holliday

Thirty shots fired in thirty seconds in the O.K. Corral left three men dead, three men wounded and turned into a thirty-day trial with some thirty witnesses before a local justice of the peace for the Earp brothers and Doc Holliday in October 1881. Since then, their gunfight with the Clantons and McLaurys has kept the town of Tombstone, Arizona alive, filled the silver screen innumerable times, occupied many pages of books, and even resulted in some poetry.

The gunfight is the stuff of legend backed up by facts. Facts, as we shall see though, are quirky things.

The ensuing 125-plus years have left as many questions unanswered about the facts as were asked in their long trial. Who fired first? Were the Earps involved in stagecoach robberies? Were the Clantons and McLaurys cattle and horse thieves deserving of their end? Why was Doc Holliday, a notorious gambler and gunslinger, deputized by Virgil Earp? Why did the Coroner's Inquest not issue a verdict? Why did the Earps and Holliday get jailed during the trial and were later freed?

For trial lawyers, the trial presents a wonderful study of trial tactics, demonstrates the dangers in the art of cross-examination, and offers innumerable insights into the minds of some of the most famous gunfighters in the wild west. As we look at the trial transcripts, finally published in 1981 on the hundred-year anniversary of the gunfight, we will see the defense team's masterful decisions about the presentation of their case, the prosecution's mistakes in both their cross-examination of witnesses and their failure to develop a coherent and cohesive theme that explained everyone's actions in the O.K. Corral and the events leading up to the famous gunfight. The case likewise demonstrates the foolishness of a lawyer in representing a family member in a highly charged case: Attorney (and Judge) Will McLaury arrived three days after the trial started to help the prosecution and vindicate his dead brothers.

The saying that an attorney who has himself for a client has a fool for a client has an apt corollary: an attorney who has a family member for a client is a fool.

Tombstone, Arizona

In 1877, a mere five years before the shootout at the O.K. Corral, a prospector named Lewis discovered silver east of the San Pedro River in the foothills of the Huachuca Mountains in southern Arizona, some thirty miles from the Mexican border. Lewis unfortunately failed to mark his claim and when he went back from town after celebrating, he couldn't find it again. Hearing tales of the discovery, another prospector dared to brave Apache territory and Geronimo to look for silver ore. Prospector "Ed Schieffelin [had] came to Camp Huachuca with a party of soldiers and [when he] left the fort to prospect, his comrades told him that he'd find his tombstone rather than silver."[1] When he instead found silver, he named his mining claim "Tombstone" and the name stuck. The boom exploded and Tombstone was born, ultimately sprouting from an encampment of 40 tents and cabins housing 100 people to a full-blown town of some 7,000 people, complete with banks, saloons, a red-light district, a photography studio and of course, a corral. The town now has just over 1,500 residents and, after several other mining booms and busts, an economy largely based on tourism. At the time of the shootout at the O.K. Corral, the town's population hovered around 1,000.

The town's silver boom attracted many elements, including both commercial and outlaw interests. As brothers seeking to find their fortune, Wyatt Berry Stapp Earp, Virgil Walter Earp, and James Cooksey Earp arrived shortly after the first silver strike in 1879 to seek their fortunes. With his background in law enforcement in Kansas, Wyatt quickly took a stake in a faro game at the Oriental Saloon in return for providing security. Morgan Seth Earp would arrive a year later, followed shortly by Wyatt's friend, Dr. John Henry "Doc" Holliday, a sometimes dentist, gambler, and notorious gunfighter.

In an interview with the Arizona Daily Star after the shootout, Virgil Earp talked about Doc Holliday:

> There was something very peculiar about Doc. He was gentlemanly, a good dentist, a friendly man, and yet outside of us boys I don't think he had a friend in the Territory. Tales were told that he had

murdered men in different parts of the country; that he had robbed and committed all manner of crimes, and yet when persons were asked how they knew it they could only admit that it was hearsay, and that nothing of the kind could really be traced up to Doc's account. He was a slender, sickly fellow, but whenever a stage was robbed or row started, and help was needed, Doc was one of the first to saddle his horse and report for duty.[2]

On the other side of this gunfight stood Joseph Isaac "Ike" Clanton, William Harrison "Billy" Clanton and Thomas McLaury, considered Cow-boys, a pejorative term quite different from the meaning applied today. Back then, Cow-boys were stage robbers, bandits, rustlers, and generally considered reckless and dangerous. The Clantons allegedly rustled cattle in Cochise County and between the United States and Mexico. Robert Findley "Frank" McLaury and Tom McLaury allegedly worked closely with the Clantons by purchasing their stock and selling it.

It takes bad guys to make good guys.

The Rivalry Between the Earps/Hollidays and the Clantons/McLaurys

Several events led up to the gunfight at the O.K. Corral, starting with a horse stolen from Wyatt Earp in 1879, which he recovered from Billy Clanton. In mid-1880, Virgil, Wyatt, and Morgan located mules at the McLaury ranch that were allegedly stolen from the Army's Fort Rucker. In response, Frank wrote an editorial in the town's newspaper and accused the Earps of acting as vigilantes instead of lawmen. In late 1880, Wyatt arrested Cow-boy William "Curly Bill" Brocius for the murder of Tombstone marshal Fred White. The case against Curly Bill was dismissed for lack of evidence and Wyatt's then-empty arrest justifiably angered the Earps. After White's death, the town council appointed Virgil Earp as its marshal.

There were three levels of law enforcement in Tombstone: Town Marshal Virgil Earp, Cochise County Sheriff Johnny Behan, and federal territory marshal Crawley Drake. Drake's only involvement with this story was to appoint Virgil as deputy federal marshal before Virgil arrived in Tombstone, a position he resigned when he assumed the town marshal job. After the O.K. Corral shootout, Wyatt Earp asked Drake to be appointed a federal territory marshal prior to his vendetta ride to track down and kill his brothers' alleged killers from the Clanton gang. Behan and Earp competed for the Governor's appointment as sheriff, but Earp withdrew his application. Earp claimed Behan had agreed to appoint him as under-sheriff, but Behan never did so, causing bad blood between them.

Words have meanings. Using "gang" continues its criminal connotations today, and the Clanton's enemies quite intentionally labeled them as a gang. Publicity is every bit a part of the law. The Earps were labeled as lawmen with badges, who society respected at one time. But loyalties were not so easily defined.

Sheriff Behan generally favored the Cow-boys and remained friends with both the Clantons and the McLaurys. The Earps—especially Wyatt—befriended Tombstone's commercial interests.

Wyatt Earp and Sheriff Johnny Behan also competed for the affections of Josephine Sarah "Josie" Marcus, an actress, after she arrived in 1879. Behan and Marcus either lived together in Tombstone for some time or she served as his housekeeper, but she left him in 1881, largely due to an affair Behan had with another woman. Beginning much earlier in about 1873, Wyatt Earp lived with Celia Ann "Mattie" Blaylock and while the 1880 U.S. census lists them as husband and wife, most believe they were not actually married. In 1882, after Mattie left Wyatt and Tombstone, Josie lived with Wyatt and adopted "Earp" as her last name. Mattie Blaylock died in July of 1888 in Pinal City, Arizona. Wyatt Earp and Josie Marcus Earp eventually married in 1888 and lived together for almost fifty years.

As the romantic rivalry between Behan and Wyatt Earp unfolded, outlaws stole $26,000 and killed the Bisbee stagecoach driver and a passenger on March 15, 1881. Virgil, Wyatt, and Morgan Earp, along with Bat Masterson and Doc Holliday, headed off in a posse after the bandits and Behan and another group headed off in a separate posse. The Earp posse captured one of the bandits who confessed his only involvement was holding horses during the crime, and the Earps turned him over to the Behan posse. Shortly later, the man escaped from Behan's unlocked jail and Behan refused to pay the Earp posse for their work.

When in doubt about how to solve a crime, one method that works well instructs us to "follow the money."

To oust Behan from his position as Sheriff and increase his own popularity, Wyatt Earp struck a deal with Ike Clanton and Frank McLaury, promising to pay the $6,000 reward for information to allow Wyatt to capture the Bisbee stagecoach bandits. Before Wyatt could make the arrest, the bandit Cow-boys died in a gunfight in New Mexico. Tensions arose between Wyatt Earp and Doc Holliday on one hand, and Ike Clanton and Frank McLaury on the other hand, over leaks of the terms of this secret deal to other Cow-boys, endangering Ike and Frank's relationships with the Cow-boys.

These tensions came to a head as one of the two local newspapers, the *Tombstone Daily Epitaph*, noted in its Earp-friendly article, *Three Men Hurled Into Eternity in the Duration of a Moment*, the day after the gunfight, on October 27, 1881:

> Since the arrest of Stilwell and Spence for the robbery of the Bisbee stage, there have been oft repeated threats conveyed to the Earp brothers—Virgil, Morgan and Wyatt—that the friends of the accused, or in other words the cowboys, would get even with them for the part they had taken in the pursuit and arrest of Stilwell and Spence. The active part of the Earps in going after stage robbers, beginning with the one last spring where Budd Philpot lost his life, and the more recent one near Contention, has made them exceedingly obnoxious to the bad element of this county and put their lives in jeopardy every month.[3]

Even the newspapers had a verbal gunfight. The other newspaper, the *Tombstone Daily Nugget* (no longer published), was not so kind in its contemporaneously published article, *A Desperate Street Fight*, favoring the Cow-boy's version of the story:

> The origin of the trouble dates back to the first arrest of Stilwell and Spencer for the robbery of the Bisbee stage. The co-operation of the Earps and the Sheriff and his deputies in the arrest caused a number of cowboys to, it is said, threaten the lives of all interested in the capture. Still, nothing occurred to indicate that any such threats would be carried into execution.[4]

Nonetheless, the confrontational history and deep-rooted animosity between the Earps and Clantons boiled over onto the streets of Tombstone next to the O.K. Corral. Facing these threats, and not willing to back down, the Earps turned to the law to disarm the Clantons and McLaurys.

The Law

Practically at the insistence of the Earps, the town fathers of Tombstone passed an ordinance several months before the shootout at the O.K. Corral, prohibiting anyone from carrying guns within the town limits. Except lawmen, of course. They typically consider themselves exempt from gun laws.

> Ordinance No.9: To Provide against Carrying of Deadly Weapons, effective April 19, 1881.
>
> Section 1. It is hereby declared to be unlawful for any person to carry deadly weapons, concealed or otherwise [except the same be carried openly in sight, and in the hand] within the limits of the City of Tombstone.
>
> Section 2: This prohibition does not extend to persons immediately leaving or entering the city, who, with good faith, and within reasonable time are proceeding to deposit, or take from the place of deposit such deadly weapon.
>
> Section 3: All fire-arms of every description, and bowie knives and dirks, are included within the prohibition of this ordinance.

The Enforcers and The Law Breakers

After a night of threats and taunts back and forth between Ike Clanton, Wyatt Earp, and Doc Holliday—and an uncharacteristically calm card game—the Earps retired in the late evening of October 25, 1881. Ike continued to drink into the next morning and armed himself with a six-shooter and a Winchester rifle. He continued to threaten the Earps and Doc Holliday. His brothers Billy and Frank, along with Tom McLaury, were also in town, apparently willing to make good on their threats against the Earps and Holliday. Alerted to the threats when they awoke on the morning of October 26, 1881, the Earps first dismissed the taunts but as they continued to receive the threatening reports, Virgil, Wyatt, and Morgan Earp gathered and with Doc Holliday, started their march toward the O.K. Corral to disarm the Clantons and the McLaurys.

Sheriff Johnny Behan attempted to intervene and stop the Earps and Doc Holliday from proceeding, warning them they would be killed and then disingenuously advising the lawmen that he had already disarmed the Clantons and the McLaurys. They brushed Behan aside and walked shoulder-to-shoulder to the O.K. Corral, their pistols and rifles ready.

What happened next is the stuff of legend, much controversy, many questions at trial, innumerable movies, and inspired prose. As the two faced one another, demands were made by the lawmen, threats were bandied back in response, and shots were fired. As the gun battle commenced, bullets flew, and grey smoke puffed out of gun barrels, and Frank McLaury and Doc Holliday ended up with guns pointed at one another.

> "I've got you now," Frank McLaury yelled to Doc.
>
> "Blaze away! You're a daisy if you do," countered Holliday.[5]

As the Tombstone Nugget story said, "The 26th of October, 1881, will always be marked as one of the crimson days in the annals of Tombstone, a day when blood flowed as water, and human life was held as a shuttlecock."[6]

Larger-than-life events tend to inspire larger-than-life quotes.

After the thirty seconds of shooting subsided, we conclusively know that Frank and Tom McLaury lie dead in the O.K. Corral on the streets of Tombstone. Billy Clanton remained alive for an hour after the editor of the *Tombstone Daily Nugget* carried him to a nearby home and reported Billy's last words, "Goodbye boys; go away and let me die."[7]

Ike Clanton had thrown down his arms and escaped unharmed, though he would later testify that bullets buzzed by his head. Morgan Earp had been shot twice, once through each shoulder, but would recover. Virgil had been shot in the calf and would also recover. A bullet grazed Doc near his hip. The town doctor took Morgan and Virgil to his office for treatment.

Sheriff Behan attempted to immediately arrest Wyatt Earp and Doc Holliday, but they would not have it. "After the firing was over, Sheriff Behan went up to Wyatt and said, 'I'll have to arrest you.' Wyatt replied: 'I won't be arrested today. I am right here and am not going away. You have deceived me. You told me these men were disarmed; I went to disarm them.'"[8]

The coroner impaneled a grand jury and started a five-day inquest. After an inconclusive verdict in his inquest, Ike Clanton instead filed murder charges against the four shooters left standing, and they next went before a judge for a preliminary hearing just days later.

The Coroner's Inquest

After the grand jury of twelve citizens and the coroner, Doctor Henry Matthews, inspected the bodies of the dead men, they conducted a brief inquiry and swore nine witnesses to testify. None of the witnesses would be cross-examined in this proceeding, which was conducted solely by the coroner. He asked the only questions, and from the two statements he obtained, it would appear he simply asked for narrative statements from the witnesses.

Typically, a Coroner's Inquest determines how and why an individual died. It is usually conducted by the coroner and includes a court reporter who transcribes the sworn statements of the witnesses who come before the grand jury. These statements can be used in later criminal or civil proceedings since they were given under oath. The grand jury consists of six to twelve jurors from the county where the death occurred. Inquests are generally open to the public and not held in private. The grand jury proceedings seek information about the victim's death so the grand jury can decide whether the victim died by suicide, homicide, accident, natural causes, or an undetermined cause.

The term "grand jury" is used to describe a jury of as many as 24 individuals who may sit and hear more than one trial or multiple types of proceedings, such as administrative, civil or criminal and decide whether to issue an indictment (criminal) or presentment (civil) to initiate a singular trial. A *petit* jury usually consists of 12 individuals and sits for one trial only and is typically referred to as simply a "jury." Today, federal court juries consist of six individuals (commonly called a "six-pack"), but most states continue to use 12 individuals. The first grand jury was formed in 977 C.E. by an Anglo-Saxon king, but England abolished grand juries in 1993 and today grand juries exist only in the United States.

Before we get too deep in this inquest, pause here for a brief moment and think about the desirability of working in a town called "Tombstone" if you're a coroner or an undertaker—here, the same person.

Two days after the shooting, October 28, 1881, the hearing in the inquest began and finished a day later. In the matter of the deaths of the McLaurys and Billy Clanton, of the nine witnesses who testified before the grand jury in the Coroner's Inquest, two of those witnesses—Ike Clanton and Sheriff John Behan—were directly involved with the shooting. Despite those witnesses' obvious biases and testimony against the Earps and Holliday, the coroner's grand jury did not return an indictment against the lawmen. Although the backgrounds of the jurors aren't well known, it seems likely they were law-abiding businessmen of Tombstone, and not predisposed to the Cow-boys. Behan testified before the grand jury first. The capitalization below is in the original—they are subheadings in the newspaper report, and show the obvious biases of the two different newspapers:

> John H. Behan, being sworn says; I am Sheriff, and reside in Tombstone, Cochise County, Arizona; I know the defendants Wyatt Earp, and John H. Holliday; I know Virg and Morg Earp; I knew Thomas McLaury, Frank McLaury, and William Clanton; I was in Tombstone October 26, when a difficulty, or shooting affray took place between the parties named. The first I knew that there was likely to be any trouble, I was sitting in a chair getting shaved in a barber shop [. . .]; someone in the shop said there was liable to be trouble between Clantons and the Earps; [. . .] I saw Marshal Earp standing there and asked what was the excitement [. . .]; he said there (were) a lot of s---s of b---s in town looking for a fight [. . .]; I said to Earp you had better disarm the crowd; he said he would not, he would give them a chance to make the fight; I said to him [. . .] I was going down
>
> TO DISARM THE BOYS.
>
> I meant any parties connected with the cowboys who had arms; [. . .] Virgil Earp had a shotgun; with the muzzle touching the door-sill, down at his side; I did not see arms on the others at the time; I then went down Fourth Street to the corner of Fremont, and I met there Frank McLaury [

. . .] I said to him: (defendants here objected to any conversation between witness and Frank McLaury, court overruled the objection at this time). I told McLaury that I would have to disarm him, as there was likely to be trouble in town and I propose to disarm everybody in town that had arms. He said he would not give up his arms as he did not intend to have trouble; I told him that he would have to give up his pistol, all the same; [. . .] about that time I saw Ike Clanton and Tom McLaury down the street below Fly's Photography Gallery; I said to Frank, 'Come with me;' we went down to where Ike Clanton and Tom were standing; I said to the boys, 'You must give up your arms!' Billy Clanton and Will Claiborne; I said to them, 'Boys you have got to give up your arms.' Frank McLaury demurred; I don't know exact language; he did not seem inclined, at first, to give up his arms. Ike told me he

DID NOT HAVE ANY ARMS.

I put my arm around his waist to see if he was armed, and found he was not; Tom McLaury showed me by pulling his coat open, that he was not armed, I saw five standing there and asked them how many there were of them; they said four of us [. . .]; I said boys you must go up to the Sheriff's office and take off your arms and stay there until I get back; I told them I was going to disarm the other party; at that time I saw Earps and Holliday coming down the sidewalk, on the south side of Fremont Street; they were a little below the post office; Virgil, Morgan and Wyatt Earp and Doc Holliday were the ones; [. . .] they did not heed me and I threw up my hands and said go back, I'm the Sheriff of this county and am not going to allow any trouble if I can help it; they brushed past me and I turned and went with them [. . .] when they arrived within a very few feet of the Clantons and McLaurys I heard one of them say

I THINK IT WAS WYATT EARP

You s---s of b---s you have been looking for a fight and now you can have it,' about that time I heard a voice say 'Throw up your hands;' during this time I saw a nickel-plated pistol pointed at one of the Clanton party - I think Billy - My impression at the time was that Doc Holliday had nickel-plated pistol; I will not say for certain that Holliday had it; these pistols I speak of were in the hands of the Earp party; when the order was given, 'Throw up your hands,' I heard Billy Clanton say, 'Don't shoot me, I don't want to fight,' Tom McLaury at the same time threw open his coat and said, 'I have nothing,' or 'I am not armed;' he made the same remark and the same gesture that he made to me when he first told me he was not armed; I can't tell the position of Billy Clanton's hands at the time he said, ' I don't want to fight,' my attention was directed just at that moment to the nickel-plated pistol; the nickel-plated pistol was the first to fire [. . .]

Two of the three fired shots were very rapid after the first shot; by whom I Do not Know; the first two shots fired by the Earp party; I could not say by whom; the next three shots I thought at the time came from the Earp party [. . .] the nickel-plated pistol went off immediately; I think V.W. Earp said, 'Throw up your hands;' [. . .]. I saw Frank McLaury staggering on the street with one hand on his belly and his pistol in his right; I saw him shoot at Morgan Earp, and from the direction of his pistol should judge that the shot went in the ground; he shot twice there in towards Fly's Building at Morgan Earp, and he started across the street; heard a couple of shots from that direction; did not see him after he got about half way across the street; then heard a couple of shots from his direction; looked and saw McLaury running and a shot was fired and he fell on his head; heard Morg say, 'I got him;' there might have been a couple of shots afterwards; but that was about the end of the fight; I can't say I knew the effect of the first two shots; the only parties I saw fall were Morg Earp and Frank McLaury. My impression was that the nickel-plated pistol was pointed at Billy Clanton; the first man that I was certain that was hit was Frank McLaury, as I saw him staggering and bewildered and knew he was hit; this shortly after the first five shots; I never saw any arms in the hands of any of the McLaury party except Frank McLaury and Billy Clanton; saw Frank McLaury on the sidewalk, within a very few feet of the inside line of the street;

did not see a pistol in the hands of any of the McLaury party until 8 or 10 shots had been fired; Frank was the first of the party in whose hands I saw a pistol; Ike Clanton broke and ran after the first few shots were fired; Ike, I think, went through Fly's Building; the last I saw of him he was running through the back of Fly's Building towards Allen Street. [Capitalization in original.][9]

Behan's testimony introduced several points not favorable to the Earps and Holliday that the prosecution later seized on in the preliminary hearing to prove their guilt. He put the Clantons and the McLaurys in the role of non-aggressors and painted the lawmen as the ones seeking a fight and firing shots without provocation. Consistent with that testimony, Behan implicated Doc Holliday for firing the first shot. Finally, he aggrandized his own involvement in the events leading up to the shooting as the role of a pacifist, and squarely placed Wyatt as the centerpiece of the troublemakers.

Of the two witnesses, the most important for the upcoming trial was the statement of Ike Clanton since the prosecution as you will see developed its theme around his testimony at the inquest hearing. The defense lawyers, therefore, could use Ike's statements at the Coroner's Inquest against him if he varied from his previous testimony. Ike testified on the night before the shoot-out, the Earps pistol-whipped him and he got into a verbal fight with the Earps and Holliday, but somehow managed to stay up all night and play cards with them. In the morning, they exchanged more threats, and at the O.K. Corral, it was the Earps and Holliday who fired first, trying to kill him. He testified he grabbed Wyatt, but his gang had no guns.

Right. When you outlaw guns, only outlaws will have guns. I think that was a bumper sticker on the back of the Wells Fargo stagecoach if I'm remembering my history correctly.

At the inquest, Ike testified as follows, as reported by the *Tombstone Daily Nugget*:

Ike Clanton, sworn;

Am a cattle dealer; was present on the 26th of the month, and am a brother of William Clanton who was killed on that day, saw the whole transaction, the killing; well, the night before the killing went into the Occidental lunch saloon for a lunch; while in there Doc Holliday came in and raised a row with me; was abusing me; he had his hand on his pistol; called me a s--- of a b---; he told me to get my gun out; I told him I had no gun; I looked around and saw Morgan Earp behind him, they began to abuse me, when I turned and got out doors; Virgil Earp, Wyatt and Morgan were all up there, Morg Earp told me if I wanted to fight to turn myself loose; they all had their hands; I told them again that I was not armed; Doc Holliday said, 'You s--- of a b---, go and arm yourself; I did then go and arm myself; I went back, saw V. Earp and T. McLowry [sic—McLaury throughout]; Virg Earp was playing poker with his pistol in his lap; we were playing poker, we quit at daylight; I followed him and said, 'I was abused the night before, and was still in town,' he said he was going to bed; the reason I followed him up was I saw him take his pistol out of his lap and stick it in his pants; I came back and passed in my chips; staid around until about 8 or 9 o'clock;

I STAID TO MEET DOC HOLLIDAY;

The next thing they, Virg and Morg Earp, slipped up and disarmed me; shortly after I met my brother; he asked me to go out of town; just then I met the man that had our team; I told him to harness up; then I went to get something left by my brother. We then went to where our team was; met the sheriff there; he told us that he would have to arrest us and take our arms off. I told him that we were just going to leave town; that I had no arms on me; he then told Billy, my brother, to take his arms up to his office, Billy told him he was just leaving the town; the sheriff then told Frank and Tom McLowry to take their arms off. Tom McLowry then opened his coat and said, 'Johnny, I have nothing.' Frank said that he was leaving town, and that he would disarm if the Earps would; that he had business that he would like to do before he left town. Just at that time Doc Holliday and the Earps appeared on the sidewalk; the sheriff stepped out to meet them; he told them that he had this party in charge; they walked right by him. I stepped out and met Wyatt Earp; he stuck his - six shooter at me and said, 'Throw up your hands!' The marshal also told the other boys to throw up their hands; Frank McLowry and Billy Clanton threw up; Tom McLowry threw open his coat and said he had nothing; they said you's s--- of b---s came here to make a fight; at the same instant Doc Holliday and Morgan Earp shot; Morgan shot Billy Clanton, and I don't know which of the boys he shot; I saw Virg shooting at the same time; I grabbed Wyatt Earp and pushed him around the corner and then ran through the photograph gallery; at the same time I saw Billy Clanton fall; when I got away.

ALL OF US THREW UP OUR HANDS.

Except Tom McLowry, who threw open his coat saying that he had nothing. There was some trouble between myself and the Earps prior to this; there was nothing between the other boys and the Earps; Doc Holliday said I had used his name; I said I hadn't; I never had trouble with the Earps; they don't like me; we once had a transaction, myself and the Earps; I know of no threats made by the Clantons and McLowrys that day; I made no threats, only as I formerly said; they, the Earps, met Billy Clanton 15 minutes before they killed him and shook hands with him and said they were glad to meet him; Billy Clanton and McLowry were only a half an hour in town; I might have made threats as said, as I felt that way; I made no worse threats at them than they did with me; I didn't expect Wyatt, I expected

MORGAN AND DOC HOLLIDAY TO ATTACK ME.

[Capitalization in original.][10]

While other witnesses testified before the Coroner's Inquest, Sheriff Behan and Clanton's testimony slanted toward a finding that the lawmen caused the deaths of the McLaurys and Billy Clanton. Ike Clanton didn't have a lawyer when he testified in the inquest, and the prosecution was now stuck with his story as told to the coroner's grand jury. Having testified under oath, Ike could not change his testimony without risking being called a liar, and he therefore cast in stone the prosecution's theory, which severely limited the prosecutor's ability to shape a strong case against the Earps and Holliday. The coroner's grand jury verdict came in, neither implicating the lawmen nor clearing them. The same verdict applied word-for-word to Tom McLaury and Billy Clanton:

> Tombstone, Territory of Arizona, }
> County of Cochise October 29, 1881. }
>
> We the undersigned, a jury of inquest, summoned by the coroner of the court of Cochise to determine whose the body is submitted to our inspection; when, where, and under what circumstances the person came to his death. After viewing the body and hearing such testimony as had been submitted to us, find that the person was Frank McLowry, 29 years of age (Editor's note: Records show his birth date as March 3, 1848, which made him 33 not 29.) and a native of Mississippi (Editor's note: Records show his place of birth as Kortright, New York.), and that he came to his death in the town of Tombstone in said county, and on the 26th day of October, 1881, from the effects of pistol and gunshot wounds inflicted by Virgil Earp, Morgan Earp, Wyatt Earp and one Holliday, commonly called Doc Holliday.[11]

The lack of any indictment or decision against either side in the inquest left "the boys" free to go, as the newspapers referred to them. Kind of like those old games of cops and robbers. But Ike Clanton would have no such result that allowed the Earps and Holliday to go free, and on October 30, 1881, swore out a warrant to arrest the lawmen for murder of his brother and the McLaurys. On the same day, the court first addressed the question of bail for the lawmen, set at $10,000 each, which they then posted. Testimony started the following day on October 31, 1881, just five days after the shooting.

Trial of the Lawmen: The Players in the Preliminary Hearing

Apart from those you have met already, local attorney and Judge Wells W. Spicer acted as a justice of the peace in the preliminary hearing. Spicer had first been admitted to the bar in Iowa and then Utah, where he defended a man accused in the then famous Mountain Meadows Massacre. That trial resulted in what Spicer considered the unjustified conviction of the defendant and his death by firing squad while conveniently seated next to his coffin. The Earps and Holliday couldn't have hoped for a better judge for their side of the case. It would have been difficult to find a judge with a better disposition with the lawlessness present in the territory, coupled with the court's requirement to enforce the law. Given Spicer's years of practice, he was considered well-versed in the law. The lawyers before him were equally skilled.

According to an interview of Virgil Earp,[12] the Cow-boys put up about $10,000 to hire the best lawyers in the territory to prosecute them, but the prosecution team included members with very different goals. The Arizona governor appointed Prosecutor Lyttleton Price. Those who thought the lawmen took unfair advantage of the Clantons and McLaurys saw Price as beholding to politicians and businessmen and favoring the Earps and Holliday. Ike Clanton brought his personal lawyer, Ben Goodrich, onto the prosecutor's team, who was not subject to the same motives as Price. Tom and Frank McLuary's brother, Will, who was both a lawyer and a judge, also joined the prosecutor's team on November 14, 1881, almost halfway through the trial in the middle of Sheriff Behan's testimony. While Price and Goodrich may have agreed on a common strategy typical of preliminary hearings, it was apparent Attorney McLaury sought only revenge for his dead brothers. As with most who have a personal stake in a particular matter, McLaury's rage blinded his otherwise skilled trial tactics. As the county prosecutor, the government paid Price's salary, much like the district and United States attorneys of the present day. Goodrich and McLaury, on the other hand, were private attorneys. In today's environment, circumstances where private attorneys assist government attorneys still happen, as when Congress appoints a special prosecutor.

Attorney Tom Fitch ably represented the Earp brothers. Fitch's biography from the U.S. House of Representatives notes that he was a Representative from Nevada, a member of the California assembly in 1862 and 1863; district attorney of Washoe County, Nevada in 1865 and 1866, and then elected as a Republican to the Forty-first Congress where he served from 1869 to 1871. After he lost the election for another term in Congress, he continued the practice of law and was an occasional editor and writer for the *San Francisco Times*.[13]

Due to a conflict of interest with the Earps, Holliday was represented by local attorney T.J. Drum. In addition to his law practice, Drum was a local federal judge and the United States

Court Commissioner of the First Judicial District. He was more than familiar with the Earps, having previously heard many criminal cases the Earps had brought before him during the performance of the Earps' regular law enforcement duties prior to the O.K. Corral shootout.

The Earps and Holliday's best defense lie in a united front that today we would call a joint defense. Prosecutors typically offer one or more of the defendants a plea to a lesser charge or sometimes outright immunity from further charges in return for that defendant's testimony and evidence against the others. It appears the Tombstone prosecutor did not use this tactic, which likely would not have been effective anyway, given the strong friendship between Wyatt and Doc. Even the Earp brothers had a technical conflict of interest, but one that was likely ignored. Facing charges that could result in hanging tends to divide the interests of joint defendants—here Virgil or Morgan could have easily blamed the fight on Wyatt and escaped their own hanging with a self-defense argument, but again, it was unlikely brothers who fought together and relied on each other for a living would betray one another.

The Preliminary Hearing

The "trial" of the Earps and Doc Holliday was a preliminary hearing, the step before an actual trial. In that preliminary hearing, which is much as the same it is today, the judge is charged with determining whether there is "probable cause" that a crime was committed, and, if so, then the defendants are "bound over" for trial. No jury is impaneled for a preliminary hearing—the judge is the sole fact finder. If the defense is successful in proving a lack of probable cause, then the case is dismissed and does not proceed to trial.

Under the Arizona territory law of 1881, the prosecution in the Earp/Holliday preliminary hearing had only to meet the minimal burden of proof of "sufficient cause to believe the defendants guilty."[14] This standard is well below the criminal trial standard of "beyond a reasonable doubt" for a guilty verdict, and even below the lesser standard of "preponderance of the evidence" (sometimes called a 51/49 percent finding) used in a civil trial.

It's hard for a prosecutor to lose a preliminary hearing. Prosecutors typically call only a few witnesses to establish the bare likelihood a crime was committed because defense counsel treats a preliminary hearing as a means to learn how the prosecution will present its case at trial. Since most preliminary hearings result in a court finding "probable cause" and given the low burden of proof, both sides use the preliminary hearing as a preview of how the other side will try their case before a jury. Wise prosecutors thus limit the evidence presented to just enough to meet their burden of proof, and defense counsel equally avoid showing their hand prior to the actual trial and frequently will not call any witnesses.

In the Earps and Holliday's case, however, the defense employed a much different tactic. They recognized Judge Spicer's predilection toward the law-abiding, commercial interests in Tombstone. Given the theory chosen by the defense, it would be easy to align the lawmen's case with Judge Spicer's predispositions. When compared to the vagaries of trial before a jury, especially when nearly 2,000 showed up for the McLaury and Clanton's funeral and burial at Boot Hill in Tombstone, defense counsel believed their best chance lay with Judge Spicer for a favorable verdict in the preliminary hearing instead of a jury.

The prosecution, on the other hand, had two main choices for a winning theory: either pin the start of the gunfight on the known renegade Doc Holliday and thus implicate the Earps by association, or show the Earps themselves as rogues trying to kill off a rival gang.

The Prosecution's Case - William Allen

The prosecutors Price and Goodrich on November 1, 1881, first called William Allen, a friend of the McLaury family, and somewhat doubtfully alleged in a later book by Josie Earp to himself have fired at the Earps and Holliday from behind. Allen testified in part that he heard one of the Earps yell, "You sons-of-bitches, you have been looking for a fight!" Then to cap off his condemnation of the lawmen, he said,

> Tom McLaury threw his coat open and said, "I ain't got no arms!" He caught hold of the lapels of his coat and threw it open. William Clanton said, "I do not want to fight!" and held his hands out in front of him [witness shows how]. He had nothing in his hands when he held them in this position. I did not notice what Frank McLaury did. I did not notice him

or Ike. Just as William Clanton said, "I do not want to fight!" and Tom McLaury threw open his coat and said, "I ain't got no arms," the firing commenced by the Earp party.[15]

The defense tried to impeach Allen's credibility with allegations that he had used an alias and been convicted of larceny under that alias, but Allen denied the charge and the prosecution's objections to continued attempts to bring it up again were sustained. The prosecution had used the generally accepted trial technique of starting strong, setting out their theory of rogue lawmen out for a personal vendetta against the Clantons and the McLaurys.

Wesley Fuller

On November 7, 1881, the prosecution called Wesley Fuller, an eyewitness of the shootout and a local gambler. After his testimony, Judge Spicer revoked the bail previously posted by Wyatt Earp and Doc Holliday and put them in jail. Fuller's testimony was fairly damning of the lawmen:

> Deposition of Wesley Fuller, a gambler, of Tombstone. He states he saw the difficulty between the Earps and Holliday on one side and the McLaury brothers and the Clantons on the other, on Fremont, near the corner of Third Street. He was right back of Fly's Gallery in the alley when the shooting began. He says he saw the Earp party, armed, at Fourth and Allen and that he was on his way to warn Billy Clanton to get out of town. He saw Billy, Frank McLaury and he thinks Behan, but did not get to speak with Billy, as just then the Earps hove into view, and he heard them say, "Throw up your hands!" Billy Clanton threw up his hands and said, "Don't shoot me! I don't want to fight!" and at the same time the shooting commenced. At this time, he had not seen Tom McLaury nor Ike Clanton.
>
> He says the Earp party fired the first shots. Two were fired right away, they were fired almost together. They commenced firing then very rapidly and fired 20 or 30 shots. Both sides were firing. Five or six shots were fired by the Earp party before the other party fired. Billy Clanton and Frank McLaury were the only two I saw fire of the Clanton party. As

> the first shots were fired by the Earp party, Billy Clanton had his hands up. [Shows the position as he stood raising his hands up to the line of his head.] Frank McLaury was standing, holding his horse when the firing commenced. He was not doing anything that I could see. He had no weapon that I saw on him. I saw his hands and he had nothing in them. If there had been, I would have seen it. I think the first two shots were aimed at Billy Clanton. I saw that he was hit. He threw his hands on his belly and wheeled around. I did not see any effect on anybody else at that time. Frank McLaury drew a weapon and was firing during [illegible]. When he drew his weapon, he was on Fremont Street, a little past the middle of the Street. [Shows on diagram.] Further talk as to relative positions. Then he says, on questions, that seven or eight shots had been fired by the Earp party before he saw Frank McLaury draw his pistol. [16]

The prosecution moved to revoke bail for Wyatt and Doc, who were then taken into custody by none other than Sheriff John Behan, and they remained in his custody for the next sixteen days. Friends of the Earps guarded the jail while the two were imprisoned. Virgil and Morgan remained at their homes recovering from their wounds.

Billy the Kid

One of the prosecution's following witnesses on November 8, 1881, was William Claiborne, known as "Billy the Kid," but not the same as the more famous character depicted in many western television shows and movies. He testified much the same way as Allen, blaming the Earps and Holliday with firing the first shot and claiming the McLaurys and Clantons were unarmed. On his cross-examination, though, he was confronted with a prior arrest, which destroyed his credibility:

> (Q) Don't you pass sometimes under the name of "The Kid?"
>
> (A) Yes sir, sometimes I do.
>
> (Q) How old are you?
>
> (A) I was 21, the 21st day of last October.
>
> (Q) What state are you from?

(A)   From Mississippi.

(Q)   Do you like the Earps?

(A)   I have nothing against them.

(Q)   Were you not in a killing scrape sometime ago in Charleston, for which you are now held under bonds?

[Objection by prosecution. Question objected to on the ground that it is immaterial, irrelevant, and not pertinent to the issue before the court, and in no manner tends to impair the credibility of the witness for truth or veracity, or show his bias. Objection overruled and excepted to.]

(A)   I decline to answer.[17]

His redirect examination by the prosecution was completely ineffectual, despite the attempt at humor, in attempting to rehabilitate him as a credible witness:

(Q)   You were asked, in your cross-examination, if one of the Earps arrested you in Charleston sometime ago upon a criminal charge. If you were arrested upon any charge, was it by Virgil Earp, Wyatt Earp, or Morgan Earp?

[Objected to by the Defense. Objection sustained.]

(Q)   You were asked in your cross-examination if [you] were not sometimes called "The Kid." Please explain how you came to be called by that name.

(A)   Well, I came to Arizona when I was small, when Tombstone was first struck. John Slaughter's men called me "The Kid," because I was the smallest one in the outfit. That is the way the name originated with me.

(Q)   When did you first come to Tombstone?

(A)   About two and a half, or three years ago.

(Q)   How much smaller were you then, than you are now?

(A)   I have grown nearly two feet since then, in height.[18]

The defense likely objected to the first question because it was not the same question Fitch had carefully asked in cross-examination. Then like now, there is a rule in successive examinations that the attorneys must stay within the scope of the prior examination. If the Earps had arrested Billy the Kid, then that fact presumably would have shown his bias against the lawmen and shouldn't have been objectionable to the defense. Nevertheless, the prosecution's attempt to rehabilitate Billy the Kid may have gotten a laugh, but not much more.

Ike Clanton

Ike and Claiborne's testimony pegged the Earps as both causing the fight and portrayed the Cow-boys as victims, difficult theories to prove together. Most murder cases require the prosecution to prove motive, which is frequently either based on money or blood relationships. Apocryphally, most murders are committed by a relative for either financial or romantic reasons. Here, pinning the murders of the McLaurys and Billy Clanton on the Earps and Holliday required the prosecution to demonstrate an entirely different motive, since none of the defendants were related to the McLaurys or the Clantons and had nothing to gain financially from their death. Ike Clanton's questioning started on November 9, 1881, immediately after Claiborne. In the first part of his testimony, his statements and claims mirrored his testimony before the Coroner's Inquest as related above, claiming that the lawmen barely gave warning before they started firing. The prosecution made its motive clear with Ike Clanton's testimony, but it was the first time Clanton's grand jury testimony would be challenged through cross-examination. On direct at trial, the prosecution attempted to establish the animosity between the two groups:

> (Q) State if there was any previous difficulty between you and the defendants or either of them; and if yes, when and where?
>
> (A) Yes sir, there was a difficulty between Holliday and Morgan Earp and I, the night before at a lunch stand in this town near the Eagle Brewery Saloon, on the north side of Allen Street. As well as I remember, it was about 1 o'clock in the morning. I went in there to get a lunch. While sitting down at the table, Doc Holliday came in and

commenced cursing me and said I was, "A son-of-a-bitch of a cowboy," and told me to get my gun out and get to work. I told him I had no gun. He said I was a damned liar and had threatened the Earps. I told him I had not, to bring whoever said so to me and I would convince him that I had not. He told me again to pull out my gun and if there was any grit in me, to go to fighting. [. . .] I then got up and went out on the sidewalk. Doc Holliday said, as I walked out, "You son-of-a-bitch, if you ain't heeled [armed], go and heel yourself." Just as I stepped out, Morgan Earp stepped up and said, "Yes, you son-of-a-bitch, you can have all the fight you want now!" I thanked him and told him I did not want any of it now, I was not heeled. [. . .]. I walked off and asked them not to shoot me in the back.

It was on cross that Ike Clanton unknowingly opened the door to a major stumble:

(Q) Did not Wyatt Earp approach you, Frank McLaury, and Joe Hill for the purpose of getting you three parties to give said Leonard, Head and Crane away-in the Arizona parlance-so that he, Wyatt Earp, could capture them?

(A) Wyatt Earp approached me, but I do not [know] that he ever approached Frank McLaury or Joe Hill. [. . .] He then told me he would put me on a scheme to make six thousand dollars. I asked him what it was. He told me he would not tell me unless I would promise to do it, or if I would not promise to do it, not to mention our conversation to anyone else. He then made me promise on my honor as a gentleman not to repeat the conversation if I did not like the proposition. I asked him what it was. He told me it was a legitimate transaction. He then made me promise the second time that I would not mention it any more. He told me he wanted me to help put up a job to kill

Crane, Leonard and Head. He said there was between four and five thousand reward for them, and he said he would make the balance of the six thousand dollars up out of his own pocket. I then asked him why he was anxious to capture these fellows. He said that his business was such that he could not afford to capture them. He would have to kill them or else leave the country. [. . .] I never talked to Wyatt Earp any more about it.

Clanton then went on to shift the blame for the killing of Bud Philpot, the driver of the Bisbee stagecoach, to Doc Holliday. The prosecutors leapt on Clanton's testimony, which offered them the motive they sought: they could now portray the lawmen as crooks themselves for robbing the stagecoach and show that Holliday was himself a killer. The prosecution's lead attorney, Littleton Price, couldn't resist asking one question too many, which as all good trial lawyers know is the danger faced when asking a question with an unknown answer:

(Q) Why have you not told what Doc Holliday, Wyatt Earp, Virgil Earp, and Morgan Earp said about the attempted stage robbery and the killing of Bud Philpot before you have told it in this examination.

(A) Before they told me, I made a sacred promise not to tell it, and never would have told it, had I not been put on the stand. And another reason is, I found out by Wyatt Earp's conversation that he was offering money to kill men that were in the attempted stage robbery, his confederates, for fear that Bill Leonard, Crane and Head would be captured and tell on him, and I knew that after Leonard, Crane and Head was killed that some of them would murder me for what they had told me.

Clanton did not realize the mistake he had just made. He had earlier claimed to have grabbed Wyatt Earp as the fighting began and when Wyatt rebuked him for being unarmed, Clanton successfully ran away to escape the gunfire. As Judge Spicer later observed in his ruling, Earp could have easily killed him at that point if Clanton's fanciful story about the lawmen robbing the stage, splitting the monies, and killing the driver and one of its passengers was true.

Moreover, Clanton's story was unbelievable in and of itself: what possible motivation would any of the Earp brothers have for disclosing their robbery and killing story to Clanton? If Clanton truly hated the Earps as he claimed, why had he not previously reported the story to Sheriff Behan and had them arrested? The prosecution's rehabilitation of Clanton's farfetched testimony failed to address any of these questions and instead failed to follow-up after Fitch's sarcastic re-cross-examination destroyed Ike's credibility:

> (Q) About what time did you hear of the killing of Philpot and Holliday's participation in it?
>
> (A) I heard of it the night it was done, [but] I did not hear of Doc Holliday's being implicated in it until several days afterwards.
>
> (Q) Did you rely upon the information which you received in reference to Doc Holliday's participation in said killing?
>
> (A) I said that after Leonard, Crane and Head were killed, I was afraid I would be murdered.
>
> (Q) Do you still entertain that fear?
>
> (A) Well, after the attempt to murder me the other day, I do.
>
> (Q) Did anybody else beside Doc Holliday, Wyatt Earp, Virgil Earp, and Morgan Earp, or anyone of them, confess to you that they were confederates in stopping the stage and murdering Bud Philpot?
>
> [Question objected to on the ground that it is immaterial.]
>
> (Q) Did not Marshall Williams, the agent of the Express Company at Tombstone, state to you, and if at Tombstone, and if so, where, that he was personally concerned in the attempted stage robbery and the murder of Philpot?

[Question objected to by prosecution.]

(Q) Did not James Earp, a brother of Virgil, Morgan and Wyatt, also confess to you that he was [a] murderer and stage robber?

[Objected to by prosecution, objection sustained on the ground that it is immaterial and irrelevant.][19]

Fitch's last two questions damned Clanton's credibility, despite the objections. The point had been made. That's one great thing about always telling the truth. You never have to remember what you said before.

Sheriff Behan next took the stand, and like Ike Clanton, largely repeated his testimony from the Coroner's Inquest. He made a rather cryptic reference at the end of his answer, which many believe is a veiled reference to his dispute with Wyatt Earp over Josephine Marcus, and explains the animosity between the two:

(Q) Were not you and Wyatt Earp applicants to General Fremont for the appointment of Sheriff of Cochise County, and did not Wyatt Earp withdraw his application upon your promise to divide the profits of the office and did not you subsequently refuse to comply with your part of the contract? [Objected to by the Prosecution. Overruled.]

(A) In the first place we were both applicants for the office. I was, and I understood Mr. Earp was. When I became satisfied that I would get the appointment, I went to Mr. Earp and told him that I knew I would get the appointment of Sheriff, and that I would like to have him in the office with me. I also told him that I did not want him to cease his efforts to get the office if he could. I told him I was sure I could get it and that if I did, I would take him in, that in case he got the office, I did not want anything to do with it. He said it was very kind of me, that if he got the office he had his brothers to provide for, and could not return the compliment if he got it. I said I asked nothing if he got it, but in case I got it, and I was certain of it, I would like to have him in the office with me. I said, "Let this talk make no difference with you in your efforts to get the office." Something afterwards transpired that I did not take him into the office.

On cross, Sheriff Behan tried to explain the "something." He claimed Wyatt Earp provided advance notice to Ike Clanton of a subpoena in a civil matter, which Behan was supposed to serve on Clanton. While plausible, the testimony was largely unbelievable because he was unable to offer a reason why Wyatt would take such an action. Fitch also got Sheriff Behan to admit to a contradiction in his testimony about Tom McLaury and how he was able to shoot back at the lawmen:

(Q) Were you satisfied when you put your arm around the waist of Ike Clanton, Tom McLaury threw the lapels of his coat aside, and Billy Clanton said he did not want to fight, that these parties had no arms?

(A) When I left the Clanton party to meet the Earps, I was satisfied that Ike Clanton and Tom McLaury had no arms on them.

(Q) Could they not have had arms and you not know it?

(A) Ike Clanton could not without my knowing it. Tom McLaury might have had a pistol and I not know it.

(Q) As you examined him simply around the waist, could he not have had a pistol in his pocket?

(A) He could not have had a pistol in his pocket, as I examined him very closely with my eye.[20]

Ike Clanton had earlier admitted that both Tom and Frank McLaury had rifles on their horses, and ample testimony exists about Tom's firing his rifle at the lawmen. By Fitch's questioning, he had shown Sheriff Behan's testimony to be suspect—why would a lawman trained to be observant have missed the rifle on McLaury's horse?

Especially if that lawman thinks the rifle might be pointed at him in a few minutes.

At this point in the proceedings, the roles of the lawyers shifted. Where previously District Attorney Price and the prosecutors first asked witnesses questions soliciting their direct testimony, the defense team of Attorneys Fitch and Drum then followed with their cross-examination. In the normal procedure of any trial, the opposite would occur after the prosecution rested. Once the defense began to present its case-in-chief, Fitch and Drum would ask questions on direct examination first, then Price and his prosecution team would follow-up with their cross-examination. As before, the respective parties could conduct re-direct and re-cross-examination to clear up points left open by the opposing side, although it appears that Judge Spicer limited the amount of re-direct and re-cross the lawyers could employ. At the end of the case, Judge Spicer injected himself into the proceedings and asked his own questions, sometimes commonplace even today, but Spicer took an unusual step of visiting the final witness without the lawyers, something that would not be allowed today.

The Defense Case

Unlike the prosecution's case, the defendants presented a different and much simpler theory of the events that not only fit well with Judge Spicer's predilection for law enforcement, but also appealed to his legal training surrounding the rule of law. Put simply, the defense argued it was the "good guys" versus the "bad guys."

In contrast, the prosecution had tried vainly to paint the Cow-boys as victims of law enforcement gone bad, a theory that Ike Clanton and Sheriff Behan's testimony couldn't pull off and was neither credible nor believable. We will see a variant of that theory against law enforcement successfully applied by the defense in the O.J. trial at the end of this book. To apply the theory of police incompetence (one of the main threads of the O.J. defense), the prosecution against Wyatt Earp failed to account for several facts in their theory, as Judge Spicer made clear in his decision.

Defense Attorney Tom Fitch pulled off a coup, citing to an Arizona statute that allowed the accused to read a prepared statement and eliminated the ability of the prosecution to cross-examine the defendant on the statement. Fitch apparently helped Wyatt Earp write his statement. There are some legal historians who believe the statute had been overruled, but Judge Spicer admitted the statement into evidence over the prosecutor's objections. Wyatt Earp, with just a few introductory questions, read his testimony as reflected in the record:

> On this sixteenth day of November, 1881, upon the hearing of the above entitled action, on the examination of Wyatt Earp and J. H. Holliday, the prosecution having closed their evidence in chief, and the defendants, Wyatt Earp and J. H. Holliday, having first been informed of his rights to make a statement as provided in Section 133, page 22 of the laws of Arizona, approved February 12, 1881, and the said Wyatt Earp having chosen to make a statement under oath and having been personally sworn, makes such statement under oath in answer to interrogatories as follows:
>
> (Q) What is your name and age?
>
> (A) My name is Wyatt Earp: 32 years old last March the 19th.
>
> (Q) Where were you born?
>
> (A) In Monmouth, Warren County, Illinois.
>
> (Q) Where do you reside and how long have you resided there?
>
> (A) I reside in Tombstone, Cochise County Arizona: since December 1, 1879.
>
> (Q) What is your business and profession?
>
> (A) Saloon keeper at present. Also have been Deputy Sheriff and also a detective.
>
> (Q) Give any explanations you may think proper of the circumstances appearing in the testimony against you, and state any facts which you think will tend to your exculpation.
>
> (A) The difficulty which resulted in the death of William Clanton and Frank McLaury originated last spring, [Objection made by prosecution against the defendant, Wyatt Earp, in making his statement, of using a manuscript from which to make such statement, and object to the said defendant being allowed to make statement without

> limit as to it relevancy. Objection overruled.] and at a little over a year ago, I followed Tom and Frank McLaury and two other parties who had stolen six government mules from Camp Rucker. Myself, Virgil Earp, and Morgan Earp, and Marshall Williams, Captain Hurst and four soldiers; we traced those mules to McLaury's ranch. [Prosecution moved to strike out the foregoing statement as irrelevant. Objection overruled.]

Wyatt explained how Doc Holliday came into the picture:

> I am a friend of Doc Holliday because when I was city marshal of Dodge City, Kansas, he came to my rescue and saved my life when I was surrounded by desperadoes.

He described the night before the shootout and the spark that ignited the fight:

> On the night of the 25th of October, Holliday met Ike Clanton in the Alhambra Saloon and asked him about it. Clanton denied it. They quarreled for three or four minutes. Holliday told Clanton he was a damned liar, if he said so. I was sitting eating lunch at the lunch counter. Morgan Earp was standing at the Alhambra bar talking with the bartender. I called him over to where I was sitting, knowing that he was an officer and told him that Holliday and Clanton were quarreling in the lunch room and for him to go in and stop it. He climbed over the lunch room counter from the Alhambra bar and went into the room, took Holliday by the arm and led him into the street. Ike Clanton in a few seconds followed them out. I got through eating and walked out of the bar. As I stopped at the door of the bar, they were still quarreling.
>
> Just then Virgil Earp came up, I think out of the Occidental, and told them, Holliday and Clanton, if they didn't stop their quarreling he would have to arrest them. They all separated at that time, Morgan Earp going down the street to the Oriental Saloon, Ike going across the street to the Grand Hotel. I walked in the Eagle Brewery where I had a faro

game which I had not closed. I stayed in there for a few minutes and walked out to the street and there met Ike Clanton. He asked me if I would take a walk with him, that he wanted to talk to me. I told him I would if he did not go too far, as I was waiting for my game in the Brewery to close, and I would have to take care of the money. We walked about halfway down the brewery building, going down Fifth Street and stopped.

He told me when Holliday [. . .] said that in the morning he would have man-for-man, that this fighting talk had been going on for a long time, and he guessed it was about time to fetch it to a close. I told him I would not fight no one if I could get away from it, because there was no money in it. [. . .] About that time the man that is dealing my game closed it and brought the money to me. I locked it in the safe and started home. I met Holliday on the street between the Oriental and Alhambra. Myself and Holliday walked down Allen Street, he going to his room, and I to my house, going to bed.

Despite their differences, Wyatt, Doc, and Ike played a card game of faro the night before and well into the morning. Why then did the shootout even happen? Ike claimed that during the card game, Wyatt and Doc insulted and "abused" him so much he wanted revenge.

I got up the next day, October 26, about noon. Before I got up, Ned Boyle came to me and told me that he met Ike Clanton on Allen Street near the telegraph office, that Ike was armed, that he said, "as soon as those damned Earps make their appearance on the street today the ball will open, we are here to make a fight. We are looking for the sons-of-bitches!" I laid in bed some little time after that, and got up and went down to the Oriental Saloon.

Harry Jones came to me after I got up and said, "What does all this mean?" I asked him what he meant. He says, "Ike Clanton is hunting you boys with a Winchester rifle and six-shooter." I said, "I will go down and find him and see what he wants." I went out and on the corner of Fifth and Allen I met Virgil Earp, the marshal. He told me how he heard Ike Clanton was hunting us. I went down Allen

Street and Virgil went down Fifth Street and then Fremont Street. Virgil found Ike Clanton on Fourth Street near Fremont Street, in the mouth of an alleyway.

Ike spoke out-of-turn to Jones as a braggart, but when he faced down Wyatt, Ike was not so confident without his brothers at his side.

> I walked up to him and said, "I hear you are hunting for some of us." I was coming down Fourth Street at the time. Ike Clanton then threw his Winchester rifle around toward Virgil. Virgil grabbed it and hit Ike Clanton with his six-shooter and knocked him down. Clanton had his rifle and his six-shooter was in his pants. By that time I came up, Virgil and Morgan Earp took his rifle and six-shooter and took them to the Grand Hotel after examination, and I took Ike Clanton before Justice Wallace.
>
> Before the investigation, Morgan Earp had Ike Clanton in charge, as Virgil Earp was out at the time. After I went into Wallace's court and sat down on a bench, Ike Clanton looked over to me and said, "I will get even with all of you for this. If I had a six-shooter now I would make a fight with all of you." Morgan Earp then said to him, "If you want to make a fight right bad, I will give you this one!" at the same time offering Ike Clanton his own six-shooter.
>
> Ike Clanton started to get up and take it, when Campbell, the deputy sheriff, pushed him back in his seat, saying he would not allow any fuss. I never had Ike Clanton's arms at any time, as he stated.
>
> I would like to describe the positions we occupied in the courtroom. Ike Clanton sat on a bench with his face fronting to the north wall of the building. I myself sat down on a bench that ran against and along the north wall in front of where Ike sat. Morgan Earp stood up on his feet with his back against the wall and to the right of where I sat, and two or three feet from me.
>
> Morgan Earp had Ike Clanton's Winchester in his hand, like this, with one end on the floor, with Clanton's six-shooter in his right hand. We had them

all the time. Virgil Earp was not in the courtroom during any of this time and came there after I had walked out. He was out, he told me, hunting for Judge Wallace.

I was tired of being threatened by Ike Clanton and his gang and believe from what he said to me and others, and from their movements that they intended to assassinate me the first chance they had, and I thought that if I had to fight for my life with them I had better make them face me in an open fight. So I said to Ike Clanton, who was then sitting about eight feet away from me. "You damned dirty cow thief, you have been threatening our lives and I know it. I think I would be justified in shooting you down any place I should meet you, but if you are anxious to make a fight, I will go anywhere on earth to make a fight with you, even over to the San Simon among your crowd!" He replied, "I will see you after I get through here. I only want four feet of ground to fight on!"

After Judge Wallace fined Ike and took his guns, Ike went looking for his brothers. Wyatt give us the lead-up to the gunfight as the insults flew through the air like the bullets later did.

I walked out and then just outside of the courtroom near the Justice's Office, I met Tom McLaury. He came up to me and said to me, "If you want to make a fight I will make a fight with you anywhere." [. . .] So I said to him, "All right, make a fight right here!" And at the same time slapped him in the face with my left hand and drew my pistol with my right. He had a pistol in plain sight on his right hip in his pants, but made no move to draw it. I said to him, "Jerk your gun and use it!" He made no reply and I hit him on the head with my six-shooter and walked away, [. . .] into Hafford's and got a cigar and came out and stood by the door.

Pretty soon after I saw Tom McLaury, Frank McLaury, and William Clanton pass me and went down Fourth Street to the gunsmith shop. I followed them to see what they were going to do. [. . .] I saw them in the gun shop changing cartridges into their belts. They came out of the shop [. . .] and went down Allen Street and over to Dunbar's Corral.

With that background, Wyatt turned to the trigger of the famous gunfight:

> About ten minutes afterwards, and while Virgil, Morgan, Doc Holliday and myself were standing on the corner of Fourth and Allen Streets, several people said, "There is going to be trouble with those fellows," and one man named Coleman said to Virgil Earp, "They mean trouble. They have just gone from Dunbar's Corral into the O.K. Corral, all armed, and I think you had better go and disarm them." Virgil turned around to Doc Holliday, Morgan Earp and myself and told us to come and assist him in disarming them.
>
> We four started through Fourth to Fremont Street. When we turned the corner of Fourth and Fremont we could see them standing near or about the vacant space between Fly's photograph gallery and the next building west. I first saw Frank McLaury, Tom McLaury, Billy Clanton and Sheriff Behan standing there. We went down the left-hand side of Fremont Street.
>
> When we got within about 150 feet of them I saw Ike Clanton and Billy Clanton and another party. We had walked a few steps further and I saw Behan leave the party and come toward us. Every few steps he would look back as if he apprehended danger. I heard him say to Virgil Earp, "For God's sake, don't go down there, you will get murdered!" Virgil Earp replied, "I am going to disarm them." he, Virgil, being in the lead. When I and Morgan came up to Behan he said, "I have disarmed them." When he said this, I took my pistol, which I had in my hand, under my coat, and put it in my overcoat pocket. Behan then passed up the street, and we walked on down.
>
> We came up on them close; Frank McLaury, Tom McLaury, and Billy Clanton standing in a row against the east side of the building on the opposite side of the vacant space west of Fly's photograph gallery. Ike Clanton and Billy Claiborne and a man I

don't knows were standing in the vacant space about halfway between the photograph gallery and the next building west.

I saw that Billy Clanton and Frank and Tom McLaury had their hands by their sides, Frank McLaury and Billy Clanton's six-shooters were in plain sight. Virgil said, "Throw up your hands; I have come to disarm you!" Billy Clanton and Frank McLaury laid their hands on their six-shooters. Virgil said, "Hold, I don't mean that!" I have come to disarm you!" Then Billy Clanton and Frank McLaury commenced to draw their pistols. At the same time, Tom McLaury threw his hand to his right hip, throwing his coat open like this, [showing how] and jumped behind his horse. [Actually it was Billy Clanton's horse.]

I had my pistol in my overcoat pocket, where I had put it when Behan told us he had disarmed the other parties. When I saw Billy Clanton and Frank McLaury draw their pistols, I drew my pistol. Billy Clanton leveled his pistol at me, but I did not aim at him. I knew that Frank McLaury had the reputation of being a good shot and a dangerous man, and I aimed at Frank McLaury. The first two shots were fired by Billy Clanton and myself, he shooting at me, and I shooting at Frank McLaury. I don't know which was fired first. We fired almost together. The fight then became general. After about four shots were fired, Ike Clanton ran up and grabbed my left arm. I could see no weapon in his hand, and thought at the time he had none, and so I said to him, "The fight had commenced. Go to fighting or get away," at the same time pushing him off with my left hand, like this. He started and ran down the side of the building and disappeared between the lodging house and photograph gallery.

My first shot struck Frank McLaury in the belly. He staggered off on the sidewalk but fired one shot at me. When we told them to throw up their hands Claiborne threw up his left hand and broke and ran. I never saw him afterwards until late in the afternoon, after the fight. I never drew my pistol or made a motion to shoot until after Billy Clanton and

> Frank McLaury drew their pistols. If Tom McLaury was unarmed, I did not know it, I believe he was armed and fired two shots at our party before Holliday, who had the shotgun, fired and killed him. If he was unarmed, there was nothing in the circumstances or in what had been communicated to me, or in his acts or threats, that would have led me even to suspect his being unarmed.
>
> I never fired at Ike Clanton, even after the shooting commenced, because I thought he was unarmed. I believed then, and believe now, from the acts I have stated and the threats I have related and the other threats communicated to me by other persons as having been made by Tom McLaury, Frank McLaury, and Ike Clanton, that these men last named had formed a conspiracy to murder my brothers, Morgan and Virgil, Doc Holliday and myself. I believe I would have been legally and morally justified in shooting any of them on sight, but I did not do so, nor attempt to do so. I sought no advantage when I went as deputy marshal [city marshal] to help disarm them and arrest them. I went as a part of my duty and under the direction of my brother, the marshal; I did not intend to fight unless it became necessary in self-defense and in the performance of official duty. When Billy Clanton and Frank McLaury drew their pistols, I knew it was a fight for life, and I drew in defense of my own life and the lives of my brothers and Doc Holliday.

Wanting to end on a high note, Wyatt drummed up his character references:

> I give here, as part of the statement, a document sent me from Dodge City since my arrest on this charge, which I wish attached to this statement and marked "Exhibit A."
>
> . . .
>
> [Signed] Wyatt S. Earp[21]

Exhibit A was pure character reference for Wyatt Earp, which today is inadmissible as hearsay evidence unless the defendant's character is first attacked. Given that the prosecution couldn't cross-examine Wyatt on his statement, it is a wonder this evidence was admitted by Judge Spicer. The townspeople from Dodge City all "certified" they had never known Wyatt Earp to be the aggressor in a gunfight. The defense's Exhibit A reads:

> To All Whom It May Concern, Greetings:
>
> We, the undersigned citizens of Dodge City, Ford County, Kansas, and vicinity do by these present certify that we are personally acquainted with Wyatt Earp, late of this city; that he came here in the year 1876; that during the years of 1877, 1878, and 1879 he was Marshal of our city; that he left our place in the fall of 1879; that during his whole stay here he occupied a place of high social position and was regarded and looked upon as a high-minded, honorable citizen; that as Marshal of our city he was ever vigilant in the discharge of his duties, and while kind and courteous to all, he was brave, unflinching, and on all occasions proved himself the right man in the right place.
>
> Hearing that he is now under arrest, charged with complicity in the killing of those men termed "Cow Boys." From our knowledge of him we do not believe that he would wantonly take the life of his fellow man, and that if he was implicated, he only took life in the discharge of his sacred trust to the people; and earnestly appeal to the citizens of Tombstone, Arizona, to use all means to secure him a fair and impartial trial, fully confident that when tried he will be fully vindicated and exonerated of any crime.

Exhibit A was signed by more than 60 Dodge City and Ford County, Kansas citizens, including a Congressional representative, several judges, the county attorney, sheriff, the local county commissioner, treasurer and clerk, attorneys, the mayor and city council members, various merchants, a pastor, the postmaster, a notary public and insurance agent, the deputy United States Marshal, a doctor and several liquor dealers, just to name a few. This Exhibit was surely designed to appeal to Judge Spicer's affinity for the local establishment, and to vouch for Wyatt Earp's good character, which impliedly had been put into question by the murder charges themselves.

H.F. Sills

On November 23, 1881, after the testimony of H.F. Sills, a locomotive engineer on layover in Tombstone and arguably the only neutral witness to take the stand, Judge Spicer released Wyatt and Doc from jail. With Sills' testimony, the defense had turned the corner:

> I saw four or five men standing in front of the O. K. Corral on October 26th, about two o'clock in the afternoon, talking of some trouble they had had with Virgil Earp, and they made threats at the time that on meeting him they would kill him on sight. Some one of the party spoke up at the time and said: "That they would kill the whole party of Earps when they met them." . . . One of the men that made the threats had a bandage around his head at the time, and the day of the funeral he was pointed out to me as Isaac Clanton. I recognized him as one of the party I had seen at the O. K. Corral.
>
> A few minutes after I had spoken to the marshal [Virgil Earp], I saw him and a party start down Fourth street. I followed them down as far as the post office. Then I got sight of the party that I had overheard making those threats. I thought there would be trouble and I crossed the street. I saw the marshal go up and speak to this other party. I was not close enough to hear their conversation, but saw them pull out their revolvers immediately. The marshal had a cane in his right hand at the time. He throwed up his hand and spoke. I did not hear the words though. By that time Billy Clanton and Wyatt Earp had fired their guns off. The marshal then changed his cane from one hand to the other and pulled his revolver out. He seemed to be hurt at the time, and fell down. He got up immediately and went to shooting. The shooting became general, and I stepped back in the hallway. I afterward saw Billy Clanton, when he was dead, and recognized him as the one who had fired at the same time with Wyatt Earp.[22]

Addie Bourland

On cross-examination, the prosecution was unable to shake Sill's story, which failure validated the testimony given by the Earps. Doc Holliday did not testify in the trial. The trial ended with testimony from Miss Addie Bourland, who Judge Spicer took a special interest in and visited her at home over lunch and then on his own motion, recalled her to the stand. Under present-day judicial ethical rules, a judge would not take such action. Nevertheless, Addie's testimony cleared up the questions over whether the dead men first threw up their hands:

> The prosecution objects to the further examination of the witness Addie Bourland after she has been examined by the defense, and cross-examined by the prosecution, her testimony read to her and signed by her and not brought before the court at the solicitation of counsel on either side. The court voluntarily states that after recess, and the witness had retired, he went to see the witness at her house and talked with her about what she might further know about the case, and that he, of his own motion, says that he believed she knew more than she had testified to on her examination, now introduces her upon the stand for the purpose of further examination without the solicitation of either the prosecution or defense.
>
> [Objection overruled, and questions asked of witness by the court as follows:]
>
> (Q) You say in your examination in chief, that you were looking at parties engaged in [the] fatal affray in Tombstone on the 26th of October last, at the time the firing commenced. Please state the position in which the party called the cowboys held their hands at the time the firing commenced; that is, were they holding up their hands, or were they firing back at the other party. State the facts as particularly as may be.

[Counsel for the prosecution objects to court questioning witness after he admits he has talked with the witness, etc., crossed out.]

(A) I didn't see anyone holding up their hands; they all seemed to be firing in general, on both sides. They were firing on both sides, at each other; I mean by this at the time the firing commenced.

While most trial lawyers would not challenge a judge's actions like the prosecution did here, they took their challenge a step further, perhaps realizing the futility of their position and ended their questioning with a misfire:

(Q) Did you say this morning, that when the first two or four shots were fired, you were excited and confused, and got up from the window and went into the back room?

(A) I didn't say how many shots were fired, for I didn't know when I went into the other room.

(Q) What conversation did you have with Judge Spicer, if any, with reference to your testimony to be given here since you signed your testimony this morning?

(A) He asked me one or two questions in regard to seeing the difficulty, and if I saw any men throw up their hands, whether I would have seen it, and I told him I thought I would have seen it.

It is rarely wise to allow a witness to repeat an answer given in direct testimony, and even more so here by impliedly questioning the judge's integrity. It's even less wise to question a female witness that has caught a male judge's eye, or vice-versa. Especially vice versa.

After hearing all the witnesses and considering all the evidence, Judge Spicer issued his decision, which emphasized my point about the vice versa. You can figure out which way.

Judge Spicer's Decision

November 30, 1881

Defendants Wyatt Earp and John Holliday, two of the defendants named in the above entitled action were arrested upon a warrant issued by me on the 29th day of October, on a charge of murder. The complaint filed, upon which this warrant was issued, accuses said defendants of the murder of William Clanton, Frank McLaury, and Thomas McLaury on the 26th day of last month, at Tombstone, in this County.

This case has now been on hearing for the past thirty days, during which time a volume of testimony has been taken and eminent legal talent employed on both sides.

The great importance of the case, as well as the great interest taken in it by the entire community, demand that I should be full and explicit in my findings and conclusions and should give ample reasons for what I do.

. . .

I find that on the morning of the 26th day of October, 1881, and up to noon of that day, Joseph I. Clanton or Isaac Clanton, the prosecuting witness in this case, was about the streets and in several saloons of Tombstone, armed with revolver and Winchester rifle, declaring publicly that the Earp brothers and Holliday had insulted him the night before when he was unarmed, and now he was armed and intended to shoot them or fight them on sight. These threats were communicated to defendants, Virgil Earp and Wyatt Earp.

Virgil Earp was at this time the chief of police of Tombstone and charged as such officer by the city ordinance with the duty of preserving the peace, and arresting, with or without warrant, all persons engaged in any disorderly act, whereby a breach of the peace might be occasioned, and to arrest and disarm all persons violating the city ordinance which declares it to be unlawful to carry on the person any deadly weapon within the city limits, without obtaining a permit in writing.

Shortly after noon of October 26th, defendant Virgil Earp, as chief of police, assisted by Morgan Earp, who was also at the time a special policeman in the pay of the city and wearing a badge, arrested and disarmed said Isaac Clanton, and in such arrest and disarmament, inflicted upon the side of his head a blow from a pistol - whether this blow was necessary is not material here to determine.

Excusing police brutality against criminals is a long-running theme in criminal law. Not until recently have police been held to respond for their excessive force during arrests, but many are still excused.

> Isaac Clanton was then taken to Justice or Recorder Wallace, where he was fined and his arms, consisting of a revolver and Winchester rifle, taken from him and deposited at the Grand Hotel, subject to his orders.
>
> While at Justice Wallace's court and awaiting the coming of Judge Wallace, some hot words passed between Isaac Clanton and Wyatt Earp. Earp accused Clanton of having previously threatened to take his life, and then proposed to make a fight with him anywhere, to which Isaac Clanton assented, and then declared that "Fight was his racket," and that when he was arrested and disarmed, if Earp had been a second later, "there would have been a coroner's inquest in town."
>
> Immediately subsequent to this, a difficulty occurred in front of Judge Wallace's courtroom, between Wyatt Earp and the deceased Thomas McLaury, in which the latter was struck by the former with a pistol and knocked down.
>
> [. . .] I am of the opinion that the defendant, Virgil Earp, as chief of police, subsequently calling upon Wyatt Earp, and J. H. Holliday to assist him in arresting and disarming the Clantons and McLaurys- committed an injudicious and censurable act, and although in this he acted incautiously and without due circumspection, yet when we consider the conditions of affairs incident to a frontier country; the lawlessness and disregard for human life; the existence of a law-defying element in [our] midst; the fear and feeling of insecurity that has existed; the supposed prevalence of bad, desperate and reckless men who have been a terror to the country and kept away capital and enterprise; and consider the many threats that have been made against the Earps, I can attach no criminality to his unwise act. In fact, as the

result plainly proves, he needed the assistance and support of staunch and true friends, upon whose courage, coolness and fidelity he could depend.

Did Judge Spicer just wrap Wyatt in a flag while heroic music played in the background? Have you seen the Tombstone movie?

> After this, the Clantons and McLaurys went to the Dexter Stables, on Allen Street, and shortly after, crossed the street to the O.K. Corral and passed through to Fremont Street. [. . .] It is claimed by the prosecution that their purpose was to leave town. It is asserted by the defendants that their purpose was to make an attack upon them or at least to feloniously resist any attempt to arrest or disarm them [. . .].
>
> Whatever their purpose may have been, it is clear to my mind that Virgil Earp, the chief of police, honestly believed [and from information of threats that day given him, his belief was reasonable], that their purpose was, if not to attempt the deaths of himself and brothers, at least to resist with force and arms any attempt on his part to perform his duty as a peace officer by arresting and disarming them.
>
> At this time Virgil Earp was informed by one H. F. Sills, an engineer from the A. T. & S. F. R. R [. . . who] had overheard armed parties just then passing through the O.K. Corral say, in effect, that they would make sure to kill Earp, the marshal, and would kill all the Earps.
>
> . . .
>
> Was it for Virgil Earp as chief of police to abandon his clear duty as an officer because its performance was likely to be fraught with danger? Or was it not his duty that as such officer he owed to the peaceable and law-abiding citizens of the city, who looked to him to preserve peace and order, and their protection and security, to at once call to his aid sufficient assistance and persons to arrest and disarm these men?
>
> There can be but one answer to these questions, and that answer is such as will divest the subsequent

> approach of the defendants toward the deceased of all presumption of malice or of illegality.
>
> When, therefore, the defendants, regularly or specially appointed officers, marched down Fremont Street to the scene of the subsequent homicide, they were going where it was their right and duty to go; and they were doing what it was their right and duty to do; and they were armed, as it was their right and duty to be armed, when approaching men they believed to be armed and contemplating resistance.
>
> [. . .] To constitute the crime of murder there must be proven not only the killing, but also the felonious intent. In this case, the *corpus delicti* [body of the crime] or fact of killing is in fact admitted as well as clearly proven. The felonious intent is as much a fact to be proven as the *corpus delicti*, and in looking over this mass of testimony for evidence upon this point, I find that it is anything but clear.

Remember our discussion from the Trial of Jesus? Sure, the actus reus/corpus delicti happened (they're dead), but did the Earps and Doc mean to kill them? Did they have sufficient intent/mens rea? Judge Spicer explained:

> Witnesses of credibility testify that each of the deceased or at least two of them yielded to a demand to surrender. Other witnesses of equal credibility testify that William Clanton and Frank McLaury met the demand for surrender by drawing their pistols, and that the discharge of firearms from both sides was almost instantaneous.
>
> There is a dispute as to whether Thomas McLaury was armed at all, except with a Winchester rifle that was on the horse beside him. I will not consider this question, because it is not of controlling importance. Certain it is that the Clantons and McLaurys had among them at least two six-shooters in their hands, and two Winchester rifles on their horses. Therefore, if Thomas McLaury was one of a party who were thus armed and were making felonious resistance to an arrest, and in the melee that followed was shot, the fact of his being unarmed, if it be a fact, could not of itself criminate the defendants, if they were not otherwise criminated.

It is beyond doubt that William Clanton and Frank McLaury were armed, and made such quick and effective use of their arms as to seriously wound Morgan Earp and Virgil Earp.

• • •

Considering all the testimony together, I am of the opinion that the weight of evidence sustains and corroborates the testimony of Wyatt Earp, that their demand for surrender was met by William Clanton and Frank McLaury drawing or making motions to draw their pistols. Upon this hypothesis my duty is clear. The defendants were officers charged with the duty of arresting and disarming armed and determined men who were expert in the use of firearms, as quick as thought and as certain as death and who had previously declared their intention not to be arrested nor disarmed. Under the statutes [Sec. 32, page 74 of Compo Laws], as well as the common law, they have a right to repel force with force.

In coming to this conclusion, I give great weight to several particular circumstances connected with [the] affray. It is claimed by the prosecution that the deceased were shot while holding up their hands in obedience of the command of the chief of police, and on the other hand the defense claims that William Clanton and Frank McLaury at once drew their pistols and began firing simultaneously with [the] defendants. William Clanton was wounded on the wrist of the right hand on the first fire and thereafter used his pistol with his left. This wound is such as could not have been received with his hands thrown up, and the wound received by Thomas McLaury was such as could not have been received with his hands on his coat lapels. These circumstances being indubitable facts, throw great doubt upon the correctness of the statement of witnesses to the contrary.

The testimony of Isaac Clanton, that this tragedy was the result of a scheme on the part of the Earps to assassinate him and thereby bury in oblivion the confessions the Earps had made to him about "piping" away the shipment of coin by Wells Fargo & Co. falls short of being a sound theory, [on]

> account of the great fact, most prominent in this matter, to wit: that Isaac Clanton was not injured at all, and could have been killed first and easiest, if it was the object of the attack to kill him. He would have been the first to fall; but, as it was, he was known or believed to be unarmed, and was suffered and, as Wyatt Earp testified, told to go away, and was not harmed.

A careful observation and logical conclusion to draw from the facts. If the Earps and Docs had the intent to kill (the *mens rea*), then why is Ike still alive, especially since he was otherwise the target of their abuse and insults the night before? Or was it the unwritten rule of frontier justice that you don't shoot an unarmed man?

> I also give great weight in this matter to the testimony of Sheriff Behan, who said that on one occasion a short time ago Isaac Clanton told him that he, Clanton, had been informed that the sheriff was coming to arrest him and that he, Clanton, armed his crowd with guns and was determined not to be arrested by the sheriff - or words to that effect. And Sheriff Behan further testified that a few minutes before the Earps came to them, that he as sheriff had demanded of the Clantons and McLaurys that they give up their arms, and that they "demurred," as he said, and did not do it, and that Frank McLaury refused and gave as a reason that he was not ready to leave town just then and would not give up his arms unless the Earps were disarmed - that is, that the chief of police and his assistants should be disarmed.

> In view of the past history of the county and the generally believed existence at this time of desperate, reckless and lawless men in our midst, banded together for mutual support and living by felonious and predatory pursuits, regarding neither life nor property in their career, and at the same time for men to parade the streets armed with repeating rifles and six-shooters and demand that the chief of police and his assistants should be disarmed is a proposition both monstrous and startling! This was said by one of the deceased only a few minutes before the arrival of the Earps.

Another fact that rises up preeminent in the consideration of this said affair is the leading fact that the deceased, from the very first inception of the encounter, were standing their ground and fighting back, giving and taking death with unflinching bravery. It does not appear to have been a wanton slaughter of unresisting and unarmed innocents, who were yielding graceful submission to the officers of the law, or surrendering to, or fleeing from their assailants; but armed and defiant men, accepting their wager of battle and succumbing only in death.

The prosecution claims much upon the point, as they allege, that the Earp party acted with criminal haste, that they precipitated the triple homicide by a felonious intent then and there to kill and murder the deceased, and that they made use of their official characters as a pretext. I cannot believe this theory, and cannot resist the firm conviction that the Earps acted wisely, discretely and prudentially, to secure their own self preservation. They saw at once the dire necessity of giving the first shots, to save themselves from certain death! They acted. Their shots were effective, and this alone saved the Earp party from being slain.

In view of all the facts and circumstances of the case, considering the threats made, the character and positions of the parties, and the tragic results accomplished in manner and form as they were, with all surrounding influences bearing upon *res gestae* [things done] of the affair, I cannot resist the conclusion that the defendants were fully justified in committing these homicides - that it is a necessary act, done in the discharge of an official duty.

• • •

I conclude the performance of this duty imposed upon me by saying in the language of the Statute: "There being no sufficient cause to believe the within named Wyatt S. Earp and John H. Holliday guilty of the offense mentioned within. I order them to be released."

[Signed] Wells Spicer, Magistrate[23]

Judge Spicer bought the defense case lock, stock, and barrel, and disregarded the prosecution's incongruous theory, which did not explain many facts, as his ruling pointed out. It also defied his concept of common sense: to "demand that the chief of police and his assistants should be disarmed is a proposition both monstrous and startling!" Simple theories, such as the one offered by the defense—lawmen doing their job in the face of danger and disarming defiant men holding guns in violation of the law and after receiving numerous threats—more than justified their actions. He pointed to Addie's testimony in a most flattering way.

Although the opinion acquitted Virgil, Spicer's opinion condemned his action deputizing his brother and Doc Holliday, saying Virgil "committed an injudicious and censurable act, and although in this he acted incautiously and without due circumspection." Despite the criticism, Judge Spicer's true belief shone through: "I can attach no criminality to his unwise act. In fact, as the result plainly proves, he needed the assistance and support of staunch and true friends, upon whose courage, coolness, and fidelity he could depend, in case of an emergency."

Aftermath

A month after Judge Spicer's verdict (who would never again practice law), Virgil Earp was ambushed and shot in the arm. He had several inches of bone removed and lost the use of it for the remainder of his life. On March 18, 1882, Morgan Earp was shot in the back while playing pool in a saloon and lived for only an hour longer. Afterward, Virgil and his wife, along with Jim Earp, left Tombstone for the Earp homestead in Colton, California, in San Bernardino County under escort by Wyatt and Doc.

After their return, Wyatt, joined by Doc and Warren Earp, Sherman McMasters, "Turkey Creek" Jack Johnson, "Texas Jack" Vermillion, and possibly others who all left Tombstone on what popularly became known as the Vendetta Ride. That Ride lasted for three weeks and resulted in at least the deaths of those suspected of killing Morgan and injuring Virgil: Frank Stillwell in Tucson, Florentino "Indian Charlie" Cruz in the South Pass of the Dragoon Mountains, and finally "Curly Bill" Brocius and Johnny Barnes in Iron Springs, Arizona.

Upon the discovering Frank Stilwell dead from a gunshot, a posse led by Cochise County Sheriff Johnny Behan along with Phineas Clanton, Johnny Ringo, and about 20 other Arizona Cow-boys (all deputized by Behan) pursued Earp and his men but never caught up with them. Johnny Ringo was later found dead, but disputes exist whether he was killed by Wyatt and Doc or committed suicide. The movie *Tombstone* pitted Doc and Johhny Ringo in a dramatic final shootout, where Doc reportedly says, "I'm your huckleberry," slang for "I'm the one you want." Behan lost the next election for Sheriff of Cochise County and died of natural causes in 1912.

Ike Clanton was later charged with cattle-rustling, along with his brother Phineas. Phin surrendered, but during the attempted arrest, Ike fired his rifle at Detective Jonas V. Brighton on June 1, 1887, and in return the Detective shot and killed Ike in Springerville, Arizona, and him buried nearby. Despite attempts to reinter his remains (allegedly discovered by a descendant in 1996) to Tombstone, Springerville officials have so far refused the offer.

You can never truly go home.

Wyatt Earp and Doc Holliday escaped the posse and fled to Colorado but despite demands from Arizona, were never extradited. Doc Holliday died in 1887 from tuberculosis at the Hotel Glenwood near the hot springs of Glenwood Springs, Colorado and is buried in nearby Linwood. He allegedly asked for a shot of whiskey on his deathbed. Wyatt Earp lived until age 80 in 1929, was cremated and buried in Colma, California in San Mateo County next to Josie Earp, who survived him. Tom Mix, a popular western movie star in the early half of the 1900s, was one of Wyatt Earp's pallbearers.

Chapter Conclusion

From the lawmen's perspective, Judge Spicer's decision saved them from the hangman's noose. The Cow-boys, on the other hand, saw the legal maneuvering as a fast-talking lawyer's trick. By avoiding a jury trial, the lawmen's lawyers likely avoided convictions for their clients, which would have destroyed the realities and the myths we now enjoy repeated on the silver screen. Had Wyatt, his brothers and Doc Holliday been convicted, the West would have taken a lot longer to tame and settle, perhaps throwing the area into a extended period of lawlessness. What marshal or sheriff would have wanted a job where he twice risked death—once by bandits and once again by courts?

Economic interests certainly played an influential role in the lawyer's strategy and Judge Spicer's decision. Court systems are set up by law-abiding citizens; outlaws of the time had little use for a system of justice other than a fast-drawn pistol. When lawyers recognize their audience, whether it be a jury or judge, and present the case in a light most favorable to the perspective of the decision-maker, the lawyer counts on a decision consistent with the predisposition of that decision-maker. Blinded by his brother's death, lawyer Will McLaury did not serve his clients well, and consequently contributed to the verdict favoring the lawmen.

Lawyers serve a dispassionate role in each case, and the Rules of Professional Conduct are designed to keep the lawyers separate from their clients. When emotion rules over reason, the case frequently turns out differently than expected; though when a dispassionate lawyer helps the jury see through the passion and emotion in a case, the decision typically reaches the right result.

Today many criminal judges are elected on a tough-on-crime platform and frequently draw from the ranks of prosecutors, who voters assume support that platform. Criminal defense attorneys frequently do not enjoy the same level of voter support.

Remember to enter your vote on the outcome of this trial on www.10FamousTrials.com and see how other readers voted.

CHAPTER 6
The Chicago Black Sox Trial

The national pastime of baseball is a living, breathing, sacrosanct being for many ardent fans, and it is so much more so today than it was in the 1920s. But the gamblers and players' fix of the 1919 World Series between the Chicago White Sox and the Cincinnati Reds added several more phrases to the American lexicon of baseball and apple pie. Consequently, we now have the derisive terms "Black Sox" and "Eight Men Out" aimed at the eight Chicago ball players who were alleged to have thrown the series for their own financial gain. But it is perhaps the words (real or imagined) of a young boy and his tug on "Shoeless Joe" Jackson's sleeve that best encapsulated the combination of our nation's simultaneous disgust and hope:

> As Jackson departed from the Grand Jury room, a small boy clutched at his sleeve and tagged along after him. "Say it ain't so, Joe," he pleaded. "Say it ain't so." "Yes kid, I'm afraid it is," Jackson replied. "Well, I never would've thought it," the boy said.[1]

Joe's response to the boy's plaintive plea confirmed our biggest fear: the fix was in. The baseball commissioner and team owner banished those eight players from the sport for the rest of their lives. Nonetheless, some of them couldn't shake the cold-turkey recusal and played in minor leagues under assumed names. Even some of the public didn't want them removed from the sport, with reportedly fifty towns sending the players telegrams during the trial asking them to play for exhibition teams.[2]

The fix of the series has inspired countless books, movies, and historical analysis of the facts as they are understood, but precious little has been written analyzing the trial. The best factual analysis of the entire event is in the book *Eight Men Out* by Eliot Asinof. To explain the facts here would take an equivalent tome, so I commend that book to you for your reading if you want the in-depth background.

This chapter presents the trial of the Black Sox as the judge and jurors received the testimony, placing you in the jury box to listen right beside the twelve men who decided the case.

Before the trial started, those jurors knew what you know: rumors of the fix, big-time gamblers involved in sports betting, and players who were investigated by a grand jury, with three of them supposedly confessing to their sins, and the grand jury then issuing indictments for the Black Sox. Perhaps no writer summed up the fix better than F. Scott Fitzgerald in *The Great Gatsby*:

> "Who is he anyhow, an actor?"
>
> "No."
>
> "A dentist?"
>
> "...No, he's a gambler." Gatsby hesitated, then added coolly: "He's the man who fixed the World Series back in 1919."
>
> "Fixed the World Series?" I repeated.
>
> The idea staggered me. I remembered, of course, that the World Series had been fixed in 1919, but if I had thought of it at all I would have thought of it as something that merely *happened*, the end of an inevitable chain. It never occurred to me that one man could start to play with the faith of fifty million people—with the single mindedness of a burglar blowing a safe.
>
> "How did he happen to do that?" I asked after a minute.
>
> "He just saw the opportunity."
>
> "Why isn't he in jail?"
>
> "They can't get him, old sport. He's a smart man."[3]

Gatsby's "smart man" is New York's Arnold Rothstein, a gangster known as "the big bankroll," due to his ability to always finance his deals from the roll of cash he kept with him. As Gatsby correctly noted, he never went to jail, although he was tangentially mentioned in the trial. His attorney's, and his own efforts to insulate himself from the Chicago trial, kept him away from the indictments. Through those efforts, Rothstein never even testified at the trial.

The prosecutors failed to follow the "follow the money" rule.

The Black Sox trial transcripts are lost, requiring today's historians to rely on newspaper reports of the testimony, which sometimes were sensationalized for their readers and at other times were directly contrary to one another. The Chicago History Museum revealed that it purchased an archive of Black Sox materials. Unfortunately, at the time of the researching, writing, and printing of this book, the Museum had not finished processing these materials and refused to make them available for review, taking them offline. [4]

Most of the reports come from stories filed for the major news services of the day (the Associated Press, United Press, and the International News Service [later combined into United Press International]) by two or three main reporters. Numerous other reporters covered the story for local papers, offering a slightly different take on the events. Without the actual transcripts, we must rely on news reporters of the day to tell us what happened, but admittedly many of the facts about the scandal are disputed. With this lawyer's eye, you can shift your seat from the jury box to right in between counsel's tables for the prosecution and the defense team.

The case was filed on October 10, 1920, in the Criminal Court of Cook County. Months of allegations flew back and forth, and the eight men were arraigned on February 14, 1921. The state's prosecution then languished until the following June.

The Black Sox Trial Begins

BLACK SOX CALLED TO FACE INDICTMENT

Ten of Eighteen Respond To Court's Order

Chicago, June 27—Ten of the 18 defendants in the baseball trial which opened here today put in an appearance. The suspended White Sox, Felsch, Cicotte, Williams, Jackson, Gandil, Weaver, and Risberg were on hand when the case was called. Fred McMullin, the other indicted player, is on the Pacific coast—and his attorneys stated that he would appear whenever the court ordered him to do so. He is under bond. With the seven players there appeared three other men, Ben Levi, Louis Levi and David Zelzer. Carl Zork and Ben Franklin, of St. Louis both of whom were under bond, were not in court, but their attorneys presented affidavits to the effect that both were ill and asked for a continuance.[5]

The Charges

At the opening day of the trial, Judge Hugo Friend (see Figure 6.1) overruled the defendant's motion to quash the five conspiracy charges:

1. Conspiracy to defraud the public;
2. Conspiracy to defraud Raymond William "Cracker" Schalk [the White Sox catcher out of his World Series bonus];
3. Conspiracy to commit a confidence game;
4. Conspiracy to injure the business of the American League; and,
5. Conspiracy to injure the business of Charles A. Comiskey [the White Sox team owner].

The lawyers made the motion to quash (dismiss) the indictment on the grounds that five conspiracies could not have been committed at the same time, but it was more for show than results. This standard style of legal argument is known as "alternative pleading," and properly employed here by the prosecution. With limited exceptions, the prosecutor (or plaintiff if it's a civil case) is allowed to argue different legal theories based on the same set of facts. The style of pleading relies on the judge or the jury to pick the applicable theory to reach a verdict. The defense then pushed the Court to force the State of Illinois to produce a "Bill of Particulars," a more detailed statement of the case. Although the motion was granted, the resulting Bill was not particularly enlightening:

1—Conspiracy to commit a confidence game on Charles Nims.

2—Conspiracy to obtain money under false pretenses from Charles Nims.

3—Conspiracy to commit a confidence game.[6]

The actual allegation of the damage to Ray Schalk, the team's catcher, was $1,700, the amount he would have received if the Sox had won the series but did not because they lost. The prosecution apparently thought Schalk would be a strong witness because Pitcher Cicotte had ignored his signals so many times during the games. Schalk inexplicably was not called to the stand.

In response to the judge's order, the prosecution detailed its case in the Bill of Particulars:

STATE OF ILLINOIS)

) SS:

COUNTY OF COOK)

IN THE CRIMINAL COURT OF COOK COUNTY:

THE PEOPLE OF THE STATE OF ILLINOIS)

vs.

Indictment No. 23912

EDWARD V. CICOTTE, *et al.*)

Bill of Particulars as to Count 1, Count 2, and Count 3, of Indictment No. 23912, filled in conformity to rule entered July 5th, 1921, by his Honor Judge Hugo Friend, one of the Judges of the Criminal Court of Cook County.

The defendants in the above entitled cause, and each of them, are hereby notified that the State will offer evidence tending to show that the defendants, Edward V. Cicotte ["Eddie" was a pitcher], Claude Williams ["Lefty" was a backup pitcher], Joe Jackson ["Shoeless Joe" played left field], Fred McMullin [utility infielder], Arnold Gandil ["Chick" played first base], George Weaver ['Buck" played third base], Oscar Felsch ["Happy" played center field] and Charles Risberg ["Swede" played shortstop], in September and October of 1919 were engaged as base ball players and were members of a base ball club known as the American League Base Ball Club of Chicago, a corporation;

That said American League Base Ball Club of Chicago was engaged to play in competition with a certain other base ball club known as the National League Base Ball Club of Cincinnati, Ohio, a certain series of games of base ball; some of the games of said series to be played in Chicago and other games of said series to be played in Cincinnati, Ohio;

That the defendants, William ["Sleepy Bill," a former ballplayer, now gambler, who turned state's evidence] Burns and Hal Chase were at various times connected with base ball as professional base ball players but were not participants in any of the games of the above mentioned series;

That the defendants, Joseph J. ["Sport"] Sullivan, Rachael Brown, Abe ["Little Champ"] Attell, Carl Zork, Ben Franklin, Ben Levi, Louis Levi, and David Zelzer were not connected with base ball as players, but were reputed to be gamblers or prized fighters and interested in the promotion of gambling enterprises and sporting events of questionable character;

That considerable public interest was manifested in the outcome of said series of games and each game of said series;

That each of said games was publicly regarded as an important sporting event and that the spectators of said games and each to them was required to pay an admission fee to the field where said games were played;

That the defendants participating in said games as players conspired, confederated and agreed together with the defendants not participating therein to so conduct themselves throughout the said games and each of said games and so manipulate their playing in each of said games as to make certain in advance of the playing in each of said games as to make certain in advance of the playing of said games the outcome thereof and the winner thereof, and so as to make certain in advance of the playing of all of the games of said series the outcome of the majority of the games of said series and the winner of the majority of said series of games;

And the defendants not participating in said games, as base ball players, conspired, confederated and agree together and with the defendants participating in said games to operate among the spectators of said games and others and the general public to procure divers large sums of money by means of and by use of the confidence game.

That one Charles C. Nims, a resident of Chicago, Illinois, was unlawfully, fraudulently and feloniously swindled out of the sum of $250.00 by the defendant, Joseph J. Sullivan, who was then and there engaged in carrying out the conspiracy aforesaid and who did then and there obtain from the said Charles C. Nims the sum of $250.00 by means and by use of the confidence game contrary to the Statute in such cases made and provided.

And further particulars, the defendants are respectfully referred to the first, second, and third counts of said indictment.

Signed: Robert E. Crowe

State's Attorney of Cook County, Illinois

Signed: Geo. E. Gorman

Assistant State's Attorney[7]

Jury Selection

At the start of the trial on June 27, 1921, and having worked out the technicalities of the pleadings, it was time to pick the jury. Nearly two hundred veniremen (potential jurors) were in the courtroom at any one time, out of a pool of some six hundred waiting around the courthouse to be called and examined. Judge Friend granted each side an unbelievably high one hundred twenty peremptory challenges, which resulted in a two-week stint to impanel the jury. As an example of today's limits, in California, each side may get ten challenges. The prosecution sought to stack the jury with ardent baseball fans.

The feature of the first day's session was the finding of a 64-year-old venireman who never played baseball, never handled a baseball, and never saw a baseball game. He was Herman Koehler, a night watchman. Koehler was excused by the state.[8]

On the other hand, the defense team of some fourteen lawyers for the seven accused baseballers who appeared in court in the first days of the trial wanted jurors who were not fans, figuring they wouldn't be so hard "on the boys."[9]

During jury selection, it's common for both sides to frame their questions to the jurors to "try their case" before calling a witness and introducing evidence. The prosecution successfully did so on the second day of jury selection by describing the "thousands of dollars of gold" required to win a pennant race, citing the "Big Money" made by the players:

> The state introduced figures showing that "Happy" Felsch received $714.60 a month during the 1919 season with $214.38 for each world's series week. He also received a bonus of $3,000 for the season and a contract for $10,000 for the 1920 season. "Lefty" Williams was paid $500 a month during 1919, given a bonus of $375 for the season and $500 for an extra bonus. His 1920 contract called for $6,999. He was paid $194.94 for the world's series week. "Chick" Gandil received $666.66 for each month of the 1919 playing season, while "Buck" Weaver was paid $7,250 for the season—the first under his three-year contract—and $141.36 for the world's series period, Fred McMullin received $500 a month and $149.94 for the extra week during which the club met Cincinnati. McMullin also received a new contract calling for $600 a month for the 1920 season. "Eddie" Cicotte was the best paid of the "Black Sox" during the year 1919. He received $952.50 a month that season with a $3,000 bonus at the end of the championship series. His 1920 contract called for $10,000 a season. He received $256.75 for the world's series games.[10]

The prosecution also attempted to taint the jurors by describing the players on trial with stories of late-night partying and carousing with girls. Rather than respond to the allegations, the defense made fun of the claims:

> Attorney Benjamin J. Short, defending the "Black Sox" ignored all sex problems, comparing his clients to the beauties of a sultan's harem. The bronzed defendants bore their new honors without blushing. "You understand, don't you, how these players are drafted?" inquired Benjamin Short of the veniremen. "The White Sox owners picked them up the same as a Sultan reaches out to get his harem."[11]

Though not all retorts may have been so beautiful. At the time the trial started, Shoeless Joe had gained some 42 pounds according to a report in the *Des Moines Register* on June 29, 1921, the reporter speculating that his lack of training contributed to his shape. The reporter may have confused Jackson with someone else. Contemporary court photographs show a fit and trim Jackson. At the time of his death at 66, then-current news reports had him back in shape at six-foot-one, 186 pounds; his regular playing weight.

You can't trust newspaper reporters to always get it right.

As of July 7, 1921, the prosecution and the defense had managed to select four jurors, including machinist Stephen Shuben, who said he was a White Sox fan but bet on the Cincinnati Reds because he thought they were the better team, a belief he still held after the series.[12] The defense had bagged at least one favorable juror. As the day closed, the defense attorneys signaled their clients weren't going down without dragging big baseball with them:

> This [world] series is now brought up by the defense with the charge that if the Black Sox are guilty they learned to fake games from persons higher up. Henry A. Berger, attorney for several of the [gambler] defendants, indicated that members of the White Sox of 1917 might be called and questioned regarding the possibilities that the alleged faking was done with the cognizance of the club managements.[13]

Jury selection continued Thursday, and the following day, Friday, July 8, 1921, the proceedings were halted due to the "press of other business" before Judge Friend, and the trial was set to resume on Monday. Attorney Berger for the gambler defendants again requested the court to issue subpoenas for the entire White Sox team, the entire team of the Sox from the 1917 World Series game, as well as the umpires for that series.[14] The Sox had earlier beat the New York Giants 4-2 for the series title in 1917. As an aside, the Sox would not win a world series again until 2005 when they beat the Houston Astros and swept the series 4-0.

The Loyals Look in on the Black Sox

The "loyal Sox" came to court with conflicting news reports. Contrary to the conclusions of a chummy reunion, some contemporary news reports of the time painted a much different picture:

> Members of the "Black Sox" today were sent to "Coventry" [shunned] by the loyal members of the 1919 White Sox when the latter appeared at the world's series scandal trial as witnesses subpoenaed by the defense. . . . Manager "Kid" Gleason, Eddie Collins, "Wee Dickie" Kerr, "Red" Faber, Ray Schalk and Harvey McClellan were the loyal Sox in court today. They entered the courtroom quietly and took seats together. They carefully ignored the "Black Sox" seated beside their counsel at the other end of the room. Not one of the loyal Sox looked at their accused former teammates. The "Black Sox," however, wistfully watched Gleason and his players enter. They appeared disappointed when the Sox failed to give them any kind of greeting. During the examination of veniremen the two parties carefully refrained from looking at each other.[15]

Other news reports give a different, perhaps propagandist view:

> The players intermingled, shaking hands and slapping each other on the back. The only mention of the baseball scandal was when some of the men now on the team wished the others good luck in their trial. The present team members in court, Manager Kid Gleason, Dick Kerr, Urban ["Red"] Faber, Roy Wilkinson, Eddie Collins and Harvey McClellan—had been called as defense witnesses, but as the jury had not been chosen they were excused for the time. Swede Risberg, indicted shortstop, was the first to see the 1921 players when they entered court. "Hello, Kid!" he called out to Gleason. "How's the boy?" "Pretty good, Swede," came back the manager as he shook hands with Risberg. "How's yourself?" "And there's old Buck Weaver!" added Gleason, sighting his former third baseman, now on trial. "Stacking up pretty good, Buck?" "Sure" began Weaver, but the other players began to tickle him—Weaver being very ticklish—and his remark was broken off. The men talked of the present season a few minutes and then as the players started out, Happy Felsch, indicted outfielder, called: "Hope you

win the pennant boys!" "Thanks, Happy," was the answer. "Good luck to you boys in your trial."[16]

The well wishes to the loyal Sox made little sense; they were seventeen games out from first place.

Jury selection continued on July 12 and 13, and the defense made motions to compel the testimony of "Sleepy" Bill Burns (a former major league pitcher) and Joe Gedeon (a friend of Swede Risberg), two gamblers alleged to have key roles in the scandal. Initially, the defense thought the prosecution would not be able to produce them.

Supposedly, Gangster/gambler Arnold Rothstein and his attorney, William Fallon, arranged to send Burns to Mexico, where he would not be found. American League President Byron Bancroft "Ban" Johnson, at the time an archenemy of Sox owner and future commissioner Comiskey (you know, the baseball park in Chicago), had an investigator track down Burns in Mexico and convince him to return to testify against Comiskey's bad boys. Just before trial Burns turned up and flipped to "State's evidence."

The spin doctor machine was working overtime during the trial, given that the trial was conducted as much in the newspapers as it was in the courtroom. "Ban" Johnson was able to catch the attention of one reporter to get his version and a few column inches:

> "Baseball's entire future is at stake,'' declared Johnson, at the time. "These men are guilty. Some confessed—and each confession involved the others. Later repudiations of these confessions were just legal tricks. The confessions, plus the evidence which has been gathered, proved the deliberate, cold-blooded and successful plan to sell the world's (series of 1919) to a clique of gamblers for a certain sum of money. If the men who disgraced baseball killed themselves entirely in the eyes of the baseball world were permitted to escape without a trial, it would be as hard a blow to the honesty of the National game as the sellout itself. For then it could be said that the men whose job it is to protect baseball and to keep it clean and honest were false to the trust imposed in them."[17]

He might as well have wrapped himself in the American flag while he was at it. While those involved in the scandal postured outside the court, the proceedings ground on inside.

After two weeks of juror questioning and frustrated that jury selection had virtually ground to a halt, Judge Friend ordered the parties to stay for night sessions on July 15 to speed up the process of impaneling a jury.[18] The lawyers got the message and agreed to seat the final four jurors by the end of the day, but not without some jabs first:

> Private detectives were working in the corridor outside the courtroom today [Friday, July 15, 1921]. Attorneys for both sides admitted the detectives were there, but each side refused to admit employing them. The matter came out when one of the attorneys for the state asked prospective juror: "Would the fact that there are detectives out in the corridor working for the defendants influence you?" "They are Pinkerton men, working for the state," shouted Attorney Nash for the defense. "They don't belong to us," retorted Attorney Gorman. "We didn't get any in time. We should have had them before the 1919 series."[19]

Even the jurors were tiring of the attorneys' antics:

> Jurors were sworn in late today amid cheers from spectators and veniremen, of the kind which greets a ninth inning rally by the home team. More than two weeks had been taken up in selecting the twelve jurors. Approximately 600 persons were questioned by state and defense attorneys.[20]

The real question, however, is which side the jury would favor. According to news reports:

> The jury is made up of two clerks, two machinists, a telephone repairman, a stationary engineer and the foreman of a motor company, a steel worker, a salesman, a florist, a hydraulic press operator and the foreman of a stock yards rendering plant. All but two are married and their ages range from 30 to 47. All said they understood baseball and occasionally saw major league baseball games, but none has ever played semi-professional or professional baseball and none is a student of the game, or of the "fan" type.[21]

The defense succeeded in stacking the jury with the jurors who best suited their theory of the case, which centered around both their denial that they intended to do anyone harm and that the conspiracy was a fabrication of American League President Bancroft, designed only to punish Sox owner Comiskey as part of their rivalry.

The Legal Wrangling

Over the weekend, the defense team was busy working on a motion "to exclude from the testimony of the Black Sox trial the alleged confessions of Eddie Cicotte, Joe Jackson and Claude Williams"[22] to present to the court on Monday. Knowing that the original signed confessions given before the Grand Jury proceedings were myseriously missing, the attorneys planned to argue that the statements were given without the benefit of their own attorneys, and they thought were receiving immunity deals instead of making confessions. The lawyers for the defense also indicated they would be filing a motion to exclude newly appointed Baseball Commissioner Judge Kenesaw Mountain Landis from the courtroom given his attempts to influence the jury and to dismiss the last two counts of the indictment dealing with the charges to defraud Sox catcher Schalk out of his World Series bonus winnings. George Gorman, assistant prosecutor for the State of Illinois, was slated to give opening statements Monday morning.

Judge Friend also granted the defense attorneys' motions to interview the state's two-star witnesses, "Sleepy Bill" Burns and Joe Gedeon, over the weekend, but required the interview to take place in the presence of the prosecutors. However, the interviews went nowhere. When the witnesses showed up on Sunday:

> The "Black Sox" greeted Burns and Gedeon cordially, all shaking hands. The two witnesses, who are to turn state's evidence refused to talk, however, and failed to disclose the nature of their testimony when questioned by defense counsel.[23]

> Burns, alleged to be one of the framers of the alleged conspiracy, gave the same answer to every question. "I do not care to discuss the case at all," the former major league pitcher replied to every question. "I have nothing to say," was Gedeon's stock reply, both men having been instructed by the State to give the same answers to every question.[24]

In response, the defense planned to ask the court to exclude their testimony on the grounds of surprise or be forced to respond to their questions, as well as arrest Bill Burns on an unanswered indictment arising out of the original Grand Jury proceedings.

When the trial started on Monday, the sparks began to fly even before the jury made it into the box. As AP correspondent Carl Victor Little colorfully put the events:

> The Chicago "Black Sox" got to first base today when they made the initial hit in their trial. Umpire Hugo Friend—criminal court judge—ruled that State's Attorney Gorman must not mention that three of the Black Sox made confessions during his opening statement to the twelve scorekeepers in the jury bleachers. This followed arguments by Attorney James C. "Ropes" O'Brien and other pinch hitters for the seven former White Sox stars charged with conspiracy to throw the 1919 world series with the Cincinnati Reds. Umpire Friend gave Gorman permission to mention everything in the confession of Eddie Cicotte, "Lefty" Williams and "Shoeless Joe" Jackson, but forbade him to let the storekeepers know confessions had been made.[25]

Judge Friend's decision split the baby, but perhaps favored the defendants a bit by excluding the pejorative word "confessions" from Gorman's lexicon, at least temporarily. The effect for the prosecution was virtually the same without the word since the ballplayers' statements smacked of admissions. For the most part, it was a distinction without a difference. Judge Friend overruled the defense motion to dismiss part of the indictment, letting all counts stand as plead.

OPENING STATEMENTS

The Prosecution

Using the tactic that there's no sense in overpromising, prosecution lawyer George Gorman virtually read the entire grand jury indictment but tripped up when he attempted to introduce the three players' confessions. Defense Attorney Michael Ahern jumped up to object, and the judge sustained his objection, excluding the confessions at this point in the trial.

Ahern lost no time making points with the jury and poking at Gorman:

> "You won't get to first base with those confessions!" Ahern said.
>
> "We'll make a home run with them," Gorman countered.
>
> "You may get a hit," Ahern said, "but you'll be thrown out at the plate."[26]

Baseball slang in the courtroom. You have to wonder who the lawyers were playing to.

The Defense

The defense lawyers were going to make it a case of over-interpretation of the law. They were counting on their working-man jury to sympathize with their clients and focus attention on the requirements of the players' contracts—or more particularly their lack of contracts:

> One of the biggest points to be made by the defense is that the players are not guilty of wrong-doing under the law. It will be emphasized that there is no law to compel a working man to work his best or nothing on the statute books to force a ball player to play his best. The defense is also prepared to attempt to prove that the "Black Sox" were not under contract during the world series and, therefore could do as they saw fit. The fact that the so-called master minds, who furnished the money supposed to have been used to buy out the Chicago players have not been haled into court is expected by the defense to have a reaction on the jury favorable to the "Black Sox."[27]

With this opening gambit, it's easy to see why the defense picked the jury it did—and spent two weeks struggling to do so. By now, a hot Chicago summer was now in full swing and had most of the courtroom spectators in their shirtsleeves, despite the decorum of the time.

The First Witness

You might as well start with a bang with your first witness, or at least a fistfight. The "Old Roman," as Chicago White Sox owner Charles A. Comiskey was known, came into the courtroom dressed in tails and a hat, studiously avoiding looking at his players, despite their attempts to make eye contact with him. The Illinois state's attorney led Comiskey through his testimony without incident, covering the points of "the fix" and his players. But sparks flew on cross-examination by Benjamin Short, attorney for the gamblers. He would pull no punches with "Old Roman," asking whether he was guilty of the same behavior of which his former players were accused:

> "Is it not true, Mr. Comiskey," the "Black Sox" lawyer asked, "that when you left the Cincinnati National league club of which you had been first baseman and manager, you jumped your contract?"
>
> Comiskey reddened.
>
> "That is not true," the witness declared. Jumping from the chair and starting toward the attorney . . . [he] shook his fist in the face of Attorney Ben Short. The tall, striking looking old gentleman, with the shock of gray hair, who has been in baseball for 47 years, and who now owns and operates one of the most magnificent ball parks in the major leagues, lost control of himself at a question from the attorney which he took as a personal insult.[28]

Other defense lawyers jumped up in a feigned effort to protect Short, the fans rose from their seats and the entire court erupted into an uproar. Judge Friend called for order and threatened to clear the courtroom. He then struck both the question and the answer from the record. After things settled down, a slightly calmer but still mad "Old Roman" continued,

> "I never jumped a contract and I never broke my word," Comiskey declared, hotly.[29]
>
> "Well, you 'jumped' from one league to another," retorted Mr. Short.
>
> "I didn't break any contract, nor did I jump," cried the club owner. "You can't belittle me."
>
> "You're trying to belittle these ballplayers," replied the lawyer.[30]

Short destroyed Comiskey's testimony. As much as Judge Friend had tried to "un-ring the bell," the jurors saw Comiskey's behavior for what it was—and the ballplayers in the courtroom knew it, laughing at Comiskey's answers. The defense had succeeded with the oldest lawyer's trick in the book: get the witness incensed. Tom Cruise and Jack Nicholson performed the same powerful cross-examination scenario in the movie *A Few Good Men:* "You want the truth? You can't handle the truth. You're goddam right I ordered the Code Red!"

The State next called the Sox's financial wizard Henry Grabiner, the club's secretary, to the stand to testify about the players' salaries. The state also tried to prove that "statistics didn't matter," as an attempt to disprove a defense theory that the players' stats during the series were not distinguishable from their stats in the regular season. The state called one of the series' official scorers (and editor of the *St. Louis Sports Journal*), Al Spink, trying to make their point. If the state intended to start with a hit, which is the general tactic of most trial lawyers, the players' salaries certainly highlighted the disparity between the defendants and the jurors, who as blue-collar workers, made much less than "the boys."

Why is it men playing games are referred to as boys?

The state then called "Kid" Gleason to the stand, and the Black Sox wasted no time playing to the jury. During Gleason's testimony, the players reacted to both Gleason and the attorneys on either side:

> Once when an attorney objected to part of the Kids' testimony, one of them [the defendants] remarked, "he has the sun in his eyes." "That's a single" was another remark when the defense scored a point, while "he booted that one" and "give him an error" were heard when the state proved a point in contention.[31]

Otherwise, Gleason said he had "the best ball club in the world" for the 1919 series. Other witnesses on the first day of the actual trial included Ban Bancroft, who testified about technical aspects of the series. The "technical aspects" revolve around the major league's use of the "reserve clause," which had the effect of preventing free agency for the players, tying them to one team, and preventing their free negotiation of contracts with other teams keeping their salaries low. The defense argued that the players' contracts had expired at the end of the regular season and that they were not actually under contract to play the World Series, but instead required to play under orders from the National Commission of Baseball, the forerunner of today's

Major League Baseball organization. The prosecution, on the other hand, would argue:

> . . . that the reserve clause of the baseball contracts cover the world's series period and to introduce evidence showing that the players were paid by the White Sox owners for playing in the series.[32]

The trial continued Tuesday, July 19, 1921, but the real trial was as much in the background, as one of the witnesses from the first day, Al Spink, wrote in a column in the *Reno Gazette*:

> Hal Chase and Abe Attell, two of the black sheep and really the two leaders in the entire baseball conspiracy, are not in attendance at the trials of the Black Sox. Chase was arrested in California and headed this way, when smart attorneys secured his release from custody by *habeas corpus* [Latin: produce the body] proceedings. Attell by the same method secured his release in New York. Those were the two the heads of organized baseball wanted to get worse than any two others, but they missed out on them.[33]

Reportedly, William Fallon, the attorney for Gangster/gambler Arnold Rothstein of New York, the man who financed the throwing of the World Series, masterminded Attell and Chase's release. Fallon did so to avoid further ties from the trial to Rothstein because Attell was Rothstein's confidante. Even without these witnesses, the state was on a roll, and next brought out its relief pitcher: a former pitcher for the Sox turned small-time gambler, "Sleepy Bill" Burns, after offering him immunity from prosecution, to close the game.

The prosecution touted Burns as the state's star witness, and after establishing the basics of the plot to throw the series, the lawyers brought out the clincher. According to a United Press report:

> The witness admitted he helped frame the deal with which the Black Sox are alleged to have sold themselves out to gamblers.
>
> "I met Eddie Cicotte in New York," said Burns. "He told me the White Sox would win the pennant and there was a plot to throw the series to the

Cincinnati series if enough money could be raised."[34]

Burns' testimony placed the genesis of the deal on the Sox, not on the gamblers, whom he identified as Arnold Rothstein, Abe Attell, and the mysterious "Bennett," another go-between gambler. Even so, the defense objected to further testimony, and the testimony initially was excluded. Judge Friend sustained the objection that the prosecution had yet to lay the foundation to establish the existence of his testimony. After further wrangling, the testimony that Cicotte had asked Burns for $100,000 to throw the series was allowed:

> Burns' testimony to this effect was admitted after Judge Friend three times had barred it temporarily while the attorneys could look up Supreme court rulings.[35]
>
> Cicotte, his shrewd eyes narrowed, tilted his chair forward as Burns disclosed bow the plot originated. "Cicotte," Burns related, "had the idea. He sprang it to me in the Ansonia on Sept. 16."[36]

The prosecution then moved Burns' testimony along to the time just before the series started. The first game was played in Ohio on October 1, 1919, at Redland Field. The deal was struck:

> In room 708 of the Hotel Sinton in Cincinnati, Burns said Eddie Cicotte, premier hurler of the Sox, agreed to "throw the first game if I have to throw the ball over the fence." It was there that Claude ("Lefty") Williams promised to toss away the second game, according to Burns.[37]

The eight players agreed to throw the series for $100,000, according to Burns (see Figure 6.4), and Cicotte demanded the first $10,000 as an up-front payment. But all did not continue to go according to the gamblers and players' plan. Attell had been unable to get all the money and was unable to deliver. Consequently, not all the members of the team who were expecting blood money got what they were promised:

> Burns spoke calmly, as he told of the part played in the conspiracy by the six "Black Sox" and the four alleged gamblers to whom they are alleged to have sold out for $20,000 a game—$20,000 that was only partly paid. The state's star witness told of the inception of the plot; of the sorry bargaining with

Abe Attell—former featherweight champion—tracing it out to "the ultimate double-cross." His testimony yesterday was confined to the first two games of the series, which are alleged to have been purposely lost by Cicotte, former idol of the South Side fans, and by Claude Williams, his lanky colleague.[38]

After throwing the first two games, according to the scheme, without the money from Attell, Burns was unable to deliver the promised bribe to throw the rest of the games. The gamblers needed more money to pay the players, Attell having received only $40,000 from Rothstein. But he took out and lost $30,000 to bet on a game and paid $10,000 to the players, which was first paid by Gandil to Cicotte. The rest of the players were not pleased that they hadn't been paid and reneged on the original deal to throw the entire series. Burns detailed the players' double-cross of the gamblers:

> Urged by the alleged "fixers" to win the third game to improve the betting odds, the players said they had lost for two regulars—Cicotte and Williams—and would not win for busher Dick Kerr [the pitcher slated for the third game], Burns said, then feeling they had been crossed by the gamblers, they double crossed their bribers by telling them they would lose the third game, but instead won it 3 to 0, with Dick Kerr pitching.[39]

Burns' carefully scripted testimony was building:

> His testimony, the most dramatic yet entered, was climaxed as he finished the details of the purchase and sale of a world series by rising dramatically to his feet at the end of the day's session and pointing out one of the defendants as the "mysterious Bennett," the alleged lieutenant of Arnold Rothstein, New York gambler, who, the state says, financed the conspiracy. Zelzer, an alleged gambler, was the man named. All afternoon Bums had spoken repeatedly of Bennett, the man who worked with Attell and Rothstein in framing the conspiracy.[40]

Not only were the Black Sox on trial, but also four gamblers were charged by the state. As with most criminal prosecutions, the prosecution was trying for guilt by association; the bad with the bad. By lumping the players with the gamblers, the prosecution tactically "tarred" the Black Sox. Again trying to end with a strong finish for the day, the prosecutors used the "identify the witness" tactic for dramatic effect:

> At the hour of adjournment, Assistant State's Attorney Gorman suddenly asked if Bennett was in the courtroom.
>
> "He is," answered Burns. A buzz of excitement ran through the room.
>
> "Do you see him?"
>
> "Yes. He's behind that post," and the former big leaguer pointed toward one of the pillars on the west side of the courtroom. "He's the man in the yellow shirt."
>
> Judge Friend ordered that the man designated arise and be identified before the jury.[41]

On cross, the defense lawyers went for the jugular. First up was James C. "Ropes" O'Brien, famous for his red tie and for obtaining murder convictions. When the case was first filed in 1920, he originally had taken the state's side, hired by Ban Johnson to assist the prosecution. "Ropes" (so named for winning a considerable number of death penalty cases as a prosecutor) switched to the defense team at the urging of Comiskey's attorney, Alfred Austrian, presumably for a price. He was dressed to the hilt, "flashing the cufflinks" at the jury and insulting his former employer:

The picturesque "Ropes" O'Brien, wearing his red necktie and a pinstriped silk shirt, started the cross examination.

> "How much money have you received from Ban Johnson!" shouted "Ropes."

The court upheld objections of the state and the questions went unanswered.

> "Ropes" then flashed some pictures on Burns and yelled: "Are these pictures of Abe Attell?

Again the state barked objections. "Ropes" was overruled again.

> "Did you get $300 from Ban Johnson?" asked "Ropes."

"Yes." said the witness. "These were my expenses for two months."

"How much of this went to your wife and how much went to you?"

"I don't know."

"Have you had any visible means of support during the last year other than Ban Johnson?"

"Yes. I worked in Mexico.

Q: You went to Mexico when you were indicted?

A: Yes.

Burns said he came back to the United States in April and met Ban Johnson on the border.

Q: What were you doing in Texas while you were getting money from Johnson?

A: I was fishing.

Q: What for witnesses?

Burns then told of coming to Chicago with Johnson.

Q: You knew you were under indictment when you came to Chicago?

A: Yes.

"Ropes" then razzed the state attorney for talking behind his back and disturbing the cross examination.

Q: Being under indictment didn't worry you, did it, Burns?

A: No.

Burns then admitted Ban Johnson's secretary registered for him under the name of "Williams" at a Chicago hotel.[42]

Burns had been escorted to and from the courthouse under armed guard as a point of drama for the jurors. Although "Ropes" O'Brien slightly dented Burns' testimony as paid for by one of the baseball magnates, the defense remained unable to crack his testimony. Six defense attorneys on cross got Burns to admit only one mistake in his testimony. As news reporter William Hutchinson put Burns' testimony:

> He denied he had visited the accused ball players following the first game in Cincinnati after

having testified to that effect while on the witness stand yesterday. The cross-examination by six different defense attorneys failed to reveal any other weakness in Burns' story.[43]

Trying to create drama where there likely was none, the lawyer emphasized Burns' minor factual mix-up over where he met the players (New York versus Cincinnati):

> "You desire now to change your testimony?"
>
> "Yes." . . .
>
> Mr. Luester [counsel for David Zelzer, previously identified as "Bennett"] failed to ruffle the witness, who replied sarcastically to many of the attorney's questions.

Burns' famous exchange with defense attorney Ben Short confirmed who held the upper hand:

> "You don't like me much, do you Bill?" questioned Short.
>
> "Sure I do Ben. You're a smart fellow, and I wish we had someone like you at the head of this deal. We'd all be rich now . . ." [Author's note: said Burns, his voice dripping with sarcasm.][44]

Some newspapers reported the back-and-forth as "drawing first blood," but the exchanges did little to damage Burns' testimony:

> Attorney Thomas B. Nash of the defense asked Burns if he had testified on direct examination that he met Risberg, Weaver and Felsch in a Cincinnati hotel on the morning before the first game of the series.
>
> "Yes," answered Burns.
>
> "Don't you know these players were out at Redland field practicing at that time?" shouted Nash. "Don't you know that most of the players went to the races that afternoon and weren't near the hotel?"
>
> "I saw them at the hotel," said Burns.
>
> The state repeatedly objected to the examination and said it would show the defense had misconstrued Burns' testimony. Mr. Nash repeatedly shook his hand at Burns shouting, "I am going to

impeach you, Bill," but Burns always retained his composure.[45]

Like I said before, you can't trust newspaper reporters.

The defense got Burns to admit he enjoyed delivering Cicotte as the lead schemer and agreed that he turned state's evidence because the players double-crossed him. Burns stepped down, his testimony intact and relatively unscathed by what the newspapers called the "wolf pack" of defense lawyers. Of note, though, was what Burns did not say: he never mentioned "Shoeless Joe" Jackson.[46]

The following day, July 22, 1921, brought mostly circumstantial evidence, and it looked like the prosecution had fired its best salvos with Burns' testimony. The prosecution next called John C. Soys, secretary of the Chicago Cubs National League club, who confirmed the testimony of William "Bad Bill" Burns, former major league pitcher, that a New York gambling clique had bet on Cincinnati to win the series. Soys said he was stakeholder of a number of bets made by Abe Attell and Louis Levi of Des Moines.

"Tell where you met Attell," Soys was asked.

"At the Sinton hotel in Cincinnati," said the Cubs secretary.

"Tell what your conversation was."

"In a casual way I asked Attell how he was betting on the series. He said he was betting on Cincinnati."

"What did Attell say?"

"He asked me to hold the stakes."

"Did Levi do any betting?"

"Yes, sir."

"What team did Levi place his money?"

"On Cincinnati."

Soys also told of meeting Attell in Chicago after Cincinnati had won the first two games. His testimony showed the Attell "gambling clique" knew the third game would be won by Chicago.

"Where did you first meet Attell in Chicago?" Soys was asked.

"At the Sox park around 1:30 o'clock the day of the first game here," he replied.

"What was said?"

"I told Attell I tried to find him in Cincinnati to turn over some of the bets he had won. I also said, 'It looks like Cincinnati will clean up on the series.' Attell said, 'I am not betting on Cincinnati today and I don't advise you to.' He added, 'I don't think they can beat Kerr.' Soys involved Clark Griffith, manager and part owner of the Washington American League team, and a "J. T. Hendricks" of Washington, were betting on the series. Soys said he had held as much as $2,350 in bets for Attell at one time.[47]

Apparently, players betting on games was rampant even among other teams, a point that benefitted the defense rather than the prosecution. This witness was a mistake for the prosecution. Following Soys' testimony, attorneys for the state and defense clashed over the admission of the confessions of Eddie Cicotte, "Lefty" Williams, and Joe Jackson as evidence. Court recessed and the jury waited while the lawyers entered the judge's chambers.

The prosecution continued to stumble with its next witness. Although the testimony certainly was sensational and high drama for a courtroom, the state's attorneys made a major mistake: they failed to present a consistent theory. The testimony of Bill Burns placed the source of the fix with Sox pitcher Eddie Cicotte. The next witness not only contradicted that testimony, but as the newspaper reporters noted, Carl Zork didn't fit the profile of a high-flying gambler capable of "fixing the series:"

The spotlight at the "Black Sox" trial was turned on a little red-headed chap named Carl Zork late Friday and, at last account Zork was still talking about it. Zork, if seems, is a gambler—at least the state, which has indicted him, so alleges. He looks more like, a private secretary to a big business man. With his slicked-back hair, nervous manner and owl-rimmed glasses. He's the last man who might be expected to be pointed out as the "bribe-series king."

Yet a fellow townsman from St. Louis, Harry Redmon, a witness, created something of a sensation when, looking across at the little fellow peering around a pillar, declared: "He's the little red head who started it all."

Zork gasped. He appeared to wilt. All eyes were on him. Hitherto he had been a lesser light in the proceedings.

"Will the witness explain?" asked Attorney Henry Berger.

Redmon said that he was in Hotel Morrison, Chicago, after the third world's series game. He had a meeting in the grill room with Zork. Joe Pesch, also of St. Louis, and another "tall man," whom he didn't remember. "We talked for three hours, or at least Zork did," said Redmon. "The rest of us talked about fifteen minutes all told. Zork said to me: 'I'm the little redhead from St. Louis who started it all. I'm the man who fixed the series.' Redmon said he and Pesch turned down a proposition from Zork to chip in $5,000 into the pot to fix the ball players.

Redmon, who said he was a motion, picture theater owner, engaged in an acrimonious debate with Attorney Berger, who accused him of being a bookmaker and a gambler.

"You lie!" shouted the witness.

A verbal tête-à-tête ensued, the witness finally saying: "You won't come outside and talk like that to me."[48] Berger's dispute with his own witness destroyed the believability of Redmon's testimony, if not defeated the prosecution's case outright. Even without putting on a defense, the case turned in the defendants' favor with this single witness. The reporter continued:

Court then returned to normalcy, and the big battle was over the admission of confessions of Eddie Cicotte, Joe Jackson and Claude Williams, ball players, to the Cook County grand jury last fall was started. Judge Hugo Friend asked the Jury to retire while Hartley L. Replogle, assistant state's attorney at the time the confessions were made, was being examined, the Judge reserving his decision as to whether the jury could hear this evidence, until Monday. Replogle said that Cicotte, Jackson and Williams confessed to their part in the alleged

> conspiracy to throw the 1919 world's series without any pressure having been brought upon them by him.
>
> "Didn't you promise Cicotte he would be taken care of?" Attorney Daniel R. Cassidy, Cicotte's lawyer, demanded.
>
> "I did not," Replogle replied.
>
> "Didn't you and I talk of immunity to Cicotte?"
>
> "We certainly did not," answered Replogle, hotly. Replogle testified that the confessions were purely voluntary; that he told all three that their admissions might be used against them as a future trial and that the trio signed immunity waivers in his presence. The defense let it be known that the three ball players would be put on the stand to refute Replogle's testimony.[49]

If, in fact, Cassidy and Replogle had talked about immunity, it should have been written down in the confession or at least another ancillary document signed by Replogle. To have failed to document such a crucial point raises at least the bare question of whether the agreement was made in the first place, a point not lost on Judge Friend. After listening to the testimony of the judge who presided over the grand jury proceedings where the confessions were given and the three players themselves, Judge Friend decided to admit the confessions, but only against the individuals who gave them, not the complete set of players. Replogle would be the prosecution's next-to-final witness as the state prepared to rest its case.

The court was dark (not open) on Monday, July 25, 1921, but resumed in earnest on Tuesday. The court—without the jury—heard the testimony of the three ballplayers to determine whether their confessions were voluntary. "Eddie" Cicotte took the stand first:

> "Attorneys Austrian and Replogle told me to come clean and tell what I knew and they would free me," Cicotte said. "They said to me: 'This is going to be a long trial. You don't want your wife and babies to suffer while you are in the penitentiary do you?' I confessed and when I was in the grand jury room, Judge McDonald said: 'Go ahead and indict him.'" "I protested and said I had been promised freedom. The judge "shouted: 'what are you trying

to do — bull me?' "They asked me to step out of the room and when I came back I was indicted."

State's Attorney Gorman then cross-examined the pitching ace. "I will show this man was panic stricken and ran to the grand jury to confess," said Gorman. "Didn't you cry and say you wanted to tell all you "knew?" Gorman asked.

"No," said Cicotte.

Q: "Didn't you read all about the ball scandal in the papers and spill everything of your own free will?"

A: "No—They promised me freedom."

Q: "Didn't you cry bitterly?"

A: "No; I may have had tears in my eyes."

Q: "Didn't you tell Judge McDonald to let you in the back way to the grand jury room so the ball players wouldn't bump you off?"

A: "No."

Q: "Isn't it a fact you signed an immunity waiver?"

A: "I signed something. I didn't know what it was."

Q: "Didn't Judge McDonald say to you: 'you haven't told all you know?'"

A: "Yes, I told him I had given all my story."

The pitching ace, who stated in his confession that he received $10,000 for his part in the baseball plot, was attired in a blue serge suit. He answered the questions after some hesitation and munched his chewing gum while evolving answers.[50]

"Shoeless Joe" next took the stand:

"Shoeless Joe," once the hero of the kids around the White Sox park, was questioned by Attorney Short on what happened in the state Attorney's office last fall. "Austrian asked me if I knew I would be indicted," said Joe. "I told him I didn't know about it. Austrian then asked if I had a lawyer. I told him I did not. Austrian then shouted: 'you better get one. You need a lawyer damned bad.'

I then was taken over where the grand jury was in session. On the way over with Replogle, he told me Cicotte was a free man. I was told the gamblers and not the ball players were the ones the law wanted. They told me to tell my story and I would be free. They said I could go anywhere I wanted to afterwards—to the South Sea Islands if I wanted to."

Q: "What happened then?"

A: "I left the court in the company of two bailiffs. I took them out and got them drunk that night. I thought I was free."[51]

The prosecution won their motion to admit into evidence the three confessions of the ballplayers given to the Grand Jury. After hearing the testimony of the players, Judge Friend ruled that they were made voluntarily, and allowed them into evidence. Given that "Shoeless Joe" Jackson, "Eddie" Cicotte, and "Lefty" Williams' original confessions had mysteriously disappeared from the State's files, the prosecution read the confessions into evidence from stenographic notes taken at the time the confessions were made. The ultimate victory for the prosecutors would have been to force the players to read the confessions to the jury rather than the lawyers reading them from notes. Either the prosecution didn't think of it or the judge wouldn't allow it, but they lost an opportunity to present the evidence in the most damning fashion.

The prosecution read "Lefty" Williams' confession:

Austrian: I want you to mention the names of the gamblers, the places, the times, and everyone you talked to about the whole subject.

Williams: This situation was first brought up to me in New York. Mr. Gandil called me to one side, out in front of the Hotel Ansonia, and put this thing to me . . . . After coming back to Chicago, I was called down to the Warner Hotel where the eight members that are named—not eight, I will take that back: I will name them for you: Eddie Cicotte, Chick Gandil, Buck Weaver, and Happy Felsch, and two fellows introduced as Brown and Sullivan.

Q: They were the gamblers?

A: They were supposed to be the gamblers, or fellows that were fixing it for the gamblers—one of the two, they didn't say which.

・・・

Q: Go on.

A: I was informed that whether or not I took any action, games would be fixed.

Q: Who informed you of that?

A: Chick Gandil.

Q: Right then and there?

A: No, not right then and there. Just right after that. Just as I got in the hall. So I told them anything they did would be agreeable to me; if it was going to be done anyway, that I had no money. I might as well get what I could. I haven't seen those gamblers from that day to this. We were supposed to get- Gandil told me we were suppose to get . . . what was it? . . . I was supposed to get ten thousand dollars after the second game, when we got back to Chicago, but I did not get this until after the fourth game; and he then said the gamblers had called it off; and I figured then that there was a double cross someplace. On the second trip to Cincinnati, for the sixth and seventh games Cicotte and I had a conference. I told him we were doubled crossed and I was going out to win if there was any possible chance. Cicotte said he was the same way. Gandil had informed me Cincinnati (before the Series began) that Bill Burns and Abe Attell was also fixing where we would get one hundred thousand dollars making twenty thousand dollars more. That I never received.

Q: You had a meeting in Cincinnati with the ballplayers? Where was that?

A: That was in the hotel.

Q: Who was there?

A: In Chick Gandil's room? We never had a meeting. We just went up there. We just dropped in one at a time; there was Buck Weaver, Eddie Cicotte, Happy Felsch, and myself.

Q: Was Weaver there?

A: Yes.

Q: And what conversation did you have there?

A: We asked him [Gandil] when he was going to get the hundred thousand that Burns and Attell was supposed to give us. He says 'They are supposed to give it to me after each game, supposed to give me twenty or thirty thousand dollars after each game,' which, if they gave him that, I know nothing of at all.

Q: When did he say you would get some money?

A: He didn't say. He didn't make no statement. I was supposed at first to get so much, get ten thousand dollars after the second game [Williams lost it 4-2]. I didn't receive it until the fourth game. I got only five.

[...]

Q: Did you know what games the Sox were to lose for all this money they were getting?

A: Why, they were supposed to lose the first two to Cincinnati, and I never did hear whether they were to lose or win the one with Kerr [the third game].

Q: Now, is that all you know about the whole thing?

A: That is all I know.

Jackson's 29-page long-winded confession came next, and equally dammed the left fielder. Jackson admitted to taking the bribe, but claimed not to have thrown any of the games and played his hardest.

BEFORE THE GRAND JURY OF COOK COUNTY,

September, A.D. 1920, Term.
In the Matter of the)
)
Investigation of Alleged)
)
Baseball Scandal.)
September 28, 1920
1.00 o'clock P.M.

Present: Mr. Hartley L. Replogle, Assistant State's Attorney, on behalf of The People.

Hon. Charles A. McDonald, Chief Justice of the Criminal Court.

BASEBALL INQUIRY

Tuesday, September 28, 1920

GRAND JURY

3:00 o'clock, P.M.

JOE JACKSON, called as a witness, having been first duly sworn, testified as follows:

EXAMINATION BY Mr. Replogle

Q   Mr. Jackson, you do understand that any testimony you may give here can be used in evidence against you at any future trial; you know who I am, I am State's Attorney, and this is the Grand Jury, this is the Foreman of the Grand Jury. Now I will read this immunity waiver to you so you will know just what it is:

"Chicago, Illinois, September 28, 1920. I, Joe Jackson, the undersigned, of my own free will make this my voluntary statement and be willing to testify and do testify before the Grand Jury with full knowledge of all the facts and of my legal rights, knowing full well that any testimony I may give might incriminate me and might be used against me in any case of prosecution or connected with the subject matter of my testimony, and now having been fully advised as to my legal rights, I hereby with said full knowledge waive all immunity that I might claim by reason of my appearing before the Grand Jury and giving testimony concerning certain crimes of which I have knowledge.

(Whereupon the witness signed the foregoing document)

Q   What is your name?

A   Joe Jackson.

Q   Where do you live, Mr. Jackson?

A   You mean in the City here?

Q   Where is your home?

A   Greenville, South Carolina.

Q   What is your business?

A   Baseball player.

Q   How long have you been playing professional baseball?

A   Since 1908.

Q   Where have you played professional baseball?

A   Why, I started out in Greenville, South Carolina; went there to Philadelphia, Philadelphia Americans.

Q   How long were you with them?

A   I went in the fall of 1908, and went to Savannah, Georgia.

Q   How long were you there?

A   Finished the season there, and I was called back by the Athletics; from there went to new Orleans, in 1910; 1910 in the fall I came to Cleveland and stayed with Cleveland until 1915, and I have been here [in Chicago] ever since.

Q   Did you play with the White Sox from 1915?

A   About the middle of the season I was there.

. . .

Q	You were playing professional ball with the White Sox in the season of 1919, were you?
A	Yes, sir.
Q	You played in the World Series between the Chicago Americans Baseball Club and the Cincinnati Baseball club, did you?
A	I did.
Q	What position did you play?
A	Left field.
Q	Were you present at a meeting at the Ansonia Hotel in New York about two or three weeks before—a conference there with a number of ball players?
A	I was not, no, sir.
Q	Did anybody pay you any money to help throw that series in favor of Cincinnati?
A	They did.
Q	How much did they pay?
A	They promised me $20,000 and paid me five.
Q	Who promised you the twenty thousand?
A	"Chick" Gandil.
Q	Who is Chick Gandil?
A	He was their first baseman on the White Sox club.
Q	Who paid you the $5,000?
A	Lefty Williams brought it in my room and threw it down.
Q	Who is Lefty Williams?
A	The pitcher on the White Sox club.
Q	Where did he bring it, where is your room?
A	At the time I was staying at the Lexington Hotel, I believe it is.
Q	On 21st and Michigan?
A	22nd and Michigan, yes.

Q	Who was in the room at the time?
A	Lefty and myself, I was there, and he came in.

Normally, testimony about discussions between married people is inadmissible at trial under the spousal privilege (just like the doctor-patient and lawyer-client privileges), but Shoeless Joe is confessing and he's not entitled to assert those privileges.

Q	Where was Mrs. Jackson?
A	Mrs. Jackson—let me see—I think she was in the bathroom. It was suite; yes, she was in the bathroom, I am pretty sure.
Q	Does she know that you got $5,000 for helping throw these games?
A	She did that night, yes.
Q	You said you told Mrs. Jackson that evening?
A	Did, yes.
Q	What did she say about it?
A	She said she thought it was an awful thing to do.
Q	When was it that this money was brought to your room and that you talked to Mrs. Jackson?
A	It was the second trip to Cincinnati. That night we were leaving.

. . .

Q	Then you talked to Chick Gandil and Claude Williams both about this?
A	Talked to Claude Williams about it, yes, and Gandil more so, because he is the man that promised me this stuff.
Q	How much did he promise you?
A	$20,000 if I would take part.
Q	And you said you would?
A	Yes, sir.
Q	When did he promise you the $20,000?

A	It was to be paid after each game.
Q	How much?
A	Split it up some way, I don't know just how much it amounts to, but during the series it would amount to $20,000. Finally Williams brought me this $5,000, threw it down.
Q	What did you say to Williams when he threw down the $5,000?
A	I asked him what the hell had come off here.
Q	What did he say?
A	He said Gandil said we all got a screw through Abe Attell. Gandil said that we got double crossed through Abe Attell, he got the money and refused to turn it over to him. I don't think Gandil was crossed as much as he crossed us.
Q	You think Gandil may have gotten the money and held it from you, is that right?
A	That's what I think, I think he kept the majority of it.

. . .

Q	And you were to be paid $5,000 after each game, is that right?
A	Well, Attell was supposed to give the $100,000. It was to be split up, paid to him, I believe, and $15,000 a day or something like that, after each game.

. . .

Q	At the end of the first game you didn't get any money, did you?
A	No, I did not, no, sir.
Q	Then you went ahead and throw the second game, thinking you would get it then, is that right?
A	We went ahead and threw the second game, we went after him again. I said to him, "What are you going to do?" "Everything is

all right," he says, "What the hell is the matter?"

Q   After the third game what did you say to him?

A   After the third game I says, "Somebody is getting a nice little jazz, everybody is crossed." He said, "Well, Abe Attell and Bill Burns had crossed him," that is what he said to me.

Q   He said Abe Attell and Bill Burns had crossed him?

A   Yes, sir.

. . .

Q   Do you know who was the first man that the gamblers approached, that Burns and Attell approached on your team?

A   Why, Gandil.

Q   What makes you think Gandil?

A   Well, he was the whole works of it, the instigator of it, the fellow that mentioned it to me. He told me that I could take it or let it go, they were going through with it.

Q   Didn't you think it was the right thing for you to go and tell Comiskey about it?

A   I did tell them once, "I am not going to be in it." I will just get out of that altogether.

Q   Who did you tell that to?

A   Chick Gandil.

Q   What did he say?

A   He said I was into it already and I might as well stay in. I said, "I can go to the boss and have every damn one of you pulled out of the limelight." He said, "It wouldn't be well for me if I did that."

. . .

Q   After the fourth game you went to Cincinnati and you had the $5,000, is that right?

A	Yes, sir.
Q	Where did you put the $5,000, did you put it in the bank or keep it on your person?
A	I put it in my pocket.
Q	What denominations, in silver or bills?
A	In bills.
Q	How big were the bills?
A	Some hundreds, mostly fifties.
Q	What did Mrs. Jackson say about it after she found it out again?
A	She felt awful bad about it, cried about it a while.

. . .

Q	And you are telling me this now, of course, of your own free will, you want to tell the truth, is that the idea, of all you know?
A	Yes, sir.

This attempt by the lawyer can be interpreted as, "you lied to us before, but you're not lying to us now, right?" A current-day example would be Michael Cohen's testimony about former President Trump's actions in the Stormy Daniels affair.

Q	In the second game, did you see any plays made by any of those fellows that would lead you to believe that they were trying to throw the game, that is the game that Claude Williams pitched with Cincinnati?
A	There was wildness, too, that cost that game. Two walks, I think, and a triple by this fellow, two or three men out.
Q	Was there any other move that would lead you to believe they were throwing the game?
A	No, sir, I didn't see any plays that I thought was throwing the game.
Q	In the third game Kerr pitched three, 1 to nothing. Did you see anything there that would lead you to believe anyone was trying to throw the game?

A No, sir. I think if you would look that record up, I drove in two and hit one.

Q You made a home run, didn't you?

A That was in the last game here.

Q The fourth game Cicotte pitched again? It was played out here in Chicago and Chicago lost it 2 to nothing? Do you remember that?

A Yes, sir.

Q Did you see anything wrong about that game that would lead you to believe there was an intentional fixing?

A The only thing that I was sore about that game, the throw I made to the plate, Cicotte tried to intercept it.

Q It would have gone to the first base if he had not intercepted it?

A Yes.

Q Did you do anything to throw those games?

A No, sir.

Q Any game in the series?

A Not a one. I didn't have an error or make no misplay.

Q Supposing the White Sox would have won this series, the World's Series, what would have done then with the $5,000?

A I guess I would have kept it, that was all I could do. I tried to win all the time.

Q To keep on with these games, the fifth game, did you see anything wrong with that or any of the games, did you see any plays that you would say might have been made to throw that particular game?

A Well, I only saw one play in the whole series, I don't remember what game it was in, either, it was in Cincinnati.

Q Who made it?

A	Charles Risberg.
Q	What was that?
A	It looked like a perfect double play. And he only gets one, gets the ball and runs over to the bag with it in place of throwing it in front of the bag.
Q	After the series were all over, did you have any talk with any of these men?
A	No, sir, I left the next night.
Q	Where did you go?
A	Savannah, Georgia.
Q	Weren't you very much peeved that you only got $5,000 and you expected to get twenty?
A	No, I was ashamed of myself.

In grand jury proceedings unlike trials, the jury, through the foreperson, gets to ask questions, too:

THE FOREMAN:

Q	What made you think that Gandil was double-crossing you, rather than Attell and Burns?
A	What made me think it was, Gandil going out on the coast, so I was told, I was surmising what I heard, they came back and told me he had a summer home, big automobile, doesn't do a lick of work; I know I can't do it that way.

. . .

Q	Does your contract with the Sox Baseball team call for $6,000?
A	$8,000.
Q	What part of the money did you get when you were sold by Cleveland to Comiskey?
A	I think they gave me $1,000 out of the sale.
Q	That's all you got out of it, just $1,000?
A	Yes.

Q	Do you know how much Mr. Comiskey paid the Cleveland Club for you?
A	I do not, no, sir.
Q	You knew it was a big sum of money, did you?
A	So they said.
Q	You were satisfied with $8,000 a year, were you?
A	That's all I could get out of them.
Q	Did you get $8,000 in 1919?
A	No, sir.
Q	What did you get in that year, that was last year?
A	I believe they gave me $8,000, last year.
Q	That is for the season, not for the year?
A	Yes, just the playing season, yes, sir.
Q	That also includes all your expenses on the trips, doesn't it?
A	Yes, sir.
Q	Railroad fare, board, room and so forth?
A	Railroad, fare, room and board.
Q	You were pretty well satisfied with that, weren't you?
A	They wouldn't give you any more, that's all you could get. I was pretty lucky to get a contract like that with him when I came over here.

...

MR. REPLOGLE: It is an off day, no game today.

(Whereupon the Grand Jury adjourned to Wednesday, September 29, 1920, at 9:30 o'clock A.M.)[52]

Finally, the prosecutors read Cicotte's confession, just as damning as the previous two. On September 28, 1920, at the law office of Alfred Austrian, Eddie Cicotte admitted he helped fix the 1919 World Series. Once he admitted his role in the fix in the attorney's office, Eddie was quickly escorted to the Criminal Courts Building where Assistant State Attorney Hartley Replogle questioned Eddie in front of Judge Charles MacDonald and the Grand Jury. The court reporter took down Eddie's confession:

> I don't know why I did it . . . I must have been crazy! Risberg, Gandil, and McMullin were at me for a week before the Series began. They wanted me to go crooked. I don't know. I needed the money. I had the wife and the kids. The wife and kids don't know about this. I don't know what they'll think.
>
> Before Gandil was a ballplayer, he was mixed up with gamblers and low characters back in Arizona. That's where he got the hunch to fix the Series. Eight of us, we got together in my room three or four days before the Series started. Gandil was master of ceremonies. We talked about it, and decided we could get away with it. We agreed to do it.
>
> I was thinking of the wife and kids. I'd bought a farm. There was a four-thousand-dollar mortgage on it. There isn't any mortgage on it now. I paid it off with the crooked money. I told Gandil I had to have the cash in advance. I didn't want any checks. I didn't want any promises. I wanted the money in bills. I wanted it before I pitched a ball. We talked quite a while about it. Yes, we decided to do our best to throw the games at Cincinnati.
>
> Then Gandil and McMullin took us all, one by one, away from the others and we talked turkey. Gandil asked me my price. I told him $10,000. And I told him $10,000 was to be paid in advance. It was Gandil I was talking to. He wanted to give me some money at the time, the rest after the games were played and lost. But it didn't go with me. Well, the argument went on for days, the argument for some now, some later. But I stood pat. I wanted that $10,000 and I got it.
>
> The day before I went to Cincinnati I put it up to them squarely for the last time that there would be nothing doing unless I had the money. That night I found the money under my pillow. There was

$10,000. I counted it. I don't know who put it there. It was my price. I had sold out "Commy". I had sold out the other boys. Sold them for $10,000 to pay off a mortgage on a farm and for the wife and kids . . . $10,000 . . . what I had asked, cash in advance, there in my fingers. I had been paid and I went on. I threw the game.

(Answering as to the manner in which the games were thrown Cicotte replied) "It's easy. Just a slight hesitation on the player's part will let a man get to base or make a run. I did it by not putting a thing on the ball. You could have read the trade mark on it the way I lobbed it over the plate. A baby could have hit 'em. Schalk was wise the moment I started pitching. Then, in one of the games, the first I think, there was a man on first and the Reds' batter hit a slow grounder to me. I could have made a double play out of it without any trouble at all. But I was slow—slow enough to prevent the double play. It did not necessarily look crooked on my part. It is hard to tell when a game is on the square and when it is not. A player can make a crooked error that will look on the square as easy as he can make a square one. Sometimes the square ones look crooked.

Then, in the fourth game, which I also lost, on a tap to the box I deliberately threw badly to first, allowing a man to get on. At another time, I intercepted a throw from the outfield and deliberately bobbled it, allowing a run to score. All the runs scored against me were due to my own deliberate errors. In those two games, I did not try to win . . .

I've lived a thousand years in the last twelve months. I would not have done that thing for a million dollars. Now I've lost everything, job, reputation, everything. My friends all be on the Sox. I knew it, but I couldn't tell them. I had to double-cross them.

I'm through with baseball. I'm going to lose myself if I can and start life over again.[53]

The bombshells had been dropped on the players. In baseball parlance, it was the bottom of the ninth, three men on, a full count and the players got thrown out at the plate to lose the game.

But hang on just a minute. The government can screw just about anything up.

Billy Maharg, who acted with "Sleepy Bill" Burns as the go-between for the players and Arnold Rothstein, took the stand as the state's final witness on Wednesday, July 27, 1921. He mostly confirmed Burns' testimony and detailed the gamblers' double-cross of the players' double-cross for not throwing the third game. The gamblers lost the money they bet on the Reds to win in third game because the Sox refused to throw it:

> Maharg, pugilistic hero of a decade ago and now an automobile mechanic at $7.60 a day, substantiated testimony of Bill Burns who turned State's evidence. Maharg, still wearing the brilliant diamonds of his heyday, charged Eddie Cicotte and Chick Gandil with being the originators of the plot. He told of taking the world's series with a "for sale" tag on it to Philadelphia and New York gamblers and his failure to find a purchaser. Maharg during this time functioned as the "good man Friday" of Burns, admitted fixer. The tale of the witness was one of cheating cheaters. He told of gamblers after promising players $100,000 for selling, threw a comparatively small sum at them to keep them quiet.[54]

Maharg's testimony closed the prosecution case as its last witness. When the prosecution rests, the defense typically makes a motion for a nonsuit, seeking to dismiss the charges against the defendants for lack of evidence. The lawyers for the players and the gamblers made these motions, which got a mixed reception:

> Evidence introduced against Buck Weaver and Happy Felsch did not warrant sending their case to the jury. Judge Friend held, and announced he would dismiss the charges against the two. The state offered no objection. The case of Carl Zork and Louis Levy, two of the alleged gamblers, were also to be dismissed the court ruled because of lack of evidence.[55]

While the state may not have made an objection:

The State refused to dismiss eases despite
Judge Friend's statement. "Zork, Weaver and Felsch
may not be deeply implicated by the evidence we
have presented," said Assistant States Attorney
Gorman, "but they have been brought into it."[56]

Ultimately, Judge Friend asked the prosecution to *nolle prosequi* (Latin: not prosecute) Weaver and Felsch due to the lack of evidence. The prosecution wanted to keep Weaver and Felsch as parties to the trial, but the judge dismissed Ben and Louis Levy due to lack of evidence presented against them. Judge Friend didn't think the cases against Weaver and Felsch were very strong.

The Defense Case-in-Chief

While defending this case, the defense attorneys had to choose whether the players or the gamblers would take the opening gambit. Given that the charges against the gamblers hinged on whether the players threw the game, it would seem to favor the players going first. But there's always the aspect of building toward a dramatic finish. The players wanted the cleanup position. Gambler David Zelzer went first:

> Zelzer testified he want to Cincinnati for the World Series on September 29, 1919. It was on this date that Bill Burns testified he met Zelzer in New York to discuss the alleged conspiracy. "I was never In Now York except in 1917," said Zelzer. "I never met Burns or Maharg in Cincinnati. I never saw either of them until they testified here. I do not know any of the defendant players. I never saw any of them except on a ball fluid until I came here for this trial." Zelzer told the prosecuting attorney that he knew Abe Attell. Zelzer said he bet on Cincinnati in the series.[57]

The other remaining gambler, Carl Zork, went next. He used the standard "alibi" defense: "it couldn't have been me; I was somewhere else:"

> The morning session was court was taken up with the examination of character witnesses for Zork, whom the state contends is the man who went by the name of "Bennett, Lieutenant of Arnold Rothstein." One of the main purposes, of the

examination of the witnesses was to impeach the testimony of Harry Redmon, East St. Louis picture exhibitor, who testified he had been told that Zork had been pointed out as "that little red headed fellow, who started the whole thing (the "throwing of the series")." Zork's main witness was Sid G. Keener, sporting editor of a St. Louis newspaper, who said on the night Redmon declared Zork had been pointed out to him at a supper in a Chicago hotel, the defendant was with him, Keener, in a billiard hall. He also said that Zork left for St. Louis that night.[58]

It's important when using the alibi defense to use a reputable witness. Although it may have been questionable to use a newspaper editor, at least the reporters bought his story.

When the time came for the players' lawyers to put on their side of the case, their first tactic was to attack the state's argument in the Bill of Particulars that the players did not play to the best of their ability. The lawyers put on two teammates and one opponent, but failed to introduce their testimony:

> John Collins and Nemo Leibold, who were with the White Sox during the alleged crooked series, were asked to testify if they believed the indicted men played to the best of their ability. Question after question was put to the two witnesses by "Ropes" O'Brien and Thomas Nash, defense attorneys, with the hope of bringing out this point. Every question was objected to by the state and upheld by the court. The witnesses were excused without being able to testify, as they apparently were ready to do, that the "Black Sox" played to the best of their ability. The court would not let [Walter Henry] "Dutch" Ruether, who played with the Cincinnati Reds during the disputed series, state his opinions as to whether the Black Sox" played to the best of their ability. Even though the three big leaguers did not get a chance to give much testimony in favor of the defendants, the defense's purpose was to introduce these experts who were willing to give the "Black Sox" a clean bill.[59]

The state's objections were based on relevance and foundation, which refers to the ability of these players to accurately testify based on personal knowledge about how the Black Sox played. The state must have argued that these other players had no ability to tell whether the error was intentional, which was the ultimate fact the jury was to determine. Nonetheless, "Ropes" and Nash had made their point to the jurors: if their teammates and an opponent were willing to testify for the Black Sox, then they must not be guilty.

Part of the alleged "con" by the Black Sox was based on their intent to deprive Sox owner Comiskey of his profits, so the defense lawyers next called the team's secretary to examine him on the issue of those profits:

> Harry Grabiner, secretary of the White Sox, was called by the defense to show the receipts of the Sox for 1919 and 1920. The purpose of this was to prove the business of the White Sox company was not injured by the fake series as charged in the Indictment. Records showed the fans paid out $910,306.68 to see the White Sox perform in 1920. This sum represents the gate receipts at home and the share of receipts while the team was abroad. The White Sox club took in $521,175.76 in 1919, exclusive of the world series share which brought the total gross receipts up to $608,232.25. Receipts for 1918, a short war season, were $128,596.54. In 1917 there was $408,914.27 registered. Charles Comiskey lost $51,673.00 on his team in 1918. A profit of $225,913.33 was made in 1920 and $107,015.97 in 1919. The profit in 1917 was $70,929.49. It was revealed under cross-examination that Comiskey was paid $50,000 in salary by the Sox company last year in addition to his profits.[60]

> The financial secrets of the Chicago American League baseball club, always guarded jealously, were revealed in the baseball trial today, the club's books showing a net profit of $409,337 during the last six years, more than $225,000 of this coming in 1919 alone.... The figures showed gross receipts of $2,622,858 for the six years. In only one year was there a loss—1918, when the war cut the season short. The deficit then was $51,878.[61]

These dollar amounts overwhelmed the jury because they were all working-class, blue collar men and it cost them just pennies to see a game. The defense tactic was to show Comiskey's greed. When the jurors heard how much Comiskey made compared to his players, the defense had driven one more nail in the coffin of the prosecution's case.

Given this shocking financial testimony and the favorable disposition on the jury instructions from Judge Friend, the lawyers wisely chose to end Grabiner's testimony. Court recessed for the evening, with closing arguments slated to start on Friday, July 29, 1921.

The Summations

The prosecution argued what was expected: the players had confessed to the scheme and were guilty as charged. The defense likewise performed as expected, blaming just about everyone else involved: Comiskey, Burns, Rothstein and even Rothstein's lawyer, Alfred Austrian. They attacked the prosecution's case, claiming the state's attorneys had not proven any fraud occurred—the boys played their hearts out in the series and lost the championship fair and square. Judge Friend instructed the jury to consider the evidence and the arguments of the attorneys.

> Summation for the prosecution by Assistant State's Attorney, Edward Prindeville (July 29, 1921):
>
> What more convincing proof do you want than the statement by the ballplayers? Joe Jackson, Eddie Cicotte, and Williams sold out the American public for a paltry $20,000. They collected the money, but they could not keep quiet. Their consciences would not let them rest. When the scandal broke, they sought out the State's Attorney's office and made their confessions voluntarily. Cicotte told his story to Chief Justice MacDonald. Then he told it to the Grand Jury. He was followed to the Grand Jury room by Jackson and Williams. On evidence which they gave the jurors, Bill Burns, the State's star witness, was indicted. They have called Burns a squealer, but I tell you that he owes his connection in the case to what these defendant ballplayers have confessed...
>
> This is an unusual case as it deals with a class of men who are involved in the great national game which all red-blooded men follow. This game, gentlemen, has been the subject of a crime. The

public, the club owners, even the small boys on the sandlots have been swindled.

. . .

Jackson tells you he got the five thousand dollars after the fourth game—

[O'Brien, interrupting: "I suppose that sharpened his batting average!"]

He certainly was batting 1000% when he got the $5,000! [. . .]

I say, gentlemen, that the evidence shows that a swindle and a con game has been worked on the American people. The crime in this case warrants the most severe punishment of the law. This country is for sending criminals to the penitentiary whether they are idols of the baseball diamond or gangsters guilty of robbery with a gun. [. . .]

The State is asking in this case for a verdict of guilty with five years in the penitentiary and a fine of $2,000 for each defendant![62]

Summation for the prosecution by Assistant State's Attorney George Gorman:

The attorneys for the defense will ask for mercy. They point out that Lefty Williams got only five hundred dollars a month for his services. They charge that Charles Comiskey, the grand old man of baseball, is persecuting the players because he has tried to clean out rottenness in the national game. [...]

Comiskey gave these men a job. And here we find the defendants deliberately conspiring to injure and destroy his business. [. . .] In his confession, Eddie Cicotte tells how the games were fixed. Then we have the spectacle of the public going to the game believing it was on the square. Thousands of men throughout the chilly hours of the night, crouched in line waiting for the opening for the first World Series game. All morning they waited, eating a sandwich, perhaps never daring to leave their places for a moment. There they waited to see the great Cicotte pitch a ballgame. Gentlemen, they went to see a ballgame. But all they saw was a con game![63]

With those summations, the prosecution team sat down. The defense attorneys next got their chance, and Defense Attorney Henry Barger opened for the gamblers and set the pace:

> Are you going to send the black sox to the penitentiary on the testimony of a "squealer?" Berger asked the jury.[64]
>
> The state's star witness appeared before you gentlemen with his concocted tale in hopes of getting the $10,000 reward offered by Charles A. Comiskey.[65]

Berger made it clear to the juror that Burns' testimony came only after a grant of immunity and that the jury couldn't trust what he said because he only wanted money. Berger didn't stop short at attacking "Sleepy Bill," he went after the "Old Roman," too:

> Another sensational assertion made by Berger in his summing up address to the Jury was the statement that Charles Comiskey, White Sox owner, started the prosecution because "he was not satisfied with getting $50,000 from the series but felt that he should have $5,000 or $6,000 more."[66]

Berger finished up on a legal technicality:

> "The state has not proved the men threw the series," said Berger. "But even if they did, there is no law against it on the statute books." Berger charged the trial was an outcome of the feud between Ban Johnson, president of the American League, and Charles Comiskey, owner of the White Sox.[67]

After Berger finished, he turned the continued summation over to Ben Short:

> August 1, 1921: Summation for the Defense by Attorney Ben Short (for the players):
>
> The State failed to establish criminal conspiracy. There may have been an agreement entered by the defendants to take the gambler's money, but it has not been shown the players had any intention of defrauding the public or of bringing the game into ill repute. They believed any arrangement they may have made was a secret one and would, therefore, reflect no discredit on the national pastime

or injure the business of their employer as it would never be detected! . . . .

Summation for the Defense by A. Morgan Frumberg (for the gamblers):

[. . .] By his own testimony, Mr. Austrian admits conducting the financier to the Grand Jury and bringing him back unindicted! ...Why was [Rothstein] not indicted? Why were Brown, Sullivan, Attell, and Chase allowed to escape? Why were these underpaid ballplayers, these penny-ante gamblers from Des Moines and St. Louis, who may have bet a few nickels on the World Series, brought here to be the goats in this case? Ask the powers in baseball. Ask Ban Johnson who pulled the strings in this case. Ask him who saved Arnold Rothstein!

Summation for the Defense by Michael Ahearn:

Ban Johnson was the directing genius of the prosecution. His hand runs like a scarlet thread through the whole prosecution. Johnson is boss. The czar of Russia never had more power over his subjects than Johnson has over the American League. He controlled the case. His money hired Burns and Maharg to dig up evidence. [. . .] Maharg came to court as an auto worker, but he flashed enough diamonds on his fingers to buy a flock of autos. And Burns has been proved a liar in a score of instances. He said he talked to Gandil in Chicago after the second game. He lied. He said he talked to the ballplayers on the morning before the opening game. He lied. He makes me think of a drink of moonshine: It looks good, but when you drink it gives you a stomachache![68]

Stomachache or not, the jury deliberated for just two hours and forty-seven minutes and found the eight men and two gamblers not guilty on August 2, 1921. When the foreman announced the eight separate verdicts for the players, cries of jubilation went up around the room, and the jurors spilled from the "bleachers" in the jury box, grabbed the boys and threw them up on their shoulders, parading them around the courtroom. Hero status has its benefits. Each of the jurors signed each of the eight verdicts, some 96 signatures in all.[69]

The other seven verdicts are all the same, save the name of the defendant. The newspapers plastered the verdict across their front pages.

The headlines may have screamed vindication, but Commissioner Kenesaw Mountain Landis (named for the site where his Civil War hero father lost a leg) would have none of it, banning the players for life as of August 4, 1921, just two days after the favorable decision, when he issued a statement which read:

> Regardless of the verdict of juries, no player who throws a ballgame, no player that undertakes or promises to throw a ballgame, no player that sits in conference with a bunch of crooked players and gamblers where the ways and means of throwing a game are discussed and does not promptly tell his club about it, will ever play professional baseball.
>
> . . .
>
> Just keep it in mind that regardless of the verdict of juries, baseball is entirely competent to protect itself against crooks both inside and outside the game.[70]

Comiskey was no less sympathetic:

> "I have no comment to offer on the outcome of the baseball trial," said Charles A. Comiskey, owner of the White Sox. "However, Cicotte confessed to me that he had helped to throw the world's series of 1919 and also implicated the other seven players and until such time as Cicotte can explain to me that confession, I will have nothing to do with him or them."[71]

The eight Chicago players never played major league ball again.

Chapter Conclusion

How the jury could have reached these acquittals is astounding, especially considering the players' confessions. Ultimately, the new commissioner took the decision away from the jury, correcting the injustice to baseball and restoring public confidence in the game. Nevertheless, sports fans continue to argue today whether certain members of the team, especially

Shoeless Joe Jackson, should have been banned for life and excluded from the Hall of Fame. The movie, *Field of Dreams* has a few thoughts about Shoeless Joe.

The players' status swayed the jury and the sniping between the lawyers didn't help either, with the jury obviously taking the team's side. The prosecution's choice to mix the trial of the gamblers in with the players added a significant twist. Although they were not convicted, the decision to try the gamblers hurt the prosecution's case—the jury did not want to paint the players with the same brush as the gamblers.

Had the prosecution separately tried the players from the gamblers, the state's attorneys may have been able to obtain convictions, but ultimately because of the sway Major League Baseball held over the players' ability to remain on its teams, the verdicts mattered little. The Commissioner and Comiskey staged the trial to convince the American public that the game was clean, a perception far from the truth at the time. Perhaps Commissioner Landis wanted both the convictions and the lifetime suspensions, but his remedy alone tried to solve the black eye delivered by the players and the gamblers. Baseball faced struggles not long ago with gambling, too as demonstrated by Pete Rose's ban from the game. With its own system of justice, big baseball plays by its own set of rules as we sit in the bleachers and watch.

Remember to enter your vote on the outcome of this trial on www.10FamousTrials.com and see how other readers voted.

CHAPTER 7
State v. Scopes ("The Monkey Trial")

He that troubleth his own house shall inherit the wind: and the fool shall be servant to the wise of heart."[1]

The character of famous attorney, former Secretary of State, Congressman, and fervent Christian William Jennings Bryan uttered the first half of this Bible quote in the movie about the Scopes trial, *Inherit the Wind.* In the movie's concluding moments, Clarence Darrow—who represented the evolution side—symbolically quoted the second half of the verse in his commentary to Algonquin-Roundtable famous newspaper reporter and critic H.L. Mencken, who covered the trial.

The two freedoms of speech and religion, both guaranteed in the First Amendment of the United States Constitution collided at once in the Scopes trial. The trial pitted these competing Constitutional provisions against one another in the dispute over whether teaching the science of evolution in our schools interfered with fundamentalist religious beliefs.

Called the "trial of the century," the trial was in a instead a manufactured test case by citizens in small-town Dayton, Tennessee. Several prominent businessmen met at Robinson's Drugstore, the hub of the town, and concocted the plan in response to a newspaper solicitation from the American Civil Liberties Union. The town's self-selected defendant, 24-year-old teacher John Scopes, offered himself up as a sacrificial lamb to decide the issue. The 1925 trial attracted the nation's attention and drew hordes of newspaper reporters from around the world. The ACLU arranged for Darrow to represent Scopes, a local high school science teacher, and Bryan stepped in to assist the prosecution on behalf of the State of Tennessee. While the case reached a verdict, the larger jury of public opinion remained out.

As we now know that trial ripped open the seam in the fabric of this dispute, sparking the debate that continues to run today, despite an intervening United States Supreme Court ruling that supposedly settled the matter. Indeed, a vote prohibiting teaching the science of evolution in public schools passed the Topeka, Kansas Board of Education as recently as 2005. The debate whether to teach creation or evolution continues to rage in several other states, including another recent battleground: Pennsylvania. Today we face book bans again.

Sometimes it takes a while to learn case law.

The significance of the trial in this chapter spans more than forty years in Tennessee, staring with the Legislature's passage of the Butler Act in 1925, which prohibited teachers from mentioning Darwin's *Origin of the Species* in any public school within the state and denying the Biblical lesson of creation. Part legislator, part spectator John Washington Butler, the author of the act and state representative from Macon, Trousdale, and Sumner Counties, attended Scopes' trial as a guest of a press syndicate to draw interest in the case. The case would ultimately wind its way up to the Tennessee Supreme Court, but despite the efforts of Scopes, Darrow and Mencken, it would not be until 1967 that the Tennessee state legislature would once again revisit the dispute and repeal the Butler Act by means of the code section quoted at the end of this chapter.

The Butler Act, also known as the Tennessee Anti-Evolution Act, but best known then as the Tennessee Monkey Law, formed the basis for the State of Tennessee's charges against Scopes for teaching evolution in Dayton High School:

> PUBLIC ACTS OF THE STATE OF TENNESSEE PASSED BY THE SIXTY-FOURTH GENERAL ASSEMBLY, 1925, CHAPTER NO. 27, House Bill No. 185
>
> AN ACT prohibiting the teaching of the Evolution Theory in all the Universities, Normals and all other public schools of Tennessee, which are supported in whole or in part by the public school funds of the State, and to provide penalties for the violations thereof.
>
> Section 1. Be it enacted by the General Assembly of the State of Tennessee, that it shall be unlawful for any teacher in any of the Universities, Normals and all other public schools of the State which are supported in whole or in part by the public school funds of the State, to teach any theory that denies the story of the Divine Creation of man as

taught in the Bible, and to teach instead that man has descended from a lower order of animals.

Section 2. Be it further enacted, that any teacher found guilty of the violation of this Act, Shall be guilty of a misdemeanor and upon conviction, shall be fined not less than One Hundred ($100.00) Dollars nor more than Five Hundred ($500.00) Dollars for each offense.

Section 3. Be it further enacted, That this Act take effect from and after its passage, the public welfare requiring it.

Passed March 13, 1925, W. F. Barry, Speaker of the House of Representatives; L. D. Hill, Speaker of the Senate, Approved March 21, 1925, Austin Peay, Governor.

The Setup

Scopes taught mathematics, coached the (winning) Dayton, Tennessee high school football team, and a acted as substitute science teacher who may or may not have actually taught evolution. His memoirs note that he and several "town fathers" responded to an American Civil Liberties Union advertisement in Tennessee newspapers to test the constitutionality of the Butler Act. The townspeople reasoned the publicity surrounding the case would boost the faltering town's economy. Despite the pivotal role religion played in the case, no clergymen were part of its instigation. Once townspeople agreed to the test case on May 5, 1925, the County Attorney arrested Scopes on May 7, 1925. County Attorney Sue Hicks, a close friend of Scopes, is also the alleged inspiration for Johnny Cash's famous song, "A Boy Named Sue." Judge Raulston held a perfunctory preliminary hearing on the 10th and bound Scopes over to appear before a grand jury to determine the indictment. Scopes was released on bond, and the rest of the players in the trial arrived.

For the prosecution, the trial team consisted of local Dayton attorneys Sue K. Hicks and his brother, Herbert E. Hicks, together with then Tennessee Attorney General Thomas Stewart, who would later become a United States Senator. The prosecution team also included Ben B. McKenzie, Assistant Attorney General of Tennessee, and a leader in the local bar. The townspeople then on May 12, 1925, recruited lifelong Presbyterian William Jennings Bryan as a fellow prosecutor, who brought along his son, William Jennings Bryan, Jr. to assist with the prosecution. By his own admission, it had been some 26 years since the senior Bryan had seen the inside of a courtroom.

The defense team was made up of former dean of the law school at the University of Tennessee at Knoxville, John R. Neal, famous trial attorney Clarence Darrow, ACLU attorney Arthur Garfield Hays and Dudley Field Malone, an international divorce attorney who had previously worked with Bryan in the state department. In the trial transcript, Judge John T. Raulston adopts the local practice of calling the attorneys "Colonel" and "General," the latter referring to Attorneys General. The honorific title "Colonel" used for all attorneys in Tennessee and "General" was a courtesy used for all attorneys general (the prosecution). The senior Bryan, however, was an actual Colonel in the Army, having fought in the Spanish-American War and is consequently buried at Arlington National Cemetery. None of the other lawyers involved in the case held any true military rank.

As an aside, the honorific "Colonel" is also used in Kentucky, which is how Colonel Sanders of chicken bucket fame claimed his title.

The Grand Jury

As part of the setup, Judge Raulston impaneled a grand jury of thirteen men (the standard twelve, plus an alternate), and charged them with investigating the alleged crime of violating the Butler Act, and instructed them in part as follows:

> Since the act involved in this investigation provides that it shall be unlawful to teach any theory that denies the divine creation of man as taught in the Bible, it is proper that I call your attention to the account of man's creation as taught in the Bible, it is proper that I call your attention to the first chapter of Genesis, reading as follows: Reads First Chapter of Genesis. [Judge Raulston read the entire 31 verses of the first chapter].

. . .

> and in making this declaration, I make no reference to the policy or constitutionality of the statute, but to the evil example of the teacher disregarding constituted authority in the very presence of the undeveloped mind whose thought and morals he directs and guides.
>
> To teach successfully we must teach both by precept and example. The school room is not only a place to develop thought, but also a place to develop discipline, power of restraint, and character.
>
> If a teacher openly and flagrantly violates the laws of the land in the exercise of his profession (regardless of the policy of the law) his example cannot be wholesome to the undeveloped mind, and would tend to create and breed a spirit of disregard for good order and the want of respect for the necessary discipline and restraint in our body politic....[2]

Not that he had an opinion one way or the other, certainly.

Typically, the prosecuting lawyer, together with the judge, will draft a set of instructions designed to instruct the grand jury at the end of the trial about the law and the factual investigation they must undertake and determine. In a full trial with defense attorneys (they're not allowed in grand jury proceedings) both sets of lawyers draft jury instructions with the judge determining what is actually ready to the jury. Jury instructions are usually required to be neutral expressions of the law.

But here, this prior-to-the-actual-trial instruction was given to a grand jury on May 25, 1925, for the purposes of determining whether a chargeable offense occurred, so the lawyers did not participate in the preparation of these instructions, which were simply created by the judge and read by him to the grand jury. Predictably, the grand jury, led by foreman John Rose, returned an indictment against Scopes for allegedly violating the Butler Act by teaching evolution in the Dayton High School. Raulston scheduled the grand jury hearing for August, but when townspeople discovered a rival evolution trial proceeding in Chattanooga, he moved up the hearing to ensure Dayton would hear the test case first.

Preparations Begin

Dayton prepared for the trial's expected publicity by converting some six blocks of Dayton's main street into a pedestrian mall, building a speaker's platform on the lawn of the courthouse (which the judge used during the trial for Darrow's examination of Bryan) and assembled a tourist camp. The town installed the latest technology in the courtroom: telegraph and telephone wiring, movie-newsreel camera platforms and radio microphones. WGN Radio broadcasted the trial live and paid more than $1,000 a day for telephone lines.

Newspaper reporters from around the world likewise arrived to cover the trial. Judge Raulston regularly played to the photographers and was the first trial judge in the United States to allow a trial to be broadcast by radio throughout the country. Baltimore Sun reporter H.L. Mencken, more famous for holding a regular seat at the Algonquin Roundtable, gave the trial its sensational name: "The Monkey Trial." On Sunday before the trial started, William Jennings Bryan delivered a sermon at Dayton's Methodist Church, attacking the defense in the Scopes case. Judge Raulston and his family dutifully sat in the church's front pew seats.[3]

He had a front-row seat for the trial, too. Attorneys preaching in church is a tactic we still see today, whether a judge is in the congregation or not.

The Trial

A circus carnival atmosphere surrounded the Rhea (pronounced "Ray") County Courthouse, complete with signs and banners encouraging attendees to "Read Your Bible" and hawkers with monkeys in cages performing for the masses. Some 1,000 people, 300 of whom were standing, crowded the courthouse on opening day as the trial started.

In the sweltering summer heat of Dayton, Tennessee at 9:22a.m. on Friday, July 10, 1925, Circuit Court Judge John Raulston of the Rhea County Court opened John Scope's trial with a prayer by the Reverend Cartwright:

> Oh, God, our divine Father, we recognize Thee
> as the Supreme Ruler of the universe, in whose hands

are the lives and destinies of all men, and of all the world ... Hear us in our prayers, our Father, this morning, for the cause of truth and righteousness, throughout the length and breadth of the earth, and Oh, God, grant that from the President of the United States down to the most insignificant officer thereof, that the affairs of church and state may be so administered that God may beget unto Himself the greatest degree of Honor and glory. . . . Amen.[4]

Only after the prayer were the out-of-state lawyers were introduced by the prosecution, and then welcomed by the court:

The court—Gentlemen: I desire to assure you that we are glad to have you. The foreign lawyers for both the state and the defendant. I shall accord you the same privileges that are accorded the local counsel and assure you again that we are delighted to have you with us.[5]

This welcome, while kind, omitted a step in the legal procedure normally required to admit lawyers not licensed to practice law in Tennessee. As we saw in the John Brown trial, these outside, foreign lawyers are typically required to produce their credentials, or *bona fides,* to assure the court they are licensed to practice law in their home state. They must also be accompanied by a locally licensed attorney to ensure the foreign (out-of-state) lawyers comply with local procedures and customs. Present-day procedure typically requires a *pro hac vice* (Latin: "for this turn" or occasion) application and verification by the state bar. Some states, like Nevada, allow an attorney to appear only a limited number of times before being required to sit and take that state's bar exam. Here, however, given the high-profile reputations of these lawyers, the court undoubtedly dispensed with this usual requirement.

Scopes used the textbook Hunter's Civic Biology, a state-approved book, which had been in use in Tennessee for almost two decades and sold by Robinson's Drugstore to the Dayton High School. In response to the Scopes trial, at least one institution of higher learning, Columbia University in New York, suggested in 1925 that it might refuse to admit any student from Tennessee high schools due to the educational limitations in place because of the Butler Act.[6]

Unlike most trials, the Monkey Trial was more about picking a jury, procedure, argument, and oratory than it was about actual witnesses and testimony. Indeed, the prosecution introduced its first witness only on the afternoon of the fourth day of the trial, and then called just four witnesses. The defense attempted to call some eleven different scientists and religious leaders, but their testimony was excluded. Instead, the defense was permitted only to submit the eleven written statements as an offer of proof for the appellate courts to consider. In fact, the 50 pages of these written statements in the transcript are more informative on the subject of evolution than the textbook at issue and available for review in the transcript, printed in the World's Greatest Court Trial© from page 230-280 of the transcript and readily available online.

On the legal point, an "offer of proof" is a statement from the attorney describing the evidence the witness expects to provide. The offer is made outside the presence of the jury and can be made either through a short statement by the attorney, presenting a written affidavit, or actually questioning the witness, who is usually not subject to cross-examination.

Ultimately, the defense succeeded in calling just two witnesses: Dr. Maynard M. Metcalf (whose testimony, along with the other scientists, was in the record but excluded from being presented to the jury) and Prosecutor William Jennings Bryan. It is highly unusual and a violation of the current-day Rules of Professional Responsibility for a member of either trial team to testify, but this trial was more for showmanship than an actual trial.

After some initial preliminaries in the trial and having extended typical Southern hospitality, Judge Raulston and the lawyers picked the jury. The prosecution almost accepted each member of the venire pool without question, confident in the fundamentalist religious background of the community members, striking only those few who said they did not go to church. The defense team, attempting to avoid being "home-towned," was more careful. Clarence Darrow (not yet granted the honorific of "Colonel" by the court) questioned Talesman (a potential juror selected by the Sheriff from bystanders, not from a pool obtained by lottery) J. G. Dagley after initial questioning by the court:

Gen. Stewart: We pass him to the defendant.

Examination by Mr. Darrow, for the defense:

Q: You are a farmer?
A: Yes, sir.
Q: Near here?
A: What is that?
Q: Do you live near here, near the town?
A: Twelve or fourteen miles.
Q: Have you lived in Tennessee most of your life?
A: I was born and raised here.
Q: In this community?
A: Yes, sir.
Q: Have you ever known anything about evolution, or read about it?
A: I have not.
Q: You don't know anything about it at this time?
A: No, sir.
Q: Are you a church member?
A: Yes, sir.
Q: Of what church?
A: Methodist.
Q: You have been for a good many years?
A: Yes, sir, a number of years.
Q: Have you ever heard it discussed in church?
A: No, sir.
Q: Did you ever hear your minister express himself on it?
A: No, sir.[7]

Mr. Darrow accepted Mr. Dagley for a seat in the jury box. Not all potential jurors were seated, however. One of the talesmen pulled for duty, Number 20, was a local minister, Reverend J.P. Massingill:

> **The Court:** What do you say to Mr. Massingill?—for the state?

> **Mr. McKenzie:** I pass him to you, Colonel.

Questions by Mr. Darrow:

Q: What is your business?

A: I am a minister.

...

Q: Did you ever preach on evolution?

A: Yes. I haven't as a subject; just taken that up; in connection with other subjects. I have referred to it in discussing it.

Q: Against it or for it?

A: I am strictly for the Bible.

Q: I am talking about evolution, I am not talking about the Bible. Did you preach for or against evolution?

A: Is that a fair question, judge?

> **The Court:** Yes, answer the question.

A: Well, I preached against it, of course! (Applause).

Q: Why, "of course?"

> **The Court:** Let's have order.

> **Mr. Darrow:** Your Honor, I am going to ask to have anybody excluded that applauds.

> **The Court:** Yes, if you repeat that, ladies and gentlemen, you will be excluded. We cannot have applause. If you have any feeling in this case you must not express it in the courthouse, so don't repeat the applause. If you do, I will have to exclude you.

Q: You have a very firm conviction—a very strong opinion against evolution, haven't you?

A: Well, some points in evolution.

Q: Are you trying to get on this jury?

A: No, sir.

Q: Have you formed a strong conviction against evolution?

A: Well, I have.

Q: You think you would be a fair juror in this case?

A: Well, I can take the law and the evidence in the case, I think, and try a man right.

Q: I asked if you think thought you could be a fair juror?

A: Yes, sir.

. . .

Q: And in your opinion he [Scopes] has been teaching contrary to the Bible?

General Stewart: If Your Honor please, I except [an "exception" is the same as an objection to preserve the record] to that. The question involved here will be whether or not—not, I apprehend if Mr. Scopes taught anything that is contrary to the Bible—that isn't the question. He has asked him whether or not he has prejudged the guilt of the defendant.

The Court: He has a right to know that.

Gen. Stewart: The man has already stated to him that he had no opinion in the case.

Mr. Darrow: Do you think he would be a fair juror in the case?

Gen. Stewart: Yes, I do, if he says so.

Mr. Darrow: I don't.

After some further questioning by the court, Reverend Massingill was excused for cause by Judge Raulston upon Darrow's challenge. A "for cause" challenge is one side's request to the court to excuse the potential juror due to that individual's inability to judge the case fairly. By challenging a potential juror "for cause," the defense or prosecution does not use up its peremptory challenges, which are purely discretionary and do not require an explanation from the attorneys. If the judge refuses to grant a "for cause" challenge, then the attorneys can exercise a peremptory challenge.

In Tennessee's civil practice in 1925, each side got three peremptory challenges. Lawyers are usually careful to use a "for cause" challenge only in situations where they believe the judge will strike the potential juror, believing that there is nothing worse than having a juror sit on the panel knowing that the lawyer does not want the juror. The lawyers will almost always hold back at least one of those peremptory challenges to ensure they can strike a juror they challenge for cause in the event the judge does not agree with the "for cause" challenge. Typically, if the judge refuses to strike the potential juror "for cause," the lawyer requesting the challenge will then exercise a peremptory challenge and strike the juror. Darrow exercised only one peremptory. News reports do not specify how many peremptory challenges the state used.

The jury consisted of farmers, a retired U.S. Marshall, one of Scope's fellow teachers, and cabinet makers. Each one testified that he was a member of a church, but only one admitted to not attending regularly. As a matter of local procedure, the jury was not immediately sworn pending the start of trial but was instructed by the judge to not discuss the matter with others or the newspapermen covering the trial. That instruction is still given today.

Famed reporter H.L. Mencken, commented on the jury selection process in his July 11, 1925 dispatch in the Baltimore Sun:

> It was obvious after a few rounds that the jury would be unanimously hot for Genesis. The most that Mr. Darrow could hope for was to sneak in a few bold enough to declare publicly that they would have to hear the evidence against Scopes before condemning him. The slightest sign of anything further brought forth a peremptory challenge from

the State. Once a man was challenged without examination for simply admitting that he did not belong formally to any church. Another time a panel man who confessed that he was prejudiced against evolution got a hearty round of applause from the crowd. . . .[8]

After impaneling the jury, the lawyers got around to the legal niceties of the trial. In the first of several procedural challenges, the defense next filed a Motion to Quash (dismiss) the indictment against Scopes on the Constitutional grounds of freedom of speech, freedom of religion and other procedural grounds arguing that the statute itself was too vague. After further briefing by both sides, much legal wrangling and handwringing, Judge Raulston denied the defense Motion, but the defense had succeeded in preserving its grounds for appeal. Colonel Neal, for the defense, argued:

> Our contention, to be very brief, is that in [the Butler] act there is made mandatory the teaching of a particular doctrine that comes from a particular religious book, and to that extent, it places the public schools of our state in such a situation, in regard to particular church establishments, that they contravene the provisions of our constitution.[9]

For the prosecution, General McKenzie responded, in part:

> There can be no question, as we view it, as to the constitutionality of the act, or the validity of the indictment. It serves notice on the defendant of what? That you were employed to teach in the public schools of Rhea County, that you taught a theory that is contrary to the record given by the Holy Writ as to the creation of man, and I insist it defines its own self. It does not need any construction. Instead, you taught that a man descended from a lower order of animals, just in the language of the statute.[10]

As part of their Motion to Quash, the defense chose to attack the word "Bible" in the statute as vague, challenging the State of Tennessee to define what it meant:

> **Gen. Stewart:** Yes, that "no preference shall ever be given, by law, to any religious establishment or mode of worship." Then, how could that interfere, Mr. Darrow?

Mr. Darrow: That is the part we claim is affected.

Gen. Stewart: In what wise?

Mr. Darrow: Giving preference to the Bible.

Gen. Stewart: To the Bible?

Mr. Darrow: Yes, Why not the Koran?[11]

General Stewart had a ready answer to the defense's questions:

> If Your Honor please, the St. James Version of the Bible is the recognized one in this section of the country. The laws of the land recognize the Bible; the laws of the land recognize the law of God and Christianity as a part of the common law.

. . .

Mr. Neal: Does not it [the statute] prefer the Bible to the Koran?

Gen. Stewart: It does not mention the Koran.

Mr. Malone: Does not it prefer the Bible to the Koran?

Gen. Stewart: We are not living in a heathen country.[12]

Darrow sarcastically countered the Attorney General's argument:

> Here, we find today as brazen and as bold an attempt to destroy learning as was ever made in the middle ages, and the only difference is we have not provided that they shall be burned at the stake, but there is time for that, Your Honor, we have to approach these things gradually.[13]

. . .

> That is what was foisted on the people of this state . . . that it should be a crime in the state of Tennessee to teach any theory of the origin of man, except that contained in the divine account as recorded in the Bible. But the state of Tennessee under an honest and fair interpretation of the

constitution has no more right to teach the Bible as the divine book than that the Koran is one, or the book of Mormons, or the book of Confucius, or the Budda *[sic]*, or the Essays of Emerson, or any one of the 10,000 books to which human souls have gone for consolation and aid in their troubles. Are they going to cut them out?[14]

. . .

If men are not tolerant, if men cannot respect each other's opinions, if men cannot live and let live, then no man's life is safe, no man's life is safe. Here is a country made up of Englishmen, Irishmen, Scotch, German, Europeans, Asiatics, Africans, men of every sort and men of every creed and men of every scientific belief; who is going to begin this sorting out and say, "I shall measure you; I know you are a fool, or worse; I know and I have read a creed telling what I know and I will make people go to Heaven even if they don't want to go with me, I will make them do it." Where is the man that is wise enough to do it?[15]

It's hard to be sarcastic following Darrow.

While the attorneys argued over the words of the Butler Act statute and their effect on the United States and Tennessee Constitutions, a separate sideshow went on in front of the judge: his penchant for being photographed. But court proceedings eventually got in the way of his vanity:

The Court: Gentlemen, the jury will not be sworn this afternoon, and you photographers will have to move out.[16]

Crowded with spectators and without modern air conditioning, the conditions in the Courtroom were stifling. By Monday afternoon, the attorneys begged the indulgence of the court:

The Court: Call the court to order.

The Court: I will hear you, Gen. Stewart.

Gen. Stewart: Your Honor, may I—

The Court: Proceed without your coat.

Gen. Stewart: Yes, sir.[17]

By Wednesday afternoon, even the jury was overcome:

Juror Thompson: If it ain't out of order, I would like to make the request, the unanimous request of the jury to take up the matter of some electric fans here. This heat is fearful. While I think I could stand my part of it:

The Court: The county judge is the man you would have to appeal to on that.

The Juror: He is a mighty nice man and some intimation from you would do some good.

Mr. McKenzie: Nothing would give me greater pleasure than to have them installed, but on account of the depleted state of the treasury I do not believe the county can do it.

Mr. Malone: I will buy some fans.

The Court: Col. Thompson, I will divide my fan. Perhaps we can borrow some small fans, and place them on the table, Mr. County Judge. Maybe we can place some small fans on the table.[18]

Ceiling fans were installed in the middle of the trial. Judge Raulston was a circuit (traveling) judge, so his reference to the "county judge" meant the magistrate judge who normally occupied the court. Judge Raulston was equally deferential to Juror Thompson by calling him "Colonel," since Thompson was the foreman of the jury. Judge Raulston was magnanimous with his use of titles:

The Court: I will hear you, Colonel.

Mr. Darrow: If the court please.

The Court: Have order in the courtroom. Get seats.

Mr. Darrow: I know my friend, McKenzie, whom I have learned not only to admire, but to love in our short acquaintance, didn't mean anything in referring to us lawyers who come from out of town. For myself, I have been treated with the greatest courtesy by the attorneys and the community.

The Court: No talking, please, in the courtroom.

Mr. Darrow: And I shall always remember that this court is the first one that ever gave me a great title of "Colonel" and I hope it will stick to me when I get back north.

The Court: I want you to take it back to your home with you, Colonel.[19]

Even H.L. Mencken attempted to put his cynicism aside for a moment in favor of Southern hospitality, but it didn't last long:

> It would be hard to imagine a more moral town than Dayton. If it has any bootleggers, no visitor has heard of them. Ten minutes after I arrived a leading citizen offered me a drink made up half of white mule and half of Coca-Cola, but he seems to have been simply indulging himself in a naughty gesture. No fancy woman has been seen in the town since the end of the McKinley administration. There is no gambling. There is no place to dance. The relatively wicked, when they would indulge themselves, go to Robinson's drug store and debate theology. . . .[20]

With the sideshows going on around him, Darrow wrapped up his pre-trial argument challenging the constitutionality of the statute with dramatic flair:

> If today you can take a thing like evolution and make it a crime to teach it in the public school, tomorrow you can make it a crime to teach it in the private schools, and the next year you can make it a crime to teach it to the hustings or in the church. At the next session you may ban books and the newspapers. Soon you may set Catholic against Protestant and Protestant against Protestant, and try to foist your own religion upon the minds of men. If you can do one you can do the other. Ignorance and fanaticism is ever busy and needs feeding. Always it is feeding and gloating for more. Today it is the public school teachers, tomorrow the private. The next day the preachers and the lecturers, the magazines, the books, the newspapers. After while, Your Honor, it is the setting of man against man and creed against creed until with flying banners and

beating drums we are marching backward to the glorious ages of the sixteenth century when bigots lighted fagots to burn the men who dared to bring any intelligence and enlightenment and culture to the human mind.[21]

The Third Day's Proceedings: July 14, 1925

As was the court's normal practice, Judge Raulston again opened the proceedings with a prayer. This time, Darrow was ready and immediately objected, but both the prosecutors took exception to the objection:

> **Mr. McKenzie:** That matter has been passed upon by our supreme court. Judge Shepherd took a case from the court, when the jury, after retiring to consider their verdict, at the suggestion of one of them to bow in prayer, asked divine guidance, afterwards delivering a verdict not excepted to, and afterwards taken to the supreme court: It was commendable to the jury to ask divine guidance.

To which Mr. Malone replied for the defense:

> Our objection goes to the fact that we believe that this daily opening of the court with prayers, those prayers we have already heard, having been duly argumentative that they help to increase the atmosphere of hostility to our point of view, which already exists in this community by widespread propaganda.

The Attorney General countered:

> **Gen. Stewart:** In reply to that there is still no question involved in this lawsuit as to whether or not Scopes taught a doctrine prohibited by the statute, that is that man descended from a lower order of animals. So far as creating an atmosphere of hostility is concerned, I would advise Mr. Malone that this is a God fearing country.

The Court tried to finally settle the matter, initially overruling the defense's objections:

> **The Court:** This court has no purpose except to find the truth and do justice to all the issues involved in this case.
>
> In answer to counsel for the defendant, as to my custom, I will say the several years I have been on the bench I have used my discretion in opening the court with prayer, at times when there was a minister present and it was convenient to do so; other times when there was no large assemblage of people and no minister present, I have not always followed this custom, but I think it is a matter wholly within the discretion of the court.
>
> I have instructed the ministers who have been invited to my rostrum to open the court with prayer, to make no reference to the issues involved in this case. I see nothing that might influence the court or jury as to the issues. I believe in prayer myself; I constantly invoke divine guidance myself, when I am on the bench and off the bench; I see no reason why I should not continue to do this. It is not the purpose of this court to bias or prejudice the mind of any individual, but to do right in all matters under investigation.[22]

So, it would seem the matter was ended, but in the afternoon session, Colonel Hays for the defense submitted to the court a petition signed by Unitarians, Jews, and Congregationalists asking the court that if it insisted on continuing to pray before opening each session, to select a minister from a denomination other than fundamentalists. While the defense lawyers were an enlightened lot, they likewise understood the inability of the court to comply with the Petition, since there were only fundamentalist ministers in the local area.

> **The Court:** I shall refer that petition to the pastors' association of this town, and I shall ask them:
>
> **(Laughter and loud applause, and rapping for order by the policeman.)**
>
> **The Court:** I shall ask the pastors' association from now on to name the man who is to conduct prayer. I shall have no voice, make no suggestions as to who they name, but I will invite the men named

by the association to conduct the prayer each morning.

...

Mr. Hays: May I ask Your Honor if this is a decision on my motion?

The Court: Yes, sir.

Mr. Hays: So that I may except, so that I may save the record.

Mr. Neal: Your Honor knows that the men Your Honor refers this motion to, are not among the class of men that signed the petition.

The Court: I see by the press one minister has resigned his post recently because Dr. Potter was not allowed to preach in his church and I take it he is in sympathy with Dr. Potter and his doctrine, the others are perhaps fundamentalists, I don't know.[23]

The court overruled the defense's objection to the prayers. Darrow and the defense team may have made their point for the record, but the prayers continued each morning of the trial, which was also finally ended with a benediction. While prayer in court is generally no longer practiced, it still occurs. The ACLU in August 2008 filed a complaint against a Covington County, Alabama Judge who dropped to his knees in court and asked the parties to pray with him prior to reaching a decision. None of the parties in that more recent case made an objection.

Prayer certainly has its place, even though it's been outlawed from schools and most government functions. In my nearly forty years of practice, I've never been in a courtroom proceeding that started with a prayer. I have attended as an attorney many board of supervisors and city council meetings started with a prayer, however.

These days it would not surprise me to learn that our Supreme Court might start the practice.

Fourth Day's Proceedings:
Wednesday, July 15, 1925

The court once again started with a prayer, and defense attorney Doctor Neal (sometimes called Judge Neal and sometimes Colonel Neal) again asserted an objection, this time citing a court case, asking the court to stop prayer in the courtroom.

> I would like that you read from a case a very well-known principle of law, and I think you will agree with me when I read it. "The courts will take judicial notice that the religious world is divided into numerous sects and of the general doctrines:" this is quoting from the case of State vs. District Board, 76 Wis., 177:"the courts will take judicial notice that the religious world is divided into numerous sects and of the general doctrines maintained by each sect; for these things pertain to general history, and may fairly be presumed to be subjects of common knowledge. Thus they will take cognizance, without averment, of the facts that there are numerous religious sects called Christian, respectively maintaining different and conflicting doctrines; that some of these believe the doctrine of predestination, while others do not; some the doctrine of eternal punishment of the wicked while others repudiate it; some the doctrines of the apostolic succession and the authority of the priesthood, while others reject both; some that the Holy Scriptures are the only sufficient rules of faith and practice, while others believe that the only safe guide to human thought, opinion and action is the illuminating power of the divine spirit upon the humble and devout heart; some in the necessity and efficacy of the sacraments of the church, while others reject them entirely; and some in the literal truth of the Scriptures, while others believe them to be allegorical, teaching spiritual truths alone, or chiefly."

. . .

> Therefore, believing as we do firmly that certain great religious questions are involved in this case and appealing to the general knowledge of the court, that any religious atmosphere injected in the proceedings must necessarily be of one particular faith: not that we are religious or irreligious, but

> simply because this is a religious question: that the whole atmosphere of the court in every respect should be neutral.[24]

The Court replied:

> The court believes that any religious society that is worthy of the name should believe in God and believe in divine guidance. The court has no purpose by opening the court with prayer to influence anybody wrongfully, but hopes that such may influence somebody rightfully. It has been my custom at times when there has been no minister in the court, I have called on some good old pious man whom I knew was good, who believed in God, to open the court with prayer. I don't think it hurts anybody and I think it may help somebody. So I overrule the objection.[25]

With all the maneuvering and legal jockeying over prayer and procedure temporarily out of the way, by the afternoon of Wednesday, the court was finally ready to start the actual trial, swear in the jury and take the Defendant's anti-climactic "not guilty" plea, almost as if it were an afterthought to the proceedings. Pleas are taken during arraignments, a step missing here. The State and the Defense opened the trial, to the extent their respective positions were not already clear, with short opening statements. The prosecution statement put the case simply:

> Gen. Stewart: It is the insistence of the state in this case, that the defendant, John Thomas Scopes, has violated the antievolution law, what is known as the antievolution law, by teaching in the public schools of Rhea County the theory tending to show that man and mankind is descended from a lower order of animals. Therefore, he has taught a theory which denies the story of divine creation of man as taught by the Bible.[26]

An easy case to prove, according to the prosecution. The defense saw the case as much more complicated, and its opening statement runs on for pages in the transcript, essentially arguing there was no conflict between science and the Bible and that the Bible could not contain all scientific truths. The defense made a technical point about the statute, claiming it required Scopes to have both taught evolution *and* denied the Bible story of creation. But the case was much more than the opening statement let on. Attorney Malone opened for the defense:

> So that there shall be no misunderstanding and that no one shall be able to misinterpret or misrepresent our position we wish to state at the beginning of the case that the defense believes there is a direct conflict between the theory of evolution and the theories of creation as set forth in the Book of Genesis.
>
> . . .
>
> The defense will also prove by credible testimony that there is more than one theory of creation set forth in the Bible and that they are conflicting. But we shall make it perfectly clear that while this is the view of the defense we shall show by the testimony of men learned in science and theology that there are millions of people who believe in evolution and in the stories of creation as set forth in the Bible and who find no conflict between the two.
>
> . . .
>
> While the defense thinks there is a conflict between evolution and the Old Testament, we believe there is no conflict between evolution and Christianity. There may be a conflict between evolution and the peculiar ideas of Christianity, which are held by Mr. Bryan as the evangelical leader of the prosecution, but we deny that the evangelical leader of the prosecution is an authorized spokesman for the Christians of the United States. The defense maintains that there is a clear distinction between God the church, the Bible, Christianity and Mr. Bryan.
>
> . . .
>
> There are indications that not 6,000 years ago, but through the long course of the ages from this order came man in one direction, and monkeys in the other. All that science says is that probably some time not 6,000 years ago, but in the course of the

ages, and all that science says today is that there are tendencies which indicate the validity of this opinion.

...

The defense denies that it is part of any movement or conspiracy on the part of scientists to destroy the authority of Christianity or the Bible. The defense denies that any such conspiracy exists except in the mind and purposes of the evangelical leader of the prosecution. The defense maintains that the book of Genesis is in part a hymn, in part an allegory and a work of religious interpretations written by men who believed that the earth was flat and whose authority cannot be accepted to control the teachings of science in our schools.

The narrow purpose of the defense is to establish the innocence of the defendant Scopes. The broad purpose of the defense will be to prove that the Bible is a work of religious aspiration and rules of conduct which must be kept in the field of theology.

The defense maintains that there is no more justification for imposing the conflicting views of the Bible on courses of biology than there would be for imposing the views of biologists [sic] on courses of comparative religion. We maintain that science and religion embrace two separate and distinct fields of thought and learning.

We remember that Jesus said: "Render unto Caesar the things that are Caesar's and unto God the things that are God's.[27]

The oratory would continue to flow as the trial went on, but first, the prosecution had to prove its case and call witnesses. Attorney General Stewart chose Dayton School Superintendent Walter White.

Q: Mr. White, do you know what particular books, or what particular subjects, Mr. Scopes taught in the high school?

A: He was a science teacher; he taught chemistry, biology and other subjects in the science course.

Q: Did he teach this book, Hunter's biology?

A: Yes, sir.

Q: Will you file that book as Exhibit 1 to your testimony?

A: Yes, sir.

. . .

Q: Did he say to you in reference to this book that he had taught that part that pertained to evolution?

A: Yes, sir.

Q: What did he say?

A: He admitted that he had taught that. He said that he couldn't teach the book without teaching that and he could not teach that without violating the statute.

Q: Did he say that it was unconstitutional?

A: He defended his course by saying that the statute was unconstitutional.

. . .

Q: Mr. White, I will ask you if this is the King James version of the Bible, and to file it as an exhibit to your testimony?

Mr. Hays: Do you mean to file that in evidence?

Gen. Stewart: We offer this in evidence, yes, sir, as explanatory of what the act relates to when it says "Bible."[28]

Colonel Hays launched into an exposition of what the word "Bible" meant.

Mr. Hays: What is the Bible? Different sects of Christians disagree in their answers to this question. They agree that the Bible is the inspired word of God, that the Creator of the universe is its Author, and that it is a book of divine instruction as to the creation of man, his relation to, dependence and accountability to, God. The historical and literary features of the Bible are of the greatest value, but its distinctive feature is its claim to teach a system of religion revealed by direct inspiration from God. It bases its demand for the reverence and allegiance of mankind upon the direct authority of God Himself. The various Protestant sects of Christians use the King James version, published in London in 1611, while Catholics use the Douay version, of which the Old Testament was published by the English college at Douay, in France, in 1609, and the New Testament by the English college at Rheims in 1582, and these two versions are often called, respectively, the Protestant Bible and the Catholic Bible. [. . .] Each party claims for its own version the most accurate presentation of the inspired word as delivered to mankind and contained in the original scriptures." Which version does the Tennessee legislature call for? Does it intend to distinguish between the different religious sects in passing this law? Does it mean the Protestant, the St. James version, rather than the Catholic or Douay Bible?

. . .

The Lord's prayer is differently translated in the two versions. Of the different translations of the Lord's prayer in later versions of the Bible, the following language of a Protestant has been quoted with approval by a Catholic author: 'Even the Lord's prayer has been tampered with and a discord thrown into the daily devotions. The inspired text is changed and unsettled, the faith of the people in God's Holy Word is undetermined, and aid and comfort given the enemy of all religion.'

. . .

Therefore, Your Honor, we object to the Bible going in evidence, or that book going in evidence, but insist that the prosecution prove what the Bible is before they put it in evidence.[29]

Perhaps not surprising, the court summarily overruled Hays' long-winded objection and admitted into evidence the

King James Version of the Bible. Mr. Darrow inquired where he might obtain a copy of the book, and General Stewart replied that it was available at Robinson's Drug Store—the same place Hunter's Biology could be purchased (and was purchased for use at the Dayton High School).

Irony of all ironies.

After the objection and exchange between counsel, General Stewart continued with the direct examination:

> Q: On Pages 194 and 195 of this book, (biology) where the doctrine of evolution and the evolutionary tree is shown by a drawing. Did Mr. Scopes say that he reviewed that about the 20th of April, with the rest of the book?
>
> A: It is my understanding that he reviewed the important parts of the book and that he reviewed that part, that refers to Charles Darwin's theory of evolution.[30]

Colonel Darrow undertook to cross-examine Superintendent White:

> Q: [. . .] This book of Hunter's, what is the name of that book?
>
> . . .
>
> A: George William Hunter's Civic Biology.
>
> Q: Where did Mr. Scopes get it?
>
> A: In the course of study, Mr. Robinson, the book man for this section handled the books.
>
> Q: That was the official book adopted by the board, was it not?
>
> A: In Tennessee, the board of education does not adopt books.
>
> Q: Who does?
>
> A: The Tennessee textbook commission adopts the book.
>
> Q: Official book adopted by the Tennessee textbook commission?

A: That was the official book adopted by the Tennessee textbook commission in 1919, but the contract expired August 31, 1924, a five-year contract.

Q: Had any other book been adopted in the meantime?

A: No, sir.

...

Q: So, [Scopes] taught this, which was the official book at that time?

A: Yes, sir.

Q: And did you ever have any talk with him before the time it was charged he taught it?

A: I did not.

...

Q: You never said anything to him about it or to any other teacher about not teaching it?

A: No, sir; I did not for these reasons:

Q: I don't care anything about the reason, but you may give it.

A: Under the Tennessee law, I have not:

Q: Nobody ever said anything to you about it, did they?

A: No, sir.

Q: You never complained of Mr. Scopes as a teacher?

A: I had no complaint against his work in general.

Q: That is what I am speaking of.

A: No complaint against his work in general.

Q: That's all, do you know how long this book has been used?

> A: It has been used since 1909, the school year of 1909.

(Witness excused.)[31]

Next the prosecution called one of Scopes' high school students, Howard Morgan. On direct, 14-year-old Howard testified that Scopes had taught the theory of evolution from Hunter's Biology. General Stewart's examination was largely perfunctory in establishing the facts, but it was Darrow's cross-examination that drove the defense's point home, starting to depart from the ACLU's original intent to argue the unconstitutionality of the statute:

> Q: [Col. Darrow] Now, he said the earth was once a molten mass of liquid, didn't he?
>
> A: Yes, sir.
>
> Q: By molten, you understand melted?
>
> A: Yes, sir.
>
> Q: Running molten mass of liquid, and that it slowly cooled until a crust was formed on it?
>
> A: Yes, sir.
>
> Q: After that, after it got cooled enough, and the soil came, that plants grew; is that right?
>
> A: Yes, sir; yes, sir.
>
> Q: And that the first life was in the sea.
>
> Q: And that it developed into life on the land?
>
> A: Yes, sir.
>
> Q: And finally into the highest organism which is known as man?
>
> A: Yes, sir.
>
> Q: Now, that is about what he taught you?
>
> Q: It has not hurt you any, has it?
>
> A: No, sir.
>
> **Mr. Darrow:** That's all.

(**Laughter in the courtroom**).

It's hard to tell whether either evolution or religion have kept man from understanding science.

The state next called another student to the stand, who likewise testified that Professor Scopes had taught him evolution from Hunter's Biology. But it was Darrow's cross-examination that once again stole the show:

> Q: (Col. Darrow) How old are you?
>
> A: Seventeen.
>
> Q: Prof. Scopes said that all forms of life came from a single cell, didn't he?
>
> A: Yes, sir.
>
> Q: Did anybody ever tell you that before?
>
> A: No, sir.
>
> Q: That is all you remember that he told you about biology, wasn't it?
>
> A: Yes, sir.
>
> Q: Are you a church member?
>
> A: Sir?
>
> Q: Are you a church member?
>
> A: Yes, sir.
>
> Q: Do you still belong?
>
> A: Yes, sir.
>
> Q: You didn't leave church when he told you all forms of life began with a single cell?
>
> A: No, sir.
>
> **Mr. Darrow:** That is all.
>
> **The Court:** No talking [to the courtroom spectators].[32]

Church-going and attending school were not mutually exclusive.

The state next called its fourth and final witness, F.E. Robinson, the drugstore owner and purveyor of Hunter's Biology to the Dayton High School. On direct, Attorney General Stewart got Mr. Robinson to testify that Scopes admitted teaching the theory of evolution to his students from Hunter's Biology. Once again, Darrow scored points with his cross-examination:

> Q: [**General Stewart**] showed you a book which has been marked "a civic biology," or entitled "A Civic Biology," which I hold in my hand?
>
> A: Yes, sir.
>
> Q: You were selling them, were you not?
>
> A: Yes, sir.
>
> Q: And you were a member of the school board?
>
> A: Yes, sir.

(**Laughter in the courtroom**.)

Mr. Darrow: I think someone ought to advise you that you are not bound to answer these questions.

Gen. Stewart: The law says teach, not sell.

(**Laughter in the courtroom**.)

· · ·

Mr. Darrow: Did you examine this evolutionary tree [on page 194]?

> A: Yes, sir.
>
> Q: You don't know whether man is in there, do you?
>
> A: Yes, sir; man is in here.
>
> Q: I am afraid they left him out. You put him in with the mammals, but nothing in there: the word man is not written in there, is it?
>
> A: I don't believe it is; the word man is not . . [33]

With that rousing end, the State rested its case. Normally, this testimony would not be an effective way to end the case, but as H.L. Mencken would observe in his column the following day, July 16, 1925:

> The high point of yesterday's proceedings was reached with the appearance of Dr. Maynard M. Metcalf of the John Hopkins. [...] the instant he was asked a question bearing directly upon the case at bar there was a flurry in the Bryan pen and Stewart was on his feet with protests. Another question followed, with more and hotter protests. The judge then excluded the jury and the show began.
>
> What ensued was, on the surface, a harmless enough dialogue between Dr. Metcalf and Darrow, but underneath there was tense drama. [...]
>
> Then began one of the clearest, most succinct and withal most eloquent presentations of the case for the evolutionists that I have ever heard. The doctor was never at a loss for a word, and his ideas flowed freely and smoothly. Darrow steered him magnificently. A word or two and he was howling down the wind. Another and he hauled up to discharge a broadside. There was no cocksureness in him. Instead he was rather cautious and deprecatory and sometimes he halted and confessed his ignorance. But what he got over before he finished was a superb counterblast to the fundamentalist buncombe. The jury, at least, in theory heard nothing of it, but it went whooping into the radio and it went banging into the face of Bryan....
>
> This old buzzard, having failed to raise the mob against its rulers, now prepares to raise it against its teachers. He can never be the peasants' President, but there is still a chance to be the peasants' Pope. He leads a new crusade, his bald head glistening, his face streaming with sweat, his chest heaving beneath his rumpled alpaca coat. One somehow pities him, despite his so palpable imbecilities. It is a tragedy, indeed, to begin life as a hero and to end it as a buffoon. But let no one, laughing at him, underestimate the magic that lies in his black, malignant eye, his frayed but still eloquent voice. He

can shake and inflame these poor ignoramuses as no other man among us can shake and inflame them, and he is desperately eager to order the charge.

In Tennessee he is drilling his army. The big battles, he believes, will be fought elsewhere.[34]

Mencken's joy at Metcalf's testimony would be short-lived. While Darrow opened the defense case as Mencken described and Metcalf skillfully describing the course of evolution across some 60 million years, the State "excepted" to his testimony. Nonetheless, the scientist Maynard F. Metcalf was at least put on the stand and gave his testimony explaining his belief in God did not contradict his belief in evolution.

Q: (Col. Darrow) Are you a member of any church organization?

A: Yes.

Q: What one?

A: The Congregationalist church. Do you want to know the particular church?

Q: Yes?

A: I am now a member of the United church, in Oberlin, which is a Congregationalist church. I have been a member of two other congregationalist [sic] churches: no, one Presbyterian and one Congregationalist.

Q: You have been a Presbyterian, too, have you?

A: Well, I joined the Presbyterian church when I was 11 years old, I think: I am not sure.

Q: And have you been connected with church activities aside from being a member?

A: Yes.

Q: In what way?

A: Well, in Baltimore I had charge of a Bible class in the church for about three years. I had charge of a Bible class of college students, well, not exclusively college students, mostly college students, in Oberlin. That is all, I think: of course I have had some church offices, but those do not mean much.

Q: Not unless it is treasurer or something like that.

A: No, nothing worse than deacon.

Q: Doctor, do you understand, or at least ever studied and read evolution?

A: Surely.

Q: For how long?

A: I cannot answer that question. I think I heard the word and the thought was long ago. I could not remember when, and an old brother with whom I used to sleep, used to discuss with me evolutionary subjects until we went to sleep at night, night after night, before I was eight years old. I guess I had been brought up on it.

Q: Did your evolutionary studies include the development and evolution of man, in a general way?

A: I have never been a student of human morphology or human physiology distinctly, but I have been somewhat of a student of evolution, and especially interested in man, and I have given some lectures here and there on prehistoric man, early man.

Q: And you have studied as to the origin of man, have you not?

A: Well, I have not studied firsthand very much as to the origin of man, I have not been an archeologist or anthropologist, but I have read on it, and such lectures as I have given have been compendia from work done by other men, not my own work.

Q: But, you are familiar with that work?

A: Yes, sir, fairly broadly.

Q: And your studies in zoology, they have naturally been connected with the study of evolution?

A: Yes, I have always been particularly interested in the evolution of the individual organism from the egg, and also of the evolution of organisms as a whole from the beginning of life, that has been a sort of peculiar interest of mine, always.

Q: Are you an evolutionist?

A: Surely, under certain circumstances that question would be an insult, under these circumstances I do not regard it as such.

Q: Do you know any scientific man in the world that is not an evolutionist?

[objections to the question]

Q: (**Mr. Darrow**) What would you say, practically all scientific men were or were not evolutionists?

A: I am acquainted with practically all of the zoologists, botanists and geologists of this country who have clone any work; that is, any material contribution to knowledge in those fields, and I am absolutely convinced from personal knowledge that any one of these men feel and believe, as a matter of course, that evolution is a fact, but I doubt very much if any two of them agree as to the exact method by which evolution has been brought about, but I think there is:I know there is not a single one among them who has the least doubt of the fact of evolution.[35]

The lawyers argued about the admissibility of Metcalf's testimony and opinion. In his only extended speech in the trial, Bryan elevated religion above science:

> Mr. Hays says that before he got here he read that I said this was to be a duel to the death, between

science: was it? and revealed religion. I don't know who the other duelist was, but I was representing one of them and because of that they went to the trouble and the expense of several thousand dollars to bring down their witnesses. Well, my friend, if you said that this was important enough to be regarded as a duel between two great ideas or groups I certainly will be given credit for foreseeing what I could not then know and that is that this question is so important between religion and irreligion that even the invoking [sic] of the divine blessing upon it might seem partisan and partial. I think when we come to consider the importance of this question, that all of us who are interested as lawyers on either side, could claim what we: what Your Honor so graciously grants: a hearing.

. . .

And yet while Mr. Scopes knew what the law was and knew what evolution was, and knew that it violated the law, he proceeded to violate the law. That is the evidence before this court, and we do not need any expert to tell us what that law means. An expert cannot be permitted to come in here and try to defeat the enforcement of a law by testifying that it isn't a bad law and it isn't: I mean a bad doctrine: no matter how these people phrase the doctrine: no matter how they eulogize it. This is not the place to try to prove that the law ought never to have been passed. The place to prove that, or teach that, was to the legislature. If these people were so anxious to keep the state of Tennessee from disgracing itself, if they were so afraid that by this action taken by the legislature, the state would put itself before the people of the nation as ignorant people and bigoted people: if they had half the affection for Tennessee that you would think they had as they come here to testify, they would have come at a time when their testimony would have been valuable and not at this time to ask you to refuse to enforce a law because they did not think the law ought to have been passed. And, my friends, if the people of Tennessee were to go into a state like New York: the one from which this impulse comes to resist this law, or go into any state: if they went into any state and tried to convince the people that a law they had passed ought not to be enforced, just because the people who went there didn't think it ought to have been passed, don't you think it would be resented as an impertinence?

. . .

We have sufficient proof in the book: doesn't the book state the very thing that is objected to, and outlawed in this state? Who has a copy of that book?

The Court: Do you mean the Bible?

Mr. Bryan: No, sir; the biology. (Laughter in the courtroom.)

A Voice: Here it is; Hunter's Biology.

Mr. Bryan: No, not the Bible, you see in this state they cannot teach the Bible. They can only teach things that declare it to be a lie, according to the learned counsel. These people in the state: Christian people: have tied their hands by their constitution. They say we all believe in the Bible for it is the overwhelming belief in the state, but we will not teach that Bible, which we believe even to our children through teachers that we pay with our money. No, no, it isn't the teaching of the Bible, and we are not asking it. The question is can a minority in this state come in and compel a teacher to teach that the Bible is not true and make the parents of these children pay the expenses of the teacher to tell their children what these people believe is false and dangerous? Has it come to a time when the minority can take charge of a state like Tennessee and compel the majority to pay their teachers while they take religion out of the heart of the children of the parents who pay the teachers? This is the book that is outlawed if we can judge from the questions asked by the counsel for the defense. They think that because the board of education selected this book, four or five years ago, that, therefore, he had to teach it, that he would be guilty if he didn't teach it and punished if he does.

. . .

What does this law teach, my friends? We have little what is the Morgan boy's first name?

A Voice: Howard.

Mr. Bryan: Little Howard Morgan :and, Your Honor, that boy is going to make a great lawyer some day. I didn't realize it until I saw how a 14-year-old boy understood the subject so much better than a distinguished lawyer who attempted to quiz him. The little boy understood what he was talking about and to my surprise the attorney's didn't seem to catch the significance of the theory of evolution and the thought: and I'm sure he wouldn't have said it if he hadn't had thought it: he thought that little boy was talking about the individuals coming up from one cell.

...

No wonder the gentleman from New York was not able to distinguish by just hearing it once, between the evolution of life that began in the ocean away down in the bottom and evolved up through animals bigger and bigger, until finally they got a land animal some way and then when it got on the land where it had a firmer footing it kept on evolving more and more and then finally man was the climax. That little boy could understand that and I wonder if the lawyers cannot understand it by this time. (Laughter in the courtroom.) That is evolution and that is what he taught. Not the growth of an individual from one cell, but the growth of all life from one cell

...

That is the great game to put in the public schools to find man among animals, if you can. Tell me that the parents of this day have not any right to declare that children are not to be taught this doctrine? Shall not be taken down from the high plane upon which God put man? Shall be detached from the throne of God and be compelled to link their ancestors with the jungle, tell that to these children? Why, my friend, if they believe it, they go back to scoff at the religion of their parents! And the parents have a right to say that no teacher paid by their money shall rob their children of faith in God and send them back to their homes, skeptical, infidels, or agnostics, or atheists.[36]

Bryan mocked Metcalf's exposition of the theory of evolution, complaining that:

> the tree of evolution then branched off into two great stems, the new world and the old world monkeys, and from the latter, at a remote period, man, the wonder and glory of the universe, proceeded not even from American monkeys, but from old world monkeys. (Laughter.) Now, here we have our glorious pedigree, and each child is expected to copy the family tree and take it home to his family to be submitted for the Bible family tree: that is what Darwin says.[37]

Dudley F. Malone responded for the defense, arguing that Bryan's theory of the world was disproved long ago:

> Are we to hold mankind to a literal understanding of the claim that the world is 6,000 years old, because of the limited vision of men who believed the world was flat, and that the earth was the center of the universe, and that man is the center of the earth. [. . .] Haven't we learned anything in seventy-five years? Are we to have our children know nothing about science except what the church says they shall know?[38]

. . .

> But these gentlemen say the Bible contains the truth: if the world of science can produce any truth or facts not in the Bible as we understand it, then destroy science, but keep our Bible." And we say "keep your Bible." [. .] Keep your Bible in the world of theology where it belongs and do not try to tell an intelligent world and the intelligence of this country that these books written by men who knew none of the accepted fundamental facts of science can be put into a course of science, because what are they doing here? This law says what? It says that no theory of creation can be taught in a course of science, except one which conforms with the theory

of divine creation as set forth in the Bible. In other words, it says that only the Bible shall be taken as an authority on the subject of evolution in a course on biology.[39]

. . .

There is never a duel with the truth. The truth always wins and we are not afraid of it. The truth is no coward. The truth does not need the law. The truth does not need the forces of government. The truth does not need Mr. Bryan. The truth is imperishable, eternal and immortal and needs no human agency to support it. We are ready to tell the truth as we understand it and we do not fear all the truth that they can present as facts. We are ready. We are ready. We feel we stand with progress. We feel we stand with science. We feel we stand with intelligence. We feel we stand with fundamental freedom in America. We are not afraid. Where is the fear? We meet it, where is the fear? We defy it, we ask Your Honor to admit the evidence as a matter of correct law, as a matter of sound procedure and as a matter of justice to the defense in this case. (Profound and continued applause.)[40]

Despite these eloquent questions and argument, the Judge struck Metcalf's testimony the following day. The court in fact struck all the testimony of the defense's experts, Maynard M. Metcalf, Jacob G. Lipham, Wilbur Nelson, Doctor Fay Cooper Cole, Doctor H. H. Newman, Doctor Winterton C. Curtis, Doctor Kirtley F. Mather, and proof by Biblical scholars, Doctor Rabbi Rosenwasser and Doctor Whitaker, allowing their testimony only by written affidavit in the record, depriving the defense of much of their "propaganda" as the State argued.

Gen. Stewart: The state moves to exclude the testimony of the scientists by which the counsel for the defendant claim that they may be able to show that there is no conflict between science and religion, or in question, and the story of divine creation of man, on the grounds that under the wording of the act and interpretation of the act, which we insist interprets itself, this evidence would be entirely incompetent.[41]

With little fanfare, the court excluded the scientific evidence and said:

> I held it was immaterial and incompetent because it would not reflect upon the issues involved in the case.[42]

Perhaps in protest, perhaps in disgust, H.L. Mencken left town after Judge Raulston's exclusion of the defense's scientific evidence. Mencken's article lamented:

> All that remains of the great cause of the State of Tennessee against the infidel Scopes is the formal business of bumping off the defendant. There may be some legal jousting on Monday and some gaudy oratory on Tuesday, but the main battle is over, with Genesis completely triumphant. Judge Raulston finished the benign business yesterday morning by leaping with soft judicial hosannas into the arms of the prosecution. The sole commentary of the sardonic Darrow consisted of bringing down a metaphorical custard pie upon the occiput of the learned jurist.
>
> "I hope," said the latter nervously, "that counsel intends no reflection upon this court."
>
> Darrow hunched his shoulders and looked out of the window dreamily.
>
> "Your honor," he said, "is, of course, entitled to hope.". . .
>
> The Scopes trial, from the start, has been carried on in a manner exactly fitted to the anti-evolution law and the simian imbecility under it. There hasn't been the slightest pretense to decorum. The rustic judge, a candidate for re-election, has postured the yokels like a clown in a ten-cent side show, and almost every word he has uttered has been an undisguised appeal to their prejudices and superstitions. The chief prosecuting attorney, beginning like a competent lawyer and a man of self-respect, ended like a convert at a Billy Sunday revival. It fell to him, finally, to make a clear and astounding statement of theory of justice prevailing under fundamentalism. What he said, in brief, was

that a man accused of infidelity had no rights whatever under Tennessee law.

...

Darrow has lost this case. It was lost long before he came to Dayton. But it seems to me that he has nevertheless performed a great public service by fighting it to a finish and in a perfectly serious way. Let no one mistake it for comedy, farcical though it may be in all its details. It serves notice on the country that Neanderthal man is organizing in these forlorn backwaters of the land, led by a fanatic, rid of sense and devoid of conscience. Tennessee, challenging him too timorously and too late, now sees its courts converted into camp meetings and its Bill of Rights made a mock of by its sworn officers of the law. There are other States that had better look to their arsenals before the Hun is at their gates.[43]

In his article, Mencken had highlighted an acrimonious exchange between Darrow and Judge Raulston, where the judge let Darrow's insult sit unhandled overnight, before considering whether to hold him in contempt. The following day, Darrow apologized for his sharp words to the judge, and Judge Raulston forgave him:

My friends, and Col. Darrow, the Man that I believe came into the world to save man from sin, the Man that died on the cross that man might be redeemed, taught that it was godly to forgive and were it not for the forgiving nature of Himself I would fear for man. The Savior died on the cross pleading with God for the men who crucified Him. I believe in that Christ. I believe in these principles. I accept Col. Darrow's apology. I am sure his remarks were not premeditated.[44]

Having narrowly avoided a contempt citation, the defense team found themselves in a quandary. The prosecution had succeeded in excluding all their witnesses and evidence, which offers of proof the court allowed in the record only outside the presence of the jury for the purpose of establishing a record on appeal. There was little sense in having Scopes testify since the prosecution had already proven he had taught evolution. Colonel Hays succeeded in introducing other Bibles into the record, but to little avail other than to prove there was more than one religion and one "Bible." While perhaps instructive, it missed the point.

But Darrow understood the bigger picture of the trial, which was to show the world that science could triumph over religion to explain the world order. Darrow recognized that faith had its place but argued that faith did not belong in the classroom. The defense team came up with a two-step, masterful strategy to prove their point.

The defense recognized that they would lose the battle of the verdict in the Scopes trial but could quite possibly win the war of science versus religion.

First, Darrow called Bryan to the stand, hoping to show religion could not explain the wonders of the universe. As their final stroke of genius, the defense team would waive closing arguments, thus depriving Bryan of his opportunity to do the one thing he had come to Dayton to do: argue that the state is entitled to not deny the Bible by teaching the theory of evolution.

In a surprising acquiescence to the defense strategy, the court moved the proceedings to the lawn in front of the courthouse, but the jury didn't follow. Indeed, court proceedings are rarely, if ever, conducted outside—usually only site visits require a court to travel outdoors, but even then, no testimony is allowed. Military courts martial on ships and in the field are one of the other rare exceptions for outdoor court proceedings. Proud of the town's arrangements for the yet-unused stage on the lawn, Judge Raulston claimed the courthouse building couldn't handle the weight of the crowd and moved the proceedings out-of-doors.

For two hours, Darrow questioned Bryan, while Bryan willingly responded, despite General Stewart's regular objections. Darrow was ready for this exchange—he had two years earlier on July 4, 1923, posted in the Chicago Tribune an open letter to Bryan consisting of some 55 questions on the Bible (those questions can be found in Appendix B). Bryan ignored Darrow's letter when he received it and failed to study it again prior to his cross-examination. For his performance, the press excoriated Bryan, but fundamentalists praised his responses. Darrow got the better of Bryan throughout the exchange:

> Q: You have given considerable study to the Bible, haven't you, Mr. Bryan?

A: Yes, sir, I have tried to.

. . .

Q: Then you have a made a general study of it?

A: Yes, I have; I have studied the Bible for about fifty years, or sometime more than that, but, of course, I have studied it more as I have become older than when I was but a boy.

Q: Do you claim that everything in the Bible should be literally interpreted?

A: I believe everything in the Bible should be accepted as it is given there; some of the Bible is given illustratively. For instance: "Ye are the salt of the earth." I would not insist that man was actually salt, or that he had flesh of salt, but it is used in the sense of salt as saving God's people.

. . .

Q: Now, you say, the big fish swallowed Jonah, and he there remained how long: three days: and then he spewed him upon the land. You believe that the big fish was made to swallow Jonah?

A: I am not prepared to say that; the Bible merely says it was done.

Q: You don't know whether it was the ordinary run of fish, or made for that purpose?

A: You may guess; you evolutionists guess.

Q: But when we do guess, we have a sense to guess right.

A: But do not do it often.

. . .

Q: But do you believe He made them: that He made such a fish and that it was big enough to swallow Jonah?

A: Yes, sir. Let me add: One miracle is just as easy to believe as another.

. . .

Q: Just as hard?

A: It is hard to believe for you, but easy for me. A miracle is a thing performed beyond what man can perform. When you get beyond what man can do, you get within the realm of miracles; and it is just as easy to believe the miracle of Jonah as any other miracle in the Bible.

Q: Perfectly easy to believe that Jonah swallowed the whale?

A: If the Bible said so; the Bible doesn't make as extreme statements as evolutionists do.

. . .

Q: Do you believe Joshua made the sun stand still?

A: I believe what the Bible says. I suppose you mean that the earth stood still?

Q: I don't know. I am talking about the Bible now.

A: I accept the Bible absolutely.

Q: The Bible says Joshua commanded the sun to stand still for the purpose of lengthening the day, doesn't it, and you believe it?

A: I do.

Q: Do you believe at that time the entire sun went around the earth?

A: No, I believe that the earth goes around the sun.

Q: Do you believe that the men who wrote it thought that the day could be lengthened or that the sun could be stopped?

A: I don't know what they thought.

Q: You don't know?

A: I think they wrote the fact without expressing their own thoughts.

...

Mr. Darrow: Have you an opinion as to whether: whoever wrote the book, I believe it is, Joshua, the Book of Joshua, thought the sun went around the earth or not?

A: I believe that he was inspired.

Mr. Darrow: Can you answer my question?

A: When you let me finish the statement.

Q: It is a simple question, but finish it.

The Witness: You cannot measure the length of my answer by the length of your question.

(Laughter in the courtyard.)

Mr. Darrow: No, except that the answer be longer. (Laughter in the courtyard.)

A: I believe that the Bible is inspired, an inspired author, whether one who wrote as he was directed to write understood the things he was writing about, I don't know.

...

Q: The [Bible] you have introduced in evidence tells you, doesn't it?

A: I don't think it does, Mr. Darrow.

Q: Let's see whether it does; is this the one?

A: That is the one, I think.

Q: It says B. C. 4004?

A: That is Bishop Usher's calculation.

Q: That is printed in the Bible you introduced?

A: Yes, sir.

Q: And numerous other Bibles?

A: Yes, sir.

· · ·

Q: When was that flood?

A: I would not attempt to fix the date. The date is fixed, as suggested this morning.

Q: About 4004 B. C.?

A: That has been the estimate of a man that is accepted today. I would not say it is accurate.

Q: That estimate is printed in the Bible?

A: Everybody knows, at least, I think most of the people know, that was the estimate given.

Q: But what do you think that the Bible, itself, says? Don't you know how it was arrived at?

A: I never made a calculation.

Q: A calculation from what?

A: I could not say.

Q: From the generations of man?

A: I would not want to say that.

Q: What do you think?

A: I do not think about things I don't think about.

Q: Do you think about things you do think about?

A: Well, sometimes. (Laughter in the courtyard.)

· · ·

Q: You want to say now you have no idea how these dates were computed?

A: No. I don't say, but I have told you what my idea was. I say I don't know how accurate it was.

...

Q: What about the religion of Confucius or Buddha?

A: Well, I can tell you something about that, if you would like to know.

Q: Did you ever investigate them?

A: Somewhat.

Q: Do you regard them as competitive?

A: No, I think they are very inferior. Would you like for me to tell you what I know about it?

...

Mr. Darrow: Oh, tell it, Mr. Bryan, I won't object to it.

Mr. Bryan: I had occasion to study Confucianism when I went to China. I got all I could find about what Confucius said, and then I bought a book that told us what Menches said about what Confucius said, and I found that there were several direct and strong contrasts between the teachings of Jesus and the teaching of Confucius. In the first place, one of his followers asked if there was any word that would express all that was necessary to know in the relations of life, and he said, "Isn't reciprocity such a word?" I know of no better illustration of the difference between Christianity and Confucianism than the contrast that is brought out there. Reciprocity is a calculating selfishness. If a person does something for you, you do something for him and keep it even. That is the basis of the philosophy of Confucius. Christ's doctrine was not reciprocity. We were told to help people not in proportion as they had helped us: not in proportion as they might have helped us, but in proportion to their needs, and there is all the difference in the world between a religion that teaches you just to keep even with other people and the religion that teaches you to spend yourself for other people and to help them as they need help.

...

The Witness: I mentioned the word reciprocity to show the difference between Christ's teachings in that respect and the teachings of Confucius. I call your attention to another difference. One of the followers of Confucius asked him "what do you think of the doctrine that you should reward evil with good?" and the answer of Confucius was "reward evil with justice and reward good with good. Love your enemies. Overcome evil with good," and there is a difference between the two teachings: a difference incalculable in its effect and in: The third difference: people who scoff at religion and try to make it appear that Jesus brought nothing into the world, talk about the Golden Rule of Confucius. Confucius said "do not unto others what you would not have others do unto you." It was purely negative. Jesus taught "do unto others as you would have others do unto you." There is all the difference in the world between a negative harmlessness and a positive helpfulness and the Christian religion is a religion of helpfulness, of service, embodied in the language of Jesus when he said "let him who would be chiefest among you be the servant of all." Those are the three differences between the teachings of Jesus and the teachings of Confucius, and they are very strong differences on very important questions. Now, Mr. Darrow, you asked me if I knew anything about Buddha.

Q: You want to make a speech on Buddha, too?

A: No, sir; I want to answer your question on Buddha.

Q: I asked you if you knew anything about him?

A: I do.

Q: Well, that's answered, then.

· · ·

Q: Do you think the earth was made in six days?

A: Not six days of twenty-four hours.

· · ·

Q: Does the statement, "The morning and the evening were the first day," and "The morning and the evening were the second day," mean anything to you?

A: I do not think it necessarily means a twenty-four-hour day.

Q: You do not?

A: No.

Q: What do you consider it to be?

A: I have not attempted to explain it. If you will take the second chapter: let me have the book. (Examining Bible.) The fourth verse of the second chapter says: "These are the generations of the heavens and of the earth, when they were created in the day that the Lord God made the earth and the heavens," the word "day" there in the very next chapter is used to describe a period. I do not see that there is any necessity for construing the words, "the evening and the morning," as meaning necessarily a twenty-four-hour day, "in the day when the Lord made the heaven and the earth."

Q: Then, when the Bible said, for instance, "and God called the firmament heaven. And the evening and the morning were the second day," that does not necessarily mean twenty-four hours?

A: I do not think it necessarily does.

Q: Do you think it does or does not?

A: I know a great many think so.

Q: What do you think?

A: I do not think it does.

Q: You think those were not literal days?

A: I do not think they were twenty-four-hour days.

Q: What do you think about it?

A: That is my opinion: I do not know that my opinion is better on that subject than those who think it does.

Q: You do not think that?

A: No. But I think it would be just as easy for the kind of God we believe in to make the earth in six days as in six years or in 6,000,000 years or in 600,000,000 years. I do not think it important whether we believe one or the other.

Q: Do you think those were literal days?

A: My impression is they were periods, but I would not attempt to argue as against anybody who wanted to believe in literal days.

Q: Have you any idea of the length of the periods?

A: No; I don't.

Q: Do you think the sun was made on the fourth day?

A: Yes.

Q: And they had evening and morning without the sun?

A: I am simply saying it is a period.

Q: They had evening and morning for four periods without the sun, do you think?

A: I believe in creation as there told, and if I am not able to explain it I will accept it. Then you can explain it to suit yourself.

Q: Mr. Bryan, what I want to know is, do you believe the sun was made on the fourth day?

A: I believe just as it says there.

. . .

Q: And they had the evening and the morning before that time for three days or three periods. All right, that settles it. Now, if you call those periods, they may have been a very long time.

A: They might have been.

Q: The creation might have been going on for a very long time?

A: It might have continued for millions of years.

. . .

Q: Mr. Bryan, do you believe that the first woman was Eve?

A: Yes.

Q: Do you believe she was literally made out of Adam's rib?

A: I do.

Q: Did you ever discover where Cain got his wife?

A: No, sir; I leave the agnostics to hunt for her.

. . .

Q: The Bible says he got one, doesn't it? Were there other people on the earth at that time?

A: I cannot say.

Q: You cannot say. Did that ever enter your consideration?

A: Never bothered me.

Q: There were no others recorded, but Cain got a wife.

A: That is what the Bible says.[45]

After Darrow and Bryan got into an argument over who was trying to slur the Bible, the court abruptly suspended Darrow's questioning and adjourned until the following morning, Tuesday, July 21, 1925, the eighth and last day of the trial. Judge Raulston then prevented Bryan from cross-examining Darrow. He also struck Darrow's questions and Bryan's answers from the record and would not allow the jury to hear them, refusing to make the exchange between the two parts of the jury's transcript (it is printed in the final record), perhaps realizing that Bryan had done more damage than good.

For closing arguments, both sides agreed to dispense with arguments and instead simply ask the jury for a guilty verdict: the State because it wanted a conviction, the defense because it wanted a test case to take to the appellate courts, virtually disregarding the jury and the lower court itself. Tactically by this maneuver the defense prevented William Jennings Bryan from presenting a closing argument to the jury. Bryan was sorely disappointed. Still, Darrow got to say "in a few words to the jury" that he wanted a verdict of guilty so the defense could file an appeal.

> I do not know how you may feel, I am not especially interested in it, but this case and this law will never be decided until it gets to a higher court, and it cannot get to a higher court probably, very well, unless you bring in a verdict. So, I do not want any of you to think we are going to find any fault with you as to your verdict. I am frank to say, while we think it is wrong, and we ought to have been permitted to put in our evidence, the court felt otherwise, as he had a right to hold. We cannot argue to you gentlemen under the instructions given by the court: we cannot even explain to you that we think you should return a verdict of not guilty. We do not see how you could. We do not ask it. We think we will save our point and take it to the higher court and settle whether the law is good, and also whether he should have permitted the evidence. I guess that is plain enough.[46]

After an eight-day trial, the jury retired for only nine minutes before finding Scopes guilty. Contrary to the court's instructions to them, they did not fine Scopes, so Judge Raulston imposed a $100 fine, the lowest possible fine, which the judge thought he had the power to do based on his experience in his "whiskey cases" arising out of prohibition laws. Attorney General Stewart disagreed about the judge's power to impose the fine but got overruled. While that fine may not seem significant now, consider that at the time Scopes' salary to teach was $150 per month from September through May. The *Baltimore Evening Sun* put up Scopes' appeal bond. Judge Raulston also overruled Hay's motion for an arrest of the judgment and for a new trial.

The players in the trial then engaged in a magnanimous showing of appreciation to the townspeople, the court and each other, including expressions of thanks by the news media. Hays offered to send Judge Raulston a copy of Darwin's books, *Origin of the Species* and *Descent of Man*, which Raulston accepted. Reports after the trial are unclear whether he ever cracked the spine of either book. The court then adjourned, and Doctor Brown pronounced a benediction.

Disappointed in his inability to present his closing argument, Bryan five days later arranged for its publication, just hours before he died in his sleep. Bryan's concluding words were eerily accurate:

> Again force and love meet face to face, and the question, "What shall I do with Jesus?" must be answered. A bloody, brutal doctrine: Evolution: demands, as the rabble did nineteen hundred years ago, that He be crucified. That cannot be the answer of this jury representing a Christian state and sworn to uphold the laws of Tennessee. Your answer will be heard throughout the world; it is eagerly awaited by a praying multitude. If the law is nullified, there will be rejoicing wherever God is repudiated, the Savior scoffed at and the Bible ridiculed. Every unbeliever of every kind and degree will be happy. If, on the other hand, the law is upheld and the religion of the school children protected, millions of Christians will call you blessed and, with hearts full of gratitude to God, will sing again that grand old song of triumph:

> "Faith of our fathers, living still,
>
> In spite of dungeon, fire and sword;
>
> O how our hearts beat high with joy
>
> Whene'er we hear that glorious word:
>
> Faith of our fathers: holy faith;
>
> We will be true to thee till death!"[47]

Bryan remained true to his beliefs.

The Appeal

The defense appealed to the Tennessee Supreme Court, but the court refused to rule on the substantive dispute (although addressing the substantive issues), instead overruling the case on the technical ground that the jury should have imposed the fine, not the judge. The court encouraged the prosecution to drop the case and not retry it.

The argument is that the theory of the descent of man from a lower order of animals is now established by the preponderance of scientific thought and that the prohibition of the teaching of such theory is a violation of the legislative duty to cherish Science.

. . .

> We are not able to see how the prohibition of teaching the theory that man has descended from a lower order of animals gives preference to any religious establishment or mode of worship. So far as we know, there is no religious establishment or organized body that has in its creed or confession of faith any article denying or affirming such a theory. So far as we know, the denial or affirmation of such a theory does not enter into any recognized mode of worship. Since this cause has been pending in this court, we have been favored, in addition to briefs of counsel and various *amici curiae* [Latin: friends of the court], with a multitude of resolutions, addresses, and communications from scientific bodies, religious factions, and individuals giving us the benefit of their views upon the theory of evolution. Examination of these contributions indicates that

Protestants, Catholics, and Jews are divided among themselves in their beliefs, and that there is no unanimity among the members of any religious establishment as to this subject.

. . .

This record disclosed that the jury found the defendant below guilty, but did not assess the fine. The trial judge himself undertook to impose the minimum fine of $100 authorized by the Statute. This was error. Under section 14 of article 6 of the Constitution of Tennessee, a fine in excess of $50 must be assessed by a jury. The Statute before us does not permit the imposition of a smaller fine than $100.

Since a jury alone can impose the penalty this Act requires, and as a matter of course no different penalty can be inflicted, the trial judge exceeded his jurisdiction in levying this fine, and we are without power to correct his error. The judgment must accordingly be reversed. *Upchurch v. State*, 153 Tenn. 198.

The court is informed that the plaintiff in error is no longer in the service of the State. We see nothing to be gained by prolonging the life of this bizarre case. On the contrary, we think the peace and dignity of the State, which all criminal prosecutions are brought to redress, will be better conserved by the entry of a *nolle prosequi* [Latin for "do not pursue"] herein. Such a course is suggested to the Attorney-General.[48]

The Attorney General took the Tennessee Supreme Court's advice and did not pursue the case further, much to the disgust of the defense team. Scopes did not pay the fine, and his bond was released back to the newspaper.

Epilogue to the Scopes Trial

Forty-two years would slip by before the State of Tennessee Legislature elected to reconsider the Butler Act that had banned teaching evolution in public schools. Finally repealed in 1967, the statute took only seven words to undo the acrimonious history of the dispute. Even so, the debate started by the Scopes trial continues today in other states across the county.

> PUBLIC ACTS OF THE STATE OF TENNESSEE PASSED BY THE EIGHTY - FIFTH GENERAL ASSEMBLY, 1967, CHAPTER NO. 237, House Bill No. 48
>
> AN ACT to repeal Section 498 - 1922, Tennessee Code Annotated, prohibiting the teaching of evolution.
>
> Be it enacted by the General Assembly of the State of Tennessee :
>
> Section 1. Section 49 - 1922, Tennessee Code Annotated, is repealed.
>
> Section 2. This Act shall take effect September 1, 1967.
>
> Passed: May 13, 1967
>
> James H. Cummings, Speaker of the House of Representatives
>
> Frank C. Gorrell, Speaker of the Senate
>
> Approved : May 17, 1967. Buford Ellington, Governor

But the United States Supreme Court had the last word. The following year, in 1968, the Court overturned a similar law in Arkansas in the case entitled: Epperson v. Arkansas, 393 U.S. 97 (1968), which ruled that a ban on teaching evolution violated the First Amendment's Establishment Clause because the primary purpose of the statute was religious. Thirty years after his death, Darrow's cause had won—at least in the courts.

Though the pulpit is another story.

Chapter Conclusion

Winning this trial was as hard as asking a candy store to stop carrying chocolate before Valentine's Day—it was a hard sell, and one Darrow did not expect to win at the trial court level. Judge Raulston did not provide a level playing field, allowing prayer in the courtroom, allowing the Bible to come in as evidence, disallowing the defense's scientific testimony, and playing up the out-of-town status of the defense team and their fanciful ideas. Even the judge's use of the higher ranking "General" title for the prosecutors and the lower ranking "Colonel" title for the defense attorneys created an appearance of bias.

Darrow and the defense team expected cooler heads on the appellate court to rule in their favor and were sorely disappointed when the Tennessee Supreme Court ruled against them. As we saw in the Salem Witch Trials chapter, religion does not mix well with court proceedings. Darrow's work laid the groundwork for a favorable resolution reached decades later, much like the changes to discriminatory laws as described in the John Brown chapter.

Where a belief system—like fundamental religion—is so pervasive and ingrained in the community that it is beyond question, only time and regular challenges can change the underlying framework. That framework virtually guaranteed the jury's decision—Darrow was tilting at a windmill. Had he chosen a community without a solid religious base and found a judge without religious biases, he may well have won the case, but without any impact. That's exactly what he intended.

Daniel first had to be thrown into the lion's den to win.

Remember to enter your vote on the outcome of this trial on www.10FamousTrials.com and see how other readers voted.

CHAPTER 8
The Lindy Chamberlain Trial

A good cross-examination reveals most, if not all, of the points a lawyer intends to prove in a case. The chapters of this book so far have started with a summary background for each trial, but one of the key cross-examinations in this case tells us what we need to know. Answering the questions in the following exchange was Lindy Chamberlain, baby Azaria's mother; the person asking them was Ian Barker, QC, senior prosecuting counsel for the Crown:

> Q: When was it you called out that the dingo has the baby?
>
> • • •
>
> A: Just before I went into the tent and again just afterwards.
>
> Q: When you called that out the first time there was no doubt in your mind that the dingo had the baby, was there?
>
> A: ... That's correct.
>
> Q: Where was the dingo then?
>
> A: ... It had left and gone, this direction. South.
>
> Q: On your story, it must have been carrying the baby?
>
> A: ... Yes.
>
> Q: You were convinced, when you yelled out, that it was carrying the baby, were you?
>
> A: ... Yes.
>
> Q: But you did not chase it?
>
> A: ... I did chase it.
>
> Q: When?

A: . . . I checked the tent first, just in case it dropped it, and then chased it.

Q: What were you checking the tent for?

A: . . . To see whether she'd been dropped.

Q: You were convinced when you saw the dingo emerge that it had the baby, were you not?

A: . . . I was convinced that it had something, right by the door, which I thought was the baby. I wasn't quite sure whether it had dropped her when I'd called and frightened it, or whether it'd taken her as soon as I got a few yards nearer from seeing the dingo in - first seeing it back here. As soon as I got up to about this area, here, I could see that the tent was empty, but I still wanted to check for myself to make certain.

Q: Do you think she might have been dropped inside the tent?

A: . . . I hoped she had.

Q: Of course, if she had been near the entrance, you would have seen her, from the rail, would you not?

A: . . . Not necessarily.

Q: Why?

A: . . . Because the pillows were - the pillows and the things on the pillows would've been 7 or 8 inches high, and she wasn't very big.

Q: What was the dog doing when you yelled out?

A: . . . Shaking its head.

Q: It was the focus of your immediate attention, of course?

A: . . . Yes.

Q: Here was a dog emerging from the tent, shaking its head, with, as you believed, your baby in its mouth? Is that right?

A: . . . With, as I believed, a shoe in its mouth.

Q:	When did you decide it was the baby?
A:	... Well, I realized just a split second after that, that she'd cried and been disturbed, and started to run, and as I neared the tent, I could see it was empty. That's when I realized it was the baby.
Q:	The dog was then, what, going past the front of the tent?
A:	... I couldn't tell you where the dog was, when I thought that.
Q:	When you were at the rail, the dog was within your vision, was it not?
A:	... I think - no; it'd gone before that.
Q:	... You watched it leave?
A:	... I watched it leave just a few feet, that's all; just in a split second.
Q:	It turned and went south, did it?
A:	... It came out the tent, going south.
Q:	You watched it?
A:	... Like I said, just for a split second. I wasn't concentrating on what it was doing.
Q:	Is it the position that you did not see the baby in its mouth?
A:	... That's correct.
Q:	Did you see anything in its mouth?
A:	... No.
Q:	Why?
A:	... Its nose was below the light level from the barbecue. It was obscured by the scrub and the railing, from where I was at that time.
Q:	Do you say that it had vanished by the time you got to the rail?
A:	... That's right.

...

Q: You say, do you, seriously, that you did not see the baby in the dog's mouth?

A: ... That's right.

Q: At any stage?

A: ... That's right.

Q: As it went past the tent, did it appear to be carrying anything?

A: ... I couldn't see what it was carrying, I could only just see the top of its head.[1]

Fans of Sir John Mortimer's *Rumpole of the Bailey* (available both as books and a grainy television series on BBC) will recognize the initials "QC," or Queen's Counsel, after Mr. Barker's name as the designation for an English barrister, or trial lawyer. Highly qualified lawyers (such as demonstrated by this cross-examination) can receive that designation after practicing for at least ten years, also commonly known as "taking silk," referring to the black silk robe typically worn by barristers in United Kingdom courts. Lawyers in practice less than ten years, generally without extensive trial experience, are referred to as Solicitors. A dingo is a feral dog in Australia, with features like coyotes and wolves.

Background

Here's the setup for the case: In August of 1980, a sometime preacher for the Church of Jesus Christ of Latter-Day Saints, Michael Chamberlain, his wife, Lindy, and their three children, six-year-old Aiden, four-year-old Reagan and 10-week-old baby Azaria went on vacation. They took an 18-hour drive over several days in the family car from Mount Isa in Queensland (an Australian state) to Uluru, in the Northern Territory (a sparsely populated federal territory in Australia), to camp and explore Uluru/Ayers Rock in Australia's Northern Territory.

The family arrived late in the evening on the 16th, and Michael and the boys went hiking on Uluru/Ayers Rock for the day. In 1980, it was known as Ayers Rock/Uluru. Lindy and Azaria visited Fertility Cave at the base of the Rock, where she believed a dingo watched her and her child. That evening, back at the campground around a barbeque grill, the Chamberlain family gathered and met other couples, including Sally and Greg Lowe from Tasmania. What happened next has been the subject of three Coroner's Inquests, a forty-five-day trial, three appeals, multiple books, one movie and innumerable newspaper articles and extensive television coverage. After Azaria disappeared the evening of August 17, 1980, Lindy Chamberlain's life changed forever, starting with a police interview trying to figure out what happened.

In her initial police interview, Lindy Chamberlain described the clothes Azaria wore that night:

> She was wearing a throwaway nappy, a singlet, white stretch suit—it was all white, with white booties underneath - and a little white matinee-jacket, with very pale lemon edging around the collar and cuffs. It was one of those matinee-jackets that's just got two or three buttons on the yoke, and then none coming down, and the button holes were a bit loose. She was wrapped up as I showed you this morning, in the blue bunny-rug and the larger of the two blankets.[2]

At her trial, tears would stream down Lindy Chamberlain's face when she once again recounted what Azaria wore the night she laid her down to sleep in the Chamberlain tent at Ayers Rock/Uluru, but those tear came far too late. In the meantime, the police inquiries did not stop.

The police report by Detective Michael Gilroy of the Northern Territory police fueled much speculation about satanic rituals and supposedly other odd behavior by the Chamberlains, including failing to complete the baby's registration, dressing in black in a Catholic hospital and choosing a name for Azaria that supposedly meant "Sacrifice in the Wilderness," all of which Mrs. Chamberlain denied.

> Azaria Chamberlain was born at 1:16 p.m. on Wednesday the 11th of June 1980 at Mt. Isa Hospital, at a weight of 2880 grams (6 pounds 5 1/2 ounces). The mother was reported to have repeatedly complained about the child being sick, stating that she was suffering from pyloric stenosis, a ailment which closes the sphinctum and causes vomiting. She would not heed hospital staff when they told her the baby was completely normal.

She allegedly told the staff that her other children suffered from the same complaint and that she had cured it herself when she had fallen down a hole carrying them as babies.

It is reported that she appeared not to have cared for the baby, and at one stage did not feed it for over eight hours. Registration of the baby was never completed.

When bringing the baby in for a check-up she astounded the Sisters by having the baby dressed completely in black. A doctor who treated the baby said that she did not react like a normal mother.

The same doctor said that he looked up the name Azaria in a Dictionary of Names and Meanings and found that it means 'Sacrifice in the Wilderness.'

On visiting the library on Saturday morning, I found that this book is in stock but has been mislaid. It is believed is should be available on Monday.

The parents appeared on the TV show 'This Day Tonight" on Channel Seven, on Friday evening, 29 August 1980. Mrs. Chamberlain allegedly made the comment that the blanket which covered Azaria was a strong one and difficult to cut with a knife. (The blanket which we took possession of at Ayers Rock had numerous small cuts in it which, even to the layman, looked more like cuts from a sharp instrument than punctures one would expect from a dog's teeth.)

To date we have actually not one witness who can say they saw the baby at Ayers Rock, but people who have assumed she was holding a baby when they have seen her holding a white bundle to her breast.

The impression given in her statement to me was that the two boys climbed the Rock with their father, and she was left at the bottom with the baby in the car. Later on in her statement, she states when she was at the Fertility Caves with the baby (when the dingo 'cased' it). The two boys were with her but the husband was not. They would appear to have descended by themselves. [To those who had visited

> Ayers Rock, they would know how dangerous it would have been, if true, for a six- and four-year-old to climb down the side of the Rock alone.] Where the clothes were found was not more than four hundred metres from there. Constable Morris was instructed to check out the floor of the caves for patches of soft earth, etcetera. Many tourists have been visited them since, and he has, no doubt, contacted them. He is also reinterviewing the ranger who saw Mrs. Chamberlain at the bottom of the climb that Sunday afternoon, who saw her holding the apparel of a baby.[3]

The Chamberlains denied dressing the baby in black and most of the rest of Detective Gilroy's report. According to the Baby Names book, the rare, mostly female name Azaria "is of Hebrew origin, and its meaning is 'helped by God,' from the male biblical name Azariah. Used occasionally in England from the 17th century, it honored the biblical prophet who recalled King Asa to a proper observance of religion."[4] Nevertheless, the police report fueled rampant speculation across the Australian nation, fanned by eager news media.

The news media's involvement in this matter, as well as other cases described here, call into question the wisdom of sensationalist reporting as compared to factual coverage of a trial. You decide for yourself each time you either pick up a tabloid or a respectable paper or not.

As with most deaths involving unusual circumstances, a Coroner's Inquest was conducted. Like most of the rest of this case, nothing went smoothly; there were three Coroner's Inquests in all. The first was favorable to the Chamberlains:

> Coroner Denis Barritt was so moved by the plight of the Chamberlains, and by public hatred, that he arranged for TV to broadcast his findings live. His identification of the dingo as the slayer, his criticism of bureaucrats for failing to protect visitors from dingoes, and his apology to the Chamberlains for appalling public bigotry, went out to the living rooms of the nation. His words angered many in government, bureaucrats, police and Territorians.[5]

Anger like that is not easily forgotten, as we will once again see at the end of the chapter. Dissatisfied with the corner's determination, however, the Crown's prosecutors sought to set the findings aside and reopen an investigation. The courts were only pleased to do so, and a second inquest began with the coroner then turning the matter over to the Crown prosecutors to file a case against Lindy Chamberlain for murder and against her husband, Michael Chamberlain, as an accessory-after-the fact. Those findings came from the second Coroner's Inquest, made by Northern Territory Coroner G. P. Galvin and contained in a February 1982 letter marked "personal and confidential" sent to Peter Tiffin, Crown Prosecutor, finding that Azaria's death was a homicide caused by Mrs. Chamberlain and Mr. Chamberlain was an accessory after the fact.

> I do find that the death of Azaria Chamberlain was a homicide. I propose to now consider what evidence, which exists to support any committal for trial for murder.
>
> 1. In relation to Michael Chamberlain, there is in my view, no case in relation to murder. He was seen when the child was alive by the Lowes and was always in their presence until Mrs. Chamberlain claimed that the dingo had taken the child.
>
> 2. On all the evidence, the child Reagan was asleep on return from Sunset Strip and remained so until after the disappearance of the child. These observations were supported by independent witnesses.
>
> 3. The child Aiden. A statement made by him was tendered in evidence at the inquest denying responsibility. The child was observed just before and again after the claimed incident of the dingo taking the child. It is clear from the evidence of the blood in the car that if such an act was carried out by a seven year old child, there would be some evidence of blood staining on his clothing or on his person. In fact there is no objective evidence linking Aiden in any way with the death of Azaria.
>
> 4. At no stage has there been any claim whatsoever that a stranger was involved in the death.
>
> 5. In relation to Mrs. Chamberlain, I find as follows:
>
>> a) She was present with the child at the barbecue when both she and Mr. Chamberlain and the independent witnesses say the child was alive.

b) She then left the barbecue area to place the child in the carry basket in the tent, which she claimed she carried out.

c) In response to what was thought to be a child's cry, she approaches the tent, claims to sight a dingo with what appeared to be something in its mouth and cries out that "a dingo has got my baby". I find that there is evidence from which it can be reasonably inferred, that this was a false claim and that in fact the child had been killed in the car prior to that time.

6. No motive has been suggested or proved and there is evidence that Mrs. Chamberlain appeared to be taking care and consideration for the child on that day. On the other hand, the killing of a child by a mother is not an uncommon happening and as is evidenced by the provision in some jurisdictions for the offence of infanticide. It is an inference that the small handprint on the child's clothing could not be any other person than Mrs. Chamberlain and there is evidence of the staining on the tracksuit and shoes.

On all these facts I find there is positive evidence linking Mrs. Chamberlain to the homicide and I find that a prima facie case of murder has been made out.

In relation to Mr. Chamberlain, there is the question of whether he should be charged with being an accessory after the fact to the murder of the child based on his knowledge of his wife's act from early after the incident and through subsequent investigations.

The relevant evidence is as follows:

1. The family car had headlights, two spotlights and a mobile spotlight. This was not used to assist the search, as the car's ignition keys could not be found. In fact the car was moved later with no reference to why the keys could not be found. It is an inference that because of the condition of the car, he did not want it lit even though to do so would have added credibility to the dingo claim.

2. There is the incident of the black vinyl bag and Roberta Downes [the Uluru Park nurse who arranged housing for the Chamberlains the night of Azaria's death and who testified at trial that despite her presence in the Chamberlain's car for three hours, did not smell blood] where he maintained the bag in a very awkward position despite offers to assist. There is also the question of the evidence of some foetal [spelling in original] blood in connection with that bag.

3. It is a reasonable inference that Mr. Chamberlain knew of the blood staining in the car, that he would have been involved in the cutting of the cloths and placing them in position to be found.

I find that a prima facie case has been made out against Mr. Chamberlain for the charge of accessory after the fact.[6]

The Trial of Lindy Chamberlain and Michael Chamberlain

Now satisfied that it had probable cause to proceed with a criminal trial, the Crown filed its case. On September 13, 1982, after opening statements, the Crown opened its case with Sally Lowe, one of the individuals who was with the Chamberlains at the Ayers Rock/Uluru campsite on the night Azaria died. The case would continue for forty-five days. Mrs. Lowe was first examined by Thomas Pauling, junior prosecuting counsel (now QC):

> Q: I want to take you to Mrs. Chamberlain going back from the barbecue to the tent, with the baby and Aidan [sic]...
>
> A: Yes, that point in time. Right. Mrs. Chamberlain had the baby in her arms, and Aidan [sic] was close behind her. I recall them walking along the footpath area towards their tent. I don't recall anything much after that. I have forgotten most of it. And I was involved in conversation. The next I recall is them coming back, along the same path. About halfway along that path, I suppose, I recall seeing them again. And

they walked back to the barbecue. Mrs. Chamberlain had a tin of something in her hand, and I saw a can-opener, or perhaps something else, in her other hand. Aidan [sic] was behind her. And the next I recall, he was beside me, between myself and the second barbecue, which Mr. Chamberlain had been using, and Lindy was just inside the railing, near the barbecue.

Q: Are you able to tell us how long Mrs. Chamberlain was away from the barbecue area?

A: Well, it's a fairly short period of time. But I've stated before, six to ten minutes would be roughly correct. Five to ten minutes away.... Well, she was just standing there. I heard the baby cry. Quite a serious cry, but not being my child, I didn't sort of say anything. Aidan [sic] said, "I think that's Bubby crying," or something similar. Mike said to Lindy, "Yes, that was the baby, you better go and check." Lindy went immediately to check. I saw her walk along the same footpath that they'd been on.

Q: What happened next?

A: She was in the area on that footpath closest to where the car and the tent were, only inside the railings, and yelled out the cry, "That dog's got my baby."

Q: Yes?

A: "That dog's got my baby." We froze for a minute. Mike and my husband Greg ran in the direction she was looking to the south side of their car, out in that general area. Then, as they went off searching, one of them shouted about a torch, and Greg said to get the torch from the car, which I did. I had my daughter on my hip.

Q: After the police arrived, a major search got underway?

A: That's right. People came from all directions.

Q: [Did you then enter the Chamberlain's tent?]

A: Yes. Aidan [sic] was close by me after the men had started searching, and he was very upset, and said that the dog had got his baby in its tummy. And I cannot recall why, now, but I took him to the tent, and I had some thought in my mind of getting him to sleep. He showed me where he slept, his sleeping-bag, inside the tent. I had my daughter. I was holding her with me at the time. I knelt at the front of the tent and leaned in a little way. I think Aidan [sic] got in when he showed me where he slept. I saw a few spots of blood around the area at that time. After he showed me where he slept, I think my eyes caught sight of the bigger pool of blood in the tent.

Q: Where was it?

A: I was leaning in from the middle of the tent, so it would have been a little off to the right, and it shocked me a bit, because it looked as if it had soaked into something padded, but was still wet on the surface. So, although the area itself wasn't large, I took it to be quite a lot of blood.

Q: Can you describe it?

A: About six by four [inches] a squashed circle, I suppose. I recall it as a dark, red, wet pool of blood.

Cross-examination by John Phillips, QC, for the Chamberlains:

Q: I suppose it is clear enough from your evidence, but the fact is that prior to meeting the Chamberlains in the way you did, you had no contact with them, directly or indirectly?

A: No, no.

Q: And no connection whatsoever, for example, with their church?

A: No.

Q: And, in the three-quarters of an hour, where had the acquaintanceship got to? First names, was it?

A: Yes, first names.

· · ·

Q: The Crown is saying that it is impossible you heard the baby when Mrs. Chamberlain returned to the barbecue.

A: I disagree with that.

Q: Not only do you disagree with it, but you are absolutely certain that is the time you heard the baby? Are you?

A. [The witness nods.] (A "nod" is universally recognized as "court reporter lingo" for an up-and-down head movement, otherwise signaling an affirmative agreement, or "Yes." When a court reporter writes, "Shook her head," it universally means a side-to-side movement, signaling a negative agreement, or "No.")

Q: Would you say, "Yes," please.

A: Yes. All the Chamberlains, Aidan [sic] and Mrs. Chamberlain and Mr. Chamberlain were present. My husband, myself and child. And we heard the cry.

Q: The cry came from the direction of the tent?

A: It definitely came from the tent.

Q: Beyond any doubt?

A: I'm positive.

Q: You knew well, from your own child, the sound of a baby crying?

A: Well, I come from a big family and am used to babies. I can tell the difference between a baby and an older child.

Q: Apart from your own baby and rearing it through the same stages as Azaria Chamberlain, what other babies of that age had you had direct contact with, prior to August 1980?

A: I come from a family of nine, and they always seem to be having children. I'm just familiar with babies and children.

Q: You are quite satisfied that the sound you heard was a baby crying out?

A: Yes. Positive.

Q: I think it has been suggested to you in the past that it might have been the little boy Reagan, who I think was then four, crying out in his sleep? Do you reject that suggestion completely?

A: Definitely. It was a small baby.

Q: What about this suggestion that Mrs. Chamberlain stood up with the baby, took it over to the car and sat in the front seat, and cut its throat? In the three-quarters of an hour you were with her was there anything, anything, that indicated to you that such a thing was likely to happen?

A: No. In fact the opposite. She sort of had a new-mum glow about her. It's hard to describe.

Q: A new-mum glow. Did she appear a loving mother to you?

A: Yes. Definitely yes.

Q: Was she in a sullen, truculent, surly mood?

A: No. She was a little tired, but she still managed to be quite cheerful and happy.

Q: Was there anything in her appearance and her demeanor, on her return, that indicated anything abnormal had happened?

A: No. She seemed to be solely concerned with feeding Aidan [sic] some more food.

Q: Was she covered in blood?

A: No.

Q: Did she have any blood on her at all that you saw?

A: Well, I didn't look all over her. But just looking directly at her, I didn't see any blood, no.

...

Q: (resumed by **Phillips**) I do not think the prosecution suggests otherwise, but there is no doubt the baby was alive during the time the mother was nursing it at the barbecue, is there?

A: Yes, the baby was definitely alive.

Q: Because you saw it kicking, did you not?

A: Yes. Also the expression it made on its face.[7]

From reading the transcript it's easy to assume Mrs. Lowe was not favorable to the prosecution's case, but rather supported the defenses' theories. Journalists covering the story noted that her in-court reactions to the questions were not comfortable, and consequently the jury could choose not to believe her, as we will see when they render their verdict. Transcripts unfortunately lose the humanity of witnesses' testimony, a fact many appellate court judges regularly point out when reviewing "dry transcripts" on appeal, and consequently defer to the judge or jury's decision whether to believe a witness. As the High Court observed about Mrs. Chamberlain's testimony cited at the beginning of this chapter:

> Her demeanour under cross-examination must have been crucial to the jury's verdict. A jury makes allowances for mistakes in recollection or observation - and the jury's view of the honesty or dishonesty of the mistakes determines whether the allowance counts in favour of one side or of the other. The jury were entitled to regard cross-examination of Mrs. Chamberlain about her raising the hue and cry as important. In the light of her earlier statements, they may have thought that her answers in cross-examination were honestly confused or they may have thought she was deliberately prevaricating, for on this occasion she

maintained that she raised the cry both before entering and after leaving the tent.[8]

Trying a case is as much about judging humanity as it is about the facts.

Scientific Evidence

The prosecution essentially had two theories, or strands as the appellate courts called them, about the case, arguing first that Mrs. Chamberlain killed her baby and second that her "dingo theory" could not be believed. Since the prosecution did not have either a body or a murder weapon, it had only circumstantial evidence to prove its case. While the popular television show, *Crime Scene Investigation* and its numerable variants hadn't yet made it to television screens, criminal courts in the 1980s were beginning to experience what lawyers have now come to call the "CSI Effect," where juries demand scientific evidence to prove a case. The prosecution provided it in spades, and the defense may have fallen prey to it, conducting an examination that is at least over the heads of many common jurors:

Forensic Scientist Joy Kuhl was cross-examined by John Phillips, QC, for the defense:

Q: Now, Mrs. Kuhl, that is a demonstration electrophoresis plate?

A: Yes...

Q: That is a demonstration photograph of a gradient gel?

A: Yes.

Q: And that is a demonstration photograph of an Ouchterlony plate?

A: Yes.

Q: What about the real thing? What about the actual electrophoresis plates that you ended up with at the end of your tests? Do you produce those?

A: No.

Q: What about the actual Ouchterlony plates that you ended up with at the end of your tests? Do you produce those?

A: No.

Q: What about the actual gradient gel that you used in your tests? Do you produce that?

A: No.

Q: What about the plate that you used for attempt at a haptoglobin grouping? Do you produce that?

A: No.

Q: They are in Sydney, are they?

A: No. . .

Q: Where are they?

A: They have been destroyed.

Q: The plates are destroyed?

A: Yes.

Q: All of them?

A: All of them.

Q: Whose decision was that? Who is to take responsibility for this?

A: I don't see it as anyone's responsibility. It is standard procedure in our laboratory.

Q: Did you take any photographs of them? Or did you direct that any photographs be taken of this evidence, before you destroyed it?

A: No. We have not the facilities for that. . .

Q: Now, at the inquest, did you swear this? "Human foetal [spelling in original] hemoglobin is different from adult hemoglobin. While a baby, or a fetus, is in uterus it does not have any adult hemoglobin."

A: Yes, I did.

Q: That was demonstrably false.

A: I used that statement for the - for purposes of making things clear and simple. It was not a false statement.

Q: I say false in the sense of incorrect?

A: It was incorrect, scientifically. It was used as an indication of the relative amounts.

Q: You are perfectly entitled to give any explanation which you have, but the fact is, scientifically that statement is utterly incorrect.

A: Scientifically, it is not correct. Yes. . . [Note, in hindsight, the trick employed by the expert witness here. On the one hand, she agrees with the examiner, but turns her answer around by using a contra-positive, confusing the jury whether she actually answered yes or no. Counsel, if he had caught the trick, could have followed up with a simple question to clarify her response: "So you lied, didn't you?"]

Q: Are you suggesting that we should, as it were, shut the door [on the possibility that the blood stains she examined could have been present in the Chamberlain car in] September 1979?

A: That would have been consistent with my opinion, yes.

Q: These stains could not date from August 1979? Do you swear that?

A: It is an opinion. Based purely on experience. I can't swear that.

Q: Do you swear they cannot date from July 1979?

A: Once again, no, I can't swear that.

Q: Do you swear they cannot date from June 1979?

A: No. . .

Q: Here are two bands [of reaction], Mrs. Kuhl?

A: A band and a smudge.

Q: There is a band, and a faint impression of a second band?

A: No, I can see only one band.

Q: That is a band, is it not?

A: It is not a band. It is an artifact in the staining procedure.[9]

The court could have excluded Mrs. Kuhl's testimony based upon the destruction of the blood evidence and the prosecution's failure to make either the car from where the blood was taken or the blood plates available to the defense to test. By preventing the defense from testing the blood, the prosecution denied the defense the right to "confront" the blood as a witness.

While I'm not licensed to practice in Australia, it seems odd this evidence wasn't either stricken from the record, or a mistrial declared. Juries tend to believe evidence written in blood.

As it was discovered much, much later, the supposed "blood" on the car was a combination of the automotive manufacturer's overspray from a sound deadener applied to the underside of a car, paint emulsion and a spilled milkshake. Despite her spectacular fall from grace based on this mistake, Mrs. Kuhl continued to work with Northern Territory police until 2003, when she retired. She passed away in November 2008. Her obituary noted,

> She was the forensic biologist whose evidence had depicted the Chamberlain's Holden Torana [their car] as riddled with foetal blood.
>
> It was later found to be sound deadener used by Holden.
>
> Ms. Kuhl told the Northern Territory News in 2005 that forensic techniques were very different in the '80s, "DNA" was an unknown acronym.
>
> "It was a different laboratory culture we were in then," she said.[10]
>
> It's never been "different" to preserve evidence.

Despite the destruction of the blood samples and Mrs. Kuhl's questionable testimony, the trial judge instructed the jury how to examine the issues surrounding the supposed blood in the car. Note, however, his basic (and we now know to be incorrect) assumption that there was blood in the car:

> You are, if you are satisfied that blood was found in the family car, still entitled to see where it leads you, even if you have a doubt that due to

denaturation or her methodology, her opinion that it was foetal blood, does not stand up, you're still entitled to ask yourselves how that blood, even though you are not convinced it had a foetal content - and to say it may or may not have - how that blood came to be there. Is it explained by Mr. Lenehan's bleeding in that car, near Port Douglas on 17 June 1979. If you find because of the location of blood in the car, that it cannot be so explained, you can still consider whether it was Azaria's blood - that is the only explanation after you - after considering the other evidence. Or, ladies and gentlemen, you must also consider that it was a family car, and the evidence of people sustaining injury in the car, and questions of projectile vomiting, bloody-noses and the like.[11]

Judges who precondition the jury are the bane of defense trial lawyers. I commend any episode of *Rumple of the Bailey* as virtual evidence of this silent maxim.

The prosecution called other eyewitnesses, Judy West, Amy Whittacker, Murray Haby, and Uluru (the Aboriginal name for Ayers Rock) National Park Chief Ranger Derek Roff, who assisted in the search for baby Azaria. Judy West, her husband Bill and daughter Catherine, a Western Australia farming family camping in nearby tent at time of Azaria's disappearance, testified that they heard a dingo give a territorial warning growl (presumably to second dingo or pack of dingoes) moments before Sally Lowe testified she heard Azaria's cry. The family testified to the Chamberlain family's unusual behavior the night Azaria died, confirming that neither Michael nor Lindy searched for Azaria.

Max and Amy Whittacker together with their daughter Rosalie, a Victoria, Australia family camping in campgrounds on the night Azaria disappeared. Amy, a nurse and social worker, stayed with Lindy the night Azaria died. Max and Rosalie searched the area and found drag marks in sand with dingo tracks, and testified they also saw impressions of a 'bundle' in sand. The prosecution next struck out to disprove the defenses' dingo theory.

The prosecution next called a forensic pathologist from London, England, not having any success locating an Australian expert to testify in favor of their case. Doctor James Cameron, the prosecution forensic expert, testified:

A: I saw no evidence on any of these garments to suggest that any member of the canine family was involved. I cannot say anything about dingoes. I speak about the canine family in general.

Q: In your opinion, is there evidence suggesting to you that the child was not killed by a member of the canine family?

A: There is evidence to suggest it was killed in another method. It suggests there was an incised wound around the neck. In other words, a cut throat.

Q: Caused by?

A: A cutting instrument across the neck, or around the neck.

Q: Held by?

A: Held by a human element.

Q: What do you say about the possibility of a dog or a dingo having savaged the child in the head?

A: I do not think there is enough evidence on the jump-suit, alone, to support that theory.[12]

The Prosecution Rests and the Defense Case Begins

At the end of Dr. Cameron's testimony, the prosecution rested and conventional wisdom among court-watchers and journalists covering the trial at the time placed the odds on a jury verdict of acquittals for both Lindy and Michael Chamberlain. Having waited two years for their trial and facing down an almost national obsession with their case, the defendants chose to testify on their own behalf, which under Australian law they were not obligated to do. Whether that decision was a wise idea is questionable, as evidenced by Mr. Barker's cross-examination:

Q: Mrs. Chamberlain, should we take it from what you said about Mrs. Ransome that you

	accept you told her to see that stains were cleaned from [your tracksuit] pants?
A:	I accept there must have been some conversation, about something with the trousers. I don't recall any of it.
Q:	I understand you do not recall it. But do you accept what she said about having stains cleaned from the pants?
A:	Yes. I just said: if she says that's what I said, I accept it.
Q:	Do you accept there was blood on the pants?
A:	No.
Q:	You do not?
A:	No.
Q:	Do you deny there was blood on the pants?
A:	I have never seen blood on the pants at all.
Q:	Do you remember [Mrs. Hansell, the drycleaner, in her testimony] indicated with her hand a sort of splashing motion?
A:	Yes.
Q:	She said they ranged in size from about her fingernail. "Sort of tapering off with little drips, sort of, and went down to very small points, very small blobs, just splattery. Between one to three dozen, all told, and they were tapering off, and running down towards the bottom." Do you remember her saying that?
A:	Yes.
Q:	Do you accept that is what she saw?
A:	Yes.
Q:	Do you deny it was blood?
A:	I have never seen any blood on them myself. There could have been blood on them because they were in the front of the tent.

Q: Is that the way you would account for it, if it were blood?

A: Well, that's the only explanation I have.

Q: Is that how you account for the blood on the tracksuit pants, if that be the case?

A: Yes.

Q: Notwithstanding that it was seen to be only below the knees, and only on one side?

A: I don't know how they were folded or placed in the tent. It's the only explanation I have.

Q: You would discount the possibility that it came from you?

A: That is not my blood, Mr. Barker.

Q: Did you have any blood on your shoes at any stage?

A: My own opinion is that there was blood on my shoes. It hasn't been confirmed by any tests, though.

Q: When did you become aware of the blood on your shoes?

A: It was the first time I went to wear them after I got home. It would have been a week later.

Q: When was that? That you became aware of blood on your shoes?

A: I said: about a week later.

Q: How do you say the blood got on your shoes?

A: I think it would be from crawling over things that were in the doorway, and things in the tent.

Q: I take it from what you said about the possible application of blood on the tracksuit pants, and the other blood you saw, that you accept that the baby was bleeding in the tent?

A: Yes. Yes. . . .

Q: Do you recall this animal going around the car? That is, on the southern side of the car?

A: No. As I said, I only watched it with my eyes for a couple of feet or so, and after that it was guesswork as to where it went.

Q: Did it just disappear?

A: I didn't watch where it went at that stage. I went into the tent.

Q: Do we take it that it had progressed at least to some part of the car?

A: Well, it had gone somewhere. I don't know where it had gone, Mr. Barker.

Q: Did you see it again at all?

A: I saw a dingo standing by the car on the southern side. The trackers told me that it was a different animal. It was the one I chased, though.

Q: There was two dingoes there, was there?

A: According to the trackers, there were two.

Q: When it was shaking its head, was it somewhere on top of the two parkas, is that right?

A: Somewhere in that area.

Q: Apparently, if it be blood, shaking blood onto your slacks?

A: Yes.

Q: Onto Aidan's [sic] parka? Do you know?

A: In my opinion, Aidan's [sic] parka had blood on the inside of it, but I don't think there have been any scientific results on that.

Q: You know that none has been detected, do you not.

A: I said scientifically. I don't think they've picked it up.

Q: You know, do you not, that Dr. Scott closely examined the tent for blood?

A: Yes. I believe it was Dr. Scott.

Q: You know he found a small spray, on the southern side of the tent?

A: No, I understand there was a couple of small sprays. Along the southern side of the tent.

Q: But then you know he said it is most unlikely that it was human blood?

A: I know he said he couldn't detect what it was, apart from the fact it was blood.

Q: If this dog, carrying the baby, ran to the south of the car, the spray or sprays on the side of the tent could have very little to do with this case.

A: If it had gone around the car. But if it had gone in between, that would be a different matter.

Q: You suggest that as a possibility?

A: Yes, I think it's a possibility. Yes.

Q: That it went between the tent and the car?

A: Yes.

Q: When did you first consider it as a possibility?

A: When I heard about the sprays on the side of the tent. During the first inquest.

Q: Before that, your view was that it had gone around the car?

A: I had thought that's where it had probably gone, yes.

Q: Because you saw it there.

A: I saw a dingo there. . . .

Q: You have heard quite a lot of evidence, have you not, about the presence of blood in the car?

A: Yes.

Q: You have heard quite a lot of evidence about the orthotolidine test?

A: Yes.

Q: And you heard Mrs. Kuhl say that she received positive reactions for blood from the carpet from the driver's side?

A: Yes.

Q: And the driver's seat?

A: Yes.

Q: If it were the case, do you know why there would be blood on the driver's side carpet?

A: No. It could have come from a number of places, I suppose. I don't know.

Q: What places would you suggest?

A: Children crawling around the car, or people moving. Or from people Michael had fixed up, with injuries. I don't know.

Q: Who did he fix up with injuries?

A: Oh, we often used to stop for road-accident victims.

Q: Often?

A: Yes.

Q: How many road-accident victims has he carried in that car, beside Mr. Lenehan?

A: I don't mean he carried them in the car. I mean he stopped to assist at the accident site, and then he -

Q: Yes? Well?

A: He had to get back in the car to drive.

Q: And you think he might have carried the blood with him.

A: He could easily have done that. It is quite possible to have some on your hands when you get in.

Q: And you heard about the positive reaction to the cross-bar under the passenger-seat?

A: I can remember a cross-bar. I'm not sure which seat it came from.

Q: You heard about the reaction to the stain on the ten-cent coin?

A: Yes.

Q: And the floor? And the bracket? And the hinge?

A: Yes.

Q: What do you say about that?

A: I don't know that I've got any opinion on it, particularly.

Justice Muirhead: You are not being asked, Mrs. Chamberlain, whether you accept the validity of the findings. It is merely that, if there were positive reactions, what have you to say about it?

A: Well, I don't know that I've really formed any opinion, Your Honor.

Q: (**Barker**) Can you account for the presence of blood on that side of the car?

A: I know Mr. Lenehan's blood was on that side of the car. And a number of other incidents I have related here in court, but other than that, I don't know anything about it.

Q: The blood around the console? Can you account for that, if indeed it was blood?

A: It could have got there when Reagan hit the dashboard. I don't know.

Q: When was that?

A: A couple of months after we bought the car, in 1979. Reagan was about twenty months old.

Q: What about the window handle?

A: Well that could've easily got there when I got back into the car after attending to Mr. Lenehan.

Q: The chamois?

A: That's been used on a number of occasions to clean up the, car.

Q: What about the spray under the dash.

A: I'm not convinced in my mind how that got there.

Q: Can you offer us any suggestions?

A: It would only be pure speculation.

Q: You prefer not to speculate. You just have no idea how it got there.

A: I'm not going to speculate on how it got there.

Q: You would not suggest it came from Mr. Lenehan, would you?

A: No.

Q: A nose bleed?

A: Not under there.

Q: What about the towel in the wheel-well at the back?

A: That had been used to clean up the car, and wipe down the car, on various occasions. One of the car towels had been on my knee when I was nursing Mr. Lenehan.

Q: The scissors?

A: I don't really know whether there's any blood on the scissors or not.

Q: The camera-bag?

A: There could've, quite possibly, been some blood on Michael's hands that night, from collecting the gear out of the tent. Zip up his camera-bag, it could easily get on the zip.

Q: What gear did he put in it that night? Do you know?

A: In the car? All the stuff out of the tent.

Q: In the camera-bag.

A: He wouldn't have put any gear in the camera-bag, but he may have zipped it up before he traveled.

Q: There were large areas in both the front two compartments which reacted to the positive screening tests for blood, the orthotolidine tests. Now, if indeed that reaction was for blood, can you account for it?

Phillips: Your Honor, I do not want to intervene, but did not Mrs. Kuhl specifically say that after four days she could not prove the presence of blood in the bag?

Justice Muirhead: I think Mr. Barker may be restricting it to the orthotolidine test.

Phillips: That last little piece that slipped in, got it into the area of actual blood.

Muirhead: Could you restrict it?

Barker: I said 'if it were blood', Your Honor.

Muirhead: If it were blood, and if the orthotolidine test did give a positive reaction. Put the question again.

Q: (Barker) She said screening-tests of the vinyl surfaces gave consistently positive results in both the front compartment and centre compartment. You cannot account for that?

A: If it was nasal secretion or something like that, I could understand it.

Q: Nasal secretion?

A: Well, it had held used handkerchiefs, and I carried used children's clothes in it, and things like that.

Q: On the night of 17 August?

A: I wouldn't expect so, on the night of 17 August, but it had been used for some four months, by us, before that, and it was about five years old when we got it.

Q: You see, you heard it put that other substances can cause a positive reaction, did you not?

A: Yes.

Q: And that one of those substances could be vomit, provided the vomit contained blood?

A: Yes.

Q: The baby had vomited in the car on about five occasions, is that right?

A: Yes.

Q: Did it ever vomit blood?

Muirhead: To your knowledge.

A: She had projectile vomiting. I've never analyzed it to see what's in it but it's rather painful.

Q: (Barker) On each occasion you were holding her?

A: No, on at least one occasion Reagan was. Reagan was burping her.

Q: Do you suggest that the vomit could account for the presence of blood? For the positive reaction in the camera-case?

A: Well, this is - There are things that had been at different times in the camera-bag.

Q: You say vomit?

A: The face washers, were used to wipe up vomit at some stage. But whether they had blood in them, I don't know. I'm just saying it's possible.

Q: You know there was no blood on the [tent's] fly screen.

A: I presume there wasn't, because it hasn't been mentioned.

Q: Do you say this dog had its head halfway through the fly screen, shaking a bleeding baby?

A: I said it was emerging through the fly screen.

Q: Shaking its head vigorously?

A: I couldn't tell you, now, whether it was shaking its head as it was going through, or before it was through. Its obvious movement was shaking the fly screen at some stage. It was all in a matter of a few seconds, from the time I first saw it to the time I was in the back of the tent, very, very fast and moving.

Q: Your evidence is that you saw it shaking its head vigorously, and it was moving the fly screen in the process.

A: I don't know whether its head was shaking the fly screen, or whether what it had in its mouth was hitting against the fly screen.

Q: And what it had in its mouth, we know now, according to you, was a bleeding baby.

A: That's my opinion.

Q: Pardon?

A: That is my opinion.

Q: Well, is there any doubt about it?

A: Not in my mind.

Q: Is it merely your "opinion" or is it something you know as a fact?

A: It is something my heart tells me is a fact. Other people don't think so.

Q: Does it surprise you there was no blood on the fly screen?

A: No. There was blood on the pole. It doesn't really surprise me there was none there. It would depend which angle the animal was, or which angle the wounds were.

Q: Mrs. Chamberlain, you say this child was in the mouth of a dingo which was vigorously shaking its head at the entrance to the tent. That is what you firmly believe, is that right?

A: That's right.

Q: The dog having taken Azaria from the bassinet?

Muirhead: Take it steady, Mrs. Chamberlain.

Q: You saw blood on the parka?

A: Yes.

Muirhead: Would you like a spell, Mrs. Chamberlain?

A: No, I'd rather get it over with, Your Honor.

Muirhead: I do not want you to have to answer questions when you are feeling distressed.

A: No, I'd prefer to go on. This has been going on for two years. I want to get it over with.

Q: (**Barker**) You say the blood on the parka must have come from the baby?

A: Yes.

Q: When it was in the dog's mouth?

A: Somewhere around that time

Q: What other time could it have come from the baby?

A: Look, Mr. Barker, I wasn't there. I can only go on the evidence of my own eyes. We are talking about my baby daughter, not some object.

Muirhead: We will adjourn for ten minutes.

. . .

Q: (**Barker**) I would like to remind you of some evidence given by Constable Morris. He told us this: "Mrs. Chamberlain said that originally she was at the barbecue-site and she'd seen a dingo near the tent. It had what seemed to be something in its mouth. She hadn't taken a great deal of notice of it, because she'd seen dogs and dingoes earlier in the day around the campsite, around the rubbish bins, and tourists feeding them to try to get photographs etcetera, and didn't take undue notice until she returned to the tent-site a short while later, and then suddenly realized that the dingo or dog must have taken her baby." Did you hear him say that?

A: I I don't recall his evidence greatly. That is not, to my knowledge, what I told him. It may have been the impression he got.

Q: Did you tell him you had seen a dingo near the tent, and it had what appeared to be something in its mouth?

A: I told - I told him I had seen a dingo in the tent with—appearing to have something in its mouth, yes.

Q: Is this the case: when you first saw the dingo you did not take much notice because you had seen them around the camp earlier in the day?

A: Yes, that's probably it. For the first half second or something like that, I thought it had a shoe. I didn't really take much notice. That's why I just yelled at it to get out of the tent.

Muirhead: When you say "much notice", you mean that you did not feel alarm?

A: Yes.

Q: **(Barker)** Did you tell him that you did not take undue notice until you "returned to the tent site a short while later", and then "suddenly" realized a dingo or dog must have taken the baby?

A: Not to my knowledge.

Q: Do you deny telling him that?

A: I said I don't remember telling him that.

Q: Do you deny telling him?

A: I just don't remember telling him anything about it. I don't know whether I did or I didn't.

Q: You might have told him?

A: It's possible, but I don't see why I would have, because it doesn't connect with any of my memories of what happened.

Q: Which is totally inconsistent with your evidence, is it not?

A: Yes.

Q: You know Constable Morris, do you not?

A: I do now, very well.

Q: I suggest to you that he came back to try and find out what the baby was wearing.

A: I can remember him running across, at one stage, and saying, "What was the baby dressed in?" and me saying, "White" and him tearing off again. There just wasn't an opportunity to give him a full description. He had to let the searchers know basically what they were looking for.

Q: Did you tell him, again, that you saw the dingo near the entrance to the tent?

A: I could have, quite possibly.

Q: Did you tell him the dingo had "nothing in its mouth"?

A: I think we've been over this a number of times before. I told him I saw nothing in its mouth.

Q: Did you correct him?

A: To - to my remembrance I, yes, I know we had several discussions on his impression, and my impression.

Q: You do now remember the conversation, do you?

A: I know that when he came to see us just before we left he was still confused.

Q: He was confused? By the way, did you tell him the baby was wearing a matinee-jacket?

A: I did mention it. But I don't know if he was close enough to have heard. He was on the move.

Q: You heard him say here that you did not say anything about a matinee-jacket at the time.

A: It was quite possible he was too far away to hear.

Phillips: Your Honor, I object to selected passages being put. My recollection is, when he was cross-examined, the constable clearly said that he may be mistaken.

Muirhead: He said that it was not verbatim. He made no notes.

Phillips: More than that, with respect Your Honor. He said he may be mistaken about that.

Muirhead: I was not trying to argue with you, Mr. Phillips. I was kind of basically agreeing.

Q: (**Barker**) I would like to remind you of what you told Inspector Gilroy the day after all this happened. Now, what you say there, do you not, is that you found the baby was missing when you entered the tent, not when you were running towards it?

A: I think it's just a matter of how it's put.

Q: Is it? What you say there is, do you not, you called to your husband that the dingo had the baby when you emerged from the tent? Not before you went into it?

A: Well, I did both.

Q: You did both. Did you see, as you approached the tent, that the baby had gone?

A: Yes.

Q: Why did you not tell that to Gilroy?

A: Well, I thought I had.

Q: Why did you say to him: "I dived straight in the tent first to see if there was anything I could do. I never thought of him taking her"?

A: To know that something's true, and to accept it, are two different things. . .

Q: You dived into the tent, did you not, and saw that she was gone? Is this what you told Gilroy?

A: Mr. Barker, that interview was a short interview, to give them some facts to work on. He told me they were coming back to take a statement with all details in it. I don't

	pretend that everything in there is exactly one after the other as it happened. I was totally confused, and still in shock, when that was taken.
Q:	Is it the case that what you say here [waving the document], "cannot be relied upon"?
A:	I am saying that it may not specifically be lined up, one thing after the other. It may be jumbled. I'm not saying it's incorrect. I'm saying it may be in the wrong order.
Q:	I suggest to you that it is not merely a matter of jumbling. It is simply incapable of being reconciled with what you say here. Do you understand that?
A:	It isn't, in my mind, Mr. Barker. . . .
Q:	Mrs. Chamberlain, may I respectfully suggest to you that the whole story is mere fantasy.
A:	You have suggested that before.
Q:	Mrs. Chamberlain, is it not the case that your husband declined to search actively on that Sunday night because he knew that the baby was dead, and he knew that you had killed her?
A:	No, definitely not.
Q:	And is it not the case that this is why you declined to actively search?
A:	No.
Q:	I suggest to you that the reason that you and your husband stayed near the car whilst people were searching was that, for some portion of that night at least, the child's body was in the car.
A:	Definitely not.
Q:	You invented the story of the dingo removing the child from the tent.
A:	I definitely did not invent that story. It's the truth, Mr. Barker.[13]

When a witness argues with the lawyer asking the questions, it's important to win the argument. Otherwise, the jury believes the lawyer, not the witness—even though the lawyer isn't testifying.

After Mrs. Chamberlain, the defense offered a blood expert to counter Mrs. Kuhl's testimony. Whether the jury understood his testimony is another question:

> Q: (**Phillips**) Professor Boettcher, in your opinion, should it be concluded, on the results of any of the tests performed by Mrs. Kuhl, that foetal hemoglobin was present in any of the samples tested by her?
>
> A: No. It is my opinion that such a conclusion should not be reached from the results presented by Mrs. Kuhl. The anti-serum known as anti-hemoglobin has in it antibodies that react with both the alpha and the beta molecular chains which are found in hemoglobin's. The alpha chains are found in all hemoglobin's, adult and foetal. The beta globin chain is found only in adult hemoglobin. Foetal hemoglobin contains both alpha and gamma hemoglobin chains, and if one is testing a blood sample that has some foetal and some adult material in it, one expects that, if you obtain a reaction with anti-foetal hemoglobin anti-serum, that should be directed only at the gamma chain, which is found only in foetal hemoglobin. If you perform a test on the same sample with an anti-hemoglobin serum which is specific for the alpha chain which is found in both adult hemoglobin and foetal hemoglobin, you would also expect to get a positive reaction..[14]

The defense also sought to counter Professor Cameron's testimony and offered a dingo expert of their own to dispel the "massive amounts of blood theory:" Les Harris, President of the Dingo Foundation, who testified:

> Q: (By **Andrew Kirkham** [now QC, then a junior defense counsel]) With your

knowledge of dingo attacks, would you expect to see a large amount of blood?

Barker: I object to that.

Justice Muirhead: [What is the basis for your objection]?

Barker: Your Honor, the man is not a pathologist dealing with the body of a baby. . . .We have already been told that the dingo grabs the head, crushes, and shakes. . . .

Q: (**Kirkham**) Have you [observed much blood from dingo killings in the field?]

A: No, there's been very little, and it's characteristic of a kill in the field that little bleeding takes place.

Q: We've heard evidence that a dingo in the Chamberlain tent was seen to shake its head, in the vicinity of the entrance. [Is that inconsistent with what you'd expect from your observations of dingo behavior?]

A: No, that's quite consistent, because they are observed to also shake it after they have made the seizure, and the shake is obviously intended to break the neck.[15]

Finally, the defense closed with Michael Chamberlain's testimony, which like his wife's testimony, may have seemed abnormally detached from the grief a jury might expect to see and hear when viewing the parents testifying about the loss of their child. Here is Mr. Chamberlain's testimony on cross, by Mr. Barker:

Q: What did your wife tell you had happened to the child?

A: That a dingo had taken her.

Q: When did she tell you in detail, Mr. Chamberlain, precisely what she had seen?

A: We talked about it, on and off, during the evening.

Q: What did she tell you?

A: I don't recall exactly the conversations we had.

Q:	There is no doubt, is there, that your wife was the last person to see the child alive?
A:	No doubt.
Q:	And do you tell us that you are unable to say just what she told you about the child's disappearance?
A:	In no detail can I tell you. We prayed.
Q:	Did you think then that the child had died?
A:	I knew she was in great danger.
Q:	From what?
A:	Dying.
Q:	Of what?
A:	Dying.
Q:	What did you think was going to cause her death?
A:	Either exposure or bleeding.
Q:	You didn't know from where she was bleeding?
A:	No.
Q:	You didn't inquire whether your wife could help you find out?
A:	No.
Q:	Why?
A:	It didn't occur to me. The fact was she was bleeding, and she was in danger of death.
Q:	Could it be because you knew that the dingo did not take her, and that she was dead at the hands of your wife?
A:	No.
Q:	Did you say to Constable Morris something like this, on the occasion he came back to make some inquiries: "It was the will of God; there was nothing that you or I or anybody else could do about it"?
A:	I don't recall saying it.
Q:	Do you deny it?

A:	I'm not going to deny it.
Q:	It's something you believe?
A:	I believe in God's will.
Q:	Did you believe it was the will of God when you told Morris?
A:	God's will is over all.
Q:	I suggest you couldn't see then, and you can't see now, why your wife would not have seen a baby dressed in white being carried in the mouth of a dingo out of the tent, and past the front of it.
A:	I believe my wife's account, Mr. Barker.
Q:	I suggest the whole story is nonsense, and you know it.
A:	No, Mr. Barker.
Q:	How do you account for the damage to the collar of the jumpsuit?
A:	I can't account for it.
Q:	Did your wife cut the sleeve?
A:	I don't think she did.
Q:	Did she cut the collar?
A:	I don't think so.
Q:	Did you bury the jump-suit with the child in it?
A:	No.
Q:	Did your wife?
A:	I don't think she did. . . .

Admittedly, this response is either the oddest or the most telling answer in the entire trial. "I don't think she did . . ." could just as easily mean "She just may have buried the child with its jump-suit on." The jury was looking for an emphatic answer of "Certainly not!" spoken with righteous indignation to Barker's question. This half-hearted, subject-to-multiple-interpretation answer falls far short of Michael Chamberlain truly trying to vindicate his wife and stand behind her.

Some criminal defense lawyers will rehearse their client's responses to a cross-examination in a mock trial situation prior to putting their client on the stand. This answer is the farthest thing from rehearsed, if not actually closer to an admission. It got worse.

> Q: Mr. Chamberlain, your wife, I suggest, told you that the story of the dingo was false, very soon after the child was killed.
>
> A: No.
>
> Q: Did she not?
>
> A: She did not.
>
> Q: She told you she was going to suggest that the dingo at the tent was the same as the dingo she saw at the Rock.
>
> A: Could you repeat that please?
>
> Q: She told you that she was going to suggest that the dingo at the tent was the same as the dingo she saw at the Rock.
>
> A: I don't remember that.
>
> Q: Did she say, "Why don't we go to the Olgas [a mountain range near Ayers Rock] so the boys will stop playing up"? Or something like that?
>
> A: No. No, that wasn't said.
>
> Q: Look, didn't it occur to you that there might have been a remote possibility, however remote, that the child was still alive on Monday morning?
>
> A: Miraculous.
>
> Q: You believe in miracles, don't you? There are plenty of precedents for them, aren't there?
>
> A: I'm also a realist.[16]

Realist or not, the jury's October 29, 1982, verdict was "guilty" for both Lindy Chamberlain and Michael Chamberlain. (See the comment above about arguing with the lawyer asking the questions). Lindy was sentenced to life in prison, Michael's sentence was suspended. "I consider it not only appropriate, but in the interests of justice to do so," Justice Muirhead explained in his opinion on Michael's sentence.

The Appeals After the Guilty Verdicts

Not everyone was so charitable. Indeed, the country was virtually split in half whether to believe the Chamberlains and not the courts. The High Court denied their appeal. Here's how the Australia High Court (the highest court in Australia) put it:

> The applicants, Alice Lynne Chamberlain [Lindy] and Michael Chamberlain apply to the Supreme Court of the Northern Territory, [and note that] Mrs. Chamberlain was charged that on 17 August 1980 at Ayers Rock in the Northern Territory. [The jury found that] she did murder Azaria Chantel Loren Chamberlain. By the second count of the indictment, Mr. Chamberlain was charged as an accessory after the fact, the particulars being that between 17 August 1980 and 16 December 1981 at Ayers Rock, Alice Springs and other places in the Northern Territory he did receive or assist another person, namely Alice Lynne Chamberlain, who to his knowledge was guilty of an offence against the law of the Territory, namely the offence of murdering Azaria Chantel Loren Chamberlain at Ayers Rock on 17 August 1980, in order to enable the said Alice Lynne Chamberlain to escape punishment. Each pleaded not guilty but the jury found both to be guilty as charged. They appealed against their convictions to the Full Court of the Federal Court. That court (Bowen C.J. [Chief Justice], Forster and Jenkinson J.J. [Junior Justices]) dismissed the appeals. They [the Chamberlains] now apply for special leave to appeal against that decision.
>
> Appeals dismissed.[17]

Not all the justices on the High Court agreed with this assessment. In his dissent, which analyzed the facts of the case differently than the majority. Justice Deane said:

> The Crown's case that Mrs. Chamberlain murdered her baby and that Mr. Chamberlain was an accessory after the fact to her crime is based upon circumstantial evidence largely provided by the testimony of expert witnesses. [. . .] It has been

common ground throughout that, if the baby was killed by human act, the person responsible must have been Mrs. Chamberlain.[18]

[. . .]

There is, however, independent and direct evidence of the circumstances surrounding the period of between five and ten minutes in which the Crown alleges that Mrs. Chamberlain murdered the baby. The most important of that evidence is that of Mr. and Mrs. Lowe who had first met Mr. and Mrs. Chamberlain less than an hour before the time of the alleged murder. They had had no previous association with the Chamberlains. Their credit was impugned by neither side. Their evidence, supported in some respects by the evidence of Mr. and Mrs. Whittacker, provides a basic factual context which is largely not in dispute.[19]

Mr. and Mrs. Lowe met the Chamberlains in a barbecue area in the vicinity of Ayers Rock around 7 p.m. on Sunday, 17 August 1980. Mrs. Chamberlain was nursing the baby, Azaria, whom she was trying to put to sleep. There was nothing in her demeanour to indicate that she was other than the loving mother of a normal child. Indeed, Mrs. Lowe, who appears to have observed her closely, gave evidence that "she sort of had a new mum glow about her" [. . .] At about 8 p.m., Mr. Chamberlain is said to have made a comment about hearing the baby cry. Mrs. Chamberlain walked towards the tent. It was as she drew near to it that she cried out that "that dog has got my baby". According to Mrs. Chamberlain, she had seen a dingo shaking its head as if it had something in its mouth at the entrance of the tent and had observed the empty bassinet within the tent. According to the Crown, her cry was the beginning of a facade of deceit, erected by Mrs. Chamberlain with the subsequent help of her husband, to conceal Azaria's murder.

It is conceded by the Crown that it is an essential part of its case that, at the time Mr. Chamberlain is said to have made a comment about hearing the baby cry, Azaria had already been killed. If, in fact, a cry from Azaria was heard at that time, the Crown concedes that its case against the Chamberlains breaks down. Mrs. Chamberlain's evidence was that she herself did not hear a cry: she "was rattling the things" at the fire place in the barbecue area and had not heard anything until Mr. Chamberlain said "that he thought he heard Azaria crying or something to that effect". Mr. Chamberlain's evidence was that he thought he heard Azaria cry and said to Mrs. Chamberlain: "Is that Azaria?" His description of the cry is perhaps too tailored to the circumstances to be likely to excite confidence in its veracity: "It was an urgent cry, not loud. It cut off. It almost seemed as if the baby was being squeezed." Another of the four witnesses to give evidence about a baby's cry was Mr. Lowe. He said that he and Mr. Chamberlain "were heavily involved in conversation" when Mr. Chamberlain made some comment to his wife to the effect: "Was that the baby?" He himself did not hear any baby's cry. The other evidence is that of Mrs. Lowe.[20]

Mrs. Lowe comes from what she describes "as a family of nine and they always seem to be having children". At the time she herself had an eighteen-month old child. She obviously had had considerable experience with babies. Her evidence as to what occurred after Mrs. Chamberlain had returned to the barbecue area with "a can of something in her hand" is clear and unqualified:

"I heard the baby cry, quite a serious cry but not being my child I didn't sort of say anything. Aiden said: 'I think that's bubby crying', or something similar. Mike said to Lindy: 'Yes, that was the baby.'"

Under further questioning, Mrs. Lowe gave evidence that she was "positive" that the sound she heard was the cry of a baby and that she was also "positive" that the cry "definitely came from the [Chamberlains'] tent". As has been said the Chamberlains' tent was only about 20 metres away from the barbecue area. The Crown does not suggest that she could have heard the cry of some other baby. Unless Mrs. Lowe's clear and definite evidence that she heard the cry of a baby is rejected as mistaken, the Crown's case against the Chamberlains must fail.

The jury in Darwin had the benefit of seeing and hearing Mrs. Lowe and the other witnesses give their evidence. [. . .] Perhaps the members of the jury were influenced by the fact that Mrs. Lowe alone claimed to have heard Aiden make a comment about hearing the baby cry. One would, however, question the significance that could be placed upon a failure by Mr. and Mrs. Chamberlain and Mr. Lowe to remember, looking back over the events of that night, the comment of a six-year-old child. Speculation as to what the jury may or may not have thought is not inappropriate however in that it underlines the fact that a starting point of the inquiry whether this court is of the view that the evidence failed to establish beyond reasonable doubt that Mrs. Chamberlain murdered her baby must be that the jury which was entrusted by the law with the determination of that question and which heard and saw the witnesses give their evidence decided that it did.[21]

Doing the best that I can, I have finally come to a firm view that, notwithstanding the jury's verdict of guilty, the evidence did not establish beyond reasonable doubt that Mrs. Chamberlain killed Azaria. That being so, the verdict that she was guilty of murdering her child is unsafe and unsatisfactory and constituted a miscarriage of justice. It necessarily follows that the evidence failed to establish beyond reasonable doubt that Mr. Chamberlain was guilty of the crime of which he was convicted.[22]

In the chronology of events, on November 12, 1985, the Northern Territory rejected the Chamberlain Innocence Committee's application for a full judicial inquiry into the case. Perhaps in response to this rejection, Lindy wrote the following letter from her jail cell, signaling her intent to go on strike and not work for the Northern Territory jails for 30 cents a day.[23]

Uluru Park rangers accidently discovered Azaria's blood-soaked matinee jacket at the base of Ayers Rock/Uluru on February 2, 1986, during an unrelated investigation after a hiker fell from the Rock and died nearby. After the discovery, Lindy

Chamberlain was released from prison within five days. Once again Lindy and Michael filed for relief from the court, and the Northern Territory agreed to undertake a further investigation and appointed a Commission, consisting of one judicial officer, Justice Trevor Morling.

As a result of that investigation, on May 22, 1987, Justice Morling issued a 379-page report entitled: "The Royal Commission of Inquiry into Chamberlain Convictions," analyzing and criticizing the evidence in the Chamberlain case, finding that the evidence against the Chamberlains was insubstantial at best. Justice Morling dealt with the new evidence and quickly disposed of the two "strands" of the Crown's case against Lindy Chamberlain: first, that Mrs. Chamberlain killed Azaria and, second, discounting her defense that a dingo killed her baby. In disposing of both parts of the Crown's case based on the new evidence, Justice Morling's reported pointed out:

> The short period during which Mrs. Chamberlain was absent from the barbecue made it only barely possible that she could have committed the crime alleged against her. On the Crown case, in the 5-10 minutes she was proved to have been absent from the barbecue she must have-
>
> Returned to the tent;
>
> Done whatever was necessary to ensure that Aidan [sic] did not follow her;
>
> Donned her tracksuit pants;
>
> Taken Azaria to the car;
>
> Possessed herself of a murder weapon;
>
> Cut Azaria's throat;
>
> Allowed sufficient time for Azaria to die;
>
> Secreted the body
>
> Done at least some cleaning-up of blood in the car;
>
> Removed her tracksuit pants;
>
> Obtained a can of baked beans for Aidan [sic];
>
> Returned to the tent;
>
> Entered the tent and done whatever was necessary for several articles in it to be spotted with blood;

> Collected Aidan [sic]; and
>
> Returned to the barbecue.

The length of time, which, on the Crown case, must have elapsed between Azaria's throat being cut and her death, is of some importance. It seems probable that if Mrs. Chamberlain murdered the child she would not have returned to the tent before she was satisfied the child was dead. If both Azaria's carotid arteries were severed it probably would have taken about 2-3 minutes for her to have died. The minimum time would have been half a minute. It would have taken much longer, up to 20 minutes, for her to have died if her jugular vein and not her carotid arteries, were severed. The blood staining on the jumpsuit indicates, according to all the experts, an absence of arterial bleeding.

• • •

Before August 1980 dingoes in the Ayers Rock area frequented the camping area. At that time there were many dingoes in the area, some 18-25 of which were known to visit the camping area. A number of attacks were made by dingoes on children in the months preceding Azaria's disappearance. In none of these did any child suffer serious injury.

About twenty minutes before Azaria disappeared Mr. Haby saw and photographed a dingo, which walked towards the Chamberlains' tent. A few minutes before the alarm was raised the Wests heard a dog growl.

On the night of 17 August dog tracks were observed on the southern side of and very close to the Chamberlains' tent. The same night Mr. Roft and Mr. Minyintiri, both experienced trackers and familiar with dingo behavior, saw tracks of a dog carrying a load, which they believed to be Azaria. It was within the bounds of reasonable possibility that a dingo might have attacked a baby and carried it away for consumption as food. A dingo would have been capable of carrying Azaria's body to the place where the clothing was found. If a dingo had taken Azaria it is likely that, on occasions, it would have put the load down and dragged it.

> Hairs, which were either dog or dingo hairs, were found in the tent and on Azaria's jumpsuit. The Chamberlains had not owned a dog for some years prior to August 1980.
>
> The quantity and distribution of the sand found on Azaria's clothing might have been the result of it being dragged through sand. The sand could have come from many places in the Ayers Rock region. The sand and plant fragments on the clothing are consistent with Azaria's body being carried and dragged by a dingo from the tent to the place where it was found. It is unlikely that, if the clothing had been taken from the Chamberlains' car, buried, disinterred, and later placed where it was found it would have collected the quantity and variety of plant material found upon it.[24]

Following the Morling report, on October 21, 1987, the Northern Territory Government enacted a statute that authorized the Chamberlains to apply to the Court of Appeal to have their convictions quashed. They promptly filed that application. The Court of Appeal issued their unanimous ruling.

> In the light of the new evidence, it is difficult to conceive how Azaria's clothing could have collected the quantity and variety of plant material found upon it if it had been merely taken from the car, buried, disinterred and later placed near the base of the Rock. It is more consistent with the new plant and soil evidence that Azaria's clothed body was carried and dragged by an animal from the camp site to near the base of the Rock, rather than that it was buried on the dune and later carried there.
>
> . . .
>
> There is no reason to doubt that when Azaria disappeared she was wearing the matinee jacket discovered in 1986. The jacket would have covered much of the jumpsuit worn by the child. The failure to detect dingo saliva on the jumpsuit is made more explicable than it was at the trial.
>
> . . .
>
> The question may well be asked how it came about that the evidence at the trial differed in such

important respects from the evidence before the Commission. I am unable to state with certainty why this was so. However, with the benefit of hindsight it can be seen that some experts who gave evidence at the trial were over-confident of their ability to form reliable opinions on matters that lay on the outer margins of their fields of expertise. Some of their opinions were based on unreliable or inadequate data. It was not until more research work had been done after the trial that some of these opinions were found to be of doubtful validity or wrong. Other evidence was given at the trial by experts who did not have the experience, facilities or resources necessary to enable them to express reliable opinions on some of the novel and complex scientific issues, which arose for consideration. It was necessary for much more research to be done on these matters to determine whether the opinions expressed at the trial were open to doubt.

Having said so much, I would like to touch on a matter peripheral to this Reference. It may be thought that the mere acknowledgment of a doubt about the guilt of Alice Lynne Chamberlain is a half-hearted way for the matter to end. I would like to examine that sentiment for a moment. It is rarely that a criminal trial positively establishes the innocence of an accused person. If it does so, it does so by accident. The task of a criminal court is to ask and answer the question whether it is satisfied beyond reasonable doubt that the accused is guilty of the crime charged. If it is not so satisfied, the verdict should be one of "not guilty": that is, a verdict of acquittal. From the point of view of a criminal court, a verdict of "not guilty" signifies that the jury is not satisfied beyond reasonable doubt of the guilt of the accused; it does not formally signify a positive jury finding upon the evidence that the accused is innocent. Such a positive finding is not the role of a criminal court, nor of this court. That is because under the criminal law a person is presumed innocent until the contrary is proved. It is not the court's function to establish innocence because, in the absence of a conviction, innocence is presumed: no finding is required. If the accused is not found guilty the presumption of innocence continues. So it is here. I have expressed the opinion that doubt exists as to the guilt of Mrs. Chamberlain. I would categorise that doubt as a grave doubt. The doubt has arisen as a result of considering fresh evidence, in particular, the findings of the Commission. It is the existence of that doubt that demands the quashing of the convictions and the verdicts and judgments I propose. The convictions having been wiped away, the law of the land holds the Chamberlains to be innocent.

Accordingly, I would quash the convictions of Alice Lynne Chamberlain and Michael Leigh Chamberlain and enter verdicts and judgments of acquittal.

Kearney J.[25]

This unanimous opinion finally quashed all convictions against Lindy and Michael Chamberlain on September 15, 1988, just months after what would have been Azaria's 8th birthday. Lindy received $1.3 million in compensation from the Northern Territory for being wrongfully jailed, although that sum covered only about twenty-five percent of the family's legal fees and costs. An ugly chapter in Australia's justice system had almost ended.

After the verdicts were overturned, the Northern Territory Coroner was required to change the reason for the cause of death on Azaria's birth certificate because it then read "murder." For reasons that are not apparent, the coroner claimed in his explanation that the Northern Territory may seek to recover its investigative costs from the Chamberlains. The reasons tangentially are an attempt to open the possibility of recovery, but the corner then discounted that possibility. In his report, the coroner said his job required him to "balance the probabilities," a civil standard, not a criminal standard:

After examining all the evidence I am unable to be satisfied on the balance of probabilities that Azaria Chamberlain died at the hands of Alice Lynne Chamberlain. It automatically follows that I am also unable to be satisfied on the balance of probabilities that Michael Leigh Chamberlain had any involvement in the death.[26]

With that lead-in, the outcome of his ruling was obvious, but first required some window-dressing to make it legally palatable:

> It is not the purpose of a criminal trial to establish the innocence of the accused: rather its purpose is to establish the person's guilt, the standard of proof being beyond reasonable doubt.
>
> . . .
>
> The first point to be made is that the laws of the Northern Territory do not preclude civil proceedings being brought against a person, previously acquitted in criminal proceedings, for compensation, arising out of the same set of facts advanced earlier with a view to establishing criminal guilt.
>
> . . .
>
> What must be kept firmly in mind is that in the above context criminal and civil courts perform different functions, and in discharging their respective tasks apply different standards of proof, and even where an allegation of criminal conduct is alleged in civil proceedings the presumption of innocence applies, and the defendant in the civil suit is presumed innocent until the allegation is proved.
>
> . . .
>
> Even a positive finding in the present case that Azaria Chamberlain died at the hands of Alice Lynne Chamberlain, provided such a finding was open on the evidence, would not violate the integrity of the Morling Report; nor would it create mischief by undermining the Chamberlain's status of innocence.
>
> . . .
>
> An open finding will, by its very nature, lead to speculation that Azaria's death was due to non-accidental causes. However, undoubtedly such speculation existed within the community even after the findings of the Morling Report and the subsequent quashing of the Chamberlain convictions. Such speculation continues to this very day. Regardless of the outcome of the present inquest, whether it were to result in a positive finding

(one implicating either Mrs. Chamberlain or the dingo), or an open finding, speculation over the cause and manner of Azaria's death would remain. What is important, however, is that any such speculation, inevitable as it is, can never disturb the unassailable fact that as a matter of public record the "law of the land holds Mr. and Mrs. Chamberlain to be innocent."

I foresee that many members of the community may disagree with the conclusion I have reached. Two factors may go a long way towards explaining that lack of unanimity. The first is the fact that I have had the advantage of having all the evidence before me. The second is that the mental processes leading up to my decision have been confined and structured by a set of legal principles governing the standard of proof in coronial cases.

...

Pursuant to the provisions of Section 34 of the Coroners Act, I make the following findings:

(1) The name of the deceased was Azaria Chantel Loren Chamberlain, the daughter of Michael Leigh Chamberlain and Alice Lynne Chamberlain.

(2) Azaria Chantel Loren Chamberlain, a female Caucasian, was born at Mount Isa Queensland on 11th June 1980. Her usual place of residence was 3 Abel Smith Parade, Sunset, Mount Isa, Queensland.

(3) Azaria Chantel Loren Chamberlain died at Ayers Rock on 17th day of August 1980.

(4) As to the cause of her death and the manner in which she died the evidence adduced does not enable me to say. I therefore return an open finding and record the cause and manner of death as unknown. Dated this 13th day of December 1995.

Mr John Lowndes
Coroner for the
Northern Territory

[Official signature from the inquest.][27]

We can make our own guesses why the Northern Territory does not want the case closed. According to Lindy Chamberlain-Creighton's website,

> Lindy was ultimately released from prison because of political pressure, and a journalist threatening to expose the way the Northern Territory government of the day had hidden and twisted the truth. Since Lindy had reached the end of all legal avenues available to her, Federal and Territory laws had to be changed to allow for a Royal Commission, and the quashing of the convictions, giving complete exoneration of the Chamberlains.[28]

Because of the Northern Territory Coroner's findings, the case officially remains open and unsolved. The cause of death on Azaria's death certificate now incongruously reads, "Unknown."

Chapter Conclusion

Lindy Chamberlain was convicted because she was different. She didn't respond to questions, she challenged them. She and her husband played immediately to the media when most people who had lost a child would have hidden from the media. She seemed not to crumble under the pressure of a trial when most people in a comparable situation would have fallen apart. In fact, her lack of emotion may have been what convinced jurors the most. A steely front is not what we expect from mothers of a missing baby. We want them to cry. When Lindy Chamberlain did not, the jurors assumed what most of the rest of Australia did: she was guilty.

The first decision convicting her went wrong for several reasons: Lindy's own behavior as well as the overconfidence of the investigators, whose one-track mind led them to exclude other possibilities and cram round pegs into square holes. The combination of the two events, one fueling the other, led jurors to the wrong conclusion.

Had Lindy and Michael Chamberlain cried on cue for the media and behaved as others expected, the investigators might have adopted their story earlier on and found the facts to be consistent with Lindy's "dingo-ate-my-baby" statement. As with most homicides, the police and investigators are trained to look first at the family members and to follow 'the money' as the two primary sources of killers. When the Chamberlains' behavior fell outside the norms of society and their story initially appeared sensational, the police and investigators turned on them and focused their efforts on the initially more believable theory that a disaffected mother was the killer. Only after almost irrefutable evidence came forward challenging that theory did the tide begin to turn. Even then, many in Australia still doubt the acquittal, largely due to Lindy's behavior.

Had Lindy Chamberlain initially cooperated with police and investigators instead of challenging them, had she not attacked their methods and work, had she behaved as expected, she would have never stood trial and engendered a nation's wrath. The other lesson here, on the other side, requires police, investigators, prosecutors, judges, and juries to accept others for their differences and understand that we are not all alike.

Unfortunately for both sides in this dispute, initial perceptions turned out quite different than reality—these initial perceptions turned into fixed conclusions that were wrong. Preconceived notions reached a fever pitch in the next chapter.

Remember to enter your vote on the outcome of this trial on www.10FamousTrials.com and see how other readers voted.

CHAPTER 9
The McMartin Preschool Trial

If perchance you're one of those readers who skip around and read chapters out of order, then beware here: you may want to read the Salem Witch Trials chapter first. If you've already read it, then great; you've done your homework and are ready to read a modern-day version of a different type of witch hunt. This one begs the question whether our society and judicial system learned anything over the last three-hundred-plus years. The parallels are frightening.

The Lead-up to the Charges of Sexual Abuse

On May 12, 1983, Billy Johnson, a two-and-a-half-year-old boy, just appeared one day at the McMartin Preschool in Manhattan Beach, California. The school had initially rejected Billy because it was otherwise full and had a six-month waiting list, but his mother, 40-year-old Judy Johnson, merely dropped him off in the preschool's yard and drove away. The teachers relented and accepted Billy. He attended preschool approximately ten times over the ensuing three-month period.

Then on August 12, 1983, Billy's mother filed a series of complaints with the local police, claiming her son had been sodomized by both her estranged husband and McMartin Preschool teacher Ray Buckey. Buckey was the grandson of school founder Virginia Steely McMartin, 79, and son of administrator Peggy McMartin, 59. Buckey was 30. The school had been open for nearly thirty years and received four community awards as well as the prestigious Rose and Scroll Award, awarded to outstanding businesswomen. Investigators would learn that Billy had showered with his brother and been fondled, but his older brother denied any sexual penetration. Despite his mother's allegations about Ray Buckey, Billy continued to attend McMartin Preschool.

Manhattan Beach Police Detective Jane Hoag investigated Johnson's call, interviewed Johnson's son, and called twelve other McMartin parents referred to by Johnson. Unfortunately, Billy was unable to identify Ray Buckey from class photos. None of the other parents reported any reason to believe their children had been sexually abused.[1] Hoag's investigations into the matter continued nevertheless.

Billy had been examined at a local hospital by an inexperienced doctor who accepted Mrs. Johnson's story and found evidence of abuse—but later, more skilled examinations revealed no visible signs of abuse.[2] He would later be taken to Children's Institute International, an agency that treated abused and neglected children. The role of the CII in interviewing child witnesses would be severely criticized in the trial and later appellate proceedings.

Following Judy Johnson's complaints, the Los Angeles County District Attorney's Office would spend nearly seven years in the preliminary hearing and three trial proceedings, and conduct investigations and institute court proceedings, including two trials that all together cost nearly $16 million. In the wake of the allegations and investigations, hundreds of children would emerge emotionally scarred, the McMartin Preschool and its adjoining lots would be dug up in searches for "secret tunnels" that would never be discovered, resulting in demolishing the school. Ray Buckey, a part-time aide at the school, spent five years in jail, and many teachers and administrators' reputations were ruined.

The ultimate irony would be that the DA would not secure any convictions in the case, which he finally abandoned after a second jury reached a hung verdict against Ray Buckey. The other teachers who were accused were acquitted. The day before the end of the three-year preliminary hearing in the case, and after having been diagnosed as a paranoid schizophrenic, Judy Johnson was found dead in her home from chronic alcoholism—in part due to her despondency over her 13-year-old son's inoperable brain tumor. She never testified in any hearing in the case.

Ray Buckey's Arrest and the Police Investigation

The police searched Buckey's home, but found no evidence of child pornography, videotapes, or photographs of children at the school or otherwise. Undeterred, on September 7, 1983, Police Detective Jane Hoag arrested Ray Buckey after confiscating a rubber duck, a graduation robe, and Playboy magazines from Buckey's home. Despite interrogations, Buckey refused to confess. The Los Angeles District Attorney's office declined to prosecute the case given the lack of evidence.[3] They released Buckey from jail.

Undaunted, the police also seized preschool records and found a mailing list. The police chief sent the following letter to parents, asking that it be treated "strictly confidential." The letter read:

> September 8, 1983
>
> Dear Parent:
>
> This Department is conducting a criminal investigation involving child molestation (288 P.C.) Ray Buckey, an employee of Virginia McMartin's Pre-School, was arrested September 7, 1983 by this Department.
>
> The following procedure is obviously an unpleasant one, but to protect the rights of your children as well as the rights of the accused, this inquiry is necessary for a complete investigation.
>
> Records indicate that your child has been or is currently a student at the pre-school. We are asking your assistance in this continuing investigation. Please question your child to see if he or she has been a witness to any crime or if he or she has been a victim. Our investigation indicates that possible criminal acts include: oral sex, fondling of genitals, buttock or chest area, and sodomy, possibly committed under the pretense of "taking the child's temperature." Also photos may have been taken of children without their clothing. Any information from your child regarding having ever observed Ray Buckey to leave a classroom alone with a child during any nap period, or if they have ever observed Ray Buckey tie up a child, is important.
>
> Please complete the enclosed information form and return it to this Department in the enclosed stamped return envelope as soon as possible. We will contact you if circumstances dictate same.

We ask you to please keep this investigation strictly confidential because of the nature of the charges and the highly emotional effect it could have on our community. Please do not discuss this investigation with anyone outside your immediate family. Do not contact or discuss the investigation with Raymond Buckey, any member of the accused defendant's family, or employees connected with the McMartin Pre-School.

THERE IS NO EVIDENCE TO INDICATED THAT THE MANAGEMENT OF VIRGINIA MCMARTIN'S PRE-SCHOOL HAD ANY KNOWLEDGE OF THIS SITUATION AND NO DETRIMENTAL INFORMATION CONCERNING THE OPERATION OF THE SCHOOL HAS BEEN DISCOVERED DURING THIS INVESTIGATION. ALSO, NO OTHER EMPLOYEE IN THE SCHOOL IS UNDER INVESTIGATION FOR ANY CRIMINAL ACT.

Your prompt attention to this matter and reply no late than September 16, 1983 will be appreciated.

HARRY L. KUHLMEYER, JR.

Chief of Police

JOHN WEHNER, Captain[4]

Just the facts, ma'am. Not that we want to predispose you.

The Interviews of the Children

In November 1983, Children's Institute International immediately spun up under the direction of associate Kee MacFarlane, who held a master's degree in social work from the University of Maryland that she earned in 1974. Although she called herself a "Psychotherapist," she later admitted in the preliminary hearing that she was not licensed as a psychologist, a social worker, nor a marriage, family, or child counselor by the State of California. In his opening statement at the trial, Buckey's attorney would claim the only licenses MacFarlane held were "a driver's license and a welder's license." She had previously obtained a welder's license as part of her avocation as a sculptor. Molding things apparently came naturally to Ms. MacFarlane. By March 1984, CII investigators had identified some 360 students as sexually abused.

Kee MacFarlane and a CII co-worker, Dr. Astrid Hager, interviewed many of the children using techniques like these in the following actual interview, using puppets and anatomically correct dolls. Here is a partial transcript of her interview of an 8-year-old boy:

> **MacFarlane:** Mr. Monkey is a little bit chicken, and he can't remember any of the naked games, but we think that you can, 'cause we know a naked games that you were around for, 'cause the other kids told us, and it's called Naked Movie Star. Do you remember that game, Mr. Alligator, or is your memory too bad?
>
> **Boy:** Um, I don't remember that game.
>
> **MacFarlane:** Oh, Mr. Alligator.
>
> **Boy:** Umm, well, it's umm, a little song that me and [a friend] heard of.
>
> **MacFarlane:** Oh.
>
> **Boy:** Well, I heard out loud someone singing, "Naked Movie Star, Naked Movie Star."
>
> **MacFarlane:** You know that, Mr. Alligator? That means you're smart, 'cause that's the same song the other kids knew and that's how we really know you're smarter than you look. So you better not play dumb, Mr. Alligator.
>
> **Boy:** Well, I didn't really hear a whole lot. I just heard someone yell it from out in the [yard]. Someone yelled it.
>
> **MacFarlane:** Maybe. Mr. Alligator, you peeked in thewindow one day and saw them playing it, and maybe you could remember and help us.
>
> **Boy:** Well, no, I haven't seen anyone playing Naked Movie Star. I've only heard the song.
>
> **MacFarlane:** What good are you? You must be dumb.
>
> **Boy:** Well I don't know really, umm, remember seeing anyone play that, 'cause I wasn't there, when - I -when people are playing it.
>
> **MacFarlane:** You weren't? You weren't? That's why we're hoping maybe you saw, see, a lot

of these puppets weren't there, but they got to see what happened.

Boy: Well, I saw a lot of fighting.

MacFarlane: I bet you can help us a lot, though, 'cause, like, Naked Movie Star is a simple game, because we know about that game, 'cause we just have had twenty kids told us about that game. Just this morning, a little girl came in and played it for us and sang it just like that. Do you think if I asked you a question, you could put your thinking cap on and you might remember, Mr. Alligator?

Boy: Maybe.

MacFarlane: You could nod your head yes or no. Can you remember who took the pictures for the naked-movie-star game? That would be a great thing to feed into the secret machine [the video camera], and then it would be all gone, just like all the other kids did. You can just nod whether you remember or not, see how good your memory is.

Boy: [Nod's puppet's head.]

MacFarlane: You do? Well, that's remarkable. I wonder if you could hold a pointer in your mouth, and then you wouldn't have to say a word and [boy] wouldn't have to say a word. And you could just point.

Boy: [Places pretend camera on adult male nude doll using alligator puppet] Sometimes he did.

MacFarlane: Can I pat you on the head for that? Look what a big help you can be. You're going to help all these little children, because you're so smart ... OK, did they ever pose in funny poses for the pictures?

Boy: Well, it wasn't a real camera. We just played...

MacFarlane: Mr. Alligator, I'm going to. . .going to ask you something here. Now, we already found out from the other kids that it was a real camera, so you don't have to pretend, OK? Is that a deal?

Boy: Yes, it was a play camera that we played with.

MacFarlane: Oh, and it went flash?

Boy: Well, it didn't exactly go flash.

MacFarlane: It didn't exactly go flash. Went click? Did little pictures go zip, come out of it?

Boy: I don't remember that.

MacFarlane: Oh, you don't remember that. Well, you're doing pretty good, Mr. Alligator. I got to shake your hand.

Interview #2 (a 6-year-old girl)

Dr. Astrid Heger: Maybe you could show me with this, with this doll [puts hand on two dolls, one naked, one dressed] how the kids danced for the Naked Movie Star.

Girl: They didn't really dance. It was just, like, a song.

Heger: Well, what did they do when they sang the song?

Girl: [Nods her head]

Heger: I heard that, I heard from several different kids that they took their clothes off. I think that [first classmate] told me that, I know that [second classmate] told me that, I know that [third classmate] told me. [Fourth classmate] and [fifth classmate] all told me that. That's kind of a hard secret, it's kind of a yucky secret to talk of-but, maybe, we could see if we could find—

Girl: Not that I remember.

Heger: This is my favorite puppet right here. [Picks up a bird puppet] You wanna be this puppet? Ok? Then I get to be the Detective Dog . . . We're gonna just figure it all out. Ok, when that tricky part about touching the kids was going on, could you take a pointer in our mouth and point on the, on the doll over here, on either one of these dolls, where, where the kids were touched? Could you do that?

Girl: I don't know.

Heger: I know that the kids were touched. Let's see if we can figure that out.

Girl: I don't know.

Heger: You don't know where they were touched?

Girl: Uh-uh. [Shakes her head]

Heger: Well, some of the kids told me that they were touched sometimes. They said that it was, it kinda, sometimes it kinda hurt. And some the times, it felt pretty good. Do you remember that touching game that went on?

Girl: No.

Heger: Ok. Let me see if we can try something else and –

Girl: Wheeee! [Spins the puppet above her head.]

Heger: Come on, bird, get down here and help us out here.

Girl: No.

Heger: Bird is having a hard time talking. I don't wanna hear any more no's. No no, Detective dog we're gonna figure this out.[5]

According to the Ninth Circuit Court of Appeals in a civil rights lawsuit filed by Peggy McMartin Buckey after the conclusion of the first trial and her acquittal:

> MacFarlane had no relevant academic, professional, or technical licenses or credentials. CII and MacFarlane proceeded seriously to mishandle the investigation, so as to violate established guidelines for child abuse investigation and to cause the children to fabricate testimony and fantasize experiences of abuse that had never occurred. The County, acting through [District Attorney] Philibosian, accepted the CII investigation as basis for launching a prosecution against Buckey and others. Meanwhile, MacFarlane leaked the story to Satz at [K]ABC [Channel 7], where it was disseminated to the public.[6]

To top off her qualifications, MacFarlane also admitted to a romantic relationship with the TV news reporter who originally broke the story, Wayne T. Satz. The Ninth Circuit allowed Buckey's case to proceed against the named defendants.

By early February 1984 during the beginning of local "sweeps month," Satz told television viewers in Los Angeles of a "massive child abuse scandal" involving 60 children at the McMartin Preschool. MacFarlane and Satz's romantic relationship was not the only one spawned by the McMartin Preschool case. Los Angeles Times Editor David Rosenzweig, who oversaw the coverage of the case for the paper, became engaged to marry Lael Rubin, the lead prosecutor, having met her in 1988. Rosenzweig later removed himself from the story. Rosenzweig died in 2007, survived by Rubin. After the trial, Los Angeles Times Reporter David Shaw wrote a Pulitzer Prize-winning expose on the case and questioned his own paper's lack of bias in its coverage.

On March 22, 1984, a grand jury indicted Ray Buckey, his mother, Peggy Buckey, his sister, Peggy Ann Buckey, Virginia McMartin, and three other McMartin teachers, Mary Ann Jackson, Bette Raidor, and Babette Spitler. The grand jury initially indicted the "McMartin Seven" on 115 counts of suspected child sexual abuse. In May 1984, District Attorney Robert H. Philibosian increased to 208 the number of charges and identified 40 additional alleged child victims. As a result of the charges, Virginia McMartin faced 96 years in jail and Raymond Buckey faced 776 years. On the civil side, some 24 parents filed lawsuits against the accused, claiming damages of nearly $24 million for their children.

During the McMartin indictments and the beginning of the preliminary hearing, Philibosian ran for election in November 1984. He had been appointed to fill former Los Angeles District Attorney John Van de Kamp's unexpired term after Van de Kamp's election as California State Attorney General in 1982. In the election, Philibosian lost to District Attorney Ira Reiner. Philibosian then went to work as "of counsel" (not a partner, not an associate) to a large Los Angeles law firm.

After filing the indictments and exchanging discovery in the case, the matter proceeded next to a preliminary hearing. Under California law, the attorneys for both parties are required to provide one another with all physical and documentary information they intend to use at the preliminary hearing and trial. The prosecution has the added burden of disclosing to the defense any exculpatory evidence they may have in their possession. Questions arose later whether the prosecution had met its burden in timely disclosing exculpatory evidence.

The Preliminary Hearing

The preliminary hearing started in August 1984 and lasted almost three years. Los Angeles County Municipal Court Judge Aviva K. Bobb presided over the hearing. Three prosecutors, including Deputy District Attorney Lael Rubin, presented witnesses for the prosecution. Three years? Remember that part earlier about presenting your case succinctly? To top it off, the Sixth Amendment to our Constitution requires a speedy trial generally to start within ten days of an arrest, but there are too many exceptions to cite.

The witnesses called included Kee MacFarlane of CII, some of the allegedly abused children, McMartin parents, therapists, and medical experts. The defense attorneys questioned each of the witnesses at length and argued to the judge that such allegedly widespread and deep-rooted abuse could not have gone on for so long undetected by parents, medical experts, and authorities.

University of Missouri, Kansas City Law Professor Douglas O. Linder observed:

> The testimony of children at the preliminary hearing was shockingly bizarre, and often riddled with inconsistencies and contradictions. Several children reported being photographed while performing nude somersaults as part of the Naked Movie Star Game. One child said that as the game was being played the children sang, "What you see is what you are, you're a naked movie star!" Others testified as to playing a nude version of "Cowboys and Indians"-- sometimes with the Indians sexually assaulting the cowboys, and sometimes vice versa. Children testified that sexual assaults took place on farms, in circus houses, in the homes of strangers, in car washes, in store rooms, and in a "secret room" at McMartin accessible by a tunnel. One boy told of watching animal sacrifices performed by McMartin teachers wearing robes and masks in a candle-lit ceremony at [nearby] St. Cross Episcopal Church. In response to a defense question, the boy added that

the kids were forced to drink the blood of the sacrificed animals. Perhaps strangest of all, was the testimony of one boy who said that the McMartin teachers took students to a cemetery where the kids were forced to use pickaxes and shovels to dig up coffins. Once the coffins were removed from the ground, according to the child, they would be opened and the McMartin teachers would begin hacking the bodies with knives.[7]

Nevertheless, at the end of the laborious hearing, Judge Bobb found probable cause that a crime had been committed and ordered the Defendants bound over for trial.

At the conclusion of the three-year preliminary hearing in 1986, Rubin's co-prosecutors expressed doubts about the continued prosecution of the case. District Attorney Ira Reiner and his senior deputies met with the trial team and elected to dismiss all charges against five of the defendant teachers, leaving only Ray Buckey and Peggy McMartin Buckey to face trial. At this point, the District Attorney's office had spent over $4 million prosecuting the case. Before the trial would end, the DA's office would spend another $11 million, and for all the time and money spent, not obtain a single conviction.

Professor Linder again reported that before the trial started:

> Independent filmmakers who produced a documentary on the McMartin trial turned over to both the California A. G.'s office and to defense attorneys copies of a taped interview with McMartin prosecutor Glenn Stevens. In the on-camera interview, Stevens acknowledges that children began "embellishing and embellishing" their stories of sexual abuse and said that, as prosecutors, "we had no business being in court." Stevens also admitted on tape that prosecutors withheld potentially exculpatory information from defense attorneys, including evidence concerning the mental instability of the original complainant in the case, Judy Johnson, as well as evidence that Johnson's son was unable to identify Ray Buckey in a police line-up.[8]

Stevens resigned from the case and revealed material that had been withheld from the defense attorneys in the preliminary hearing, including claims by the original accuser's mother, Judy

Johnson, that people had flown through windows, killed lions, and had sexual encounters with giraffes. Stevens also revealed wild and untrue allegations against Ray Buckley that had him beating a giraffe to death with a baseball bat. Based on this withheld and exculpatory evidence, the defense attorneys made a motion to dismiss the charges, but the judge denied the motion.[9] The trial was set to proceed.

The First Trial

After the unusually and inordinately long preliminary hearing, the first of two trials began on July 14, 1987, just shy of five years since the first allegations. The parties picked a jury, which itself took weeks. Finally, the parties selected eight males and four females, half of which were white, three African American, two Asian, and one Hispanic. All but two jurors had some college education.

Opening statements began with the lead prosecutor, Deputy District Attorney Lael Rubin:

> Your honor, ladies and gentlemen, this is a case about trust and betrayal of trust . . . trust placed in the hands of Ray Buckley and Peggy Buckey. Parents who will testify will tell you. . . they didn't ask about activities that were going on at the preschool. They didn't piece together the clues they were getting from their children. These parents will tell you they now understand the importance of listening. The case contains one hundred felony counts of Section 288-A and B, and one count of conspiracy. . . .
>
> Betrayal! These innocent children placed their trust in these two teachers and the teachers betrayed them. . . . One mother observed her two daughters performing oral copulation on each other. Another mother saw a sore rectum in her child. She will tell you [her child] did not want to go to school, did not want to sit on her father's lap and that she ran through the house singing. "What you see is what you are/ You're a naked movie star."
>
> One mother will tell you that she saw her daughter masturbating with a wooden pole. One mother will tell you that her children had nightmares. One mother will tell you that her child had a rectal

fissure. Another mother will tell you she saw bloody stools when her child went to the bathroom. Then, the people will ask you to bring back verdicts on all one hundred counts. . . .[10]

Dean Richard Gits, the attorney for Peggy McMartin Buckey had a different approach:

> Ladies and gentlemen, yesterday, Miss Rubin told you this is a case about trust. I'm here to outline Mrs. Buckey's defense. This is not a case about trust. This is a case about victims. It is your job to decide who are the victims, and what I call 'the enemy. . . .'
>
> It is the theory of the defense that all these people are victims. There is one more victim I will not name, but before this case is over you will know who he is.
>
> You will come to know Mrs. Buckey. You will find out she is not a perfect person. Some say she talks too much, that she is nosy. But under all of it you will see a warm and kind heart. You will come to know that Mrs. Buckey does not molest children. She loves children. You will come to know that Mrs. Buckey does not slaughter animals. The D.A. seems to talk about games and mentions that someone dug up a lot, and someone left the school with a bunch of boxes, suggesting that pornography was somehow secreted. You will come to know exactly what was taken out. Also, you will come to know the money that was spent and the people utilized. It's what I call the nonevidence in this case.
>
> The people interviewed included 450 children and 150 adults. Also, forty-nine photo lineups were prepared, bank account records were seized and examined. Eighty-two locations were photographed, one church was investigated. Three churches were implicated, two food markets, two car washes, two airports, and one national park. Thousands of pornographic photographs and movies, confiscated by police, were examined in a search for pictures of the McMartin children. Laboratory tests were conducted of twenty blankets from the school, children's clothing, sheets, rags, and a long list of other items, including mops, kitchen rags,

notebooks, soil samples, sponges, animal bones, quilts, underwear, and an archeological dig was conducted.

All of these investigations came up negative. They were looking for secret tunnels, trap doors. They conducted surveillance of Ray Buckey, his family, and friends, which consumed 135 hours. They consulted with a satanic expert, U.S. Customs agents. They contacted pedophiles; they checked real estate records, utilities records, relatives, friends, associates of the Buckey family, other possible offenders, vehicles, uncharged suspects.

They attempted a pornography buy. All of this cost more than one million dollars. The results? Zero! We believe the money was well spent. It was well worth it. Everything they investigated and found nothing-- [this is] defense evidence! It was well worth it.

Between August 17 and September 7, 1983 . . . Detective Hoag will tell you she contacted twelve families, and you can imagine what impact that would have. But the result of the investigation was zero molestation. Peggy's name was never mentioned. So, as of September 7, 1983, there was no molestation. There was a search, and the purpose of the search was to find pornography. So she executed a search warrant. A letter was sent out stating that Ray Buckey was arrested for child abuse. It told the parents 'ask your child. . . .' As of that date, nobody indicated any molestation was going on at that school.

Within the CII structure, many things happened that you have to know. . . . And when Kee MacFarlane said a child had been molested, the mother would talk to another mother. . . . The interviewers gave the parent a nine-page questionnaire, and while the parent was filling out the questionnaire, they took the child into a separate room and interviewed the child for an hour, or two hours!

You need to look at that tape carefully. . . . Why did the parents take their children there? They were told that they were experts. They had an impressive building. They had a separate unit called 'Child Abuse Diagnostic Center.' These people must know what's going on. The parents were told and believed they were experts.

The interviewer in every case walks in the door and says, "Mr. and Mrs. [Parent], I have some bad news for you. Your child has been molested." You will see the tape. Each and every parent was told, "You have to be supportive of the child." It is hard to disagree with that, but the result is that it reinforces the child.

And they wouldn't look at the whole tape. They would fast-forward so that the parents never saw the denials. . . the parents were convinced that it happened. . . . The child gets love and affection. You will see that they were referred to a therapist. One of those people was an employee of the very agency that did the evaluation, connected ideologically. . . .

The involvement of the CII didn't end there. They brought in an employee of CII, Dr. Heger. She will testify her findings. She will conclude [that] they are consistent with sexual abuse. She will testify the children were molested . . . .Medical evidence does not exist.

You will find further reinforcement of the child. . . . It provides a bonding with other families. They have been told and they believe their children were molested in these cases.

You will see from the tape how [a child] testified in the preliminary hearing that she was locked in a closet. There are no closets in the preschool!

• • •

Why were the Manhattan Beach Police, and CII victims? Because they believed in what they were doing. They were not entirely victims, because they should have known better.

There is one more victim, and that last victim is the same as the enemy. And when you get to know this person you will have solved this case.[11]

Ray Buckey had his own attorney, required by California law in each criminal case to avoid the potential for a conflict of interest, a momentous change since John Adams first tried cases as described in the Boston Massacre chapter. Defense Attorney J. Daniel Davis, opened for Mr. Buckey, attacking the prosecution's case before it even got started:

> Good morning, ladies and gentlemen . . . I have heard negative things about betrayal of trust. There was something very, very wrong about what happened. The truth never really had a chance because children were artificially traumatized by interviewers into falsely believing they were molested.
>
> The evidence itself will be a source for you to decide. There are people who are primarily responsible for what is very wrong in this case. . . . What is the effect of telling parents that their child has been molested? If the child has not been molested, could you ever convince the parents thereafter that the child was not molested? Can winning a trial at all costs be consistent with justice?
>
> The evidence . . . will tell you that Ray Buckey was not at the school at the critical times . . . Ray Buckey was not even there at the school when [a boy who accused Buckey] was there. The teachers who have died were not accused. Those who are living were all accused.
>
> There were good reasons for people putting their trust in the school. There will be testimony that naked games were played. The children played good, wholesome, healthy games. The children went on field trips. Parents came along. . . . Songs were sung. There was a music environment. No guns were permitted. . . . There were projects. Individual pieces were put up on the bulletin board. There were drawings and paintings these children did. . . . There were pets. Turtles, rabbits, guinea pigs, dogs, bird feeders. It was a happy environment.
>
> The D.A. sent [the families] to CII. CII said they were molested and referred them to therapists. . . . They were directed to Manhattan Beach Police Department and made statements. . . and parents

were told to go to an agency that provides funds for victims. That led to payments to CII and therapists. . . . Witnesses were generated. The D.A. is putting on his case with witnesses almost entirely from CII. CII provided the witnesses.

Ray Buckey is twenty-nine. He was born in 1958 in Hawthorne. He attended the Virginia McMartin Preschool. He is an athletic person. You will find that he has been active in a number of sports. He attended El Camino College for two years. He has coached a variety of sports.

When he was at home he kept a number of pets. He is not a person who could likely harm an animal. They secretly taped conversations between Ray and his mother for hundreds of hours, hoping to hear conversations of crimes. Instead, they talked about animals. He began as a teacher at McMartin Preschool in 1981, took classes at UCLA. He became a teacher in 1981 until he was arrested. He was living with his parents. The house he lived in was searched. Ray Buckey rushed to a hiding location and pulled out some pornography and attempted to flush it down the toilet. It was not child pornography. It was pictures of nude adults. He was caught trying to flush it. Nude adults.

I am Ray Buckey's attorney and I do speak for him, so I would like to tell you that I will not be testifying in this case. He will be testifying. And we ask that you keep an open mind and that you await all the evidence in this case, and that he fully intends to reveal all he knows about the case, and that there may be victims on both sides.

. . . Mrs. Johnson told authorities that [her boy] was molested at a time when Ray Buckey was in jail. [Her boy] gave no testimony at the preliminary hearing. He was interviewed on videotape by Dr. Gloria Powell. That videotape has disappeared.

. . . We were told that they were experts, that they had expert credentials. . . . Kee MacFarlane's only credentials were a driver's license and a welder's license.[12]

The attorneys on both sides had the benefit of a three-year preliminary hearing to study their case, so they knew exactly where the holes in the case lay. Davis obviously expected to attack Kee MacFarlane's credentials.

On August 8, 1988, Kee MacFarlane took the stand in the trial, and was cross-examined by the defense attorneys, first by Dean Gits, counsel for Peggy Buckey:

Q: When [name of girl] says she doesn't remember any[naked games] you said, "I know 'em all because other kids told me." Do you think that puts pressure on ----- to remember games that she might otherwise not remember?

A: Yes.

Q: Do you think that having naked dolls with anatomical parts tends to suggest to the child naked games, naked people?

A: No, I don't believe that.

Q: You made the statement, "Every kid from the preschool came in and told me." Do you think that statement puts pressure on a child?

A: No.

Q: You said, "That's why we wanted to use puppets. We wanted them to get real brave because more than sixty kids have come in and told yucky secrets, and every day more kids come in and tell us what went on down there." Do you think that statement might put undue pressure on [name of girl] to comply with what other kids said?

A: That statement was true.

[...]

Q: In this interview, you are the source of contagion, right?

Prosecution attorney: Objection.

Judge William R. Pounders: Sustained.

Q: (by Gits) "All the kids' mommies and dads now know what happened at the school, all the

	touching, all those sneaky little games." Do you think by using that statement, and authority figures as sources of knowledge is putting pressure on her?
A	I'm telling her all the parents came to see me and now it's okay.
Q:	Before that did [name of girl] make any statement about touching?
A:	I don't really remember.
Q:	"Well, I'm glad you're not so dumb, Snake." Do you think by telling [the interviewed girl] that, you are telling her she's dumb if she didn't agree?
A:	No.
Q:	"The mommies and daddies are so glad the kids are telling." When you say "this stuff happened," are you telling ------ touching happened at the preschool?
A:	I think I'm trying to tell her I know something happened. I use the word, "stuff," on purpose.
Q:	Do you believe these statements tell the children you believe molestation happened at the preschool?
A:	No.

• • •

Q:	"Well, Mr. Snake, you and any puppets you want to use can help us figure it out so no more kids will have that yucky stuff happen to them. . . ." Do you think this is one of the most fundamental pressure points? "All the other kids said it happened." Parents, Kee, authority figures. Isn't that telling [the interviewed girl] that kids are getting raped and molested? "Secret police are watching Ray all the time." Don't you think that statement might influence [the interviewed girl] to believe that Ray is a bad person?
A:	Yes.

Q: ". . . and we're gonna make sure that no more kids get hurt." What did you mean, "we"?

A: I was referring to myself.

Q: "If you have a good memory like all the other kids." Isn't that putting pressure on [the interviewed girl]?

A: I'm not asking [her] to comply with my statement...

Q: "I think we should beat up Mr. Ray. . . . What a bad guy! Don't you think he's a bad guy? He's not gonna do this any more to kids, is he?" Did you encourage [the interviewed girl] to beat up the Ray doll?

A: In a manner of speaking, yes.

Q: Is there a clinical reason for doing that? A therapeutic reason?

A: It can be. . . .

Q: Looking back on [this] interview. . . do you think Raymond Buckey ever had a fair chance?

A: The issue of "fair" may have to be left to the courts to decide.

Q: No further questions at this time, your honor. Then Daniel Davis, counsel for Ray Buckey, took up the cross-examination:

Q: You indicated you had training from the FBI.

A: No, I was the trainer.

Q: And who trained you before you trained the FBI?

A: I attended numerous workshops.

• • •

Q: Do you think that by disrobing a doll and exposing a child to what appears to be an erect penis, that that's suggesting things to the child?

A: Well, we worked very hard on the dolls to have them not appear to be an erect, stimulated penis. In fact we tied them down. If you're asking about whether it can ever affect a child, it's one the research of the last five years has been investigating and . . . there's absolutely no evidence in the research that they do that. . . providing incorrect or false information just because they've got these dolls. . . .

• • •

Q: Do you see any harm in telling a child what other children said?

A: Harm? Well I can see it can become a problematical issue in legal cases but it doesn't have any effect one way or the other. You cannot say that it is harmful. In fact I did it because I saw a potential for children sitting and clamming up. I did it to prevent that.

Q: . . . You can't distinguish whether what the child says thereafter is something they actually experienced or something you're telling them other kids said. Isn't that one of the issues?

Prosecution attorney: Objection. Speculation.

Judge Pounders: Sustained.

• • •

Q: Just taking the act of a child beating a doll, do you feel there is a difference in interpreting what is going on when a child beats a doll of their own volition, as opposed to a child beating a doll at the suggestion of an adult?

A: It can be different. It can be the same. It depends on the child. . . . It may be the same, whether they're invited to do it or whether they do it on their own.

Q: To the extent that you adopted this doll-beating technique, you cannot direct us to the identity of any child in the McMartin case that initiated it in their own right-right?

A: Not off the top of my head.

Q: And did any of these children, of their own volition, initiate the doll-beating?

A: Not that I recall.

Q: You suggested it to the children?

A: I don't remember.

. . .

Q: You accept, don't you, that in some of these interviews you urged these little children to beat up on these dolls?

A: Yes.

Q: And at the beginning of this piece you're introducing the name of a game and the fact it may or may not be a naked game, correct?

A: Correct.

Q: Don't you feel that that is overly suggestive to a child to tell the child that it's naked?

A: Absolutely not!

. . .

Q: And did you make an effort to force little [name of boy] to make an accusation of oral copulation on my client in that interview?

A: Absolutely not.

Q: Your sequence in the technique with [the interviewed boy] was to first talk about sexual acts and then attempt to have him demonstrate them - correct?

A: No. . . . The goal was to take it all and show anything significant to the parents.

Q: What we saw [the boy] doing, demonstrating a little doll with its penis in the mouth of another little doll, do you think that had any pornographic effect?

Prosecuting attorney: Objection.

Judge Pounders: Sustained. . . .

Q: (Davis) "MacFarlane: When Ray comes out, what does Ray do? How does something get in that little hole?" [Boy]: "Well, nothing gets in that little hole." MacFarlane: "Remember when we figured all that out? That's already in the secret machine?" [Boy]: "Do yeah. Lemme think. . . ." MacFarlane: "Remember that? How did that get in there? Let's just show how that happened. That'll be easy. And that can be in the secret machine, all gone. How did it happen?" [Boy]: "Well, Ray kicked him." Does it seem apparent to you at this time, that. . . he's saying nothing happened to his bottom?

A: No. It doesn't seem apparent. It seems to me that he's having a hard time with those questions. . . .

Q: What you were really trying to do was to get him to demonstrate sodomy with the dolls so you could show it to the parents. Wasn't that really what you were doing?

A: Mr. Davis! I never set out to try to prove to three hundred plus parents that I could make them believe by looking at some segment of tape that their children had been molested! I wanted them to see what I saw because they know their kids better than I did. . . so they could know in their own minds whether something happened to their children. . . .

Q: Do you see yourself as a link in the process that led to the children making these accusations?

A: I believe that I enabled children who had not been able to describe things, before they came to me. . . . My job was to uncork the bottle, to see what they had to say, once they had gotten over the fear they had.[13]

Remember, Ms. MacFarlane was a sculptor.

The Jailhouse Informant

Beyond offering MacFarlane's so-called expert testimony, the DA's team explored every avenue to convict Ray Buckey, including putting a known perjurer, George Freeman, on the stand. While in prison, Freeman and Ray Buckey were cellmates for a time. In deciding whether to offer an informant's testimony, prosecutors must weigh the balance of testimony by jailhouse informants against the damage defense attorneys will do to the informant on cross-examination. Given the fact that the informant is in prison, the defense attorney will almost always be able to impeach the credibility of the witness with prior felony convictions. When an informant admits to committing perjury as well, however, the witness has hardly any value.

The DA knew that Freeman had committed perjury in three prior cases but granted him immunity from prosecution for perjury in those cases to obtain his testimony against Ray Buckey in the McMartin trial. The California Rules of Professional Conduct, like most other states, prohibits an attorney from putting a witness on the stand if the attorney knows the witness will commit perjury. In this situation, the DA had no direct knowledge that Freeman's story about Ray Buckey's jailhouse confession constituted perjury. When she offered his testimony, it became immediately obvious the testimony was made up, and the cross-examination resulted in Freeman's admission that he made up his story. Prosecutor Lael Rubin took Freeman on direct:

Q: . . . Mr. Freeman, have you been convicted of any felonies?

A: Yes, I have.

Q: How many?

A: Five felonies . . .

Q: Are you on parole?

A: Yes, I am.

Q: Were you recently arrested?

A: Yes, I was.

Q: When?

A: November 10, 1987. . . ..

Q: Have any promises been made to you in order to get you to testify in this case?

A: No promises whatever. . . .

Q: Did Ray [Buckey] tell you [while Buckey was in jail with Freeman] he left town?

A: Yes he did.

Q: Why?

A: He said he was told to leave town and took the pictures and films to South Dakota. He was told to burn them but he buried them.

Q: Did Ray Buckey say that molestations actually occurred in the preschool?

A: Yes, he did.

Q: When?

A: At naptime.

Q: Did he tell you he used anything to help him molest children?

A: Yes, he did.

Q: What did he use to help him molest children?

A: KY [jelly] and baby oil. . . .

Q: You told Ray Buckey you had molested children in order to make him comfortable. Why is it you wanted to make him comfortable?

A: I was curious. . . . I have kids. . . .

Q: What did he tell you?

A: He said he fucked a two-year-old boy in the butt. . .

Q: Did Ray Buckey tell you he took pictures to South Dakota?

A: Yes, he did.

Q: Did he tell you what was on the pictures and films?

A: Kids in sex acts.

Q: Did he tell you what was done with any other pictures?

A: Yes, he did. He said some of them were in Denmark.

Q: Did you talk to Ray Buckey about church?

A: Yes, he did. He said he belonged to a church I couldn't get into-like a cult.

Q: Did Ray Buckey say anything about hurting animals?

A: Yes, he did.

Q: What did he say?

A: If the kids told on him. . . . He slaughtered a cow at a ranch.

Q: Were there kids present?

A: Yes, there were.

Q: How did you get to know Sgt. Dvorak?

A: I met him in 1983.

Q: Was this in another case?

A: Yes, it was.

Q: Did he help you out on your case?

A: Yes, he did. . . . He went and talked to the judge in San Fernando and instead of three years in prison I got one year in county jail. ["Prison" refers to state prison for hardened criminals and serious felony crimes. "Jail" refers to county jails that typically house criminals convicted of misdemeanors.]

Q: On March 28, did a sheriff come and take you to see an attorney?

A: Yes, he did.

Q: When you got to the attorney room did you see any person you see here today?

A: Yes, I did.

Q: Who did you see?

A: Danny Davis and Ray Buckey.

Q: And what was said?

A: He said the Aryan Brotherhood want my ass and two Mexicans in San Fernando and the BGF [Black Guerilla Family prison gang] in Soledad [at the Salinas Valley State Prison] wanted to get me and he said he would put me on TV and the newspapers where everybody could see what I look like. He told me to get my ass out of Ray Buckey's room. He said there would be two men waiting for me on the day of my release.

Q: Did you tell Sgt. Dvorak about your meeting with Mr. Davis?

A: Yes, I did.

Q: Did he look at your notes?

A: Yes, he did. . . . He said he couldn't read 'em. . . .

Q: Did someone suggest that you move out of L.A.?

A: Yes, they did.

Q: And did anyone give you assistance?

A: Yes, they did. Mr. Gil Brunetti of the D.A.'s office paid the first month's rent, approximately one thousand dollars.

Q: Did you contact a TV station?

A: Yes, I did.

Q: What did Dan Leighton tell you?

A: He told me I could make a lot of money from a movie or a book. . . .

Q: Did you talk to reporter Wayne Satz at Channel 7 [KABC]?

A: Yes, I did. . . . Satz wanted to put me on TV.
. . .

Ray Buckey's attorney Daniel Davis, took Freeman on cross-examination, and destroyed his credibility:

Q: . . . Mr. Freeman, are you a rat?

A: They say I am in different places . . .

Q: Mr. Freeman, how would anybody in the world know how many lies you told in the preliminary [hearing]?

A: Only God.

Q: And you're a strong-arm robber, aren't you? [A strong-arm robber is someone who uses physical force to overcome the victim of a crime as opposed to using a weapon.]

A: Depends.

Q: Depends on what?

A: If I'm drunk enough.

Q: You were an informant in the Bailey case?

A: Yeah.

Q: And you lied in front of the jury.

A: One thing, I believe.

Q: Did you consider that a serious lie?

A: I had my reasons.

Q: Those reasons you carried throughout your criminal career, right?

A: Right . . .

Q: I'm going to list cases in which you committed perjury. . .Is there any case in which you didn't perjure yourself?

A: I don't know.

Q: Was there any case where the D.A. didn't know you were lying under oath?

A: I don't know.

Q: The D.A., Watts, used you as a witness after he knew you lied.

A: Yes, he did.

Q: He wrote a letter for you after you told him you lied to him?

A: Yes, he did.

Q: In [the] Bailey [case], did you get up and say he made a confession. . . like you did in this case?

A: Yeah.

Q: I'd like to talk about what you did with some sheep. (Laughter in the courtroom)

Rubin: Objection! Assumes facts not in evidence...

Q: You said you had only five felony convictions. Isn't it the truth that you've had nine felony convictions?

A: Yeah, maybe. . . the way you calculate, yeah.

Q: Have you ever said that a man committed murder when he did not?

A: That goes back to Soledad [at the Salinas Valley State Prison]. I didn't see him stab anybody . . .

Q: You were afraid being seen in newspapers and television [discussing the McMartin case] would endanger you, right?

A: Yes.

Q: Two days after you got out of county jail, whom did you call?

A: Channel 7 Eyewitness News.

Q: And that interview was broadcast on TV, right?

A: Yes.

Q: You were under a court order not to have any interview with news media.

A: Yes.

Q: And you deliberately disobeyed that order.

A: Yes.

Q: And you had a relationship with Sgt. Dvorak and that's the reason you weren't afraid of disobeying an order from a judge?

A: [Inaudible answer.] . . .

Q: You say you were concerned for the safety of your family and that was why you committed your perjuries. Would that be principally your mother and sister?

A: Yes, it was.

Q: And isn't it true that in 1983 you tied up your mother and your sister and robbed them and burglarized their home? . . .[14]

Freeman admitted to nine felony convictions and prior perjurious testimony. Nothing is worse than robbing your own mother, as Davis gleefully pointed out after Freeman not only admitted to that crime, but also concocting his testimony against Buckey. The jury later reported that they completely disregarded Freeman's testimony.

When the prosecution stoops to desperate attempt like offering this kind of testimony, the jurors judge the quality of the remainder of the case, and that judgment is usually reflected in the verdict, as it was here.

Freeman's testimony was not the only accusation of bad lawyering hurled at the DA's team. The prosecutors faced allegations that could also ruin a prosecutor's career. In December 1986 and January 1987, the defense team discovered that for a ten-month period, Chief Prosecutor Lael Rubin and her assistants withheld potentially exculpatory evidence regarding the mental illness of Judy Johnson. Information allegedly came to light that Johnson had told the Los Angeles County DA's investigators that her son claimed to have been molested by a well-known member of the Los Angeles School Board, that some of the defendants were witches, that instructors at a local fitness club were witches, and that he drank blood from the chopped open head of a baby, as well as information about other bizarre allegations.[15]

Apparently not much came of these allegations, which may not have even been true. Lael R. Rubin continued to practice law in the Los Angeles District Attorney's Office and her record with the California State Bar showed no disciplinary proceedings brought against her because of these disclosure issues.

The Children as Witnesses

To top off the testimony of the "experts" and jailhouse informant the DA offered the children's version, putting nine child witnesses on the stand. Both prosecution and the defense attorneys asked simplistic questions, designed not to overwhelm the children. The following testimony is a typical example of the allegations, as examined on direct by Chief Prosecutor Lael Rubin (dashes represent the child's name, omitted from the transcript):

> Q: . . . Did Ray put anything in your mouth?
>
> A: Yes.
>
> Q: Which part?
>
> A: His penis.
>
> Q: In a classroom?
>
> A: I don't know.
>
> Q: Do you remember seeing Miss Peggy without clothes on?
>
> A: Yes. . . . I looked in the window. She had her bra on. . . .

Cross-examination by Daniel Davis:

> Q: ------ [name omitted], did you see a horse get killed?
>
> A: Yeah.
>
> Q: Was it a full-grown horse?
>
> A: Yes.
>
> Q: Do you know what color it was?
>
> A: I don't know.
>
> Q: How did the horse get killed?
>
> A: Ray hit it with a bat.
>
> Q: Where?
>
> A: I don't remember.
>
> Q: Did they ride the horse before it got killed?
>
> A: I don't know.

Q: Were other kids there when the horse got killed?

A: I don't know.

Q: Who was your teacher when Ray killed the horse with the bat?

A: I don't know.

Q: Who was your first teacher at McMartin?

A: I don't know.

Q: Before today you had a meeting at your home?

A: Yeah.

Q: Did you go over your questions with Lael Rubin?

A: Yeah.

Q: Lael Rubin asked you questions and you'd practice answers?

A: Yes.

Q: Some of the answers you gave, you talked about with Ms. Rubin?

A: Yes.

Q: Did you practice the names of the teachers?

A: Yes.

Q: Was your mom there practicing with you?

A: Yes.

Q: Did you practice with Lael?

A: Yes.

Q: Did you have other meetings with Lael?

A: Yes.

Q: You remember how far from the horse you were when it got killed?

A: No.

Q: Did the horse make a sound?

A: I don't know.

Q: Was the horse standing?

A:	Laying down.
Q:	How many times did he hit the horse?
A:	I don't know.
Q:	Did the horse jump around?
A:	I don't know.
Q:	Was there any grownup there when it happened?
A:	I don't know.
Q:	How did Ray touch you?
A:	With his finger.
Q:	Did he touch your wiener?
A:	**Yes.**
Q:	How long did he touch your wiener?
A:	**I don't know.**
Q:	Did Lael Rubin practice your testimony with you?
A:	**No.**
Q:	Did anybody practice your testimony with you before the trial?
A:	**No.**
Q:	Last Friday, Lael was at your house showing you pictures?
A:	**Yes.**
Q:	Did you practice questions and answers?
A:	**Yes.**
Q:	Was there a time you forgot about molestation?
A:	**I forgot everything.**
Q:	Did grownups help you remember?
A:	**Lael?**
Q:	Were there other grownups that helped you remember?
A:	**Yes.**

Q: How about the puppet lady? Did she help you remember?

A: Yes.

Q: Would it be fair to say you didn't remember anything about molestation?

A: Yes.

Q: Did your mother tell you were molested at the preschool?

A: Yes.

Q: Did she tell you [other children] were molested at the school?

A: Yes.

Q: Did you believe her?

A: Yes.

Q: Do you remember some twenty adults told you what happened?

A: Yes. . . .

[. . .]

Q: Do you think, when you talked to the puppet lady, that you were guessing answers?

A: I don't know.

Q: Back when she asked you about the "tickle game" do you remember saying [that] Ray didn't touch you?

A: No.

. . .

[Davis read from the transcript of a CII interview:]

Kee: Did anybody put something yucky in your mouth?

-----: (No response)

Kee: Can you remember?

------: I'm not sure.

Kee: How about a finger in your hole?

------: Yes.

Kee:	Boy! I bet it did! We'll see how smart you are. Did anything come out of Ray's wiener?
------:	(No response)
Kee:	What did the stuff taste like?
------:	He never did that. . . .
Q:	You knew Ray Buckey had been accused of doing things, didn't you?
A:	I don't know.
Q:	Did the puppet lady help you remember that you were molested?
A:	I think so.
Q:	Do you believe Ray Buckey put his penis inside your bottom?
A:	I don't know. . . .[16]

Some of the children who testified told the jury that Lael Rubin spent up to four hours with them practicing their answers.

The Defense Case

The District Attorney presented so many witnesses that it took an entire book to cover all of them - *The Abuse of Innocence*, by Paul and Shirley Eberle. On October 18, 1988, the defense started its case-in-chief and put on several witnesses as well, including the two defendants and its own expert, to counter Kee MacFarlane's testimony. During the defense case, Ray Buckey's bail was set at $1.5 million, enabling him to post bail. He had previously been held without bail. When he was released on bail, Ray Buckey had been sitting in a Los Angeles County jail cell for five years, the same jail where O.J. Simpson was held during his trial for murder. Alleged and convicted child abuser frequently do not survive in jail, themselves abused by other prisoners.

Defense Attorney Dean Gits questioned defense expert Dr. Michael Maloney, a physician, clinical psychologist, and professor of psychiatry at University of Southern California School of Medicine:

> Q: If you would take these scripts that you have isolated or identified here, how would

you characterize them in terms of the propriety of the interview?

A: ... With that many things wrong, with that significant amount of negative influence, I would say that these were very inappropriate interviews for this purpose.

Q: If we were to take the various aspects of this script that you have isolated, and put those together, is there a joint conclusion that you can reach in terms of the propriety of the interviews?

A: I think the risk that you run, very strongly in this case, is getting kids to acquiesce in saying things, or point to things that we are not sure of at all. There's a great deal of pressure on them to do that. . . . In evaluation for sexual abuse, this would be an inappropriate way to proceed for all the reasons I have given. . . in summary, it presents information to the children that we don't know if they had or did not have before. It tells them that things happened at the school. It gives the general nature of the things. It presents the players in the situation and, essentially, presents all the pieces to a puzzle. And there was very strong motivation for the children to solve the puzzle. The motivation comes out of things like, "Are you smart or dumb?", "Are you a good detective?", "Are you going to please your mother and father?" And then, finally, it gives a vehicle for solution, which are these puppets, these dolls. So what you're doing is presenting a situation that you could take with any children, and not know why you got the results you got out of it, no matter what their experience was before that.

Q: And is it your view that these nine CII interviews are worse than just plain useless?

Prosecution: Objection.

Judge Pounders: Sustained.

Q: Would it be fair to say, doctor, that the only end result of these interviews is that they can't be relied upon because of the techniques that were utilized?

Prosecution: Objection.

. . .

Q: Doctor, are you aware of any recognized body of experts in the field of interview methodology who espouse the interview techniques that you've isolated in this particular case?

A: No.[17]

While it's not surprising to have dueling experts disagreeing with one another, one of these experts was credentialed, the other was not. Why believe the one without credentials?

The Defendants Take the Stand

Differences of opinion among criminal defense attorneys vary widely whether defendants in a criminal case should ever take the stand. Ultimately, it's the defendant's own decision, but typically subject to heavy counseling from the attorney. There's a general assumption (which is not true) that only innocent defendants take the stand willingly, and even if true as we saw in the last chapter, that decision turned out poorly for Lindy Chamberlain. In this case, though, both Ray Buckey and Peggy Buckey elected to take the stand in their own defense.

In May 1989, Defense Attorney Dean Gits examined Miss Peggy Buckey on direct, and she denied all the charges brought against her and against the school's teachers.

Q: Did you ever molest any of those children?

A: Never.

Q: Did you ever touch them on any part of their bodies for the purpose of sexual gratification either of yourself or of anybody else?

A: No.

Q: Were you ever naked in front of any of these children?

A: Was I ever what?

Q: Were you ever naked in front of these children?

A: No.

Q: Did you ever make any of these children get naked?

A: No.

Q: Did you ever make any of these children get partially naked?

A: No.

Q: Did you ever transport any of these children off the school grounds for the purpose of molesting them?

A: Never.

Q: Did you ever transport any of these children off the school grounds for the purpose of permitting other adults to touch them?

A: No.

Q: Did you ever transport any of these children off the school grounds for the purpose of engaging in satanic acts at a church?

A: Never.

Q: Did you ever threaten these children in any manner?

A: No.

Q: Did you ever see any person molest these children while you were at the preschool?

A: Never.

Q: Did you see any other person any place in the world molest these children?

A: No.

Q: Did you ever see these children naked with any other teacher at the preschool?

A: No.

Q: With any other adult at the preschool?

A: No.

Q: Did you ever see anything at the preschool that ever once gave you the slightest suspicion that any of those children were being molested in any manner whatsoever?

A: Never.

Cross-examination by Lael Rubin:

Q: You told the court that, as director of the preschool, you were interested in having your son work at the preschool because he had some interest in working with children and that he had the potential to be a good teacher, correct?

A: Yes.

Q: What was it at the time that caused you to believe that he had an interest in working with children?

A: He had a very gentle, loving way with children, which you need when you work with children.

Q: Your honor, I move to strike the answer as nonresponsive.

Judge Pounders: Overruled. The answer will stand.

. . .

Q: Now, you told us that you never saw anything that gave you the slightest suspicion that children were being molested at the preschool. Were you aware that your son didn't wear underwear? Isn't that right?

Q: And you were aware that his penis was seen, correct?

A: No.

Q: And you had the belief that it was okay for Raymond Buckey to be in the preschool and not wear underwear?

A: I do not remember that.

...

Q: Now, Mrs. Buckey. . . did you recognize that there may be a difference between not wearing underwear at the beach and not wearing underwear at the preschool?

A: Never gave it a thought.

Q: Now, did you make statements in the past that some women don't wear bras so it's no big deal?

A: I don't remember that.

Q: Now, with a child sitting on his lap and his not wearing underwear, might that make it easier for a child to touch his genitals?

A: No. . . .

Q: Now one of the differences might be that having a child sitting on your son's lap and his not wearing underwear might make it easier for him to get aroused, correct?

A: No.

Q: Are you aware that ----- grabbed your son in his penis or had you heard that she grabbed your son in his penis?

A: I certainly did.

Q: Was that something that you observed?

A: No.

...

Q: When you checked, that one time, you saw he did have a hard on, correct?

A: He certainly did not!

Q: Would you agree it is an unusual event when the director of a preschool checks her son for an erection?

A: I told you I did it one time and one time only. It's such a dumb question!. . . .It had to do with his being male.

Q: Have you ever seen your son with an erection on any other occasion?

Gits: Objection. Assumes facts not in evidence. . . .

Q: Was she [a mother with a child enrolled in the McMartin Preschool who made accusations against Ray] lying?

A: Yes, she was lying.

Q: Why would she lie?

A: Why did everybody lie in this case?

Q: Do you have a reason to lie in this courtroom?

A: I don't lie. . . . I'm telling the truth. I've heard the word, "lie," so much in this case I've learned to say "lie" like the rest of you. . . .

Q: Are you accusing me of lying?

A: No, I'm not. . . .

• • •

Q: Now, from the thirtieth or thirty-first of August, within the next few days after that, on the second of September, that was when your residence was searched, correct?

A: Yes.

Q: And before the search actually began, you told one of the police officers that "You can't believe little kids. They'll lie." Correct?

A: I do not recall saying that.

Q: Mrs. Buckey, showing you this document, I would ask you to read the end of the first paragraph. . . . And doesn't that refresh your recollection that, shortly after Det. Hoag arrived at your residence, you remarked that "You can't believe little kids. They all lie."?

A: I do not remember saying that.

Q: Mrs. Buckey, if Detective Hoag put that in her police report, would that be untrue?

A: It certainly would be. She lied about a lot of things. . . .[18]

Wow. That was effective cross-examination.

Ray Buckey took the stand on July 28, 1989, and was examined in the defense case-in-chief by his attorney Daniel Davis:

Q: During the time that you were at the McMartin Preschool, did you ever reach an agreement of any kind with other teachers. . . that you would attempt to conceal children being molested at the preschool?

A: No.

Q: You heard [------] describe your mother as being in her bra at the preschool. . . . Did you ever see anything like that at the preschool?

A: No.

Q: From what you know of your mother, is she the type of person who would do that at the preschool?

A: She would not even do it at home.

Rubin: Objection.

Judge Pounders: Sustained. The answer is stricken.

Q: (Davis) You heard suggestions that your mother was naked at the preschool. Is that something you ever saw at the preschool?

A: No.

Q: Have you ever been in St. Cross Church? [Author's note: there were allegations of satanic rituals performed in this church.]

A: Never in my life.

Q: Have you ever touched a child to arouse or obtain sexual gratification?

A: No.

Q: Have you ever knowingly exposed your penis to a child?

A: No.

Q: Did you ever hurt ------ [name of alleged victim]?

A: No.

Q: Did you ever molest ------ in any way?

A: No.

Q: Did you ever sodomize -------?

A: No.

Q: Did you ever sodomize anybody?

A: No. . . .

Q: Have you ever been a member of any type of network of child molesters or involved in the sale or production of kiddie porn?

A: No.

Q: Have you ever seen kiddie porn?

A: No.

Q: Did you ever put your finger into the vaginal opening of a child?

A: No.

Q: Did you ever kill a horse with a baseball bat?

A: No.

Q: Were you ever there when [one of the child witnesses] was at the preschool?

A: No.

Q: Have you ever been in the men's room at the Red Carpet Car Wash?

A: No.

Q: Have you ever been inside the women's room at the Red Carpet Car Wash?

A: No. . . .

Q: Did George Freeman ever talk to you about sex?

A: His sex. He told me about his ex-wives. He told me about the women he had sex with and the men he had sex with. . . .

Cross-examination by Lael Rubin:

Q: Did you tell George Freeman that you screwed [-----] in the ass?

A: No, and I don't use your kind of language, Miss Rubin. . . .

Q: Did you have sexual intercourse with [your adult girlfriend] Barbara?

A: Yes, we did.

Q: Mr. Buckey, did you see that portion of a [D.A.] report that states that Barbara said that she did not have sexual intercourse with you that night?

A: Yes.

Q: Would you describe your sexual relationship with Barbara?

A: In which location?

Q: The Fantasy Motel.

A: Sexual intercourse.

Q: Is there any reason that Barbara would say that you did not have sexual intercourse with her?

A: I'm sure she has her reasons. I'd like to hear them.

Q: Now, you're aware of the fact that Barbara told the district attorney investigator that she. . .

Davis: Objection! Hearsay.

Judge Pounders: Overruled. It's not offered for the truth of the matter.

Q: (Rubin) Are you aware of the fact, Mr. Buckey, that Barbara has told district attorney investigators that she tried to seduce you but that you wouldn't be seduced?

A: I believe the report says that. I don't know her reasons. . . .

Q: Did you and Barbara sleep under your pyramid?

A: Yes. . . .

Q: Mr. Buckey, have you talked with any of your friends about your relationship with Barbara?

Davis: Objection. Vague as to time. Otherwise irrelevant.

Judge Pounders: Sustained. . . .

Q: (Rubin) Did Barbara get along with your mother?

A: I don't remember.

Q: Mr. Buckey, isn't it true that your mother told you to get rid of Barbara?

A: I know she wasn't happy that I had a woman living in my apartment with me. The whole family wasn't too happy about it.

Q: Why is that?

Davis: Objection. Calls for speculation.

Judge Pounders: Overruled.

A: It was their morals. I didn't think it was immoral. . .I was very much in love with Barbara.

Q: Mr. Buckey, do you have a belief that child molesters do not have relationships with adult females?

A: It's common sense. If you have a perversion for children you wouldn't have a desire for female adults.

Q: Is that your belief based on your experience?

A: What experience?

Q: Having a perverted interest in children and therefore not having an interest in women?

> A: . . . I can't imagine it. . . . It's like mixing apples and oranges. It's like homosexuality. You wouldn't have an interest in females.
>
> Q: Have you met or heard about individuals who are bisexual?
>
> A: I've heard of it but I can't imagine it.
>
> Q: Now, isn't it true, Mr. Buckey, that in order to counter a claim that you had a sexual interest in children, you came up with and fabricated this account of sexual intercourse with Barbara?
>
> A: I have no sexual desire for children, never had and never will. . . .[19]

Another riveting cross-examination. No "Perry Mason" moment here or with Mrs. Buckey.

When the matter was finally submitted to the jury some thirty months after it started, the jury then deliberated for two-and-one-half months. On January 18, 1990, the jury acquitted Peggy Buckey on all charges. She was released after having spent two years in jail. On fifty-two of the sixty-five charges against Ray Buckey (prosecutors dropped the other charges during the trial), the jury returned an acquittal. On the thirteen remaining charges, the jury announced a deadlock, with the majority (seven jurors) favoring a not guilty verdict for Ray Buckey. The deadlock resulted in a mistrial.

The Second Trial

With a hung jury in the first trial on thirteen counts, District Attorney Ira Reiner made the decision in late January of 1990 to try the case again against Ray Buckey. Two new DAs were assigned to the case, and the defense attorneys filed a successful motion to obtain a new judge. The second trial mirrored the first, with three notable exceptions: the second trial charged Ray Buckey with only eight counts arising out of alleged abuse of three children, it took only thirteen days and the prosecution elected not to call Kee MacFarlane. She was instead called by the defense.

The jury once again hung along the same lines as before, with the majority favoring acquittal, but unable to agree on a verdict, leaning toward acquittal on six counts and conviction on one. Facing a second mistrial, the DA gave up and dismissed the charges.

The Tunnels

Rounding out this case, some parents of the McMartin Preschool children undertook an almost obsessive effort to dig up the "secret tunnels" in March 1985. After several failed efforts on their own, the parent group finally convinced the DA to conduct a search. The DA hired an archeological firm, Scientific Resource Surveys, Inc., to unearth the ground under and around the McMartin Preschool. No tunnels were located, but the firm did find two trash dumps under the property dating from the 1940s.

Still not satisfied, the parents hired their own expert, Dr. E. Gary Stickel, to search further. Dr. Stickel was famous for his claim of locating human bones in California's Santa Clara Valley, dating back some 40,000 years. Most archeologists believe humans did not occupy either North or South America before 25-30,000 years ago. The day the McMartin verdicts were announced at the end of the first trial, Dr. Stickel released a one-page summary claiming to have located tunnels but refused to release his 186-page report to the DA, citing a "lack of trust." Later analysis of the report resulted in conflicting conclusions, but the consensus remains that no secret tunnels ever existed under or around the McMartin Preschool.

Aftermath

At the end of the second trial, all charges against Ray Buckey were dismissed. In 1991, the McMartin Preschool was demolished. Ray Buckey finished college. Virginia McMartin died in December of 1995 at age 88. Peggy Buckey regained her teaching credentials and was awarded $180,000 from the state in lost pay. She moved to Anaheim, California, where she taught extreme-case disadvantaged children, and died in December 2000 in Torrance, California.

The preliminary hearing and trials left the seven defendants financially destitute. The DA's office did not recover the nearly $16 million it spent.

Defense Attorney Dean Gits worked at the Los Angeles Federal Public Defender's office. Defense Attorney J. Daniel Davis opened a private practice in Los Angeles. Assistant

Deputy District Attorney Lael Rubin was later promoted to Special Prosecutor in the Los Angeles District Attorney's Office. Kee MacFarlane, MSW, continued to participate in the field of child forensic interviews.[20]

The predecessor entity to CII was founded in 1906, and in 1981, CII operated on a $900,000 budget of mostly private donations. CII continues to operate today as Children's Institute, Inc. but its website history does not refer to the McMartin trial.[21] After Kee MacFarlane's involvement with CII, the Institute received $350,000 in state funding in 1985, becoming the first publicly funded training center for the diagnosis and treatment of child abuse.

In all, CII received $15,356,797 in donations, grants, and funding while the McMartin matter was pending.[22]

Chapter Conclusion

The decision went wrong initially with the assumptions made by the police, who simply accepted as true the allegations made against the school and fanned flames of suspicion with their letter to the parents of the schoolchildren. Critical thinking was lacking not only in the police force, but also at CII, who appeared to have simply encouraged the children and then selectively made presentations to the parents of the preschoolers. The District Attorney's Office likewise did not question the allegations and findings. Even the judges did not control their cases, a criticism we will see leveled again in the next chapter. At every stage, the system favored the laudable goal of protecting children, but like the Salem Witch Trials, did little to analyze the foundations for the children's allegations.

Children generally make believable witnesses and consequently the law enforcement system tends to trust their statements implicitly. But a critical view of the testimony presented by the children failed to see their testimony filtered by adults at crucial steps. First, Billy Johnson's mother filtered his statements if they were even his in the first place. Police investigators interpreted the children's statements. CII further adjusted the children's statements, and finally the District Attorney put a prosecution-style spin on their statements. When the children were finally put on the stand and subjected to cross-examination—apparently the first time their statements had been truly questioned, we can see how the allegations fell apart. Had anyone—at any step during this long and tedious and overly expensive process—critically reviewed the children's statements, the matter presumably would have ended early on. But at each critical step, the children's stories went untested.

It was an expensive lesson to learn.

Remember to enter your vote on the outcome of this trial on www.10FamousTrials.com and see how other readers voted.

CHAPTER 10
The O.J. Simpson Trial for the Murder of Nicole Brown Simpson and Ronald Goldman

The O.J. Simpson trial for the murder of his divorced wife, Nichole Brown Simpson, and Ronald Goldman, affected opinions of the criminal judicial system more than any other case in the previous chapters of this book, and perhaps more than any other famous criminal trial. It is certainly one of the most written-about trials, having spawned innumerable books by just about everyone involved with it, and a few that were not, all seemingly directed at the performance of one side or the other, arguing why O.J. was acquitted. Websites instantly popped up, some favoring acquittal, some conviction, while still others tried to figure out what happened. New Yorkers and others on the East coast infatuated with the TV coverage of the trial adjusted their entire schedules to Pacific time just to watch the proceedings. The Internet had yet to take off.

This chapter, like the others, seeks instead to allow you an unbiased, inside look at what happened by viewing the critical testimony yourself. You get to sit in the jury box and see why the jury decided as it did. It's interesting, isn't it, that the chapter heading must be specific enough to identify which of the several O.J. trials will be discussed – his two criminal trials, his civil trials, and his child custody hearings?

But before you take your seat, we need to get the murder case on file. Sunday, June 12, 1994, was at first a relatively calm day in LA; the Gay Pride parade in West Hollywood was in full swing, the third game of the NBA finals was on TV and, ironically, the movie *Speed* was in theaters.

Another day in LA where everything is normal.

That evening, sometime after 10:00 p.m. some thirty years ago, 35-year-old Nicole Simpson Brown and 25-year-old Ronald Lyle Goldman were fatally stabbed at Brown's swanky, $650,000, two-story condominium at 875 South Bundy Avenue. Her house was on a palm-tree-lined, two-lane road in Brentwood, a tony and expensive neighborhood in Los Angeles,

California where houses now have prices with two commas. Sidney and Justin Simpson, Nicole, and O.J.'s children, were asleep upstairs. At 10:15 p.m., a neighbor heard Nicole's dog, describing the noise as a "plaintive howl." At 10:55 p.m., Nicole's dog, an Akita named Kato (who occasionally went with kids when they stayed with O.J. at his Rockingham estate), again barked and attracted the attention of a neighbor who saw the dog with blood on its paws. Then, around ten minutes after midnight, a different neighbor found the dog still barking with blood on its paws and underbelly.

That neighbor walked with the dog and followed it to Nicole's condo to discover the two bodies, describing the scene as a "river of blood." Bloody footprints were found leading from the crime scene down the north walkway to the alley behind her condo. Nicole's head had almost been severed (her arteries and one jugular were sliced so deep the knife wound nicked her spine) and Ron Goldman's body had been stabbed nearly 30 times. Both bodies showed defensive wounds. Ron Goldman had worked as a waiter at the nearby Mezzaluna restaurant and knew both O.J. and Nicole.

Burgers and Fries

Earlier that evening at 9:10 p.m., 47-year-old O.J. and everyone's favorite houseguest, Brian "Kato" Kaelin, went to a McDonald's near O.J.'s home at 360 North Rockingham (a $5 million Tudor-style mansion with three guesthouses), also in Brentwood, in O.J.'s Rolls Royce and had burgers, shakes and fries. O.J. had confided to Kato earlier in the afternoon that he and Nicole were no longer together. While out for food, O.J. complained to Kato that Nicole had been wearing "tight" clothes earlier that evening at their daughter's dance recital. Kato and O.J. arrived home around 9:45 p.m. and went their separate ways.

O.J.'s book, *If I Did It,* may not say, but Google maps report that Nicole's condo and O.J.'s estate are six minutes apart by car, just two miles. Timed runs by the LAPD, however, put the time as much as fifteen minutes with traffic and stop lights, according to one of O.J.'s attorneys F. Lee Bailey. Locals will confirm distances in L.A. are measured in time, not miles.

According to Google Maps (complete with satellite photos of the streets and houses), to get to Nicole's from the estate, travel north on North Rockingham Avenue toward Ashford

Street for 82 feet, turn right at Ashford Street and go 0.2 of a mile, then turn right at North Cliffwood Avenue and travel for 0.9 of a mile, turn left at West San Vicente Boulevard for 0.5 of a mile, and finally turn right at South Bundy Drive for 0.2 of a mile. Nicole's condo is on the right. By choosing the "walking" option, Google Maps reports a slightly different route of 1.9 miles, a 34-minute walk, one-way. There were no bloody footprints found along this walking route.

Later that evening, a limo arrived at O.J.'s estate at 10:25 p.m. to drive him to the airport for a pre-scheduled trip to Chicago, but the driver did not see O.J.'s Ford Bronco parked out front. He waited, and then rang the buzzer on the electronic security system between 10:40-10:50 p.m., but no one responded. Meanwhile, while on the phone with his girlfriend, Kato heard three thumps on the outside wall of the guesthouse, hung up and went to investigate. According to Kato and the driver, they ran into each other between 10:56-10:57 p.m. in front of O.J.'s estate.

At virtually the same time, the driver noticed someone about six feet tall and 200 pounds arrive at O.J.'s house and cross the driveway. The driver couldn't identify the individual, but noticed the individual was about six feet tall, black, and wearing dark clothes. O.J. Simpson's football statistics listed him at 6'2" and 212 pounds. At 11:01, the lights in the house came on, and O.J. then stepped outside and apologized for oversleeping. Kato, Simpson, and the driver loaded Simpson's bags into the back of the limo. O.J. carried a black carry-on bag in the limo with him. At 11:15., the limo driver drove O.J. to the Los Angeles International Airport, where he caught an 11:45 p.m. American Airlines red-eye flight to Chicago for a Hertz-sponsored golf tournament the following day.

Nicole and Ron Goldman's Timeline

Court papers in the trial revealed that Nicole Brown Simpson had moved out of the Simpson mansion in March 1992 and divorced in October 1992, but returned January 15, 1994, and remained there until May 24, 1994, nineteen days before her June 12th death. Her sister, Denise, reported that the two Simpsons had tried to reconcile, but failed.

On the night of her murder, Nicole dined at Mezzaluna restaurant with her party-of-ten family and children after her daughter's 5:00 p.m. dance recital Sunday night (which O.J. had attended as well) at the local Paul Revere Junior High School in Brentwood. The restaurant is a few blocks from Nicole's condo. Nicole spoke by phone to her mother, Juditha Brown, at 9:45. Nicole's mother had lost her prescription reading glasses just outside the restaurant, and after Nicole talked to Goldman and discovering that another waiter found them outside, he agreed to return the reading glasses to Nicole at her condo that evening. Goldman left Mezzaluna around 9:50.

Goldman lived at 11663 Gorham Avenue, also in Brentwood, in an apartment just slightly northwest of the restaurant, and apparently briefly stopped there after his shift to change his clothes before delivering Nicole's mother's reading glasses. Again, according to Google, Goldman's apartment was just six-tenths of a mile from Nicole's condo, a quick two-minute drive by car. Ron Goldman's car was found parked in the alley behind Nicole's condo.

The Police Investigate, So to Speak

After being notified by the neighbor who discovered the two bodies, police began investigating the scene of the double murder around 2:00 a.m. Monday, June 13, 1994, and found five drops of blood along the sidewalk, bloody shoe prints, a cap (with hairs on it), and a bloody left-hand glove outside Nicole's condo on Bundy. When the police went upstairs in Nicole's condo, they found a tub full of water, candles burning and the two children asleep. The police covered Nicole's body with a blanket from inside her condo.

At 4:30, the police left the primary crime scene and went to O.J.'s Rockingham estate. There they found blood drops on O.J.'s driveway and his white Ford Bronco. O.J. had registered at the Chicago O'Hare Plaza Hotel about fifteen minutes earlier.

At 6:00, Detective Mark Fuhrman walked down a path at O.J.'s Rockingham estate (the only place he walked around on the property) and found a second bloody, right-handed glove that seemed to match the one found at the Bundy crime scene. He then located other officers and took them to the glove to point it out. No bloody drops or footprints were found near the second glove. Neither of the two bloody gloves bore any cuts. The police also discovered bloody socks in O.J.'s bedroom.

The LA police next located O.J. in the morning at his hotel and informed him of his ex-wife's death. O.J. returned later in the day, was handcuffed briefly outside his home and his attorney, Howard Weitzman, convinced the police to unlock the cuffs and take them off. The police then took O.J. to their downtown Parker Center station for a three-hour interview, where he went unassisted by an attorney. According to famous attorney F. Lee Bailey, another Simpson defense lawyer, the police would not allow Weitzman to attend the interview, and contrary to Weitzman's advice, Simpson voluntarily underwent questioning alone. There are various other accounts of this scenario. The interview would not be introduced at trial and there were no "fruit of the poisonous tree" defense challenges for evidence gained from that interview.

Without an attorney present, a suspect has the right to remain silent, a right enshrined in our Fifth Amendment, and criminal defense attorneys regularly advise their clients to exercise: "I don't answer questions without my attorney." The police are trained and skilled at interrogation. Criminal suspects have no such defensive training.

During the interview, police officers noted a bloody cut on the middle finger of O.J.'s left hand; he alternately claimed to have cut it both the night before on a cell phone and then again that morning on a glass in the Chicago hotel room. The Plaza Hotel manager found a broken glass and bloody sheets in O.J.'s hotel room.

The Media Explosion

By 8:30 a.m. on Monday, the media found out about the killings and the celebrity status of those involved, and immediately flocked to both the Bundy and Rockingham locations. The circus came to town and would not leave until after the famous "not guilty" verdict in September the following year.

Nicole and Ron Goldman were both buried mid-week on June 16. With his children, Sidney and Justin, O.J. attended Nicole's funeral, appearing distraught. Juditha Brown asked him whether he murdered her daughter, and O.J. reportedly said in response, "I loved her too much." Media coverage of the funerals was a disgrace to the further grief of the families.

On Friday, June 17, 1994, the LAPD alleged it had found O.J.'s blood in samples taken from the Bundy crime scene and issued an arrest warrant for him. Fleeing from his attorney friend

Robert Kardashian's home, O.J. penned what appeared to be a suicide note. At a hastily called 5:00 p.m. press conference, Kardashian read O.J.'s note to the media, and the search for O.J.-turned fugitive was on.

That evening, about 6:20, a motorist in Orange County some forty-five miles south of LA spotted O.J. in a white Ford Bronco, which turned out to be driven by his friend and fellow football star, Al Cowlings. With an hour of daylight remaining, the media intercepted a mobile call from Cowlings that placed O.J. in the back seat with a gun to his head. In what only can be described as surreal, a low-speed, hour-long chase began from Orange County to O.J.'s Rockingham estate in Los Angeles, crossing county lines. Counties in California are the equivalent size of East coast states.

Every local media helicopter was in the air, plus a few last-minute charters, following Cowling and O.J. in the white Bronco on its hour-long travels. The chase took so long that at one point, TV Channel 7's helicopter had to break off to refuel, resulting in that station borrowing the Channel 5 feed and re-broadcasting the chase on its station with the Channel 5 logo emblazoned on the picture. Radio stations broke into regular programming to broadcast pleas from fellow sports personalities begging, "O.J., don't do it." People lined up along the freeways and bridges to watch. Signs appeared on freeway overpasses reading "Go, O.J., Go," an obvious reference to Hertz Rent-a-Car's slogan in its O.J. commercials of the time. Cars ahead of the chase even moved out of the way as Cowlings drove by slowly, flanked and followed by dozens of black-and-white police cars. Indeed, more people reportedly watched the O.J. chase than saw Neil Armstrong take his first step on the moon; a sad commentary on our media-crazed, celebrity-obsessed culture.

Not that I have an opinion, mind you.

O.J. ultimately surrendered just inside his Rockingham estate after an hour-long cell-phone negotiation with police. In their search of the Bronco after the arrest, police found a fake goatee beard and mustache, a change of clothes, $8,750 in cash, a loaded .357 magnum, Simpson family photos, and a passport. The police took O.J. downtown and booked him for double murder, both in the first degree.

O.J.'s sullen mugshot shows his booking number: 4013970 06-17-94, the last six digits referring to the date of the photo. Side note here: never smile in a mugshot—the jury will see it.

Simpson spent the next 474 days at the Los Angeles County Men's Jail, where he was held without bail until his acquittal. Initially, jailers confined O.J. to concrete-walled, 9x7 foot Cell #7033 (smaller than his bathroom at his estate). He wore a red wristband, signifying a "special care inmate" who was initially put on suicide watch in the "Penthouse" or "Celebrity Row" section of the county jail. He was later transferred to a traditional barred cell. When his attorneys couldn't all fit into the jail's existing conference room, at the cost of $3,000, the room was modified to allow four of his lawyers to meet with him at the same time. While O.J. was able to ride back and forth to the trial in a special van, escorted by two unmarked cars, not all prisoners were so lucky.

Other prisoners of the same jail, which previously included five-year veteran Ray Buckey, jailed during the McMartin Preschool proceedings, complained about O.J.'s special treatment of being ferried back and forth to court. Most other inmates were held in the "tank," as the courthouse lockup is known, to wait for the Sheriff's transport bus back to the jail, sometimes waiting until ten or eleven at night for their ride. Former LA County Jail prisoner Rickey Ross told *People* magazine, "It's a big, huge, filthy, stinking, urine-smelling, fecal-matter-smelling room with all kinds of obscene writing on the wall. It's right behind those courtroom doors. On the other side of those doors is hell."[1]

In September, while in jail, O.J. granted temporary custody of his two children to Louis and Juditha Brown, Nicole's parents.

The Grand Jury Proceedings

Between June 17 and June 23, 1994, the Los Angeles District Attorney convened a grand jury to determine whether to indict O.J. Simpson. This tactic is generally adopted by the government to ensure an "independent body" of citizens makes the decision to prosecute a defendant instead of the District Attorney and is usually employed in high-profile cases. Since the defense is prohibited from participating, indictments are usually foregone conclusions and give the DA 'shelter' against public opinion if the grand jury fails to issue an indictment.

In this instance, the DA ultimately dismissed the grand jury due to heightened media coverage and its influence on the grand jury's neutrality. Two witnesses who testified before the grand jury sold their stories to the tabloid press, and ultimately were never called during the trial itself. Grand Jury Witness Jill Shively, a Brentwood resident, testified she saw Simpson speeding away from Nicole's house at 10:39 on the night of the murders, with some dispute over the time of her sighting. Shivley reportedly received $5,000 from *Hard Copy* and additional monies from other media outlets for her story. Jose Camachio, a knife salesman, claimed in the Grand Jury proceedings to have sold a 15-inch German-made knife to Simpson three weeks before the murders, but was unable to produce a receipt. Camachio reportedly received $12,500 for his story.

The Preliminary Hearing

As with all felony criminal trials, and as we saw in prior chapters, the court held a preliminary hearing to determine whether probable cause existed sufficient to believe crimes had been committed. The prosecution, which included Deputy District Attorney Marcia Clark, presented just 22 witnesses (an additional witness testified in an evidentiary hearing before the preliminary hearing started), including several we will see in this chapter: Allan Park the limo driver, Brian "Kato" Kaelin the houseguest, Los Angeles Police Department Detectives Philip Vannatter and Mark Fuhrman as well as Criminalist Dennis Fung. The defense, presented by attorneys Robert Shapiro and Gerald Uelmen, offered no witnesses, which is a typical tactic in preliminary hearings.

Preliminary hearings are notoriously easy for prosecutors to win, and conversely exceedingly difficult for defendants to win. Defense counsel use the hearing to get "free discovery," since defendants are not allowed to depose criminal witnesses. Prosecutors must put on a "passable" case to bind the defendant over and proceed to trial. In addition, most criminal defense attorneys prefer to play their cards "close to the vest" and not reveal their case strategy to the prosecutors.

Nevertheless, the defense filed and argued a motion to suppress all the evidence found at O.J.'s Rockingham estate, but the judge denied the motion and instead admitted the evidence. The defense argued that there was no emergency reason to enter O.J.'s property (which, if true, would allow into evidence things found "in plain sight"), noting that the police did not enter with guns drawn, bulletproof vests or call for backup. The defense likewise pointed out that Detective Mark Fuhrman had jumped the fence and turned his back on the house to "buzz" the rest of the team through the electronic gate. The prosecution disingenuously argued that the police feared for the safety of the occupants, theorizing that O.J. and his family members might also be dead or in danger from a hostage situation. Only after discovering the blood drops and bloody glove did the police get a search warrant. Kato and Simpson's daughter Arnelle (also on O.J.'s estate in a different bungalow) testified that after the police awoke them, the police did not express either of these concerns, or express concern about either murder or suicide.

There was no emergency other than to get evidence.

Criminalist Dennis Fong testified in the preliminary hearing that he never encountered any errors in some 10,000 tests which he has conducted over the course of previous criminal investigations. His testimony would be different at the trial.

Reality must have set in.

Holding it in the air, the judge waved around a sealed envelope presented to her by the defense, allegedly containing evidence. She then ordered it to be filed in the proceedings, unopened. At the time, media speculation abounded over what the envelope contained; some believed it was the murder weapon; some believed it was a knife found in O.J.'s medicine cabinet matching the description of the murder weapon, but with no blood to be found on it. No murder weapon was introduced by the prosecution at the trial. It would not be until March 17, 1995, during the trial that the defense attorneys would again mention the envelope and admit it contained a knife taken from the Rockingham estate after police searched the property twice and failed to find it. The knife had no blood on it.

As an aside to this knife-in-the-envelope tactic, giving a murder weapon to your attorney requires the attorney to turn the knife to the police as part of their investigation. O.J.'s attorneys bent that ethical rule and turned the knife over to the court, using another evidentiary tactic, filing it under seal. That tactic prevented the police from conducting a forensic investigation of the knife during their investigation and a sizable portion of the prosecution since the knife remained in the court file, sealed.

The O.J. preliminary hearing took just six days. At its conclusion, on July 8, 1994, at 3:15 p.m., Judge Kathleen

Kennedy-Powell bound O.J. over for trial, facing the death sentence as alleged by prosecutors. She ruled as follows:

> The defendant will please stand. It appearing to me from the evidence presented that the following offenses have been committed, and there is sufficient cause to believe this defendant guilty of Count 1, a violation of [California] Penal Code section 187(a), with a special allegation pursuant to Penal Code section 12022(b); and Count 2, a violation of Penal Code section 187(a), with a special allegation pursuant to Penal Code section 12022(b); and also that there is sufficient evidence of a special allegation pursuant to Penal Code section 190.2(a)(3), the court holds that the defendant be held to answer therefor, that there be no bail allowed in this case, and that the defendant be committed to the custody of the Sheriff of Los Angeles County. Date of arraignment in Superior Court will be July the 22nd at 8:30 in Department 100. The defendant is remanded at this time, and this court is adjourned.[2]

"Count 1" referred to Nicole Simpson and "Count 2" to Ron Goldman. California Penal Code section 187(a) reads: "(a) Murder is the unlawful killing of a human being ... with malice aforethought." The most interesting aspect of the charges initial brought against O.J. is the ruling's notation to "special allegations," which is legal lingo for the prosecution's intent to seek a death sentence.

Like defense attorneys, not all prosecutors are willing to take on death penalty cases. But some are. As an example, a well-known prosecutor and friend, in adjoining Riverside County, who regularly took special allegation cases was nicknamed, "Doctor Death."

Simpson was apparently arraigned more than once where he would enter his plea to the charges. At one of his delayed arraignments, either July 22 or August 8, 1994, O.J. loudly pled, "Absolutely, 100 percent not guilty" in response to the charges of murder in the first degree against him. Members of Simpson's attorney team offered a $500,000 reward for information leading to the conviction of the real murderers and set up an 800- number tip line. The reward was never paid, the phone number another tactic. The team also hired investigator John McNally, who apparently was not licensed as a private investigator in

California. The defense team never offered up a different killer, either, but a P.I. "was looking into it."

Strategies

Ultimately, several significant developments occurred in this case: by the time the trial started, the prosecutors withdrew their "special allegations," no longer seeking the death sentence for O.J., instead asking the court to impose life in prison as a punishment. Celebrity may have its benefits. By withdrawing the death penalty, the prosecution gave up the opportunity to have a "death-qualified" jury: one that would be willing to find him guilty knowing he might face the death penalty.

Juries so qualified during the *voir dire* process are questioned by the judge to ensure on the one hand they are not categorically opposed to the death penalty, but on the other hand will consider life in prison as an acceptable alternative. These death-qualified juries typically have disproportionately less women and minorities, including African Americans, than standard criminal juries. Members of a death penalty-qualified jury are also more likely to convict than non-qualified jurors. If the prosecution had kept the "special allegations" against O.J. in place, then they could have ensured they enpaneled this type of jury at the start of the case. At any later time, the prosecutors could have withdrawn the death penalty allegation but kept the qualified jury intact, increasing their chances of a conviction. On the other hand, withdrawing the death penalty mid-trial is usually viewed by the jury as the prosecutor's acknowledgement of weaknesses in their evidence.

In another unusual move, the prosecution elected not to file this case in Santa Monica, which would have been the proper venue for the trial since the crime occurred in that judicial district, a determination made solely by location. Santa Monica is largely white and wealthy. The case was instead filed in downtown Los Angeles, where the jury pool would more accurately reflect the racial and financial makeup in the city, but not the suburb where O.J. lived among his wealthy peers. One of the considerations for this decision may have arisen out of the prosecution's concern to avoid a repeat of the six days of riots, looting, and arson that broke out in LA after the practically still-fresh April 29, 1992, jury decision acquitting four white police officers for the beating of Rodney King. Rodney King's verdict sparked outrage over what was considered a racist-based decision as the powder keg for the riots. The prosecution thought it more likely a downtown jury would vote to convict O.J. than his tony Santa Monica neighbors and not trigger riots again. Prosecutors instead blamed the change of venue on earthquake damage to the Santa Monica Courthouse, which oddly enough was able to continue to try other criminal and civil cases while O.J.'s case was heard downtown.

Looking at the case overall, the prosecution had several things in its favor: two dead bodies, lots of evidence (both physical and circumstantial), motive and opportunity. It did not, however, have either a direct eyewitness, a weapon or the bloody clothes supposedly worn by the murderer the night Nicole and Ron Goldman were murdered. The bloody gloves Detective Fuhrman found would play a key role, however.

The Pre-trial Warmup

With in-court cameras rolling all but twice during the proceedings (when cameras accidently caught a juror on tape), Judge Lance Ito opened the proceedings on January 13, 1995. Ito's credentials include a 1972 bachelor's degree with honors from UCLA and a 1975 law degree from another UC school, Berkeley's School of Law at Boalt Hall. Ito had previously served as a Los Angeles Deputy DA and worked as a prosecutor in the gang unit as well as the organized crime and terror unit and married a high-ranking LAPD officer. He had earlier presided over the infamous Charles Keating, Jr. criminal trial arising out of the 1980's savings and loan scandal. Keating's ten-year jail sentence, imposed by Ito, was later overturned on appeal due to judicial error arising out of Ito's incorrect jury instructions.

O.J.'s pre-trial proceedings started with the prosecution team of Marcia Clark, Christopher Darden, and William Hodgman in place, along with others in the LA DA's office. On the other side was the so-called "Dream Team" of defense lawyers, Johnnie Cochran, Jr., a well-known personal injury lawyer who filed civil cases over police brutality; F. Lee Bailey, a lawyer famous for nationally prominent criminal trials; Alan Dershowitz, a Harvard law professor; Robert Shapiro, a locally prominent criminal lawyer; Barry Scheck, a professor at the Cardozo School of Law in New York; Robert Kardashian (yes, *that* family), a local attorney and friend of O.J.; Gerald Uelmen, a law professor at Santa Clara University, and several other ancillary lawyers. Cochran took over the lead of the defense team after deposing Shapiro from that position, winning favor from O.J. for frequently visiting him in jail, something Shapiro rarely did. Kardashian ultimately resigned to his "close personal friendship" with O.J. Sheck and Uelmen were the lawyers who would challenge the prosecution's DNA evidence, which evidence was a relatively new phenomenon at the time. Dershowitz and the other ancillary lawyers handled much of the written motion work as law professors.

As the trial got underway in January 1995, and outside the presence of the jury, Judge Ito ruled on two preliminary motions. He rejected O.J. Simpson's request to individually address the jury after Prosecutor Marcia Clark denounced the idea as "a blatant attempt to impress the jury with his charisma and star appeal."[3] Judge Ito ruled, "The motion to allow the defendant to directly address the jury will be denied. The motion to allow him to exhibit to the jury his knee injuries or the result of the scarring and the surgeries will be allowed."[4]

His performance in the Hertz TV commercials must have been done by a stunt double.

The Goldmans and Nicole Simpson's family attended the trial proceedings at various times. O.J.'s mother, Eunice Simpson, also showed up and testified on behalf of her son like warm apple pie. His father died well before the murders took place.

Choosing a Jury

The non-death-qualified jury was initially comprised of nine African Americans, one Caucasian, one Hispanic and two of mixed race. Of those twelve jurors, eight were women; four were men. The lawyers also picked twelve alternates. The jury and the alternates were sequestered together in a local LA hotel for nearly nine months and had a difficult time getting along.

Judge Ito removed jurors regularly throughout the case for assorted reasons. On Wednesday, March 1, 1995, Judge Ito removed an African American male from the panel and replaced him with a white female. With that removal, the ethnic balance on the jury shifted from nine African Americans, one white, one Hispanic and one mixed race to eight blacks, two whites, the Hispanic, and a mixed-race juror. On March 17, 1995, Judge Ito replaced a self-described "mixed-race" juror with a white woman, 60, who had been divorced since 1968, believed in the accuracy of DNA evidence, and said that during a 911 call that Nicole Brown Simpson "seemed to need help and wasn't taken seriously."[5] Near the end of the trial, there were only two alternates left, and the case was in danger of a mistrial for lack of jurors. Although it would have been possible under California law to proceed with just six jurors (as federal courts do with what is called a "six-pack" jury), the prosecution refused. The trial barely finished with a full jury intact.

Opening Statements

Trial started on January 24, 1995, and would finally end more than eight months later on September 3, 1995, when the jury found Simpson not guilty. In O.J.'s murder trial, the Prosecution team addressed the jury first:

> He killed her out of jealousy. He killed her because he couldn't have her. Simpson is an extremely controlling and possessive man.[6]

Deputy DA Darden told the jury they would find out why O.J. murdered his ex-wife and Goldman. Deputy District Attorney Marcia Clark then described the evidence against Simpson:

> There is a path of blood where there should be no blood. That trail of blood from Bundy through his own Ford Bronco and into his house in Rockingham is devastating proof of his guilt.[7]

Defense counsel Johnnie Cochran spoke following Mr. Darden and Ms. Clark and proclaimed O.J. an innocent man wrongfully accused. He also chose to open with a salvo attacking the evidence:

> Nowhere, I think will you find in this case, is the problem of the evidence being contaminated, compromised, and corrupted more important than the area of DNA testing. This is a - the evidence will show is a very new and powerful technology. In the past five years, police departments and crime labs have tried to transfer this DNA test that has been used for research and medical diagnosis and apply it to crime scene samples. We expect all of you will hear in the course of the evidence, this transfer of technology has not been simple or easy. And so, I

want to share with you in the course of my opening statement now, some differences between DNA testing for medical purposes and forensic DNA testing on crime scene samples. Numbering, as we- in the graphic, that all evidence passes through first the L.A.P.D.'s hands. If it's compromised when it starts, it's compromised when it comes out. If the evidence was contaminated at the scene, or mishandled by the Los Angeles Police Department, it doesn't matter what DNA test was done afterwards, how many times they're done, or which laboratories did them. The results would not be reliable, we expect the evidence to show.[8]

Cochran's refrain that the evidence was "contaminated, compromised and ultimately corrupted" came to represent the defense's initial main attack. What at first would seem polar-opposite approaches by the defense team and the prosecutors is not that far apart. Clearly, the prosecution claimed O.J. committed the murders. The defense, on the other hand, said the evidence didn't prove that O.J. committed the murders. While I'm parsing as most attorneys do, the distinction is important. The defense didn't try to blame another, unknown assailant (the SODDI defense—"Some Other Dude Did It"). The defense didn't try to prove O.J.'s innocence, although it "said" O.J. was innocent. Instead, the defense tried and succeeded by instead showing the prosecution couldn't prove O.J.'s guilt. In a criminal trial, let alone a murder trial, not attempting to prove your innocence is a daring tactic, but one that must be frequently employed given the choice if the defendant won't testify.

Cochran presented O.J.'s alibi: he was practicing his golf swing out back at his Rockingham estate. He had no witnesses to back up his alibi. More troubling is the inconsistency of this attempt at an alibi when compared with O.J.'s claim that he overslept as the reason he didn't immediately come to the door when the limo driver first rang the bell at the front gate on the night of the murders. As it developed in the trial itself, the defense was able to add another theory—that the evidence had been planted by a racist cop.

Trial Testimony Starts

O.J.'s defense suffered an early blow when Judge Ito ruled that evidence of his spousal abuse could be admitted in the trial.

The prosecution lost no time in capitalizing on that ruling, and introduced as their first witness 911 operator Sharyn Gilbert, who took the stand Tuesday, January 31, 1994. A police detective next testified that when he responded to a 911 call years before the murders in 1989, Nicole Simpson ran toward him wearing only a bra and sweatpants yelling "he's going to kill me, he's going to kill me."[9]

According to her sister, Denise Brown, Nicole broke up with O.J. Simpson a week and a half before she died. On Friday, February 3, 1995, and the following Monday, Prosecutor Christopher Darden put Denise on the stand to describe the relationship between O.J. and Nicole and his history of abuse:

> **Mr. Darden:** Is there a bar in the Red Onion?
>
> **Ms. Brown:** Yes.
>
> **Mr. Darden:** And did you have something to drink?
>
> **Ms. Brown:** Yes, I did.
>
> **Mr. Darden:** Really. What did you drink?
>
> **Ms. Brown:** We were all – well, actually, we were all doing shots of tequila.
>
> **Mr. Darden:** The Defendant was doing shots of tequila?
>
> **Ms. Brown:** Yes.
>
> **Mr. Darden:** Was Nicole doing shots of tequila?
>
> **Ms. Brown:** Yes.
>
> . . .
>
> **Mr. Darden:** So, the drinks were free?
>
> **Ms. Brown:** I'm not saying all of them were. I'm not sure, but people do tend to buy him drinks and buy us – and they were buying us drinks too because we were with him.
>
> **Mr. Darden:** And did you see the Defendant drink shots of tequila?
>
> **Ms. Brown:** Uh-huh. Yes.
>
> **Mr. Darden:** Did anything unusual happen that night in the Red Onion?

Ms. Brown: Yes.

Mr. Darden: What was that?

Ms. Brown: Well, we all started – well, we were all drinking and goofing around and being loud and dancing and having a great time. And then at one point, O.J. grabbed Nicole's crotch and said, "This is where babies come from, and this belongs to me." And Nicole just sort of wrote it off as if it was nothing, like – you know, like she was used to that kind of treatment and he was like – I thought it was really humiliating if you ask me.

Mr. Shapiro: Move to strike the last part as being nonresponsive, calling for speculation, narrative.

The Court: Overruled.

Mr. Darden: And when he grabbed your sister's crotch and said, "This is where babies come from" – is that what he said?

Ms. Brown: "This is where babies come from and this belongs to me," and, "This is mine."

Notice what Mr. Darden did here. O.J.'s attorney, Robert Shapiro, and the judge interrupted the flow of his questions and back-and-forth with Denise Brown. By Darden asking the question again, he gets Ms. Brown to repeat her answer for the jury, emphasizing it, and then re-establishing his rapport with the witness.

Mr. Darden: And when he said this and when he grabbed her in the crotch, were there people around?

Ms. Brown: Oh, yeah. The bar was packed.

Mr. Darden: Strangers?

Ms. Brown: Yeah. Yeah. He was talking to the strangers.

. . .

Mr. Darden: What reaction if any was there by the Defendant when you told him that he took your sister Nicole for granted?

Ms. Brown: He got extremely upset. He—

Mr. Darden: And what happened next?

Ms. Brown: He started yelling at me, "I don't take her for granted. I do everything for her. I give her everything," and he continued, and then a whole fight broke out and pictures started flying off the walls, clothes started flying – he ran upstairs, got clothes, started flying down the stairs and grabbed Nicole, told her to get out of his house, wanted us all out of his house, picked her up, threw her against the wall, picked her up, threw her out of the house. She ended up on her – she ended up falling. She ended up on her elbows and on her butt. Then she – he threw Ed McCabe out. We were all sitting there screaming and crying, and then he grabbed me and threw me out of the house.

Mr. Darden: Are you okay, Miss Brown?

Ms. Brown: Yeah. It's just so hard. I'll be fine.

Mr. Darden: Your Honor, if it pleases the Court, can we adjourn and continue this Monday morning?

By stopping at a dramatic point, Mr. Darden left the jury with high-impact testimony as the last thing they'd remember over the weekend and left them wanting more damaging testimony to be presented again on Monday. This technique is not always easy to time out, but when it works, it works well, in part because the lawyer gets to repeat Friday's testimony again when trial restarts on Monday to remind the jury what happened when the trial adjourned.

Mr. Darden: Miss Brown, when we left off last Friday you told us about the crotch grabbing incident at the Red Onion. Do you recall that?

Ms. Brown: Yes.

Mr. Darden: And you also talked to us about an incident that occurred after you and your sister, Nicole, and Ed McCabe returned to the defendant's house after an evening at the La Cantina?

Ms. Brown: Yes, I did.

. . .

Mr. Darden: And was he saying anything to – did the Defendant say anything as he threw those—

Ms. Brown: He wanted her out of his house.

Mr. Darden: That is what the Defendant said?

Ms. Brown: He wanted her out of his house and he continued going up the stairs and he grabbed the clothes out of her closet and started throwing them down onto the foyer where we were down on the bottom and came back down and grabbed Nicole. He threw her up against the wall and then he grabbed her. And the only thing I remember is that it was – he looked so – his whole facial structure changed. Everything about him changed.

Mr. Darden: Let me stop you there.

Mr. Shapiro: Your Honor, we would object. That is nonresponsive.

The Court: All right. Ladies and gentlemen, the witness' comments regarding facial structuring and change of expression is stricken from the record and it was not in response to the question. You are to disregard that answer. Mr. Darden.

Mr. Darden: Okay. Did you see the Defendant's face immediately after you told him that he took your sister for granted?

Ms. Brown: Yes, I did.

Mr. Darden: Okay. And what, if anything, unusual did you notice about his face at that time?

Ms. Brown: At that time he got very upset and he started screaming.

Mr. Darden: Now, was his anger manifested in any way other than the fact that he became – other than the fact that he began screaming?

Ms. Brown: Yeah. His whole facial structure changed. I mean, everything changed about him.

Mr. Darden: Okay. When you say his facial structure changed, what do you mean? Elaborate on that for us, please.

Ms. Brown: It was calm, quiet, normal conversation, like we were sitting here right now, and then all of a sudden it turned into – the eyes got real angry. It was as – his whole jaw, everything started, you know – his whole face just changed completely when he got upset. Umm – it wasn't as if it was O.J. anymore. He looked like a different person and that is what Nicole had always said when he gets angry.

• • •

Mr. Darden: Miss Brown, showing what you has been marked People's 10 for identification, is that a photograph of your sister, Nicole?

Ms. Brown: Yes, it is.

Mr. Darden: Is that a photograph that you have seen before?

Ms. Brown: Yes, it is.

Mr. Darden: Do you know who took that photograph?

Ms. Brown: I did.

Mr. Darden: Do you recall when it was that you took that photograph?

Ms. Brown: Yeah. It was right after the '89 incident.

Mr. Darden: Was on it New Year's Day itself?

Ms. Brown: Yeah. I think it was a couple of days later.

Mr. Darden: That photograph depicts certain injuries to your sister; is that correct?

Ms. Brown: Yes, it does.

Mr. Darden: The swelling over her right eye, that isn't how she usually looked, is it?

Ms. Brown: No, it is not.

Mr. Darden: Your Honor, may I show the jury People's 11 for identification?

The Court: Yes, you may. [Mr. Darden then showed the jury the photograph, which is called "publishing" the photograph to the jury.]

Mr. Darden: Miss Brown, showing you People's 11 for identification, in this photograph your sister has her right arm raised; is that correct?

Ms. Brown: Yes.

Mr. Darden: Do you see any injury to her right arm there?

Ms. Brown: Yes, I do.

Mr. Darden: What do you see?

Ms. Brown: A bruise, a big bruise.

Mr. Darden: And directing your attention to the right side of her – of her head or forehead, do you see any injuries to the right side of her head?

Ms. Brown: Yes, I do.

Mr. Darden: That is not how she usually looked, is it?

Ms. Brown: No, it is not.

Mr. Darden: You told us a moment ago that you took these photographs; is that correct?

Ms. Brown: Yes, I did.

Mr. Darden: Okay. Would you describe for us, please, the circumstances that lead to your taking these photographs?

Ms. Brown: Nicole asked me to take them for her.[10]

The DAs also introduced other evidence of another spousal abuse incident involving O.J.'s earlier 1993 attack on Nicole Simpson through LAPD officers who responded to calls again from Nicole and would utilize that evidence in their closing argument.

As the case continued, the prosecution introduced evidence to establish the time the murders were committed by calling Nicole's neighbors on South Bundy Avenue who heard, observed, and found the dog, as well as the neighbor who found the two bodies and called the police. The defense team on cross-examination then used photographs of the murder scene, attempting to show that the police moved and tampered with the bloody glove and other evidence. O.J.'s lawyers pointed out at every chance they got how the police's investigation of the crime scene was both sloppy and incomplete. Judge Ito suspended the trial at one point when one of the jurors was overcome by the gruesome testimony and graphic pictures of the bloody victims.

A Field Trip

The court, jury, prosecutors, defense team, and court staff took a bus tour on February 12, 1994, and went to the crime scene and Simpson's Rockingham estate so they could better understand what was to be discussed in the courtroom. According to Professor Douglas O. Linder's review of the event:

> The defense saw it [the tour] as an opportunity to put a favorable spin on Simpson's life. Before the jury arrived at Simpson's home, down came a picture of Paula Barbieri, O.J.'s girlfriend. In its place, up went a Norman Rockwell print from Johnnie Cochran's office that depicted a black girl being escorted to school by federal marshals. Pictures of Simpson standing with white golfing buddies were replaced with pictures of his mother and other black people. A Bible was installed conspicuously on an end table in the living room. The tour seemed to go wonderfully well for the defense. As the group toured his home, Simpson pointed to a backyard play area and said, "That's where I practiced my golf swing."[11]

Then on February 15, 1994, the prosecution dropped a bombshell. They disclosed for the first time that blood found on the rear gate leading to Nicole Simpson's condo matched O.J. Simpson's blood. The defense argued the blood could have come from the couple's children, either Sidney or Justin. At the time, DNA testing may not have been advanced enough to allow such fine distinctions to be made, and the question was not resolved at the trial through expert testimony.

Sidebars, Objections, and the Heat of the Trial

Trial attorneys frequently get frustrated with one another, and sometimes even more so with the judge when they believe the judge hasn't made the right decision or sufficiently controlled the courtroom testimony. While lawyers generally respect judges, trial lawyers know that judges have no more legal education than they do, so after you've tried several cases, you're not as afraid of the judge as you are when you're handling your first ten or so trials.

As TV trial-watchers know, the judge called many sidebars out of the presence of the jury, mostly to admonish the lawyers or resolve a thorny evidentiary issue. In this instance, the two prosecutors, and particularly Mr. Darden, got frustrated with Mr. Cochran's "speaking objections" when he objected to testimony, essentially injecting his own "testimony" in the form of argument into the testimony of the witnesses.

The proper way to assert an objection is to say the word "objection," followed by a one- or two-word shorthand for the basis of the objection, like, "objection, hearsay." Trial lawyers will frequently, when they believe they can influence the jury, speak a longer objection that runs on and on to interject their own statements to prove a point, much to the frustration of the lawyers on the other side if the judge refuses to control and prevent it.

Typically, Mr. Darden was considered a master at needling the defense team, especially Mr. Cochran, who himself likewise fought back masterfully, ultimately instead succeeding in goading Mr. Darden, despite objections from all the other prosecutors on the team, to ask O.J. Simpson to demonstrate to the jurors that the gloves fit. Prior to that huge mistake, however, Mr. Darden lost his temper at sidebar, building up to his fatal mistake with O.J.'s bloody glove demonstration.

Mr. Darden was at one point particularly frustrated with Mr. Cochran's speaking objections and their collective effect on the jury. So frustrated, in fact, that at sidebars he regularly interrupted the judge and other counsel and at one point insulted the judge. Despite several warnings, Mr. Darden didn't get the message from Judge Ito. After violating the court's orders for a third time, Judge Ito considered holding him in contempt of court. Jurors may not know exactly what is said during a sidebar, but they carefully observe how the judge and attorneys interact with one another when the jurors return to the courtroom. They knew Darden had incurred Judge Ito's wrath, even though they might not have known exactly why.

Many legal observers pointed out that Judge Ito lost control of the courtroom, starstruck with the "Dream team" of defense lawyers and allowing too many delays, objections, and sidebars. Here's how the sidebar described above played out:

Ms. Clark: Objection, hearsay.

The Court: Let me see counsel at sidebar.

(Side bar.)

The Court: Ladies and gentlemen, be seated. Mr. Lange, you can step down.

(Witness excused.)

The Court: All right. The record reflects the jury has withdrawn from the jury room. Mr. Darden, let me give you a piece of advice. Take about three deep breaths, as I am going to do, and then contemplate what you're going to say next. Do you want to take a recess for a moment?

Mr. Darden: I don't require a recess, your Honor.

The Court: All right. I will hear your comment at this point. I've cited you [for contempt]. Do you have any response?

Mr. Darden: I would like counsel, your Honor.

The Court: You can have counsel. You have counsel. Do you want to call your counsel? Do you want to have somebody from your appellate division come down?

By referring to the "appellate division," Judge Ito insulted Mr. Darden. The "appellate division" or "writs and appeals" in other prosecutor's offices, is the group of government lawyers who write the briefs on appeal and are generally considered the more educated attorneys in the office and who value reason over passion. They are not typically trial lawyers, like Mr. Darden, who occasionally let his passions get in the way.

Ms. Clark: I would like to know—

(inaudible).

The Court: Do you represent Mr. Darden in this matter?

Ms. Clark: I don't know if I'm legally entitled to, but I would like to be heard on his behalf.

The Court: All right.

Ms. Clark: What we are all concerned about here, your Honor, is that there is a method of cross-examination that is being conducted by Mr. Cochran that has –

The Court: That's not what I'm interested in, Ms. Clark.

Ms. Clark: That is the impetus for the exchange at side bar, your Honor, and we are – all of us, greatly concerned about what the jury is getting. They're getting -- that is the impetus. That is what led to –

The Court: I don't want to hear this, Ms. Clark. No. Ms. Clark, I don't want to hear about that. I'm not interested in that. I'm interested in the refusal to avoid -- the refusal to obey the court's order not to address that issue, not to speak to the court as I was hearing from one counsel, not to interrupt the court, and the court gave three admonitions, and Mr. Darden chose to ignore those.

Ms. Clark: Mr. Darden did not choose to ignore them. I think Mr. Darden was simply, at that time, overcome with what has been transpiring with Mr. Cochran's cross-examination. It was not a desire to flaunt the court's authority, although I would point out to the court that the court's order to stop and desist has been ignored by the defense time and time and time again with no citation. No citation. Mr. Darden is simply responding to the events that have been occurring in this courtroom today and have been occurring throughout cross-examination. I myself have become overwhelmed by the fact that the jury has been given hearsay, has been given – and the record will stand by what I said, slop in the form of counsel testifying before every witness.

The Court: Counsel, didn't I tell you I didn't want to hear that? I'm interested in a contempt proceeding.

Ms. Clark: If the court would like to set the matter for OSC [an Order to Show Cause, which means that the matter would both be delayed and Mr. Darden would have an opportunity to present a written response to Judge Ito's contempt citation], then we will proceed to OSC. I don't think it's required.

The Court: It's not required. I can do it summarily. Do you want to push it to that?

Ms. Clark: No.

The Court: Then how come you haven't taken the opportunity? When I invite counsel to take three deep breaths and think carefully about what they are going to say to the court next, that's an opportunity to say gee, I'm sorry, I lost my head there. I apologize to the court. I apologize to counsel. When you get that response, then we move on. When you tell the court you want to have an order to showcause, that's a different response. That says you want to fight. You want to fight some more with the court, you're welcome to do so. I'm going to take a recess. I'm going to give you and Mr. Darden an opportunity to think about this carefully with about 10 deep breaths perhaps. Have I made myself clear?

Ms. Clark: You have. Shall I take off my watch and my jewelry?

This smart-ass remark to the judge just as easily could have landed Ms. Clark into trouble. She was "short handing," a reference to the judge that she was ready to be handcuffed and go to jail if necessary. When a judge remands someone to the custody of the bailiff to send that person to jail, they are required to remove their watch, jewelry, and all other valuables for safekeeping.

The Court: Ten minutes.

(Recess taken.)

The Court: Mrs. [Diedre] Robertson [the court clerk, who keeps track of the courtroom], do we have anybody for the People?

Mrs. Robertson: (Inaudible).

The Court: There is probably bad karma with Mr. Neufeld [one of the defense lawyers] today.

Mr. Cochran: We will ask him to step outside, your Honor.

The Court: Good afternoon, counsel.

Ms. Clark: Good afternoon, your Honor.

The Court: Any further comment?

Ms. Clark: We would ask leave of the court to recess at this time, so that we can be present with appellate counsel tomorrow morning. [This response signals to the judge that both Ms. Clark and Mr. Darden are ready for a fight.]

The Court: It's a pretty simple procedure. Do you wish to pursue this? [The Judge is inviting an apology and at the same time signaling that a fight will mean bigger monetary sanctions.] Ms. Clark: We are only asking for the opportunity at this time to confer with counsel. [She signals that they're willing to back down.]

The Court: Well, you seem to have two options. Either you offer an apology to the court and we proceed or we proceed to a contempt hearing. Those are your choices. Request for a continuance is denied. [In other words, are you really sure you want to pick a fight with me?]

Ms. Clark: May we have a moment, your Honor? [Ms. Clark got it.]

The Court: Sure.

(Pause.)

Ms. Clark: We would like the opportunity to confer with counsel before we resolve this matter, your Honor, and is the court not going to afford us that opportunity? [Mr. Darden did not get the message. He's still blinded by his temper.]

The Court: Nope.

Ms. Clark: We could proceed with a trial and resolve the matter at the conclusion of the day or in the morning tomorrow, and that way we wouldn't have to take up any more court time with this matter at this time.

The Court: There is a simple way to terminate this, Ms. Clark. [He really means Mr. Darden.]

Ms. Clark: I'm aware of that. [She's definitely got the picture and is signaling to the Judge both that she doesn't want to be sanctioned but Mr. Darden may need to be.]

The Court: I think I've offered it to you twice already now. I don't know I have to do it a third time, but I'm prepared to go forward if you choose otherwise.

Ms. Clark: Even if the court is prepared to go forward with the contempt proceeding, we're entitled to counsel, are we not?

The Court: This is civil contempt, counsel. It has to be adjudicated immediately, unless you want to make it a criminal contempt and have a jury trial. Love to see the *voir dire* [the court's own questioning of a new criminal jury] in that case.

Ms. Clark: Me too. Can we use the same jury, your Honor?

The Court: Ms. Clark, all levity aside, I've offered you now three times an opportunity to end this right now. This is very simple, and perhaps as Mr. Darden had the opportunity to review the transcript I had before me, he would see the wisdom of that.

Ms. Clark: And perhaps we would like to review it as well, but – why don't we review the transcript, your Honor?

. . .

The Court: Let me see counsel at the side bar without the reporter, please. Mr. Hodgman, would you join us, please?

(Side bar.)

[The transcript they reviewed revealed the following exchange]:

Mr. Cochran: We will prove it, your Honor. They know. This is such –

Ms. Clark: Why doesn't he prove it then. Let him call a witness.

Judge Ito: No, no.

Mr. Cochran: I can choose the witness that I want. They obviously haven't tried any cases in a long time, and obviously don't know how, but this is cross-examination.

Mr. Darden: Who is he talking about doesn't know how to try the case?

Judge Ito: Wait, Mr. Darden.

Mr. Darden: Is he the only lawyer that knows how to try the case?

Judge Ito: I'm going to hold you in contempt.

Mr. Darden: I should be held in contempt. I have sat here and listened to –

Judge Ito: Mr. Darden, I'm warning you right now.

Mr. Darden: This cross-examination is out of order.[12]]

The Court: All right. Thank you, counsel. Mr. Darden.

Mr. Darden: Your Honor. Thank you for the opportunity to review the transcript of the side bar. It appears that the court is correct, that perhaps my comments may have been or are somewhat inappropriate. I apologize to the court. I meant no disrespect, however, I did have some concerns, and concerns I would like to take up with the court when the court is available to hear my concerns. I apologize.

The Court: Mr. Darden. I accept your apology. I apologize to you for my reaction as well. You and I have known each other for a number of years, and I know that your response was out of character, and I'll note it as such. Thank you.

Mr. Darden: Thank you, your Honor.

The Court: Let's have the jury, please.

[Signaling that all is right in the world of the courtroom once again.]

(Whereupon the jury enters the courtroom.)

The Court: Ladies and gentlemen, be seated. All right. Mr. Cochran, proceed.

Mr. Cochran: Thank you very kindly, your Honor. When we broke I believe I was asking you [the witness, Mr. Lange] whether or not you were aware, became aware at some point that Faye Resnick moved in with Nicole Brown Simpson on or about June 3, 1994.

Ms. Clark: Objection, hearsay. [She at least got the picture.]

The Court: Sustained. ["There's one just for the sake of rewarding you, Ms. Clark."] Rephrase the question. ["But I'm still going to allow the information to come into evidence."][13]

With that issue aside, the parties turned back to the matter at hand. In early March 1995, the prosecution put lead investigator Detective Tom Lange on the stand (the contempt exchange above interrupted his testimony). As Cochran pounded away at Lange, Cochran got Lange to admit the police had not pursued any leads that would suggest someone other than O.J. committed the murders. By getting Lange to make that admission, Cochran was able to show the police rushed to judgment and concluded O.J. was guilty. The defense theory involved a drug crime as a potential motive, and sought to drag in one of Nicole's houseguests, Faye Resnick (who had checked into rehab for cocaine abuse just days before Nicole's death). Statistics show, however, that wives are the most frequent victims in family murders and that some 62% of family murders occur at night.[14]

Rosa Lopez

Outside the presence of the jury, the defense offered testimony from Rosa Lopez, a housekeeper who worked and lived nearby O.J.'s Rockingham estate testified on February 27 that she saw O.J.'s white Ford Bronco parked outside his estate at the time the prosecutors said he committed the murders. In response, on March 2nd and 3rd, again outside the presence of the jury, prosecutors attacked her statements and drilled home inconsistencies in her story. The cross-examination eliminated her as an alibi witness for O.J. The prosecution scored a point not seen by the jury.

Detective Fuhrman Give the Defense a Point for Their Closing Argument

For five days in early to mid-March, Detective Mark Fuhrman took the stand. He had served on the LA police force for nearly twenty years after a stint in the Marines, where he was honorably discharged as a sergeant. Before enlisting, Fuhrman earlier dropped out of high school in Washington, where he was born. At the time he took the stand, he had earned 55 commendations while on the force.

The defense pounded away at Fuhrman, who they believed to be a racist; complaining so much that Judge Ito required them to make an offer of proof concerning the questions they intended to ask Fuhrman on the stand. The defense team first filed what's commonly called a "Pitchess Motion" (named after a party in an appellate case) to obtain Fuhrman's confidential personnel records to see if he'd been disciplined for behavior that could be classified as racist. Judge Ito partially granted the defense motion and ordered the release of Fuhrman's personnel files.

On March 10, 1995, the prosecution put Detective Fuhrman on the stand to show he wasn't alone and didn't have the opportunity to plant evidence:

> Q: (Clark) At that point, sir, had you already been to Rockingham and come back to Bundy?
>
> A: Yes, ma'am.
>
> Q: So at the point that you wrote the ski mask, how close had you gotten to that item?
>
> A: No closer than the landing where I observed the two victims from where the first shoeprint—
>
> Q: That was the closest observation you had at that point?
>
> A: Yes.
>
> . . .
>
> Q: Okay. So Item No. 17 is based on your observation of these two items that you got a look at from the vantage point of the gate with Officer Riske and Detective Phillips and from the landing with Officer Riske and Detective Phillips?
>
> A: Yes, ma'am. . . .
>
> Q: All right. So you got as far as Item No. 17 documenting your observation of a ski mask, one glove by the feet of the male victim. Had you completed your notes at that point? Were you all done?
>
> A: No.

Q: What happened to interrupt you?

A: Well, before – while I was still writing my notes, Detective Roberts entered, he had just arrived on scene and he came into the – into the living room, he was directed by Detective Phillips, and he said, "Can you update me or bring me up to speed?" I did that briefly. I told him – I informed him what I had seen in the house. I took him onto the landing very quickly, pointed out there was a glove, a cap, there was a male victim, a female victim, a menu. I showed him the shoeprints. I walked him back the path. I showed him on the gate the blood. And this is at this time is when Detective Roberts and I both saw the smudge and that possible visible fingerprint.[15]

F. Lee Bailey, a nationally well-known criminal attorney even before he represented O.J. Simpson, cross-examined Detective Fuhrman on what may very well be one of the first of several turning points in the trial. Kathleen Bell, a Los Angeles real estate agent, earlier sent the following letter to Johnnie Cochran (misspelling Detective Fuhrman's name), which Judge Ito allowed into evidence:

> I'm writing to you in regards to a story I saw on the news last night. I thought it ridiculous that the Simpson defense team would even suggest that their might be racial motivation involved in the trial against Mr. Simpson. I then glanced up at the television and was quite shocked to see that Officer Ferman was a man that I had the misfortune of meeting. You may have received a message from your answering service last night that I called to say that Mr. Ferman may be more of a racist than you could even imagine.
>
> Between 1985 and 1986 I worked as a real estate agent in Redondo Beach for Century 21 Bob Maher Realty, (now out of business). At the time, my office was located above a Marine recruiting center off of Pacific Coast Highway. On occasion I would stop in to say hello to the two Marines working there. I saw Mr. Ferman there a couple of times. I

remember him distinctly because of his height and build.

While speaking to the men I learned that Mr. Ferman [*sic*] was a police officer in Westwood, and I don't know if he was telling the truth, but he said that he had been in a special division of the Marines. I don't know how the subject was raised, but Officer Ferman said that when he sees a "nigger" (as he called it) driving with a white woman, he would pull them over. I asked would if he didn't have a reason, and he said that he would find one. I looked at the two Marines to see if they knew he was joking, but it became obvious to me that he was very serious.

Officer Ferman went on to say that he would like nothing more than to see all "niggers" gathered together and killed. He said something about burning them or bombing them. I was too shaken to remember the exact words he used, however, I do remember that what he said was probably the most horrible thing I had ever heard someone say. What frightened me even more was that he was a police officer.

I am almost certain that I called the LAPD to complain about Officer Mark Ferman, yet I did not know his last name at the time. I would think that the LAPD has some record of this.

Now that I know Mr. Ferman was the investigating officer, I must suggest that you check into his background further. I am certainly not a fan of Mr. Simpson, but I would hate to see anyone harmed by Officer Ferman's extreme hatred.[16]

Sometimes critical evidence arrives outside normal discovery channels between the attorneys.

In the media, Bailey compared Fuhrman's remarks to Adolph Hitler's, which comparison Johnnie Cochran would repeat in closing, much to the disgust of fellow defense team member Robert Shapiro, who accused Cochran of "dealing the race card from the bottom of the deck."[17] But the tactic apparently worked despite Shapiro's objection. First, Bailey would confirm Fuhrman's denial that he ever knew Kathleen Bell.

Q: ...You say you're sure you never met a woman named Kathleen Bell?

A: Yes, sir. . . .

Q: Did you ever meet a woman that looks like the lady on the Larry King show by some other name?

A: No.

Q: In looking at that face – how long did you watch the show that night?

A: About five minutes.

Q: Was that enough to satisfy you that you had never seen this woman before?

A: I did not recognize her.

Q: That wasn't my question. Were you satisfied after five minutes – and I take it you discontinued viewing the show – that the woman being interviewed by Larry King and identifying herself as Kathleen Bell was someone you had never met?

A: That's correct.

Q: Okay. Is it not true that you would have recollected such a person if you had met them under the circumstances she described without going into what they were?

A: Yes, I would.

Q: That kind of thing would impress your memory the same way the meeting of O.J. Simpson would; would it not?

A: I don't think in the same way, but similar, yes.

Q: Well, what she was discussing was fairly outrageous conduct; is it not?

A: Yes, sir.

Q: Okay. And if you had engaged in that conduct with the woman whose image you were looking at, that's not something you would soon forget, is it?

A: No. . . .

Q: Detective Fuhrman, would you take a look at this photograph of a blond woman and tell me whether or not that is the person that was being interviewed by Larry King when you watched the show at the request of the prosecution.

A: Yes. . . .

Q: . . . And do you have no recollection of Joe Faus [one of the Marines] being in your company and hers in the recruiting station in 1986 or thereabouts?

A: I do not.

Q: Or at any time in your life?

A: I do not.

Q: All right. [Author's note: This "all right" is sloppy questioning and sloppy lawyering. Responding to a witness' answer with "all right" or "O.K." signals to the jury that the lawyer is confirming the witness' testimony, which in many of these questions, is not what Mr. Bailey is trying to do, and is sending the wrong message. Luckily for Mr. Bailey, Fuhrman hung himself with these answers, as we will see in a moment.] So that if he were to say that he did in fact introduce the two of you, you say that can't be true, true?

A: If he said that, I do not recall ever meeting this woman in the recruiting station or anywhere else.

Q: All right. Well, I'm trying to get the distinction between a lack of recollection, a faded memory and an absolute certainty that you have never seen this woman before until you saw her on television. Which is it?

A: I do not recognize this woman as anybody I have ever met.

Q: All right. You testified on direct examination that not only did you not know this woman and had never met her, but you

	had never said the things that were displayed on the Elmo [a courtroom display device, quite like an overhead projector] in her letter, true?
A:	Yes, sir.
Q:	All right. And is it fair to say there can be no mistake in your mind about your testimony in this particular?
A:	That's correct.
Q:	All right. Now, do you know a woman named Andrea Terry [Kathleen Bell's girlfriend, who she tried to set up with Fuhrman.]?
A	No, I do not.
Q:	Did you ever meet a woman standing six feet one inch named Andrea Terry in a bar down there where you [Fuhrman is six feet two inches] live?
A:	No, sir.
Q:	Is there a bar down in that area that you frequent?
A:	No longer, but yes, there is.
Q:	Back in '85?
A:	Yes, sir.
Q:	What was the name of it?
A:	Hennessey's Tavern.
Q:	Hennessey's Tavern. Now, I ask you whether or not on an occasion in the middle 80's related in time to your going to the Marine recruiting station for whatever purpose you met with a woman named Andrea Terry and Kathleen Bell, an independent second occasion.
A:	No.
Q:	Have you been shown any photographs of Andrea Terry by anyone?
A:	No, I have not.[18]

On March 15, 1995, Bailey got to the heart of it and confirmed Fuhrman's words:

> Q: (**By Mr. Bailey**) Do you use the word "nigger" in describing people?
>
> **Ms. Clark:** Same Objection.
>
> **The Court:** Presently?
>
> **Mr. Bailey:** Yes.
>
> **The Court:** Overruled.
>
> **The Witness:** No, sir.
>
> Q: Have you ever used that word in the past ten years?
>
> A: Not that I recall, no.
>
> Q: You mean if you called someone a nigger you have forgotten it?
>
> A: I'm not sure I can answer that question the way you phrased it, sir.
>
> Q: You have a difficulty understanding the question?
>
> A: Yes.
>
> Q: I will rephrase it. I want you to assume that perhaps at some time since 1985 or 1985, you addressed a member of the African American race as a nigger. Is it possible that you have forgotten that act on your part?
>
> A: No, it is not possible.
>
> Q: Are you therefore saying that you have not use that word in the past ten years, Detective Fuhrman?
>
> A: Yes, that is what I'm saying.
>
> Q: And you say under oath that you have not addressed any black person as a nigger or spoken about black people as niggers in the past ten years, Detective Fuhrman?
>
> A: That's what I'm saying, sir.
>
> Q: So that anyone who comes to this court and quotes you as using that word in dealing

> with African Americans would be a liar, would they not, Detective Fuhrman?

A: Yes, they would.

Q: All of them, correct?

A: All of them.[19]

The defense called Ms. Bell late in their case on September 5, 1995. She testified about the same things she had written in her letter to Johnnie Cochran and that Fuhrman also met Andrea Terry.

> **Mr. Bailey:** All right. And did you talk any further about that hypothetical of a black man riding with a white woman being pulled over?
>
> **Ms. Bell:** Yes.

Q: What else was said?

A: I asked, "What if they are in love?"

Q: And what did he say to that?

A: He said, "That is disgusting."

• • •

Q: After the word "disgusting" was uttered, what was next said by either of you?

A: Well, again I looked at the Marines because I had spoken to them before and they didn't seem to be mean people, and so I was waiting for some kind of reaction from them, and then, umm, I just was kind of--I just kind of paused and then he said, "If I had my way I would gather":"All the niggers would be gathered together and burned."[20]

The defense also found Natalie Singer, an aspiring screenwriter who had once been a personal assistant to Superman movie star Christopher Reeve and who testified in concert with Ms. Bell:

> **Mr. Bailey:** What did he [Fuhrman] say?
>
> **Ms. Singer:** It is okay to say that?
>
> **Mr. Bailey:** Yes.

Ms. Singer: He said, "The only good Nigger is a dead Nigger."[21]

Celebrities live all over L.A. and these Hollywood connections run rampant through Tinseltown. Every local knows a star or is a friend of someone who does. And everyone's a screenwriter.

The defense then put Laura Hart McKinny (at the time of her interviews of Fuhrman, "Laura Hart") on the stand because she had interviewed—on tape and with his consent—Mark Fuhrman for the purposes of a screenplay she was writing on women police officers. The interviews occurred over a ten-year period from April 1985-July 1994.

McKinny Transcript No. 4, p. 1 (Tape No. 4, p. 1) contains the following exchange:

> **Hart:** I just transcribe you.
>
> **Fuhrman:** Verbatim.
>
> **Hart:** I have to.
>
> **Fuhrman:** All the cocksuckers. Everything. That's important. That's policeman's talk.
>
> **Hart:** It's life talk. It's not just policemen's talk.
>
> **Fuhrman:** But, we have mastered it. No, the Marine corps mastered it.[22]

In the defense case-in-chief on August 29, 2008, the court allowed the defense to play the only two snippets of the most recent tapes from the McKinny interviews where the jury could hear Fuhrman, in his own words, say the very same things as Kathleen Bell had alleged, and Ms. Singer also testified. Judge Ito ruled that "The specific racial epithet at issue is perhaps the single most insulting, inflammatory and provocative term in use in modern-day America."[23]

On August 31, 1995, the judge admitted these two recent statements as impeachment evidence because Fuhrman had denied ever using the racial epithet at issue in the ten years preceding the 1995 trial. All told, the defense offered 41 examples of Fuhrman using the racial epithet, 18 examples of misconduct on the issue of Fuhrman's credibility and willingness to fabricate evidence. Fuhrman made the two comments in late July of 1994. The judge excluded his older statements from evidence, but were much more prejudicial:

(. . .speaking of changes in composition of L.A.P.D.).

"That we've got females . . .and dumb niggers, and all your Mexicans that can't even write the name of the car they drive."

(McKinny Transcript No. 1, p.11.)

(. . .speaking of the physical risks to officers).

"If I'm wrestling around with some ___ nigger, and he gets me in my back, and he gets his hands on my gun. It's over."

(McKinny Transcript No. 1, p. 12)

(. . .describing arrest of a suspect).

"She was afraid. He was a big nigger, and she was afraid."

(McKinny Transcript No. 1, p. 20)

(. . .explaining arrest of a suspect in Westwood).

"He was a nigger. He didn't belong. Two questions. And you are going: Where do you live? 22nd and Western. Where were you going? Well, I'm going to Fatburger. Where's Fatburger. He didn't know where Fatburger was? Get in the car."

(McKinny Transcript No. 1, p.33)

(. . .commenting on L.A. P. D. politics).

"Commander Hickman, was a dickhead. He should be shot. He did that for one thing. He wants to be chief, so he wants the city council, and the police commissioner, and all these niggers in L.A. City government and all of 'em should be lined up against a wall and fuckin' shot."

(McKinny Transcript No. 1, p.41)

(. . .discussing American aid to drought victims in Ethiopia).

"You know these people here, we got all this money going to Ethiopia for what. To feed a bunch of dumb niggers that their own government won't even feed."

(McKinny Transcript No. 1, p. 44)

(...discussing where he grew up in the state of Washington).

"People there don't want niggers in their town. People there don't want Mexicans in their town. They don't want anybody but good people in their town, and anyway you can do to get them out of there that's fine with them. We have no niggers where I grew up."

(McKinny Transcript No. 1, p.45)

(...speaking of women as training officers).

"When I came on the job all my training officers were big guys and knowledgeable, some nigger'd get in their face, they just spin 'em around, choke 'em out until they dropped."

(McKinny Transcript No. 1., p. 47)

(...discussing use of chokehold by L.A.P.D.).

"Now, we have to eliminate a choke hold because a bunch of niggers down in the south end of L.A. said this is bad."

(McKinny Transcript No. 1., p. 49)

...

[Continuing the argument in the defense's offer of proof] The "Fuhrman Tapes" contain eighteen examples of Detective Fuhrman admitting participation in police misconduct, or offering approving comments with respect to misconduct. This misconduct includes illegal use of deadly force, beating suspects to extract confessions, planting evidence, framing innocent persons, and lying or covering up misconduct by others.[24]

Fuhrman apparently didn't know when to stop. Even as the case was pending, he continued with his interviews with McKinny. Again, according to the offer of proof:

The "Fuhrman Tapes" contain two references to Detective Fuhrman's role as a key witness in this case. These statements were made on July 28, 1994, after his testimony at the Preliminary Hearing.

1. **(. . .explaining police department reaction to the suggestion he planted the glove).**

> Q: You're them.
>
> A: I'm the key witness in the biggest case of the century. And, if I go down, they lose the case. The glove is everything. Without the glove – bye, bye.
>
> *(Tape No. 12, p. 7; McKinny Transcript No. 12, p. 22)*
>
> 2. Well, the funny thing about it is just like the attorney said, "For the rest of your life, this is you: you're 'bloody-glove Fuhrman,'" that's it . . . He says, "You might as well make it pay off, if you don't make it pay off, all you're doing is going through all this heartache for nothing. Go for Shapiro, he's an asshole."
>
> *(Tape No. 12, p. 12; McKinny Transcript No. 12, p. 22)*[25]

To continue with this thread and wrap it up, let's fast forward even further into the trial before we jump back to the ongoing chronological order. On September 6, 1995, Detective Fuhrman killed the prosecution's case when he testified without the jury present, but now with his own lawyer, Darryl E. Mounger, in tow:

> **Mr. Uelmen**: Detective Fuhrman, was the testimony that you gave at the preliminary hearing in this case completely truthful?
>
> **Det. Fuhrman:** I wish to assert my 5th amendment privilege.
>
> **Mr. Uelmen:** Have you ever falsified a police report?
>
> **Det. Fuhrman:** I wish to assert my 5th amendment privilege.
>
> **Mr. Uelmen:** Is it your intention to assert your 5th amendment privilege with respect to all questions that I ask you?
>
> **Det. Fuhrman:** Yes.
>
> . . .
>
> **Mr. Mounger:** Your Honor, further questions don't serve any purpose since my client has already answered that he will not answer any question and

will assert his 5th amendment privilege. Anything further can only be a show.

Mr. Uelmen: I only have one other question, your Honor.

The Court: What was that, Mr. Uelmen?

Mr. Uelmen: Detective Fuhrman, did you plant or manufacture any evidence in this case?

Det. Fuhrman: I assert my 5th Amendment privilege.[26]

A true *Perry Mason* moment, a rarity in real trials.

California Attorney General Dan Lungren took over the prosecution of Fuhrman for perjury in the O.J. Simpson trial to avoid the conflict of interest between Fuhrman and the Los Angeles District Attorney's Office. On October 2, 1996, Fuhrman accepted an offered plea bargain in the case, and plead *nolo contendre* (no contest) to a felony for his testimony in the O.J. trial about racial epithets.

No action was taken because of Fuhrman's assertion of his Fifth Amendment rights, although in a civil case, he would initially be presumed (subject to rebuttal proof) to have taken the actions alleged. He was sentenced to three years' probation, fined $200 and barred from ever working in California for a law enforcement agency. As a convicted felon, Fuhrman lost his right to vote and own a gun, and most likely will never work on a police force again or obtain professional employment, according to his plea bargain agreement. Like almost everyone else in the trial, he has since authored several books, including one about the O.J. trial and now receives a pension from the LAPD.

Fuhrman holds the ironic distinction of being the only person convicted of a crime related to the deaths of Nicole Simpson and Ron Goldman.

While it may be reasonable to infer that Fuhrman planted evidence (the glove, socks, and blood in Simpson's Bronco) at the Rockingham estate, we will see later that the prosecution introduced evidence that tended to show Simpson's blood at Nicole's condo on Bundy alongside the bloody shoe prints leading away from the victims and on the back gate. If true, then there is likely only one way that blood could have gotten there, unless it belonged to Simpson's children or blood samples taken from Simpson during the investigation, as the defense argued.

But I wasn't on the jury.

Calling Kato Kaelin

Now that we've finished the Fuhrman diversion, like the lawyers in the Simpson trial do when they get interrupted, let's get back to where we were before. Fuhrman had just testified that he found the first bloody glove at the Bundy crime scene and Detective Lange admitted that the LAPD hadn't pursued any leads other than ones that led to Simpson. In the middle of March 1995, the prosecution put LAPD Chief of Investigations Juan Jiminez on the stand, but on cross, he admitted the LAPD detectives were lax in notifying the coroner of the bodies of Nicole Brown Simpson and Ronald Goldman. Jiminez said, "They've dropped the ball. They've done this on numerous occasions."[27] Had they notified the coroner more promptly, Jiminez said, the time of death would have been pinpointed more accurately than "between 9 p.m. and midnight,"[28] an important point for the trial. We've been taught these details by the TV show *CSI*.

As the trial progressed in late March, the prosecution called O.J.'s houseguest, Kato Kaelin, to the stand, who testified much as outlined in the facts at the beginning of this chapter. He was glib on the stand, and jurors laughed when prosecutor Marcia Clark asked Kaelin if he was nervous and Kaelin responded, "I feel great."[29] Kato was unable to testify to O.J.'s whereabouts between 9:35 p.m. - 11 p.m. the night of the murders. A neighbor of O.J.'s testified that he did not see O.J.'s white Ford Bronco outside the Rockingham estate front gates between 9:30 and 9:45 on the evening of the murders.

Ringing the Bell and Unringing the Bell

As the trial pressed on into April, the evidence turned to the physical things found at the scene of the crimes and O.J.'s Rockingham estate. The defense team forced Criminalist Dennis Fung to acknowledge that O.J. Simpson's hair could have been brought into the crime scene accidentally—by unfolding a blanket from inside the condo to cover her body on the night of the murders. Simpson admittedly had been legitimately inside her home at various times and could have easily sloughed off his hair on the blanket.

As the prosecution began to introduce its blood evidence and DNA analysis in April, the one of the prosecution lawyers made a mistake and violated an agreement not to show the jury an airline ticket and luggage ticket that both sides agreed not to introduce into evidence because of its potential adverse effect on the jury. The court earlier ruled that the police seizure of the luggage was improper and shouldn't go before the jury and suppressed that evidence—a significant defense victory. The issue was important because the luggage may have had blood evidence that the court had ruled was not to go before the jury. The jury could assume relevant blood samples implicating Simpson were on the luggage when that evidence had been ruled inadmissible.

After much legal wrangling at the sidebar where the defense wanted the judge to instruct the jury that the prosecution had violated a court order and the prosecution claimed they had done nothing wrong, the judge ruled. Splitting the baby, the judge simply tried to unring the bell, which had already been rung:

> The Court: Thank you, ladies and gentlemen, please be seated. Let the record reflect we have been rejoined by all of the members of our jury panel again. Ladies and gentlemen, the reason for our brief recess is that the exhibit that was on the evidence display system, People's Number 175, made reference to two items that the court has previously deemed to be irrelevant and that the parties had agreed not to present to you and that exhibit was shown to you by mistake and you will not be shown that exhibit until it has been corrected, to delete mention of those two items. I know that you are very diligent jurors and I saw you looking up and reading the item; you are to disregard the mention as to items 15 and 16, if you wrote it down, read it or recollect it. You are to disregard mention of those two items. . . . I might add you are not to speculate as to what those items were.[30]

Right. Like that's possible.

Criminalist Dennis Fung Testifies about Gathering Evidence at the Scene

On cross-examination, Simpson Defense Attorney Barry Scheck grilled Los Angeles County Criminalist Dennis Fung about the cross-contamination of Nicole Brown Simpson's body with hairs of O.J. Simpson to explain away how O.J.'s hair ended up at the scene—the blanket that covered her body had been retrieved from her condo, cross-contaminating her body with hairs from O.J., who likely had sat on the blanket. Fung admitted that decision had been a mistake. Compared to never seeing a mistake in 10,000 investigations, that's quite an admission.

Q: Now, when you arrived at the crime scene, you saw that there was a blanket over the body of Nicole Brown Simpson.

A: I don't recall being there that soon. When I got there, the body of Ms. Simpson was being processed.

Q: When was the first time you saw the blanket?

A: I saw the blanket when it was on the ground.

Q: It was on the ground in the area where Ms. Simpson's body was?

A: Yes.

Q: And you came to learn in your investigation that day that the blanket had been used to cover the body?

A: Yes.

Q: And you came to learn that that blanket had come from the home of Nicole Brown Simpson?

A: I did not know that.

Q: Have you found that out?

A: Since then, yes.

Q: And did you make any inquiry on that day about where that blanket had come from?

A: No, I didn't.

Q: And would you agree, sir, that a blanket that kind can be source of, possible source of secondary transfer?

A: Possibly.

Q: And that if Mr. Simpson had been in that home and been sitting or lying on that blanket, his hairs could be in that blanket?

Mr. Goldberg: Calls for speculation, your Honor.

The Court: Sustained.

Q: Well, within that expertise, is that the kind of blanket that if somebody were sitting on it, lying on it, one would expect to find hairs that they had shed on the blanket?

Mr. Goldberg: Objection, calls for speculation.

The Court: Sustained.

Q: In your expertise as a criminalist, do you have to make judgments about different kinds of items that can be sources of possible secondary transfer?

A: Yes.

Q: You have to worry about such objects being brought into crime scenes?

A: Yes.

Q: You have to be worried about such objects being brought into crime scenes, because they can be a source of contamination?

A: Yes.

. . .

Q: All right. And would you agree it would be important to know if that blanket contained hairs and fibers from Mr. Simpson, Ms. Nicole Brown Simpson, their children or the dog, Kato?

Mr. Goldberg: Objection, your Honor. It's argumentative (Inaudible).

The Court: Overruled.

A: Yes.

> Q: It would be important to know if that blanket contained fibers that would be consistent with Mr. Simpson's Bronco?
>
> A: Possibly, yes.
>
> Q: It would be important if it even had hairs or fibers that were consistent with Mr. Goldman, if he had ever been in the house and lay or sat on that blanket?
>
> A: Possibly.
>
> Q: But that blanket was left at the crime scene and never picked up for future analysis?
>
> A: That's correct.
>
> Q: That was a mistake, wasn't it?
>
> A: It could be considered one.[31]

When the criminalist left the stand, and in front of the jury, he shook hands with the defense team, who greeted him as a hero for their case. That was not exactly the impression the prosecution wanted to leave with the jury. The defense next hacked away at Criminalist Trainee Andrea Mazzola, who collected evidence with Dennis Fung, impeached her credibility and ability to properly gather evidence, claiming she contaminated it as she gathered it by failing to change her latex gloves between taking samples, failed to gather blood samples from the back gate because she didn't see it, and changed numbering on blood samples. The prosecution attempted to repair that damage on redirect, but her testimony had been impaled, along with their theory of the case.

Could O.J. be found innocent?

One of the members of O.J.'s defense team, William C. Thompson, a Professor in the Department of Criminology, Law & Society at the University of California, Irvine, explained the problem with Ms. Mazzola's handling of the samples this way:

> After they were used to collect blood at the crime scene, the Bundy swatches were sealed in plastic bags and stored in a truck. At the end of the day, they were returned to the LAPD crime laboratory and left in test tubes overnight to dry. The next morning, criminalist Andrea Mazzola packaged the dried swatches in paper bindles. In a pretrial hearing about

two months thereafter, Mazzola testified that she had placed her initials on each of the bindles.

When defense experts examined the bindles containing the Bundy swatches, they made two startling discoveries: none of the bindles bore Mazzola's initials . . . but some bore what renowned criminalist and defense expert Dr. Henry Lee later characterized as wet transfer stains - the sort of stains that would be produced by contact with swatches that were wet with blood. These observations led Dr. Lee to a memorable conclusion: "something is wrong."

The Bundy swatches should not have been wet when they were placed in the bindles, the defense argued. According to laboratory notes, the swatches had been allowed to air-dry in open test tubes for fourteen hours before they were placed in the bindles. Dr. Lee testified that the swatches should have been completely dry within three hours. A study produced by the prosecution stated that swatches dry within fifty-five minutes.[32]

The DNA Evidence

According to the testimony offered by the prosecution, here's how the DNA and blood evidence stacked up by location:

O.J. Simpson's Ford Bronco - DNA matching Nicole Brown Simpson, Goldman and O.J. Simpson's.

O.J. Simpson's Ford Bronco (instrument panel and inside door) - O.J. Simpson

O.J. Simpson's Ford Bronco (steering wheel)—O.J. Simpson and Nicole

O.J. Simpson's Ford Bronco (front console)— all three

Socks in O.J.'s bedroom—O.J. and Nicole

Glove found at Rockingham—all three

Nicole's condo (walkway and rear gate)—O.J. Simpson

Bruno Magli Shoe print of Goldman's shoe at condo—Nicole Brown Simpson

Nicole's fingernails—Nicole Brown Simpson

The prosecution offered evidence from DNA experts that an RFLP test (Restriction Fragment Length Polymorphism analysis and pronounced "rif-lip") was done from a blood drop found at the condo that was large enough to be tested on through the procedure. The RFLP test cuts a DNA molecule at a specific location, then measures base pair lengths for comparison. According to this test, the blood found at the crime scene could have come from 1 of 170 million sources of blood, and O.J.'s blood fit that one-in-170 million chance.

The other four blood drops were tested by the PCR method (Polymerase Chain Reaction). The PCR method essentially clones the DNA sample, allowing millions of copies of the DNA strand. There was a 1-in-5,200 match to O.J. from only the fifth drop.

These five drops were among the most noteworthy evidence against Simpson because they were collected on June 13, 1994, prior to when the police obtained a sample of Simpson's blood. The defense nevertheless argued that these samples were cross contaminated at the lab.

The other blood sample found at the Rockingham scene the prosecution admitted into evidence presented an even stronger statistical chance—one in 6.8 billon. The prosecution argued that statistical DNA match made Nicole Simpson the only person on earth who matched that DNA blood sample.

Given these DNA statistics and presumed reliability, the defense had several options to attack the samples. The defense could claim the samples were either planted or contaminated and quite possibly degraded—or worse yet, both. The defense team wisely argued that the blood evidence from the Bronco was contaminated from two break-ins while it was impounded at police facilities. Again, Professor Thompson explained the problems with the DNA samples, as asserted by the defense team, showing cross-contamination of the blood samples in the laboratory setting.

> LAPD criminalist Collin Yamauchi admitted that he spilled some of Simpson's blood from a reference vial while working in the evidence processing room and that shortly thereafter he

handled the Rockingham glove and the cotton swatches containing the blood from the Bundy drops. The defense proposed that some of Simpson's blood was inadvertently transferred to these evidentiary samples, perhaps on Yamauchi's gloves or instruments.

DNA of the person who left the blood drops (possibly the true perpetrator) could not be detected, the defense argued, because it was degraded and destroyed due to mishandling of the Bundy samples. LAPD criminalists collected the blood drops by swabbing them with wet cotton swatches. The swatches were then put in plastic bags and left several hours in a hot truck. The prosecution's experts all acknowledged that DNA degrades rapidly when blood samples are left in a moist, warm environment, that degradation can render the DNA originally in a sample untypeable, and that subsequent contamination of such a sample by a second person's DNA can cause it falsely to match the second person on a DNA test.

The defense argued that the pattern of the DNA test results fits neatly with the cross-contamination theory. The quantity of DNA found on the evidentiary items was small enough to be consistent with such an inadvertent transfer. On the glove, the allele matching Simpson was found in samples from the wrist notch, in an area where Yamauchi wrote his initials, and nowhere else. In the blood swatches, the quantity of DNA consistent with Simpson declined in the order in which Yamauchi handled them - that is, the first sample he handled had the most DNA, and the later samples contained much less DNA.

To bolster further the cross-contamination theory, the defense presented evidence of sloppiness in the LAPD's handling of samples prior to DNA testing. The criminalists were poorly trained with respect to sample handling, were not following a written protocol, did not understand the purpose and importance of precautionary measures, such as changing gloves, and made serious errors even when attempting to demonstrate proper sample collection and handling techniques. Defense expert Dr. John

> Gerdes, who reviewed DNA test results at the LAPD laboratory during the year prior to the Simpson case, found a history of serious contamination problems that he attributed largely to cross-contamination of DNA due to poor sample handling procedures.
>
> Dr. Gerdes also found startling evidence of cross-contamination in the DNA test results of the Simpson case itself: it appeared that the reference vials containing the blood of Nicole Brown Simpson and Ronald Goldman were contaminated with the DNA of O.J. Simpson! Extra alleles consistent with O.J. Simpson's appeared when the victims' blood was typed both at the LAPD laboratory and at two other laboratories to which the same vials were later sent.[33]

The prosecution put Dr. Bruce Weir, a genetic statistician, on the stand. Defense team member Peter Neufeld destroyed the value of Dr. Weir's testimony:

> Q: (by Nuefeld) . . .by failing to include the additional pairings in these samples, in these items, which do not exclude Mr. Simpson, the number that are arrived at by you and put on that board are biased against Mr. Simpson; isn't that correct?
>
> A: As it turns out, it looks that way, yes.[34]

Compared to the testimony offered about the blood evidence in the Lindy Chamberlain trial, this evidence was simple to understand. The investigators had perhaps botched the investigation.

The Gloves are Off

On June 15, 1995, the prosecution made what many consider to be its biggest blunder of the trial: Christopher Darden orchestrated a demonstration after identifying Bloomingdales as the exclusive seller of the Aris Isotoner brand glove found at both the Bundy crime scene and O.J.'s Rockingham estate. Unfortunately for the prosecution's case, Darden's demonstration inspired the defense a snappy refrain: "If the glove doesn't fit, you must acquit."

To put the gloves on O.J.'s hands, Brenda Vemich from the New York Bloomingdales store testified:

Mr. Darden: I would like to show you a pair of gloves that have already been marked. Where can we do this, your honor?

The Court: Where would you like to do it, Mr. Darden? Do you want to do it here on the shelf in front of the witness?

Mr. Darden: Okay.

. . .

Q: Miss Vemich, given the description you have provided us of the Aris Isotoner leather light glove, are you able to identify that glove when you see it?

A: Yes.

Q: Let me show you the glove that has been marked People's 164-A. It is LAPD Item No. 9, the Rockingham glove. Showing you People's 164-A, looking at that glove, can you tell us whether or not that glove is an Aris Isotoner Leather Light glove?

A: Can you turn it over?

(Mr. Darden complies.)

A: Yes. This is an Aris Leather Light glove.

Q: Now, does this glove have the "V" indentation in the palm area that you described earlier?

A: Yes, the vent palm.

Q: Okay. How about the stitching?

A: The stitching is the Brossier stitching, the lining is [cashmere].

Q: And does the leather appear to be particularly light, as you described earlier?

A: Very thin for a glove, yes.

Q: And this glove is a glove exclusive to Bloomingdales?

A: Yes.

. . . [After excruciatingly detailed testimony about the dates, numbers, sizes, colors, receipts and microfiche records about the receipt for two particular pairs of this type of Aris Isotoner gloves, Ms. Vemich testified further about who purchased this type of glove, but not necessarily the ones in the courtroom. Mr. Darden next showed the witness a credit card receipt] . . .

Q: Now, at the bottom to the right of the document do you see some numbers beginning with "3713"?

A: Yes.

Q: And what are those numbers?

A: It appears to be an American Express number.

Q: Okay. And is there a signature on the credit card receipt?

A: Yes.

Q: Can you read that signature to us?

A: Nicole Brown.[35]

The prosecution next called a former Vice President of Isotoner to testify about the limited number of gloves sold. Once they proved Nicole had bought the gloves for O.J., the prosecution then had O.J. try on the gloves. In the courtroom. In front of the jury. Without knowing in advance whether the bloody glove would fit.

While O.J. could have objected to the prosecution's request for a demonstration because to do so would violate his Fifth Amendment right not to testify, apparently the defense knew ahead of time what would happen, perhaps having conducted their own, out-of-court experiment. However, the jury would not understand the fine points of this Constitutional argument but would view O.J.'s demonstration as his "testimony" during the trial.

In any event, as you will see, O.J. did "testify," although not under oath, another point probably lost on the jury. Undoubtedly, though, the jury understood the defense's main point well enough—the gloves did not fit. To get a good fit and as a scientific control, the prosecution should have tried to force O.J. to try on a matching size of Aris Isotoner Leather Light gloves that were not blood soaked and without wearing latex gloves underneath. The defense would have likely succeeded in preventing that demonstration from the Constitutional perspective, and fearful in any event that those gloves would have fit. All speculation aside, this exchange is how it happened:

(By Mr. Darden) Your Honor, at this time, the People would ask that Mr. Simpson step forward and try on the glove recovered at Bundy as well as the glove recovered at Rockingham.

The Court: All right. (To defense counsel) do you want to do that?

Mr. Cochran: No objection, Your Honor.

The Court: All right. He can do that seated there. All right. And I think so the jury can see, I'll ask Mr. Simpson to stand. All right. Mr. Darden, which glove do you have?

Mr. Darden: This is the Bundy glove, your honor.

The Court: All right.

Mr. Darden: And after Mr. Simpson tries on the gloves, I would ask that he be required to step back over to the jury and again show him his bare hands.

The Court: Well, we'll get to that in a second. All right. The record should reflect that, as is our practice with these gloves, Mr. Simpson will have a pair of latex gloves on while doing this.

Mr. Darden: I'm handing Mr. Simpson the left glove, Rockingham.

The Court: That's people's 77?

(The Defendant complies.)

Mr. Darden: Your Honor, apparently Mr. Simpson seems to be having a problem putting the glove on his hand.

Mr. Cochran: Your honor, I object to counsel's statements. [Just for effect.]

The Court: Sustained.

Mr. Cochran: Thank you. Move to strike.

Mr. Darden: I'd also like to hand Mr. Simpson the other glove. What exhibit number?

The Court: This is people's 164-a? Is that the right-hand glove?

Mr. Darden: Yes, your Honor.

(*The Defendant complies.*)

The Court: All right. Deputy Jex, would you just take a step back, please. Thank you. All right. The record should reflect that Mr. Simpson has both gloves [on].

Mr. Darden: May he show his hands in front of the jury so that they can see –

The Court: Yes.

Mr. Darden: Mr. Simpson is indicating that his fingers aren't all the way into the gloves, your Honor.

The Court: All right. Thank you, counsel.

Mr. Darden: Mr. Simpson told the jury that the gloves are too small. [Notice here a second blunder—Darden could have easily moved to strike Mr. Simpson's statements, or gone further and ask the court to cross-examine him on the fit of the gloves, a point the judge would have most likely denied, but the jury would have gotten the point that Simpson's statements weren't testimony. In any event, the visual of the gloves not fitting would have made any attempt to remedy the problem moot. The jury saw and understood the gloves didn't fit. There was no way to unring that bell.]

The Court: All right.

Mr. Darden: Your Honor, before Mr. Simpson goes back, can we ask him to replace the left glove onto his hand?

The Court: All right.

Mr. Darden: Can we ask him to straighten his fingers and extend them into the glove as one normally might put a glove on?

The Court: Yes.

Mr. Cochran: Your honor, object to this statement by counsel.

(*The Defendant complies.*)

> **The Court:** All right. He appears to have pulled the gloves on, counsel. [And the gloves still didn't fit. Ouch.] All right. Would you show that to the jury, Mr. Simpson, in that manner?
>
> (*The Defendant complies.*)
>
> **The court:** Thank you. Other hand, please.
>
> (*The Defendant complies.*)[36]

Right then and there, the gloves became irrelevant, and irreparably damaged the prosecution's case.

The Bruno Magli Shoes and a Trip to Italy

Nothing appeared out of reach for the prosecution, who managed to send FBI Agent Bill Bodziak to the Bruno Magli shoe factory in Italy to get the actual shoe to compare with the bloody footprint leaving the scene of the crime at Nicole's condo. O.J. denied owning such shoes during the trial, but as we know now, tabloid photos of O.J. appeared in the media coverage of the trial. O.J. contends the photos were faked; an allegation made well before artificial intelligence readily enabled tampering.

Mr. Goldberg examined the FBI Agent:

> Q: All right. Now, based upon all of the information that you had from your visit to Italy from the lasts [the impressions used to make the soles] and the soles and the photographs of the Bundy crime scene location, were you able to form an opinion regarding the size of the shoe – the size of the shoes that caused the shoeprints at Bundy location?
>
> A: Yes, I was.
>
> Q: What is that opinion?
>
> A: That size was an American size 12 with the European size 46 sole attached to it.[37]

O.J. also wore size twelve shoe. The tread on the bloody footprint matched the tread of the Bruno Magli shoe. The gloves might not have fit, but the shoes appeared to match.

The End of the Prosecution

On July 6, 1995, after presenting testimony for five months and offering 72 witnesses, the prosecution rested, failing to understand two of the most basic trial requirements: keep it simple and end with a bang. Instead, the prosecution dragged on and whimpered to an end. Despite valiant efforts to introduce convincing testimony about the hairs found at the crime scene and at Rockingham, defense attorney F. Lee Bailey questioned prosecution witness Chief of the FBI's hairs and fibers unit, Douglas Deedrick. In that cross-examination, Bailey gained admissions from Deedrick that police found no hair from Nicole Brown Simpson in O.J. Simpson's Bronco. Deedrick likewise admitted that there was no hair consistent with O.J. Simpson's hair on either the Bundy or Rockingham gloves. To add insult to injury, Deedrick once again confirmed the defense's contentions that there were no hairs from Ronald Goldman or Nicole Brown Simpson on a sock found at Simpson's mansion.

The prosecution's case ended gasping for air.

O.J.'s Defense

Despite warnings that the best defense to this prosecution was no defense at all, the Dream Team mounted an attack in July and August on prosecution eyewitness testimony about the night of the murder and challenged the prosecution's scientific evidence with experts of its own. In all, O.J.'s defense team called 54 witnesses.

Defense DNA expert John C. Gerdes, Ph.D., of Immunological Associates in Denver Colorado took the stand and stated that the LAPD has "persistent and chronic" contamination problems.[38]

Ouch.

The defense pointed out that the LAPD had been unable to match any of the fingerprints at the Bundy crime scene to O.J. LAPD fingerprint expert Gilbert Aguilar testified that none of the latent fingerprints found at the crime scene matched Simpson's prints.[39]

Perhaps the most effective defense witness was Dr. Henry Lee:

> **Mr. Scheck**: Dr. Lee, could you tell us what present position you hold?
>
> **Dr. Lee**: Currently, I'm the chief criminalist for state of Connecticut. Also, I'm the laboratory director for Connecticut State Police forensic laboratory. However, today, I come here as act as an independent consultant, nothing to do with my official capacity.
>
> . . .
>
> **Mr. Scheck**: Now, Dr. Lee, in terms of the side that you're usually on in criminal cases in terms of percentages, what percentage of the time are you called by the Prosecution and what percentage of the time are you called by the Defense?
>
> **Dr. Lee**: Uh, approximately 95 percent is for the Prosecution, less than five percent for the Defense.[40]

Dr. Lee was the ideal witness for the defense: he testified mostly for the prosecution side, so the prosecution could not accuse him of a defense-oriented bias. Dr. Lee went on to confirm that he found bloody shoe imprints on a piece of paper at the Bundy crime scene (after the police had left) and determined that they did not match Bruno Magli shoes. He also put the time of the murders closer to 11:00 p.m. to match O.J.'s alibi, and finally condemned the evidence-gathering techniques of the LAPD, pointing out that the samples appeared to have been tampered with.

Double ouch.

After examining evidence found by the LAPD, Doctor Lee said he found transfer stains inside paper packaging holding what were supposed to be dry blood samples indicating that transfer stains existed inside paper packaging that was supposed to hold dry blood samples:

> **Dr. Lee**: Something, somebody . . . put the swatch in the [package to] cause such a transfer. Who did it? What happened? I don't know. Only opinion I can give you under these circumstances: Something's wrong.[41]

The jury would ultimately determine who was wrong, but Dr. Lee gave them a pretty good idea.

Closing Arguments and Missed Opportunities

No evidence came before the jury of the contents of O.J.'s Ford Bronco found after the chase. O.J.'s suicide note was not offered by the prosecution, either. In her closing, Prosecutor Marcia Clark spoke for five hours. Christopher Darden spoke for about an hour and followed up with a rebuttal after Johnnie Cochran. Johnnie Cochran spoke for about five hours and defense attorney Barry Scheck briefly inserted a few words amid Cochran's closing argument.

Racism and Mark Fuhrman

On one of the hot-button issues in the case, both Clark and Cochran spoke about Fuhrman, but attacked him in different ways. Even Darden dealt with Fuhrman's racism.

Clark tried both to vilify Fuhrman and to save him at the same time, an almost impossible task:

> Let me come back to Mark Fuhrman for a minute, just so it's clear.
>
> Did he lie when he testified here in this courtroom saying that he did not use racial epithets in the last 10 years? Yes.
>
> Is he a racist? Yes.
>
> Is he the worst L.A.P.D. has to offer? Yes.
>
> Do we wish that this person was never hired by L.A.P.D.? Yes.
>
> Should L.A.P.D. have ever hired him? No.
>
> Should such a person be a police officer? No.
>
> In fact, do we wish there were no such person on the planet? Yes.
>
> But the fact that Mark Fuhrman is a racist and lied about it on the witness stand does not mean that we haven't proven the defendant guilty beyond a reasonable doubt. And it would be a tragedy if, with such overwhelming evidence, ladies and gentlemen, as we have presented to you, you found the

defendant not guilty in spite of all that because of the racist attitudes of one police officer.[42]

Cochran took it much further, comparing Fuhrman to Hitler:

> There was another man not too long ago in this world who had those same views, who wanted to burn people, who had racist views, and ultimately had power over people in his country. People didn't care. People said he's crazy. He's just a half-baked painter. And they didn't do anything about it. This man, this scourge, became one of the worst people in the world, Adolf Hitler, because people didn't care, didn't stop him. He had the power over his racism and his anti-religionism. Nobody wanted to stop him. . . .And so Fuhrman. Fuhrman wants to take all black people now and burn them or bomb them. That's genocidal racism. Is that ethnic purity? We're paying this man's salary to espouse these views.[43]

. . .

> We've seen a number of big lies in this case in their so-called rush to judgment. We've seen lie after lie, so much so that at least two of the major witnesses, Vannatter ... and Fuhrman, their testimony by you may be totally disregarded, further dismantling the people's case. You have that right, you know, in this search for truth.
>
> In times like these, we often turn to the Bible for some answer ... I happen to really like the Book of Proverbs. And in Proverbs, it talks a lot about false witnesses. It says that, "A false witness shall not be unpunished. And he that speaketh lies shall not escape." That meant a lot to me in this case because there was Mark Fuhrman, acting like a choir boy, making you believe he was the best witness that walked in here, generally applauded for his wonderful performance. Turns out he was the biggest liar in this courtroom during this process. But the Bible had already told us the answer, that "a false witness shall not be unpunished. And he that speaketh lies shall not escape."
>
> In that same book it tells us that a faithful witness will not lie, but a false witness will utter lies.

> And finally, in Proverbs, it says that, "He that speaketh truth showeth the forthrightfulness, but a false witness shows deceit."
>
> So when we're talking about truth, we're talking about truth and lies and conspiracies and cover-ups. I always think about one of my favorite poems which I think is so very appropriate in this case, you know, "When things are at the darkest, there is always light the next day." In your life, in all of our lives, you have the capacity to transform all Mr. Simpson's dark yesterdays into brighter tomorrows. You have that capacity. You have that power in your hands. And James Russell Lowell said it best about wrong and evil. He said that, "Truth forever on the scaffold. Wrong forever on the throne. Yet that scaffold sways the future. And beyond the dim unknown standeth God within the shadows keeping watch above his own." You walk with that every day. You carry that with you. And things will come to you. And you'll be able to reveal people who come to you in uniforms in high positions who lie and are corrupt. That's what happened in this case.[44]

In his rebuttal, Darden tried to undo the damage Cochran had done:

> Let me ask you this: If you were to acquit [O.J. Simpson], what explanation would you give the day after that acquittal if someone said, "Why did you acquit him?" Would you say racism? Would you say because there's racism in the LAPD? That's what they want you to say. That's what they want you to think.
>
> You heard all the speaking and the fiery rhetoric and the quotes from Proverbs and the like. You heard all of that yesterday, all of that fiery rhetoric.
>
> Well, let me tell you what Marcia Clark and I are, let me tell you who we are. We are the voices of calm and reason in all of this. You just need to calm down. Take that common sense God gave you, go back in the jury room. Don't let these people get you

all riled up and all fired up because Fuhrman is a racist.

Racism blinds you. Those epithets, they blind you. You never heard me use that epithet in this courtroom, did you? I'm not going to put on that kind of show for you-know-who, for people who watch. That's not where we're coming from.

I am eternally grateful that Mr. Fuhrman was exposed to be what he is, because I think we should know who those people are. I've said it once, I've said it before, we ought to put a big stamp tattooed on their forehead, "Racist," so that when we see them we know who they are, so there is no speculation - we don't have to guess.

But what they want you to do and what they've done in this case is they've interjected this racism. And now they want you to become impassioned, to be upset. And they want you to make quantum leaps in logic and in judgment. They want you to say Fuhrman is a racist, he planted the glove.

You can't get from point A to point B if you just sit down and use your common sense. If you're logical, if you're reasonable, you can't do that.

It is true that Fuhrman is a racist. And it is also true that he [Simpson] killed these two people. And we proved that he killed two people and they proved that Fuhrman is a racist.[45]

Once again, now that we're finished with the Fuhrman diversion, let's return to our regularly scheduled programming.

The Rest of the Closings

Marcia Clark conceded sloppy police work:

The defense has thrown out many, many other questions. They've thrown out questions about whether L.A.P.D. has some bad police officers; does the scientific division have some sloppy criminalists; does the coroner's office have some sloppy coroners. And the answer to all these questions is: Sure, yes, they do. That's not news to you. I'm sure it wasn't a big surprise to you.

But those are not—they're important issues. You know, we should look into the quality control. Things should be done better. Things could always be done better in every case, at every time. There's no question about that.

We're not here to vote on that today.

The question is what the evidence that was presented to you that relates to who killed Ron and Nicole – what does that tell you? Does that convince you beyond a reasonable doubt?[46]

Finally, she wrapped up, ignoring the faults in her case:

And now let me summarize for you what we have proven:

One piece of the puzzle: We've proven the opportunity to kill. We've given the time window in which he was able to kill because his whereabouts were unaccounted for during the time when we know the murders were occurring.

We have the hand injuries that were suffered on the night of his wife's murder – to the left hand, as we know the killer was injured on his left hand.

We have the post-homicidal conduct that I told you about: lying to Allan Park [the limousine driver], making Allan Park wait outside. Not letting Kato pick up that little dark bag. His reaction to Detective Phillips when he made notification. When Detective Phillips said to him, "Nicole has been killed," instead of asking about a car accident, the defendant asks no questions.

We have the manner of killings, killings that indicate that it was a rage killing, that it was a fury killing, that it was not a professional hit. The manner of killing that indicates one person committed these murderers. One person with the same style of killing.

We have the knit cap at Bundy. We have the evidence on Ron Goldman's shirt of the blue-black cotton fibers, the defendant's hair.

We have the Bruno Magli shoe prints, size 12 – all of them size 12, his size shoe – all of them consistent going down the Bundy walk.

> We have the Bundy blood trail: his blood to the left of the bloody shoe prints. We have the blood in the Bronco – his and Ron Goldman's.
>
> We have the Rockingham blood trail, up the driveway, in his bathroom, in the foyer.
>
> We have the Rockingham glove with all of the evidence on it: Ron Goldman, fibers from his shirt; Ron Goldman's hair; Nicole's hair; the defendant's blood; Ron Goldman's blood; Nicole's blood. And the Bronco fiber. And the blue-black cotton fibers. We have the socks and we have the blue-black cotton fibers on the socks. And we have Nicole Brown's blood on the socks.
>
> There he is. [Pointing to the Defendant, O.J. Simpson, in true dramatic fashion, just like the TV movies.][47]

Prosecutor Christopher Darden took his turn next, and talked about the spousal abuse Nicole Brown Simpson suffered through, replaying the 911 tape from 1993 and again showing the jury photographs depicting the abuse:

> Of course, you're probably wondering, 'Well hey, if he did all these things to her, if he said all of these things to her, why did she stay?'
>
> There's this old song, and the words used to go that - I think it was the Dramatics, I can't really recall. But there was a couple of lines in the song where they said the strong give up and move on and the weak give up and stay.
>
> You know, if you badger a person long enough, if you beat them down long enough, if you wear them down long enough, pretty soon you strip them of their dignity, their self-esteem and they are weak, and they are submissive, and they can't go, they can't stay. And you know how that is, everybody knows how that is. We've all been in bad relationships before. You have friends, you see them in these bad relationships. Why, why do they stay? Why do they stay?
>
> Usually they feel they don't have a choice. They don't know that they have a choice. They

forgot that they had a choice. In their minds, they have no choice. . . .

But we talked about that yesterday and we talked about justice. And we talked about what the real issue in this case was about and I pointed the defendant out to you and I told you he killed her. And you've heard the evidence in this case.

He killed Ron Goldman. O.J. Simpson's a murderer. That's what the evidence indicates. That is what the evidence indicates, that is what the evidence shows. It shows that he's not just a murderer, but he's a double murderer. And that's unfortunate, it's unfortunate that I have to stand here and tell you this. Because I'd rather be somewhere else. I'm sure you'd rather be somewhere else. Who wants to really have to confront and deal with these issues.

But we have to because we have a duty. Marcia and I have a duty and you have a duty as well. Your duty is to look at all the evidence, to be fair, be conscientious, be objective. Your duty is to look at all the evidence, the totality of circumstances, everything. We don't want you to just look at one piece, don't just look at the prosecution's case. Look at the entire case. Look at everything.

Because when you do, when you do, what can you say, except he did it, and we've proven it and we've proven it beyond a reasonable doubt?[48]

Unlike the thrust of his attack on Fuhrman, Johnnie Cochran took the high road for the beginning of his opening, just like "Ropes" in the Black Sox trial:

That's what we're going to be talking about this afternoon as I seek to address you. The final test of your service as jurors will not lie in the fact that you have stayed here more than a year. It will lie in the quality of the verdict that you render, and whether or not that verdict bespeaks justice, as a move towards justice. . .

Listen for a moment, will you please, one of my favorite people in history is the great Frederick Douglas. He said, shortly after the slaves were freed, quote: In a composite nation like ours as before the law, there should be no rich, no poor, no high, no low, no white, no black, but common country, common citizenship, equal rights and a common destiny.

This marvelous statement was made more than 100 years ago. It's an ideal worth striving for and one that we still strive for. We haven't reached this goal yet, but certainly, in this great country of ours, we're trying. With the jury such as this, we hope we can do that in this particular case.

Now, in this case, you are aware that we represent Mr. Orenthal James Simpson. The prosecution never calls him Mr. Orenthal James Simpson. They call him "defendant."

I want to tell you right at the outset that Orenthal James Simpson, like all defendants, is presumed to be innocent. He's entitled to the same dignity and respect as all the rest of us.

As he sits over there now, he's cloaked in a presumption of innocence. You will determine the facts of whether or not he is set free to walk out those doors or whether he spends the rest of his life in prison.[49]

. . .

Thank you for your attention during this first part of my argument. I hope that during this phase of it I have demonstrated to you that this really is a case about a rush to judgment, an obsession to win at all costs, a willingness to distort, twist, theorize in any fashion to try to get you to vote guilty in this case where it is not warranted. That these metaphors about an ocean of evidence or mountain of evidence is little more than a tiny, tiny stream, if at all, that points equally towards innocence. That any mountain has long ago been reduced to little more than a molehill under an avalanche of lies and complexity and conspiracy. This is what we have shown you. And so, as great as America is, we have not yet reached the point where there is equality and rights or equality of opportunity.

I started off talking to you a little bit about Frederick Douglass and what he said more than 100 years ago, for there are still the Mark Fuhrmans in this world and in this country who hate and are yet embraced by people in power.

But you and I, fighting for freedom and ideals and for justice for all, must continue to fight to expose hate and genocidal racism and these tendencies. We then become the guardians of the Constitution.

As I told you yesterday . . . if we, as the people, don't continue to hold a mirror up to the face of America and say: "This is what you promised; this is what you delivered," if you don't speak out, if you don't stand up, if you don't do what's right, this kind of conduct will continue on forever, and we'll never have an ideal society, one that lives out the true meaning of the creed of the Constitution of life, liberty and justice for all."

I'm going to take my seat, but I get one last time to address you. As I said before: This is a case about an innocent man who wrongfully accused. You have seen him now for a year and two days. You observed him, the good times and the bad times. Soon it will be your turn. You have the keys to his future. You have the evidence by which you can acquit this man. You have not only the patience, but the integrity and the courage to do the right thing.

We believe you will do the right thing, and the right thing is to find this man not guilty of both of these charges.[50]

After Johnnie Cochran sat down, Defense attorney Barry Scheck, who led the attack on the DNA evidence and the quality of the evidence-gathering, said his piece:

The integrity of this system is at stake. You cannot convict when the core of the prosecution's case is built on perjurious testimony of police officers, unreliable forensic evidence and manufactured evidence.

It is a cancer at the heart of this case, and that's what this evidence shows when you go through it patiently, when you go through it carefully, when you go through it scientifically, logically. That's what the evidence shows.

And you cannot convict on that evidence. There are many, many reasonable doubts buried right in the heart of the scientific evidence in this case, and we have demonstrated them. And we don't have to prove them, but the evidence shows it.

So, in the words of Dr. Lee, something is wrong. Something is terribly wrong with the evidence in this case. You cannot trust it; it lacks integrity. It cannot be a basis for a verdict of beyond a reasonable doubt.

. . .

The other lead detective in this case is taking shoes home. . . . This could be critical evidence, the shoes that their suspect is wearing that night - taking it home.

Now, you know, it was amazing when Mr. Fung testified the extent to which, you know, they've lost all track of the rules. At one point I asked him, "Well, would it have been all right if they took the blood home?" And he said, "Sure, as long as you put it in the refrigerator overnight." Do you remember that answer? I mean there's—there's no sense of what has to be done in order to give you reliable evidence, none…

It's just plain that they didn't know what they were doing here and you can have the most sophisticated technology in the world, and if you don't apply it correctly, you can't trust the results. There's no compliance with the NRC [National Research Council] report. There's no compliance with the kind of standards that you would require in a life-and-death situation. And this is a life-and-death situation. And that's what you have to demand of a laboratory. [51]

Cochran then fervently wrapped up the defense's closing argument, almost preaching:

By your decision, you control his very life in your hands. Treat it carefully. Treat it fairly. Be fair.

Don't be part of this continuing cover-up. Do the right thing, remembering that if it doesn't fit, you must acquit; that if these messengers have lied to you, you can't trust their message. That this has been a search for truth that no matter how bad it looks, if truth is out there on a scaffold and wrong is in here on the thrown, remember that the scaffold always sways the future. And beyond the dim unknowns standeth the same God for all people keeping watch above his own. He watches all of us, and he'll watch you in your decision and thank you for your attention. God bless you.[52]

Darden handled the last word for the prosecution in his rebuttal:

See now, I'll go back to Martin because, you know, I feel comfortable with Martin Luther King. . . . [To Martin Luther King] justice was a critical issue in his life here on Earth, in his life, and it was more than a legal issue, and it was more than a moral issue. It was a spiritual issue. . . .

Read along with me what Martin Luther King said about justice. "Justice is the same for all issues. It cannot be categorized. It is not possible to be in favor of justice for some people and not be in favor of justice for all people. Justice cannot be divided. Justice is indivisible." . . .

You don't need a Ph.D. to see what's going on here. Your life experience, I think, will help you understand what's going on here. Just what you know, just what you read in the papers, just what you learned in schools and just what you heard from your friends and your girlfriends.

Someone suggested that that pathway, this pathway of death, this walkway of death, where these two people lay, wasn't pitch black that night, that it would have been easy to see two bodies laying there. That ain't true. That's not the evidence in this case.[53]

But the lawyers would not get the last word in the closing. While fending off the lawyers fighting with one another arguing about Darden's remarks in his rebuttal, Judge Ito finally took control of the courtroom, perhaps too late in the process:

Scheck: . . . I think it's improper to make an argument "everybody knows he's guilty." . .And another one I think they came perilously close with is in respect to the discussion of darkness at Bundy...

Ito: ..The argument's concluded, counsel.

. . .

Scheck: I understand that. I'm just saying –

Ito: Sit down.

Scheck:- perilously close.

Ito: That's a fair inference that can be drawn from the record. Also I'm going to admonish counsel on both sides not to make any gestures, head shaking, grimaces or any other responses to counsel's argument. I've seen it on both sides. And if I see it again, I'm going to stop in front of the jury and I'm going to upbraid you in front of the jury. Let's have the jurors.[54]

After closing arguments and a final admonishment from Judge Ito, the judge read the jury instructions to the jury and sent them off to deliberate.

The Jury Verdict

Despite predictions from the legal talking heads on the TV that the jury would be out for up to two months, they instead took just under four hours to reach their verdict. On October 3, 1995, Judge Ito's clerk read the jury's verdict, finding O.J. not guilty of all crimes charged. Again celebrity has its benefits.

Superior Court of California, County of Los Angeles. In the matter of People of the State of California versus Orenthal James Simpson, case number BA097211. We, the jury, in the above-entitled action, find the Defendant, Orenthal James Simpson, **not guilty** of the crime of murder in violation of penal code section 187(A), a felony, upon Nicole Brown Simpson, a human being, as charged in Count I of the information.

Superior Court of the State of California, County of Los Angeles, in the matter of People of the State of California versus Orenthal James Simpson. We, the jury, in the above-entitled action, find the Defendant, Orenthal James Simpson, **not guilty** of the crime of murder in violation of penal code section 187(A), a felony, upon Ronald Lyle Goldman, a human being, as charged in Count II of the information. "We, the jury, in the above-entitled action, further find the special circumstances that the Defendant, Orenthal James Simpson, has in this case been convicted of at least one crime of murder of the first degree and one or more crimes of murder of the first or second degree to be **not true**." Signed this 2nd day of October, 1995. "Juror 230." Ladies and gentlemen of the jury, is this your verdict, so say you one, so say you all?

The Jury: Yes. [Emphasis added.][55]

Judge Ito then polled the jurors individually to determine whether they had properly voted for acquittal. Each juror responded with a "yes."

Television cameras focused on O.J., who many say appeared shocked at the verdict. One African American juror pumped his fist in the air while looking at O.J. in an apparent show of solidarity. The defense team celebrated and Cochran also pumped his fist, but the Goldmans, who were in the audience, were crushed.

Jurors would later say in interviews that the prosecution bumbled the case.

No kidding.

Statistics as Compiled by
The Associated Press

Just so you don't think the media missed anything, the Associated Press complied this list:

Days Simpson spent in jail: 474

Days jurors were sequestered: 266

Length of closing arguments: 4 days

Length of opening statements: 4 days

Length of deliberations: less than 4 hours

Average age of juror: 43

Number of jurors picked: 12 plus 12 alternates

Number of jurors dismissed: 10

Witnesses: defense 54; prosecution 72

Days of testimony: defense 34; prosecution 99

Exhibits presented during testimony: defense 369; prosecution 488

Number of motions filed: 433 total (no breakdown available)

Number of attorneys who presented evidence in court: defense 11; prosecution 9.

Number of times judge pulled plug on television: 2

Cost: estimated $9 million for Los Angeles County, includes costs for court and prosecution; defense figures not available. [Defense costs were later calculated at between $4 and $7 million]

Amount earned by each of the 12 jurors and two alternates: $1,330 (at $5 a day for time of sequestration)

Length of official court transcript: more than 50,000 pages

Number of media credentials issued: more than 1,000

Number of telephone lines installed in press room: 250

Seating capacity in courtroom: 80

Fines imposed on defense: $3,000

Fines imposed on prosecution: $850

Fines imposed on others: $1,800[56]

The Aftermath

O.J.'s legal troubles related to the death of his ex-wife and Ron Goldman were far from over after the "not guilty" verdict. The parents of both victims sued O.J. in civil court for their wrongful deaths. He lost the Goldman's case and had judgment taken against him for $33.5 million, which was not dischargeable in bankruptcy due to the award of punitive damages component ($25 million of the award). Punitive damages require a finding of malice, and damages arising from intentional conduct like malice cannot be discharged under United States bankruptcy laws.

Many wonder why O.J. won in the criminal case but lost in the civil case. The difference between his criminal trial and his civil trial is the level of the burden of proof. In his criminal trial, the prosecution had to establish proof of the crimes "beyond a reasonable doubt," which criminal defense lawyers frequently argue in closing is equivalent to being 99.9 percent sure the defendant committed the crimes. In their civil court trials, on the other hand, the Browns and the Goldmans were required to prove only that it was "more likely than not" Simpson committed the murders. This civil standard sets level of proof at a "preponderance of the evidence," frequently handicapped as 51 percent to 49 percent.

His criminal jury reasonably doubted O.J. committed the murders, while his civil jury balanced the scales and believed he did.

The Goldmans have been the most diligent of the two sets of parents in pursuing their judgment but have been paid only a fraction of the court award. O.J. moved to Florida, where state law prevents judgment creditors (the Browns and the Goldmans) from seizing a judgment debtor's home (Simpson). In addition, under California law—where the judgment was obtained—a judgment creditor cannot take a judgment debtor's pension. After the trial, O.J. received his $25,000-a-month pension from the National Football League—not that it did him much good in jail, but he continued to receive that monthly pension until his death in April 2024.

On top of these two wrongful death lawsuits, O.J. engaged in a protracted battle with Nicole's parents over the custody of his children. Arguing the "best interests of the children" required them not to be with their father, the Browns sought custody. Ultimately, though, the California family law preference for children to remain with their biological parent won out, and an Orange County, California judge friend of mine, Judge Nancy Wieben Stock, awarded Simpson custody and he moved his then young children from Dana Point, California (where the Browns live) to Florida to live with him.

O.J. went through a number of other legal scrapes, including an allegation by the State of California, which claimed Simpson owed $1.44 million in past-due taxes. The State filed a tax lien filed against O.J. in September 1999, which prevented the Goldmans from recovering their judgment from O.J. until that lien was paid. Then in March 2004, satellite television network DirecTV accused Mr. Simpson in a Miami federal court of using illegal electronic devices to pirate its broadcast signals. It won a $25,000 judgment, topped off by $33,678 in attorneys fees and costs. O.J. also ran into problems with road rage allegations and other minor traffic scrapes.

Despite O.J.'s acquittal in at least this murder trial, he was convicted in his Las Vegas kidnapping and robbery case, where the judge called him both "arrogant and ignorant" and sentenced to him to 33 years in prison with the possibility of parole in nine years at his sentencing in December 2008. You may remember that O.J. and a friend broke into a Vegas hotel room with guns drawn to retrieve his allegedly stolen football memorabilia—trophies and rings. He held the alleged thieves hostage, but it was O.J. who got prosecuted, not the alleged thieves. Like 1920s gangster Al Capone who was convicted in 1931 on tax fraud, not murder and racketeering, many thought O.J. had finally been held to account for killing Nicole and Ron.

Chapter Conclusion

While O.J. steadfastly maintained his innocence and vowed to hunt down his wife's killer, many others believe the ensuing years after parole that he spent on the golf course did little to back up his claim. Still, we can't blame just O.J.

Several critical missteps occurred in the case. First, the prosecutors elected to proceed in a court not where the crime was committed, but one that would be seen as fairer to O.J. and prevent riots. That downtown jury turned out to be more sympathetic than a jury in Santa Monica likely would have been. Second, the prosecution withdrew the death penalty and gave up a jury more likely to convict before the trial began. Next, Detective Mark Fuhrman buried the prosecution's case by introducing the race card and allowing Johnnie Cochran to boil the case down and pit a white detective against an African American defendant to a racially diverse jury. Cochran took every advantage of that mistake and successfully implied Fuhrman planted evidence. The prosecutors staged an unrehearsed demonstration requiring O.J. to try on the bloody gloves, which obviously didn't fit, again allowing Cochran to capitalize on the prosecution's final and most major mistake. Judge Ito allowed that sideshow to proceed, and like Judge Raulston in the Scopes trial, may have played a bit too much to the cameras.

The media had its fair share of blame to shoulder here, too. The case was first tried to the media and the rest of the world, starting with the infamous low-speed chase. But was it truly the media we should blame, or do we only need to look in the mirror to see the cause of that coverage? Given the mass media and our insatiable appetite for celebrity news, we will never be able to discount this possibility.

Imagine instead a flawless prosecution trial with none of these missteps. Would O.J. have been convicted long before he was convicted of kidnapping and robbery in Las Vegas?

Wouldn't we all have liked to been on that jury and signed a big, fat book deal?

Remember to enter your vote on the outcome of this trial on www.10FamousTrials.com and see how other readers voted.

CONCLUSION

Although the Simpson murder trial was dubbed by many as the "trial of the century," this writer cautions that at one time or another, every other trial discussed in this book has borne that moniker, many not discussed were so labeled and many will again in the future. I am not sure which trial would deservedly bear that title of the trials in this book, but I do not believe the Simpson trial deserves it. Certainly, the interest of the public in the judicial system could easily vault the Simpson trial into that category if that level of interest was the sole criterion. Some would argue that the celebrity of those involved should serve as a criterion, too, but there are many arguments to the contrary that celebrity alone would disqualify a trial from such a title.

Other criteria may include the issues involved, such as interpreting the constitution of a particular country (Dred Scott, Plessy v. Ferguson, and Brown v. Board of Education in the U.S.) or one of its more important laws (the Kelo litigation involving the Fifth Amendment to the U.S. Constitution and the government's taking of private property). Issues such as the type of crime also may qualify a trial, such as murder (the Boston Massacre, Lizzie Borden, Sam Sheppard, Charles Manson, and Lindy Chamberlain trials, to name a few), treason (Aaron Burr), or other betrayal (the Rosenbergs). Religion (the trials of Jesus, Joan of Arc and Sir Thomas Moore as well as the Salem Witch trials), discrimination (the Amistad trial), and perhaps pivotal moments in history such as war crimes trials (the Nuremberg or Mai Lai trials) may come to mind.

Certainly the performance of the lawyers (John Adams or Clarence Darrow and any one of the latter's trials: Leopold & Loeb, the Sweet trials, the Massie trial, and the Scopes trial), the judge (Judge James Edwin Horton, Jr., the judge in the Scottsboro Boys trial who set aside the verdict and ruined his career), or the testimony of the witnesses (John Brown, who died for his beliefs) likewise may earn a trial points toward the award.

Trials outside the normal course of human events, such as sports (the Black Sox trial), mutiny on the high seas (the H.M.S. Bounty comes to mind) or resulting from bravery—or foolishness—in the face of danger (the O.K. Corral shootout) also may qualify a trial as the Trial of the Century. Perhaps even timelessness should be a criterion (the trials of Socrates and Galileo). Lawyers and other scholars could certainly propose other trials and categories; this list is not exhaustive and, by definition, more than one trial would qualify given the stretch of centuries covered in this book.

At the end of the day, however, it is you, dear reader, who should judge. My vote is just one among many. This book gives you a lawyer's insight into ten famous trials that changed history, each in their own way, allowing you the luxury of determining the winner of the Trial of the Century title and which one—or more—was a wrong decision.

Although I won't presume to pick the winner for you, I will say that I most enjoyed writing the chapter on the Salem Witch Trials, largely because of what I learned about our early judicial system and the need for the rule of law. From a purely entertainment perspective, my other favorite was the trial of Wyatt Earp, his brothers and Doc Holliday, perhaps more due to watching old TV and movie Westerns and the ease of picturing in my mind what happened.

From the opposite perspective, I also would award the Salem Witch Trials as a series of wrong decisions, if not the worst, because society and the judicial system failed us and innocent individuals needlessly died as a result. Although we hope we have now learned the lessons from that dreadful experience, other recent trials call that hope into question.

The presence of the media and our insatiable appetite for the trials and tribulations of others feeds the media frenzy, which continuously spirals downward in a vicious circle. High-speed police vehicle chases regularly fill entire half-hour local news broadcasts as if there was no news, weather, or sports that day. Like NASCAR races, we just watch to see the crash. We all complain about media coverage, but seemingly never turn off the broadcast. As my father once reminded me, "if you don't like it, vote with your feet." Perhaps it would be better to simply pick up another book rather than flip on the TV or scroll endlessly on your phone.

As this book ends, one takeaway from it revolves around the never-ending struggle for justice, recognizing the efforts of all who have gone before us to ensure we live in a world where justice is available for all. These trials light the path toward that common goal.

Thanks for turning the pages on this journey with me. Thank you too for the privilege of your time.

J. Craig Williams

About the Author

Author J. Craig Williams has tried innumerable cases, starting his career as a Certified Practicing Law Clerk while in law school. As a law student at the University of Iowa College of Law, he practiced in Iowa's Linn County Public Defender's Office, where he tried and won a week-long jury trial, 15 trials before a judge and earned a published opinion in his client's favor from the Iowa Supreme Court.

As a newly-minted lawyer in California, he switched sides and volunteered for the District Attorney's Office in the state's largest county, San Bernardino, and prosecuted numerous criminal cases, all to favorable verdicts. As a civil lawyer who's practiced for more than twenty years, he now regularly tries cases for corporate defendants in complex business litigation cases and criminal matters for white-collar defendants, continuing his winning streak. He has been recognized as one of the top 100 lawyers in Southern California, and has taught Trial Advocacy at his alma mater, the University of Iowa College of Law, where he graduated with distinction a year early.

Craig is best known for creating a new copyright law that requires websites to pay artists for their streaming music. His seminal appellate case before the Ninth Circuit, Fonovisa v. Cherry Auction, established for the first time the law of contributory copyright infringement. His case was cited as the precedent to shut down Napster, the first streaming music platform caught ripping off songs and distributing them across the Internet for free. He's still waiting for his honorary Emmy, Grammy, Oscar, and Tony awards for ensuring those artists are paid for the audio and video that streams their performances.

Appendix A

Boston Gazette and Country Journal report on Monday, March 12, 1770, of the facts of the March 5, 1770 Boston Massacre:

The Boston Gazette and Country Journal No. 779

Monday, March 12, 1770

A few minutes after nine o'clock four youths, named Edward Archibald, William Merchant, Francis Archibald, and John Leech, jun., came down Cornhill together, and separating at Doctor Loring's corner, the two former were passing the narrow alley leading Mr. Murray's barrack in which was a soldier brandishing a broad sword of an uncommon size against the walls, out of which he struck fire plentifully. A person of mean countenance armed with a large cudgel bore him company. Edward Archibald admonished Mr. Merchant to take care of the sword, on which the soldier turned round and struck Archibald on the arm, then pushed at Merchant and pierced through his clothes inside the arm close to the armpit and grazed the skin. Merchant then struck the soldier with a short stick he had; and the other person ran to the barrack and brought with him two soldiers, one armed with a pair of tongs, the other with a shovel. He with the tongs pursued Archibald back through the alley, collared and laid him over the head with the tongs. The noise brought people together; and John Hicks, a young lad, coming up, knocked the soldier down but let him get up again; and more lads gathering, drove them back to the barrack where the boys stood some time as it were to keep them in. In less than a minute ten or twelve of them came out with drawn cutlasses, clubs, and bayonets and set upon the unarmed boys and young folk who stood them a little while but, finding the inequality of their equipment, dispersed.

On hearing the noise, one Samuel Atwood came up to see what was the matter; and entering the alley from dock square, heard the latter part of the combat; and when the boys had dispersed he met the ten or twelve soldiers aforesaid rushing down the alley towards the square and asked them if they intended to murder people? They answered Yes, by G-d, root and branch! With that one of them struck Mr. Atwood with a club which was repeated by another; and being unarmed, he turned to go off and received a wound on the left shoulder which reached the bone and gave him much pain. Retreating a few steps, Mr. Atwood met two officers and said, gentlemen, what is the matter? They answered, you'll see by and by. Immediately after, those heroes appeared in the square, asking where were the boogers? Where were the cowards? But notwithstanding their fierceness to naked men, one of them advanced towards a youth who had a split of a raw stave in his hand and said, damn them, here is one of them. But the young man seeing a person near him with a drawn sword and good cane ready to support him, held up his stave in defiance; and they quietly passed by him up the little alley by Mr. Silsby's to King Street where they attacked single and unarmed persons till they raised much clamour, and then turned down Cornhill Street, insulting all they met in like manner and pursuing some to their very doors. Thirty or forty persons, mostly lads, being by this means gathered in King Street, Capt. Preston with a party of men with charged bayonets, came from the main guard to the commissioner's house, the soldiers pushing their bayonets, crying, make way! They took place by the custom house and, continuing to push to drive the people off pricked some in several places, on which they were clamorous and, it is said, threw snow balls. On this, the Captain commanded them to fire; and more snow balls coming, he again said, damn you, fire, be the consequence what it will! One soldier then fired, and a townsman with a cudgel struck him over the hands with such force that he dropped his firelock; and, rushing forward, aimed a blow at the Captain's head which grazed his hat and fell pretty heavy upon his arm. However, the soldiers continued the fire successively till seven or eight or, as some say, eleven guns were discharged.

By this fatal manoeuvre three men were laid dead on the spot and two more struggling for life; but what showed a degree of cruelty unknown to British troops, at least since the house of Hanover has directed their operation, was an attempt to fire upon or push with their bayonets the persons who undertook to remove the slain and wounded!

Mr. Benjamin Leigh, now undertaker in the Delph manufactory, came up and after some conversation with Capt. Preston relative to his conduct in this affair, advised him to draw off his men, with which he complied. The dead are Mr. Samuel Gray, killed on the spot, the ball entering his head and beating off a large portion of his skull.

A mulatto man named Crispus Attucks, who was born in Framingham, but lately belonged to New-Providence and was here in order to go for North Carolina, also killed instantly, two balls entering his breast, one of them in special goring the right lobe of the lungs and a great part of the liver most horribly.

Mr. James Caldwell, mate of Capt. Morton's vessel, in like manner killed by two balls entering his back.

Mr. Samuel Maverick, a promising youth of seventeen years of age, son of the widow Maverick, and an apprentice to Mr. Greenwood, ivory-turner, mortally wounded; a ball went through his belly and was cut out at his back. He died the next morning.

A lad named Christopher Monk, about seventeen years of age, an apprentice to Mr. Walker, shipwright, wounded; a ball entered his back about four inches above the left kidney near the spine and was cut out of the breast on the same side. Apprehended he will die.

A lad named John Clark, about seventeen years of age, whose parents live at Medford, and an apprentice to Capt. Samuel Howard of this town, wounded; a ball entered just above his groin and came out at his hip on the opposite side. Apprehended he will die.

Mr. Edward Payne of this town, merchant, standing at his entry door received a ball in his arm which shattered some of the bones.

Mr. John Green, tailor, coming up Leverett's Lane, received a ball just under his hip and lodged in the under part of his thigh, which was extracted.

Mr. Robert Patterson, a seafaring man, who was the person that had his trousers shot through in Richardson's affair, wounded; a ball went through his right arm, and he suffered a great loss of blood.

Mr. Patrick Carr, about thirty years of age, who worked with Mr. Field, leather breeches-maker in Queen Street, wounded; a ball entered near his hip and went out at his side. [Carr would also die.]

A lad named David Parker, an apprentice to Mr. Eddy, the wheelwright, wounded; a ball entered his thigh.

Appendix B

Text of Clarence Darrow's July 4, 1923 Letter to the Editor of the Chicago Tribune (printed by the Tribune on its front page):

July 4, 1923

Editor of the Tribune: I was very much interested in Mr. Bryan's letter to The Tribune and in your editorial reply. I have likewise followed Mr. Bryan's efforts to shut out the teachings of science from the public schools and his questionnaires to various college professors who believe in evolution and still profess Christianity. No doubt his questions to the professors, if answered, would tend to help clear the issue, and likewise a few questions to Mr. Bryan and the fundamentalists, if fairly answered, might serve the interests of reaching the truth--all of this assumes that truth is desirable.

For this reason I think it would be helpful if Mr. Bryan would answer the following questions:

> Do you believe in the literal interpretation of the whole Bible?
>
> Is the account of the creation of the earth and all life in Genesis literally true, or is it an allegory?
>
> Was the earth made in six literal days, measured by the revolution of the earth on its axis?
>
> Was the sun made on the fourth day to give light to the earth by day and the moon made on the same day to give light by night, and were the stars made for the benefit of the earth?
>
> Did God create man on the sixth day?
>
> Did God rest on the seventh day?
>
> Did God place man in the Garden of Eden and tell him he could eat of every tree except the tree of knowledge?
>
> Was Eve literally made from the rib of Adam?
>
> Did the serpent induce Eve to eat of the tree of knowledge?

Did the eating of this fruit cause Adam and Eve to know that they were naked?

Did God curse the serpent for tempting Eve and decree that thereafter he should go on his belly?

How did he travel before that time?

Did God tell Eve that thereafter he would multiply the sorrows of all women and that their husbands should rule over them?

Did God send a flood covering the whole earth, even the tops of the highest mountains and destroy "all flesh that has the breath of life," excepting the inmates of the ark?

Did God command Noah to build and ark for him and his family and to take on board a male and female of every living species on earth?

Did he build the ark and gather the pairs of all animals on the earth and the food and water necessary to preserve them?

As there were no ships in those days, except the ark, how did Noah gather them from all the continents and lands of the earth?

Did he then cause it to rain forty days and forty nights and destroy every living thing on the earth?

[While I wouldn't presume to alter Darrow's questions, it occurs to me to ask Bryan whether God also intended to destroy the fish in the ponds, lakes, streams, rivers and oceans.]

Did all these living things enter the ark on the second month and 17th day of the month?

Were all the high mountains on all the earth covered?

Did the waters prevail on the earth for 150 days?

Did the ark rest on Mount Ararat in the seventh month and the tenth day of the month?

Did God set a rainbow in the heavens for a token that the world would not again be destroyed by flood?

Was this the first rainbow that ever appeared?

According to the old testament, was this not about 1,750 years B.C.?

Is not history full of proof that all colors and kinds of people lived over large and remote parts of the earth within fifty years after this time?

Were the pairs of animals sent to every quarter of the earth after the flood?

How could many species that are found nowhere but in Australia or other far off places get there and why did they not stop on the way?

Was there any more water on the earth in Noah's day than any other time before or since?

Is not all the water that falls drawn from the reservoirs of water on the earth?

Is it possible to increase the amount of water in any part of the earth without drawing it from another part?

Does not water seek its level?

Shortly after the flood was the whole earth of one language?

Did the inhabitants begin to build the Tower of Babel so that they might reach the heavens?

Did God confound their language so they could not complete the tower?

How high would the tower have had to be to reach the heavens?

Was the confounding of tongues at the Tower of Babel the cause of the many languages spoken by the people of the earth?

Did the Lord prepare a big fish to swallow Jonah and did he lie for three days and three nights in the whale's belly when he was spewed out on dry land?

Was Lot's wife turned into a literal pillar of salt for turning back and looking at Sodom and Gomorrah when she was fleeing from their destruction?

Did Balaam's ass speak to him in human language?

Did the walls of Jericho fall down flat from the soldiers and priests marching around it and blowing on the ram's horn?

Did the sun stand still to give Joshua time to fight a battle?

If the sun had stood still, would that have lengthened the day?

If instead of the sun standing still, the earth had stopped revolving on its axis, what would have happened to the earth and all life thereon?

Under the biblical chronology [by Bishop Usher], was not the earth created less than 6,000 years ago?

Are there not evidences in writing and hieroglyphics and the evidence of man's handiwork which show that man has been on the earth more than 50,000 years?

Were there not many flourishing civilizations on the earth 10,000 years ago?

According to the same chronology, was not Adam created less than 6,000 years ago?

Are there no human remains that carry their age on the earth back to at least 100,000 years?

Has not man probably been on earth for 500,000 years?

Does not geology show by fossil remains, by the cutting away of rock for river beds, by deposit of all sorts, that the earth is much more than a million years and probably many million years old?

Did Christ drive devils out of two sick men and did the devils request that they should be driven into a large herd of swine and were the devils driven into the swine and did the swine run off a high bank, and were they drowned in the sea?

Was this literally true, or does it simply show the attitude of the age toward the cause of sickness and affliction?

Can one not be a Christian without believing in the literal truth of the narrations of the Bible here mentioned?

Would you forbid the public schools from teaching anything in conflict with the literal statement referred to?

Questions might be extended indefinitely, but a specific answer to these might make it clear what one must believe to be a "fundamentalist."

Very truly yours,
Clarence Darrow

Electronic Version, Book websites and Bonus Materials

How Would You Decide? 10 Famous Trials That Changed History

www.10FamousTrials.com

This website gives you the chance to vote chapter-by-chapter how you would have decided the outcome of the trials and help pick the Trial of the Century. Visit the website to see how other readers voted!

At the time of the first edition's publication, How Would You Decide? will be published in three versions. First it will be published as both a hardbound book and an electronic version, which will be available online through Amazon, Kindle, and Barnes & Noble, as well as all other major booksellers. These links as well as a sample chapter from the book are available on 10FamousTrials.com.

This book has also been adapted by Nathan Todhunter into a chapter-by-chapter podcast series to be broadcast on the *Legal Talk Network* over the course of the year following the publication of book's first edition. In that adapted and abridged podcast series, the author narrates the adaptation and approximately 100 voice actors play the live-action parts of the judges, lawyers, and witnesses from testimony quoted in the book.

Finally, the author anticipates recording an audio version of the book after its publication. Stay tuned! When available, the link will be posted to 10FamousTrials.com

You can see all the available versions on the book's website.

In the electronic version, you'll get an expanded version of How Would You Decide?. The book's uncut electronic version includes links to author's selections from the opening statements, trial testimony and closing arguments. There are nearly 400 endnotes, which contain hyperlinks and citations to the complete, unedited version of the trial transcripts in their original form, allowing you full access for expanded research and to the entire context of the quoted material.

On the book's website www.10FamousTrials.com, you can also find the links to the author's occasional blog, *May It Please The Court*, press materials and contact information.

How to Get Sued: An Instructional Guide

www.howtogetsued.com

This is the author's first hardcover book, which consists of short, humorous vignettes about the foolish things that people do to get in trouble with the law. The author offers advice how to avoid similar situations and how the law can affect you. The book makes a great present for anyone involved with the law and is sure to generate a good laugh.

On this book's website, you can find a sample chapter, bonus materials including a free bonus chapter (*So You've Been Sued?*) information about the author J. Craig Williams, press materials and contact information.

The Sled

www.thesled.online

The author and his wife, Christine Bartley Williams, wrote this paperback children's book for their first batch of grandchildren, Naomi Jo, and Kingston. Their grandchildren star as the characters in the book, who along with several of the family's animals try to save Christmas. They must prevent Santa, his elves, and reindeer from being frozen by the Frost King.

The book was illustrated by Amelia Bernstein, a former Disney artist. It too is available on Amazon, Barnes & Noble, and all major booksellers, and links to purchase it are available on its website.

Endnotes

Chapter 1

[1] *Jewish Antiquities, Testimonium Flavianum:* Volume 18, pages 63-64, by Josephus Flavius, 94 C.E.

[2] *The Annals,* Vol. XV, page 44, by Publius Cornelius Tacitus, 62-65 C.E., translation based on Alfred John Church and William Jackson Brodribb, 1876.

[3] *The Trial of Jesus from a Lawyer's Standpoint, The Roman Trial,* volume II, page x, by Walter Marion Chandler, The Empire Publishing Company, 1908.

[4] *The New Testament of the Bible*, Mark, chapter 14, verses 57 - 58.

[5] *The New Testament of the Bible*, Luke chapter 22, verses 70–71.

[6] *History of the Synoptic Tradition,* by Rudolph Bultmann, 1921.

[7] *The New Testament of the Bible*, Matthew chapter 26, verses 57—75 and chapter 27, verses 1 - 26; Mark chapter 14, verses 53—72 and chapter 15, verses 1 - 15; and, Luke chapter 22, verses 52—71 and chapter 23, verses 1—25.

[8] *The New Testament of the Bible,* John chapter 2, verses 13—22; chapter 11, verses 47—57; and, chapter 12, verses 12—42.

[9] *The New Testament of the Bible,* Mark chapter 11, verses 15—19 and chapter 11, verses 27—33; Matthew chapter 21, verses 12—17 and chapter 21, verses 23—27; and, Luke chapter 19, verses 45—48 and chapter 20, verses 1—8.

[10] *The New Testament of the Bible*, John chapter 18, verses 12—28 and chapter 19, verses 1—16.

[11] Mark chapter 15, verses 1-2.

[12] Mark chapter 15, verses 3-15.

[13] *The New Testament of the Bible*, Matthew, chapter 26, verses 60-61.

[14] *The Trial of Jesus from a Lawyer's Standpoint, The Roman Trial,* volume II, page 30, by Walter Marion Chandler, The Empire Publishing Company, 1908.

[15] *The New Testament of the Bible,* Luke chapter 2, verse 46.

[16] *The Trial of Jesus from a Lawyer's Standpoint, The Roman Trial,* volume II, page 106, by Walter Marion Chandler, The Empire Publishing Company, 1908.

[17] *The New Testament of the Bible,* Matthew, chapter 22, verse 21.

[18] *The New Testament of the Bible,* Paul, chapter 25, verse 16.

[19] See <u>People v Bretagna</u>, 298 N.Y. 323, 325 (1949). Those studied in the law will immediately recognize the basic Harvard Blue Book citation format used

here. For those who only see occasionally see case citations, the format is readily understood as Name v. Name, WWW Reporter XXX, YYY (ZZZZ), with "W" representing the volume number, "Reporter" representing both the court that heard the case and the name of book where the published report can be found, "W" representing the page where the opinion starts, "Y" representing the page where the point cited can be found (sometimes called the "point page" or the "jump cite"—not included in this citation above), and finally Z representing the year when the opinion was published. Any search engine, such as Google, will readily find the opinion using this format, which form can vary so wildly that the students on Harvard's Law Review take hundreds of pages to explain through the Harvard Blue Book.

[20] *International Adjudication: Procedural Aspects*, volume 4, page 202, by V.S. Mani, 1980.

[21] California Civil Code §§ 3509-3548.

[22] California Civil Code § 3521.

[23] *European Convention of Human Rights*, Article 4, Protocol 7, The Fifth Amendment of the United States Constitution and Article 20 of the Constitution of India.

[24] *The Trial of Jesus from a Lawyer's Standpoint, The Roman Trial*, volume II, page 55, by Walter Marion Chandler, The Empire Publishing Company, 1908.

[25] *The Old Testament of the Bible*, Exodus, chapter 21, verses 23—25; Leviticus chapter 24, verses 18—20; and Deuteronomy, chapter 19, verse 21, see also the Code of Hammurabi, the Quran, chapter 5, verse 45 and the Torah.

Chapter 2

[1] *Memorable Providences, Relating to Witchcrafts and Possessions*, by Cotton Mather, 1689.

[2] *Ergotism: The Satan Loosed in Salem?*, Science magazine, by Linda Caporeal, volume 192, pages 21-26, April 2, 1976.

[3] *The Salem Witch Trials: a biographical sketch of Tituba*, by Professor Douglas Linder, http://www.law.umkc.edu/faculty/projects/ftrials/salem/ASA_TIT.HTM.

[4] *Narratives of the Witchcraft Cases, 1648-1706*, page 343, edited by George Lincoln Burr, Charles Scribner's Sons, 1914.

[5] *The New England Historical and Genealogical Register*, pages 131—153, volume XI, April 1857; pages 316—321, volume XII, July 1858; pages 127—128 and pages 245—248, volume XII, January 1858.

[6] *Salem Witch Museum Education*, http://www.salemwitchmuseum.com/education/.

[7] *Witchcraft in Salem Village in 1692*, pages 56—57, by Winfield S. Nevins, North Shore Publishing Company, 1892.

[8] *Op. cit., Witchcraft in Salem Village in 1692*, pages 57-59.

[9] *Op. cit., Witchcraft in Salem Village in 1692*, page 75.

[10] *Op. cit., Witchcraft in Salem Village in 1692*, page 65.

[11] *Neuman and Baretti's Dictionary of the Spanish and English Languages*, volume I, page 345, William Kerr & Co., New York, 1842.

[12] *Witchcraft in Salem Village in 1692*, page 153, by Winfield S. Nevins, North Shore Publishing Company, 1892.

[13] Photograph by Margo Burns, reproduced with permission.

[14] National Archives (Great Britain), CO5/785, page 336-337.

[15] *Salem Witchcraft and Cotton Mather, A Reply*, page 19, by Charles W. Upham, 1869.

[16] *A Complete Collection of State Trials and Proceedings for High Treason and Other Crimes and Misdemeanors from the Earliest Period to the Year 1783, with Notes and Other Illustrations*, page 673, by Thomas Bayly Howell, Longman, Hurst, Rees, Orme and Brown, 1816.

[17] *Ibid.* pages 673—674.

[18] *Constitutional Free Speech Defined and Defended in an Unfinished Argument in a case of Blasphemy*, page 370 by Theodore Albert Schroder, The Free Speech League, 1919.

[19] *Op. cit., Witchcraft in Salem Village in 1692*, page 65.

[20] *Ann Pudeator*, by Alex Williams and Maren Douglass, http://xela218.googlepages.com/annpudeator.

[21] *Salem Witch Trials*, http://socialscience.cypresscollege.edu/~lyerby/witch.htm.

[22] *Narratives of the Witchcraft Cases, 1648-1706*, pages 216-217, edited by George Lincoln Burr, Charles Scribner's Sons, 1914.

[23] *Salem Witchcraft: With an Account of Salem Village, and a History of Opinions on Witchcraft and Kindred Subjects*, page 301, By Charles Wentworth Upham, Wiggin and Lunt, 1867.

[24] *Records of Salem Witchcraft, Copied from the Original Documents*, volume II, pages 44—46, by William Elliot Woodward (printed privately), 1864.

[25] *Op. cit., The New England Historical and Genealogical Register*.

[26] *The New England Historical and Genealogical Register*, volume XLIV, pages 168 - 170, 1890.

[27] *The Witchcraft Trials in Salem: A Commentary*, by Professor Douglas O. Linder, http://www.law.umkc.edu/faculty/projects/ftrials/salem/sal_acct.htm.

[28] *Cases of Conscience Concerning Evil Spirits Personating Men, Witchcrafts, infallible Proofs of Guilt in such as are accused with that Crime*, by Increase Mather, 1693.

[29] *Op. cit., The New England Historical and Genealogical Register*, volume XI, page 246.

[30] *Ibid.*

[31] *Cotton Mather, Keeper of the Puritan Conscience*, page 142, by Ralph Philip Boas and Louise Schutz Boas, Harper, 1928.

[32] *More Wonders of the Invisible World Part V*, pages 144-145, by Robert Calef, 1700.

Chapter 3

[1] See *Key Figures in the Boston Massacre Trials*, by Professor Douglas Linder, http://www.law.umkc.edu/faculty/projects/ftrials/bostonmassacre/keyfigures.html.

[2] "You'll be Back," Hamilton lyrics, song 7, p. 24. https://www.blumenthalarts.org/assets/doc/Hamilton-Lyrics-ACT-I1-e82b4f261a.pdf

[3] *The Records of Oxford Massachusetts: Including Chapters of Nipmuck, Huguenot and English History. Accompanied With Biographical Sketches and Notes, 1630-1890 With Manners and Fashions of the Time*, page 360 by Mary Dewitt Freeland, Genealogical Publishing Comm., 2003, originally published Albany, N.Y., Joe Munsell's Sons, 1894.

[4] *History of the Boston Massacre, March 5, 1770,* page 195, by Frederick Kidder and John Adams, published Albany, N.Y., Joe Munsell, 1870.

[5] *Ibid.*

[6] *Ibid.*

[7] *The Boston Massacre Trials, An Account* by Professor Douglas Linder, at http://www.law.umkc.edu/faculty/projects/ftrials/bostonmassacre/bostonaccount.html.

[8] *Captain Thomas Preston's Account of the Boston Massacre, 13 March 1770*, pages 750-53, by Captain Thomas Preston, from British Public Records Office, C.O. 5/759, reprinted by Merrill Jensen, Editor in *English Historical Documents*, Volume IX. (London, 1964), from the WWW Virtual Library at http://www.vlib.us/amdocs/texts/preston.html.

[9] *Deposition of Captain Thomas Preston*, March 12, 1770, page 1, at http://www.newberry.org/K12maps/module_13/images/preston_boston_massacre.pdf.

[10] *Ibid.*, page 1.

[11]   *Ibid.*, page 2.

[12]   *A Short Narrative of the Horrid Massacre in Boston, Printed by Order of the Town of Boston,* pages 13-19, 21- 22 and 28-30, republished by John Doggett, Jr., New York, 1849.

[13]   *Ibid.*

[14]   See Footnote 3 of Crawford v. Washington, 541 U.S. 36 (2004).

[15]   *Summary of the Boston Massacre* by the Boston Massacre Historical Society at http://www.bostonmassacre.net/trial/trial-summary2.htm.

[16]   *Ibid.*

[17]   See, for example, Professor Douglas Linder's collection of Boston Massacre documents at http://www.law.umkc.edu/faculty/projects/ftrials/bostonmassacre/bostonmassacre.html.

[18]   *Other Boston Massacre Trial Depositions (Daniel Calef)* at http://www.bostonmassacre.net/trial/d-more.htm.

[19]   *Ibid.*

[20]   *Other Boston Massacre Trial Depositions (Peter Cunningham)* at http://www.bostonmassacre.net/trial/d-more.htm.

[21]   *Deposition of Captain Thomas Preston, March 12, 1770,* by Professor Douglas Linder, at http://www.law.umkc.edu/faculty/projects/ftrials/bostonmassacre/prestontrialexcerpts.html.

[22]   *Ibid.*

[23]   *Boston Massacre Trials: 1770 - Captain Preston's Trial,* Law Library - American Law and Legal Information, at http://law.jrank.org/pages/2359/Boston-Massacre-Trials-1770-Captain-Preston-s-Trial.html.

[24]   *Summary of the Boston Massacre* by the Boston Massacre Historical Society at http://www.bostonmassacre.net/trial/trial-summary3.htm.

[25]   *Ibid.*

[26]   *Ibid.*

[27]   *What Really Happened in the Boston Massacre? The Trial of Captain Thomas Preston,* Faulkner University, at http://faulkner.liquidmatrix.com/academics/artsandsciences/socialandbehavioral/readings/hy/boston.asp.

[28]   *Deposition of Theodore Bliss,* by the Boston Massacre Historical Society at http://www.bostonmassacre.net/trial/d-bliss.htm.

[29]   *Boston Massacre Trials: 1770 - Captain Preston's Trial,* Law Library - American Law and Legal Information, at

http://law.jrank.org/pages/2359/Boston-Massacre-Trials-1770-Captain-Preston-s-Trial.html.

30   *American Eloquence: A Collection of Speeches and Addresses by the Most Eminent Orators of America*, page 843, by Frank Moore, published by D. Appleton & Company, 1857.

31   *Ibid.*, page 247.

32   *The Trial of the British Soldiers, of the 29th Regiment of Foot, for the Murder of Crispus Attucks, Samuel Gray, Samuel Maverick, James Caldwell, and Patrick Carr, on Monday-evening, the 5th of March, 1770, before the Honorable Benjamin Lynde, John Cushing, Peter Oliver, and Edmund Troweridge, Esquires, Justices of the Superior Court of Judicature, Court of Assize, and General Goal Delivery, held at Boston, by adjournment, November 27, 1770, Boston*, page 9, published by William Emmons, 1824 from the United States Library of Congress website: http://www.loc.gov/law/help/rare-books/pdf/john_adams_1824_version.pdf.

33   *Ibid.*, pages 79—81.

34   *History of the Boston Massacre, March 5, 1770, Consisting of the Narrative of the Town, The Trial of the Soldiers, A Historical Introduction Containing Unpublished Documents of John Adams and Explanatory Notes*, page 283, by Frederic Kidder, Albany, N.Y., Joel Munsell, 1870.

35   *Op. cit., The Trial of the British Soldiers*, page 110.

36   *Ibid.*, page 117.

37   *American Eloquence: A Collection of Speeches and Addresses by the Most Eminent Orators of America*, page 227, by Frank Moore, published by D. Appleton & Company, 1857.

Chapter 4

1   Those studied in the law will immediately recognize the basic Harvard Blue Book citation format used here. For those who only see occasionally see case citations, the format is readily understood as Name v. Name, WWW Reporter XXX, YYY (ZZZZ), with "W" representing the volume number, "Reporter" representing both the court that heard the case and the name of book where the published report can be found, "W" representing the page where the opinion starts, "Y" representing the page where the point cited can be found (sometimes called the "point page" or the "jump cite"—not included in this citation above), and finally Z representing the year when the opinion was published. Any search engine, such as Google, will readily find the opinion using this format, which form can vary so wildly that the students on Harvard's Law Review take hundreds of pages to explain through the Harvard Blue Book.

2   The Slaughter-house Cases: The Butchers' Benevolent Association of New Orleans v. the Crescent City Live-stock Landing and Slaughter-house Company; and, Paul Esteben, L. Ruch, J. P. Rouede, W. Maylie, S. Firmberg, B.

Beaubay, William Fagan, J. D. Broderick, N. Seibel, M. Lannes, J. Gitzinger, J. P. Aycock, D. Verges, the Live-stock Dealers' and Butchers' Association of New Orleans, and Charles Cavaroc v. the State of Louisiana, *ex rel.*, 83 U.S. 36 (1872).

[3] Frederick J. Blue in American Historical Review, April 2006, volume 111, pages 481-482.

[4] *John Brown, 1800-1859, with Illustrations*, page 432, by Oswald Garrison Villard, A.M., Litt.D., Doubleday, Doran & Company, Inc., New York, 1929.

[5] National Archives, Records of the Adjutant General's Office, 1780's-1917.

[6] October 25, 1859 trial testimony taken from *The Life, Trial and Execution of Captain John Brown known as "Old Brown of Ossawatomie," being a full account of the attempted insurrection at Harper's Ferry, VA.*, page 58, compiled from official and authentic sources. New York. Robert M. De Witt, publisher. Entered according to Act of Congress, in the year 1859, by Robert M. De Witt, in the Clerk's Office of the United States District Court for the Southern District of New York. The Clerk's report has been slightly edited for clarity.

[7] *Op. cit., John Brown, 1800-1859*, pages 463-466.

[8] *John Brown*, page 148, Second Edition, by Dr. Hermann von Holst, Professor at the University of Freiburg in Baden, edited by Frank Preston Stearns, Cupples and Kurd, Publisher, The Algonquin Press, New York, 1888.

[9] Columbia Encyclopedia, Sixth Ed. 2008.

[10] *Op. cit., The Life, Trial and Execution of Captain John Brown known as "Old Brown of Ossawatomie," being a full account of the attempted insurrection at Harper's Ferry, VA.*, page 58.

[11] *Ibid.*

[12] *The Trial of John Brown*, http://www.law.umkc.edu/faculty/projects/ftrials/johnbrown/browntrial.html, by Professor Douglas O. Linder.

[13] *Op. cit., The Life, Trial and Execution of Captain John Brown known as "Old Brown of Ossawatomie," being a full account of the attempted insurrection at Harper's Ferry, VA.*, page 92.

[14] *Op. cit., The Life, Trial and Execution of Captain John Brown known as "Old Brown of Ossawatomie," being a full account of the attempted insurrection at Harper's Ferry, VA.*, page 77.

[15] *Op. cit., John Brown, 1800-1859,* page 494.

[16] *Op. cit.*, October 27, 1859 trial testimony.

[17] *Remarkable Trials of All Countries*, Volume II, page 75, by Thomas Dunphy and Thomas J. Cummins, New York: S. S. Peloubet & Company, 1882.

[18] *Op. cit., The Life, Trial and Execution of Captain John Brown known as "Old Brown of Ossawatomie," being a full account of the attempted insurrection at Harper's Ferry, VA.*, page 80.

[19] *Op. cit., The Life, Trial and Execution of Captain John Brown known as "Old Brown of Ossawatomie," being a full account of the attempted insurrection at Harper's Ferry, VA.*, page 71.

[20] *Op. cit., Remarkable Trials of All Countries,* page 70.

[21] *Op. cit., The Life, Trial and Execution of Captain John Brown known as "Old Brown of Ossawatomie," being a full account of the attempted insurrection at Harper's Ferry, VA.*, page 72.

[22] *Ibid.*

[23] *Ibid.*, page 74.

[24] *The Virginia Rebellion.; Further Testimoney [sic]. Trial Of John Brown. Counsel from the North Appears for his Defence [sic]*, page 8, New York Times, October 29, 1859, http://query.nytimes.com/gst/abstract.html?res=9907E1DF1630EE34BC4151DFB6678382649FDE.

[25] *Op. cit., The Life, Trial and Execution of Captain John Brown known as "Old Brown of Ossawatomie," being a full account of the attempted insurrection at Harper's Ferry, VA.*, page 70.

[26] *The Trial of John Brown,* http://www.law.umkc.edu/faculty/projects/ftrials/johnbrown/browntrial.html, by Professor Douglas O. Linder.

[27] *Op. cit., The Life, Trial and Execution of Captain John Brown known as "Old Brown of Ossawatomie," being a full account of the attempted insurrection at Harper's Ferry, VA.*, pages 76–77.

[28] *Ibid.*, page 77.

[29] *Ibid.*, page 80.

[30] *Ibid.*, page 80.

[31] *Ibid.*, page 83.

[32] *Ibid.*, page 90.

[33] *Ibid.*, page 98.

[34] *Ibid.*

[35] *Ibid.*, pages 94-95.

[36] *Ibid., November 2, 1859 trial testimony.*

[37] *A Plea for Captain John Brown, read by Thoreau to the citizens of Concord, Massachusetts, Sunday evening, October 30, 1859,* by Henry David Thoreau, http://www.transcendentalists.com/thoreau_plea_john_brown.htm, last visited September 2, 2008.

38   *John Brown and His Men; with some account of the roads they traveled to reach Harper's Ferry*, page 398, by Hinton, Richard Josiah, New York and London, Funk & Wagnalls Company, 1894. Author's note: this last sentence is typically incorrectly omitted from this quote.

39   Strauder v. West Virginia, 100 U.S. 303 (1879).

40   *Ex parte* Virginia, 100 U.S. 339 (1879).

41   The Civil Rights Cases, 109 U.S. 3 (1883); United States v. Stanley; United States v. Ryan; United States v. Nichols; United States v. Singleton; and, Robinson and Wife v. Memphis & Charleston R. Co.

42   Plessy v. Ferguson, 163 U.S. 537 (1896).

43   Brown v. Board of Education of Topeka, 347 U.S. 483 (1954).

Chapter 5

1   The City of Tombstone website, http://www.cityoftombstone.com/.

2   Arizona Daily Star, page 1, May 30, 1882.

3   Tombstone Daily Epitaph, page 1, *Three Men Hurled Into Eternity in the Duration of a Moment*, October 27, 1881.

4   Tombstone Daily Nugget, page 1, *A Desperate Street Fight*, October 27, 1881.

5   *Ibid.*

6   Tombstone Daily Nugget, page 1, October 26, 1881.

7   Tombstone Daily Nugget, page 1, *A Desperate Street Fight*, October 27, 1881.

8   Tombstone Daily Epitaph, page 1, *Three Men Hurled Into Eternity in the Duration of a Moment*, October 27, 1881.

9   Tombstone Daily Epitaph, page 1, *Coroner's Inquest*, October 29, 1881.

10   Tombstone Daily Nugget, page 1, *Coroner's Inquest, Further Testimony Regarding The Late Tragedy*, October 30, 1881, reporting on the answers of the witnesses' testimony of October 29, 1881.

11   Tombstone Daily Nugget, page 1, *Coroner's Inquest, Further Testimony Regarding The Late Tragedy*, October 30, 1881.

12   San Francisco Examiner, *Arizona Affairs*, May 28, 1882.

13   Biographical Directory of the United States Congress, http://bioguide.congress.gov/scripts/biodisplay.pl?index=F000159.

14   Arizona Statutes, Chapter XI, sections 128, 142 and 143 (1877).

[15] *Testimony of William Allen*, November 1, 1881, http://www.law.umkc.edu/faculty/projects/FTrials/earp/allentestimony.html.

[16] https://www.famous-trials.com/earp/517-fullertestimony

[17] *Testimony of William F. Claiborne*, November 8, 1881, http://www.law.umkc.edu/faculty/projects/FTrials/earp/clairbornetestimony.html.

[18] *Ibid.*

[19] *Testimony of Ike Clanton*, November 9—15, 1881, http://www.law.umkc.edu/faculty/projects/FTrials/earp/clantontestimony.html, including all preceding quoted testimony from Ike Clanton.

[20] *Testimony in the Earp Preliminary Hearing*, http://www.law.umkc.edu/faculty/projects/FTRIALS/earp/behantestimony.html.

[21] *Statement of Wyatt Earp*, November 17, 1881, http://www.law.umkc.edu/faculty/projects/FTrials/earp/wearptestimony.html.

[22] *Testimony of H.F. Sills*, November 22—23, 1881, http://www.westernoutlaw.com/stories/files/sillstestimony.pdf.

[23] *Decision of Wells Spicer in the Earp and Holliday Case*, http://www.tombstonehistoryarchives.com/?page_id=24.

Chapter 6

[1] Chicago Herald and Examiner, page 1, September 30, 1920.

[2] The Atlanta Constitution, page 11, July 24, 1921.

[3] *The Great Gatsby*, page 49, Charles Scribner's Sons, 1925.

[4] https://collections.carli.illinois.edu/digital/collection/chm_fa/id/474/rec/1

[5] Daily Globe, page 1, June 27, 1921.

[6] The Cedar Rapids Evening Gazette, page 6, July 5, 1921.

[7] Bill of Particulars, Chicago Black Sox Trial, http://www.law.umkc.edu/faculty/projects/ftrials/blacksox/particulars.html.

[8] The Cedar Rapids Evening Gazette, page 1, International News report, July 8, 1921.

[9] Des Moines Daily News, page 3, United Press report, July 6, 1921.

[10] The Cedar Rapids Evening Gazette, page 15, International News report, July 7, 1921.

[11] Waterloo Evening Gazette, page 14, July 7, 1921.

[12] The Oil City Derrick, page 14, July 8, 1921.

[13] New Castle News, page 19, July 7, 1921.

[14] The Kingston Daily Freeman, page 8, July 9, 1921.

[15] San Antonio Evening News, page 9, International News report, July 11, 1921.

[16] The Atlanta Constitution, page 11, July 12, 1921.

[17] San Antonio Evening News, page 8, report by Frank G. Menke of the King Features Syndicate, Inc., July 26, 1921.

[18] Logansport Pharos-Tribune, page 3, July 15, 1921.

[19] The Lima News, page 3, July 16, 1921.

[20] Galveston Daily News, page 8, Associated Press report, July 16, 1921.

[21] *Ibid.*

[22] Dunkirk Evening Observer, page 1, July 16, 1921.

[23] Logansport Pharos-Tribune, page 3, July 18, 1921.

[24] The Lima News, page 6, July 18, 1921.

[25] The Oakland Tribune, page 10, July 18, 1921.

[26] Daily Northwestern, page 8, July 18, 1921.

[27] Wisconsin State Journal, page 7, report by Carl Victor Little, July 19, 1921.

[28] The Atlanta Constitution, page 7, July 19, 1921.

[29] *Ibid.*

[30] Wisconsin State Journal, page 7, report by Carl Victor Little, July 19, 1921.

[31] The Cedar Rapids Evening Gazette, page 1, report by William K. Hutchinson, International News Service correspondent, July 19, 1921.

[32] *Ibid.*

[33] The Reno Evening Gazette, page 5, report by Al Spink, July 19, 1921.

[34] Evening Chronicle, page 1, July 19, 1921.

[35] Capital Times, page 10, July 22, 1921.

[36] Galveston Daily News, page 9, United News report, July 22, 1921.

[37] Racine Journal-News, page 1, July 20, 1921.

[38] Capital Times, page 8, July 20, 1921.

[39] Racine Journal-News, page 10, July 20, 1921.

[40] *Op. cit.*, Capital Times

[41] *Ibid.*

[42] Port Arthur Daily News, pages 1 and 3, July 20, 1921.

[43] The Cedar Rapids Evening Gazette, page 1, report by William K. Hutchinson, International News Service correspondent, July 21, 1921.

[44] *Trial Testimony in the Chicago Black Sox Trial*, http://www.law.umkc.edu/faculty/projects/ftrials/blacksox/trialtestimony.html.

[45] Iowa City Press-Citizen, page 2, July 21, 1921.

[46] Dunkirk Evening Observer, page 8, July 22, 1921.

[47] The Cedar Rapids Evening Gazette, page 1, report by William K. Hutchinson, International News Service correspondent, July 22, 1921.

[48] The Atlanta Constitution, page 9, report by James L. Kilgallen, United News correspondent, July 23, 1921.

[49] *Ibid.*

[50] The Lima News, page 2, United Press report, July 25, 1921.

[51] *Ibid.*

[52] *Joe Jackson Transcript*, http://www.1919blacksox.com/transcripts5.htm.

[53] *Eddie Cicotte Transcript*, http://www.1919blacksox.com/transcripts2.htm.

[54] The Star Journal, page 7, July 27, 1921.

[55] Moberly Evening Democrat, page 1, July 27, 1921.

[56] Alton Evening Telegraph, page 2, Associated Press report, July 27, 1921.

[57] *Ibid.*

[58] The Evening Gazette, page 1, July 28, 1921.

[59] Wisconsin State Journal, page 1, July 28, 1921.

[60] *Ibid.*

[61] The Evening Gazette, page 1, July 28, 1921.

[62] The Black Sox Trial: Trial Summations (Excerpts) https://www.famous-trials.com/blacksox/960-excerpts

[63] *Black Sox Trial Summations*, http://www.law.umkc.edu/faculty/projects/ftrials/blacksox/trialsummations.html.

[64] Moberly Evening Democrat, page 1, August 1, 1921.

[65] Lima News, page 6, August 1, 1921.

[66] The Evening Gazette, page 13, August 1, 1921.

[67] Woodland Daily Democrat, page 1, August 1, 1921.

[68] The Evening Gazette, page 1, July 28, 1921.

[69] *Cook County Clerk of Court Famous Trials website,* http://www.cookcountyclerkofcourt.org/gifs/verd1.gif.

[70] The Evening Gazette, page 1, August 3, 1921.

[71] *Ibid.*

Chapter 7

[1] *Proverbs* 11:29, King James version.

[2] *The World's Greatest Court Trial,*© pages 5-7, Cincinnati, Ohio, 1925.

[3] *"I do not think about the things I don't think about,"* The Edge of the American West, July 21, 2008, http://edgeofthewest.wordpress.com/2008/07/21/i-do-not-think-about-things-i-dont-think-about/.

[4] *The World's Greatest Court Trial,*© page 3, Cincinnati, Ohio, 1925.

[5] *The World's Greatest Court Trial,*© page 4, Cincinnati, Ohio, 1925. [Author's note: The trial transcript has been edited throughout to eliminate typographical mistakes that appear in the original.]

[6] *A Civic Biology: Presented in Problems*, page 194, by George William Hunter, American Book Company, 1914 (digitized by Google).

[7] *The World's Greatest Court Trial,*© page 11, Cincinnati, Ohio, 1925.

[8] *Mencken Likens Trial to a Religious Orgy, with Defendant a Beelzebub,* by H.L. Mencken, Baltimore Evening Sun, July 11, 1925.

[9] *The World's Greatest Court Trial,*© page 52, Cincinnati, Ohio, 1925.

[10] *The World's Greatest Court Trial,*© page 59, Cincinnati, Ohio, 1925.

[11] *The World's Greatest Court Trial,*© page 66, Cincinnati, Ohio, 1925.

[12] *Ibid.*

[13] *The World's Greatest Court Trial,*© page 75, Cincinnati, Ohio, 1925.

[14] *The World's Greatest Court Trial,*© page 76, Cincinnati, Ohio, 1925.

[15] *The World's Greatest Court Trial,*© page 84, Cincinnati, Ohio, 1925.

[16] *The World's Greatest Court Trial,*© page 70, Cincinnati, Ohio, 1925.

[17] *The World's Greatest Court Trial,*© page 61, Cincinnati, Ohio, 1925.

[18] *The World's Greatest Court Trial,*© pages 111 - 112, Cincinnati, Ohio, 1925.

[19] *The World's Greatest Court Trial,*© page 74, Cincinnati, Ohio, 1925.

[20] *Yearning Mountaineers' Souls Need Reconversion Nightly, Mencken Finds,* by H.L. Mencken, Baltimore Evening Sun, July 13, 1925.

[21] *The World's Greatest Court Trial,*© page 87, Cincinnati, Ohio, 1925.

22	*The World's Greatest Court Trial,*© pages 87-93, Cincinnati, Ohio, 1925.
23	*The World's Greatest Court Trial,*© page 93, Cincinnati, Ohio, 1925.
24	*The World's Greatest Court Trial,*© pages 94 - 95, Cincinnati, Ohio, 1925.
25	*The World's Greatest Court Trial,*© page 95, Cincinnati, Ohio, 1925.
26	*The World's Greatest Court Trial,*© page 112, Cincinnati, Ohio, 1925.
27	*The World's Greatest Court Trial,*© pages 112—116, Cincinnati, Ohio, 1925.
28	*The World's Greatest Court Trial,*© pages 120 -121, Cincinnati, Ohio, 1925.
29	*The World's Greatest Court Trial,*© pages 121 -122, Cincinnati, Ohio, 1925.
30	*The World's Greatest Court Trial,*© page 123, Cincinnati, Ohio, 1925.
31	*The World's Greatest Court Trial,*© pages 124 -125, Cincinnati, Ohio, 1925.
32	*The World's Greatest Court Trial,*© page 129, Cincinnati, Ohio, 1925.
33	*The World's Greatest Court Trial,*© pages 130 -131, Cincinnati, Ohio, 1925.
34	*Mencken Declares Strictly Fair Trial Is Beyond Ken of Tennessee Fundamentalists*, by H.L. Mencken, Baltimore Evening Sun, July 16, 1925.
35	*The World's Greatest Court Trial,*© page 136—137, Cincinnati, Ohio, 1925.
36	*The World's Greatest Court Trial,*© page 175, Cincinnati, Ohio, 1925.
37	*The World's Greatest Court Trial,*© page 176, Cincinnati, Ohio, 1925.
38	*The World's Greatest Court Trial,*© page 183, Cincinnati, Ohio, 1925.
39	*The World's Greatest Court Trial,*© page 185, Cincinnati, Ohio, 1925.
40	*The World's Greatest Court Trial,*© pages 187 - 188, Cincinnati, Ohio, 1925.
41	*The World's Greatest Court Trial,*© page 147, Cincinnati, Ohio, 1925.
42	*The World's Greatest Court Trial,*© page 223, Cincinnati, Ohio, 1925.
43	*Battle Now Over, Mencken Sees; Genesis Triumphant and Ready for New Jousts*, by H.L. Mencken, Baltimore Evening Sun, July 18, 1925.
44	*The World's Greatest Court Trial,*© page 226, Cincinnati, Ohio, 1925.
45	*The World's Greatest Court Trial,*© pages 284 - 303, Cincinnati, Ohio, 1925.
46	*The World's Greatest Court Trial,*© page 311, Cincinnati, Ohio, 1925.

47   *The World's Greatest Court Trial,*© page 339, Cincinnati, Ohio, 1925.

48   John Thomas Scopes v. The State of Tennessee, 154 Tenn. (1 Smith) 105, 289 S.W. 363 (1927).

Chapter 8

1   Chamberlain v. The Queen (No.2) [1984] HCA 7; (1984) 153 CLR 521, 592. [Author added "Q" and "A" designations for ease of reading. These designations are not in the original.] See also, http://www.austlii.edu.au/au/cases/cth/high_ct/153clr521.html.

2   *Chamberlain Interview,* http://www.law.umkc.edu/faculty/projects/FTrials/chamberlain/chamberlaininterview.html.

3   *First Police Report on the disappearance of Azaria Chamberlain NT 1980,* Policing Australia Since 1788—In the Line of Duty, Report of Inspector Michael Gilroy of the Northern Territory Police, Mt Isa, August 30, 1980, http://www.inthelineofduty.com.au/timeline.asp?startyear=1980&iID=873.

4   *Baby Names,* http://www.thinkbabynames.com/meaning/0/Azaria, last visited November 29, 2008.

5   *Evil Angels* by John Byson, copyright 2005, http://www.lindychamberlain.com/files/Bryson-The_Tactician.pdf.

6   *Coroner G.P. Galvin's findings,* http://www.law.umkc.edu/faculty/projects/FTrials/chamberlain/galvinfindings.html.

7   *Chamberlain testimony transcript,* http://www.law.umkc.edu/faculty/projects/ftrials/chamberlain/chamberlaintranscript.html (Edited by the author to remove HTML code and slight clarifications).

8   Chamberlain v. The Queen (No.2) [1984] HCA 7; (1984) 153 CLR 521, 590. See also, http://www.austlii.edu.au/au/cases/cth/high_ct/153clr521.html.

9   Chamberlain testimony transcript, http://www.law.umkc.edu/faculty/projects/ftrials/chamberlain/chamberlaintranscript.html (Edited by the author to remove HTML code and slight clarifications).

10   *Key Forensic Expert Mourned,* by Daniel Bouchier, November 20, 2008, Northern Territory News, http://www.ntnews.com.au/article/2008/11/20/17245_ntnews.html.

11   Chamberlain v. The Queen (No.2) [1984] HCA 7; (1984) 153 CLR 521, 559.

12   *Chamberlain testimony transcript,* http://www.law.umkc.edu/faculty/projects/ftrials/chamberlain/chamberlaintranscript.html.

[13]   *Chamberlain testimony transcript*, http://www.law.umkc.edu/faculty/projects/ftrials/chamberlain/chamberlaintranscript.html (Edited by the author to remove HTML code and slight clarifications).

[14]   *Chamberlain testimony transcript*, http://www.law.umkc.edu/faculty/projects/ftrials/chamberlain/chamberlaintranscript.html.

[15]   *Testimony of Les Harris, examined by Andrew Kirkham*, The Trial of Lindy and Michael Chamberlain: Selected Excerpts, http://www.law.umkc.edu/faculty/projects/FTRIALS/chamberlain/chamberlaintranscript.html.

[16]   *Chamberlain testimony transcript*, http://www.law.umkc.edu/faculty/projects/ftrials/chamberlain/chamberlaintranscript.html.

[17]   Chamberlain v. The Queen (No.2) [1984] HCA 7; (1984) 153 CLR 521. See, http://www.austlii.edu.au/au/cases/cth/high_ct/153clr521.html.

[18]   *Ibid.*, at 623.

[19]   *Ibid.*, at 624.

[20]   *Ibid.*, at 625.

[21]   *Ibid.*, at 626.

[22]   *Ibid.*, at 630.

[23]   *Strike statement by Lindy Chamberlain*, Darwin Prison, Papers of Lindy Chamberlain, 1980-1996 (bulk 1980-1988), Files of Lindy Chamberlain (selectively digitized), National Library of Australia, MS 9180, http://nla.gov.au/nla.ms-ms9180-1-3x.

[24]   See the [Third] *Inquest Into the Death of Azaria Chamberlain*, pages 62—63 and 65—66, http://www.nt.gov.au/justice/courtsupp/coroner/findings/other/chamberlain_3.pdf, December 13, 1995, citing The Royal Commission of Inquiry into Chamberlain Convictions (known as "The Morling Report"). See also http://www.lindychamberlain.com/files/1995_Inquest_into_the_death_of_Azaria_Chamberlain.pdf.

[25]   In Re: Conviction of Chamberlain, The Supreme Court of the Northern Territory of Australia, September 15, 1988, 93 FLR 239, 1988 WL 858795. See also http://www.austlii.edu.au/au/cases/nt/NTSC/1988/64.html.

[26]   *Op. cit.*, [Third] *Inquest Into the Death of Azaria Chamberlain*, page 97, December 13, 1995.

[27]   *Op. cit.*, [Third] *Inquest Into the Death of Azaria Chamberlain*, pages 101—107, December 13, 1995.

[28]   *Lindy Chamberlain*, http://www.lindychamberlain.com/content/legal.

Chapter 9

[1] *A Case of Dominoes?*, by Mary A. Fischer pages 128—129, Los Angeles Magazine, September 25, 1989.

[2] *Op. cit.*, Mary A. Fischer, pages 128-135.

[3] Easy Reader/Redondo Beach News, March 25, 1994.

[4] http://www.law.umkc.edu/faculty/projects/ftrials/mcmartin/lettertoparents.html.

[5] *McMartin Preschool trial victim interviews*, http://www.law.umkc.edu/faculty/projects/ftrials/mcmartin/victiminterviews.html.

[6] Buckey v. County of Los Angeles, City of Manhattan Beach; Robert Philibosian; Children's Institute International; Wayne T. Satz; Capital Cities/ABC, Inc.; and, Kathleen "Kee"

MacFarlane, 968 F.2d 791 (1992).

[7] *The McMartin Preschool Abuse Trial: A Commentary*, by Doug Linder (2003), http://www.law.umkc.edu/faculty/projects/ftrials/mcmartin/mcmartinaccount.html.

[8] *The McMartin Preschool Abuse Trial: A Commentary*, by Doug Linder (2003), http://www.law.umkc.edu/faculty/projects/ftrials/mcmartin/mcmartinaccount.html.

[9] *Keep McMartin Case In Mind As Hysteria Looms*, page B1, by Paul Carpenter, The Morning Call newspaper, Allentown, PA, May 19, 2002.

[10] *Opening statement of Lael Rubin*, http://www.law.umkc.edu/faculty/projects/ftrials/mcmartin/openingstatements.html#Lael.

[11] *Opening Statement of Dean Gits*, http://www.law.umkc.edu/faculty/projects/ftrials/mcmartin/openingstatements.html#Dean.

[12] *Opening Statement of Daniel Davis*, http://www.law.umkc.edu/faculty/projects/ftrials/mcmartin/openingstatements.html#Daniel.

[13] http://www.law.umkc.edu/faculty/projects/ftrials/mcmartin/macfarlanetestimony.html. (The Author has edited the transcripts throughout this chapter to add "Q" and "A" where appropriate to designate "Question" and "Answer," restored spacing to make the testimony appear consistent with the actual court transcript and has edited out and added quotation marks for ease of reading.)

[14] http://www.law.umkc.edu/faculty/projects/ftrials/mcmartin/freemantestimony.html.

[15] Los Angeles Herald Examiner, December 18, 1986, and January 22, 1987; and, Orange County Register, January 6, 1987.

[16] *Testimony of 11-year-old boy*, http://www.law.umkc.edu/faculty/projects/ftrials/mcmartin/boy11testimony.html.

[17] *Testimony of Dr. Michael Maloney in McMartin Preschool Trial*, http://www.law.umkc.edu/faculty/projects/ftrials/mcmartin/maloneytestimony.html.

[18] *Testimony of Peggy McMartin Buckey in the McMartin Preschool Trial*, http://www.law.umkc.edu/faculty/projects/ftrials/mcmartin/peggybuckeytestimony.html.

[19] *Testimony of Ray Buckey in the McMartin Preschool Trial*, http://www.law.umkc.edu/faculty/projects/ftrials/mcmartin/raybuckeytestimony.html.

[20] *American Professional Society on the Abuse of Children*, http://www.apsac.org/mc/community/eventdetailsPrint.do?print=true&eventId=187093.

[21] *About Us*, by Children's Institute, Inc., http://www.childrensinstitute.org/about/history.php.

[22] *The Dark Truth About the Dark Tunnels of McMartin*, by the Institute for Psychological Therapies, http://www.ipt-forensics.com/journal/volume7/j7_2_1_7.htm#en29r.

Chapter 10

[1] *Marking Time*, http://www.people.com/people/archive/article/0,,20103992,00.html, September 26, 1994.

[2] July 8 1994 Preliminary Hearing, http://walraven.org/simpson/ph_jul08.html.

[3] *Court TV Files: O.J. Simpson Trial*, http://www.courttv.com/casefiles/simpson/criminal/summary/week01.html

[4] *CNN O.J. Simpson Trial, Opening statements, testimony begins*, http://www.cnn.com/2007/US/law/12/11/court.archive.simpson1/index.html.

[5] *CNN O.J. Simpson Trial News: March Transcripts*, http://www.cnn.com/US/OJ/trial/mar/index.html.

[6] *CNN O.J. Simpson Trial, Opening statements, testimony begins*, http://www.cnn.com/2007/US/law/12/11/court.archive.simpson1/index.html.

7   *CNN O.J. Simpson Trial, Opening statements, testimony begins*, http://www.cnn.com/2007/US/law/12/11/court.archive.simpson1/index.html.

8   *CNN O.J. Simpson Trial News: January Transcripts*, January 30 .zip file, http://www.cnn.com/US/OJ/trial/jan/index.html.

9   *CNN O.J. Simpson Trial News: January Transcripts*, January 31 .zip file, http://www.cnn.com/US/OJ/trial/jan/0131OJTR.ZIP.

10   *Denise Brown testimony*, http://www.law.umkc.edu/faculty/projects/ftrials/Simpson/browntest.html.

11   *Trial of Orenthal James Simpson*, by Doug Linder, 2000, http://www.law.umkc.edu/faculty/projects/ftrials/Simpson/Simpsonaccount.htm.

12   *Jack Walraven's Best of the Sidebars*, http://walraven.org/simpson/sb-best.html#sanctions.

13   *CNN O.J. Simpson Trial News: February Transcripts*, February 23 .zip file, http://www.cnn.com/US/OJ/trial/feb/0223OJTR.ZIP.

14   Sunday, July 10, 1994 United States Department of Justice Press Release, http://www.ojp.usdoj.gov/bjs/pub/press/mif.pr.

15   *CNN O.J. Simpson Trial News: March Transcripts*, March 10 .zip file, http://www.cnn.com/US/OJ/trial/mar/0310OJTR.ZIP.

16   *Jack Walraven's Simpson Trial Transcripts—Letter from Kathleen Bell to O.J. Simpson's lawyer*, http://walraven.org/simpson/bell.html.

17   *Shapiro, Dershowitz Add To O.J. Pile*, Seattle Times, by Kevin J. Hamilton, Seattle Times, April 19, 1996, http://community.seattletimes.nwsource.com/archive/?date=19960419&slug=2325048.

18   *Mark Fuhrman testimony*, March 9-16, 1995 http://www.law.umkc.edu/faculty/projects/ftrials/Simpson/fuhrman1.htm.

19   "Defense Amended Offer of Proof" dated August 25, 1995, http://web.mit.edu/dryfoo/www/Info/fuhrman.html.

20   *Jack Walraven's Simpson Trial Transcripts—September 5, 1995*, http://walraven.org/simpson/sep05.html.

21   *Ibid.*

22   "Defense Amended Offer of Proof" dated August 25, 1995, http://web.mit.edu/dryfoo/www/Info/fuhrman.html.

23   *Jack Walraven's Simpson Trial Transcripts— Ito's Final Decision on the Fuhrman Tapes*, http://walraven.org/simpson/fhr_tps2.html.

24   *Ibid.*

25   *Ibid.*

26   People v. Simpson Court transcript. See also, *Murder in Brentwoood*, by Mark Fuhrman, Kensington Publishing Co., 1997.

27 *CNN O.J. Simpson Trial News: March Transcripts*, March 17 .zip file, http://www.cnn.com/US/OJ/trial/mar/0317OJTR.ZIP.

28 *CNN O.J. Simpson Trial News: March Transcripts*, http://www.cnn.com/US/OJ/trial/mar/index.html.

29 *Ibid.*

30 *CNN O.J. Simpson Trial News: April Transcripts*, April 4 .zip file, http://www.cnn.com/US/OJ/trial/apr/0404OJTR.ZIP.

31 *CNN O.J. Simpson Trial News: April Transcripts*, April 5 .zip file, http://www.cnn.com/US/OJ/trial/apr/0405OJTR.ZIP.

32 *Proving The Case: The Science Of DNA: DNA Evidence In The O.J. Simpson Trial*, by William C. Thompson, 67 U. Colo. L. Reverend 827 (1996).

33 *Proving The Case: The Science Of DNA: DNA Evidence In The O.J. Simpson Trial*, by William C. Thompson, 67 U. Colo. L. Reverend 827 (1996).

34 *CNN O.J. Simpson Trial News: June Transcripts*, June 23 .zip file, http://www.cnn.com/US/OJ/trial/jun/0623OJTR.ZIP.

35 *CNN O.J. Simpson Trial News: June Transcripts*, June 15 .zip file, http://www.cnn.com/US/OJ/trial/jun/0615OJTR.ZIP.

36 *Ibid.*

37 *CNN O.J. Simpson Trial News: June Transcripts*, June 19 .zip file, http://www.cnn.com/US/OJ/trial/jun/0619OJTR.ZIP.

38 *CNN O.J. Simpson Trial News: August Transcripts*, August 2 .zip file, http://www.cnn.com/US/OJ/trial/aug/0802OJTR.ZIP

39 *CNN O.J. Simpson Trial News: August Transcripts*, August 17 .zip file, http://www.cnn.com/US/OJ/trial/aug/0817OJTR.ZIP.

40 *CNN O.J. Simpson Trial News: August Transcripts*, August 23 .zip file, http://www.cnn.com/US/OJ/trial/aug/0823OJTR.ZIP.

41 *CNN O.J. Simpson Trial News: August Transcripts*, August 25 .zip file, http://www.cnn.com/US/OJ/trial/aug/0825OJTR.ZIP.

42 *Excerpts of Marcia Clark's Closing Arguments*, http://www.times.com/books/97/06/15/reviews/clark-excerpts.html.

43 *The Trial of Orenthal James Simpson*, http://www.law.umkc.edu/faculty/projects/ftrials/Simpson/Simpsonaccount.htm.

44 *Cochran Concludes his closing arguments*, http://www.usatoday.com/news/index/nns039.htm.

45 *Darden's rebuttal begins*, http://www.usatoday.com/news/index/nns040.htm.

46 *Op. cit., Excerpts of Marcia Clark's Closing Arguments.*

47 *Op. cit., Excerpts of Marcia Clark's Closing Arguments.*

[48] *Prosecutor Darden begins his closing arguments*, http://www.usatoday.com/news/index/nns35.htm.

[49] *Defense Attorney Johnnie Cochran begins closing arguments*, http://www.usatoday.com/news/index/nns20.htm.

[50] *More of Cochran's closing arguments*, http://www.usatoday.com/news/index/nns17.htm.

[51] *Ibid.*

[52] *Cochran concludes his closing arguments*, http://www.usatoday.com/news/index/nns039.htm.

[53] *Prosecutor Darden concludes his rebuttal*, http://www.usatoday.com/news/index/nns041.htm.

[54] *Prosecutor Darden concludes his rebuttal*, http://www.usatoday.com/news/index/nns041.htm.

[55] *Jack Walraven's Simpson Trial Transcripts—October 2 to October 31, 1995*, http://walraven.org/simpson/oct02-31.html.

[56] *Jack Walraven's Simpson Trial Transcripts—Simpson Trial Statistics*, http://walraven.org/simpson/ojstats.html.

That's it. The end.

If you're a moviegoer:

Books aren't like movies where they put the bloopers at the end of the reel.

It's ok to close the book and put it back on the shelf now.

Or better yet, give it to a friend.

Thanks for reading.

Goodbye.

www.ingramcontent.com/pod-product-compliance
Lightning Source LLC
Chambersburg PA
CBHW072143070526
44585CB00015B/990